Collins

CSEC®
SOCIAL STUDIES

Shoba Marsha Gayah and Meritta Hyacinth
Reviewers: Dennise Bascom and Farah Christian

Collins

William Collins' dream of knowledge for all began with the publication of his first book in 1819. A self-educated mill worker, he not only enriched millions of lives, but also founded a flourishing publishing house. Today, staying true to this spirit, Collins books are packed with inspiration, innovation and practical expertise. They place you at the centre of a world of possibility and give you exactly what you need to explore it.

Collins. Freedom to teach.

Published by Collins
An imprint of HarperCollins*Publishers*
The News Building
1 London Bridge Street
London
SE1 9GF
UK

HarperCollins*Publishers*
Macken House,
39/40 Mayor Street Upper,
Dublin 1,
D01 C9W8,
Ireland

Browse the complete Collins Caribbean catalogue at
collins.co.uk/caribbeanschools

© HarperCollins*Publishers* Limited 2025

10 9 8 7 6 5 4 3 2

ISBN 978-0-00-866705-4

Collins CSEC® Social Studies is an independent publication and has not been authorised, sponsored or otherwise approved by CXC®. CSEC® is a registered trademark of the **Caribbean Examinations Council (CXC®)**.

All rights reserved. No part of this publication may be reproduced, stored in a retrieval system, or transmitted in any form by any means, electronic, mechanical, photocopying, recording or otherwise, without the prior written permission of the Publisher or a licence permitting restricted copying in the United Kingdom issued by the Copyright Licensing Agency Ltd., Barnard's Inn, 86 Fetter Lane, London, EC4A 1EN.

Without limiting the exclusive rights of any author, contributor or the publisher of this publication, any unauthorised use of this publication to train generative artificial intelligence (AI) technologies is expressly prohibited. HarperCollins also exercise their rights under Article 4(3) of the Digital Single Market Directive 2019/790 and expressly reserve this publication from the text and data mining exception.

British Library Cataloguing in Publication Data

A catalogue record for this publication is available from the British Library.

The publishers gratefully acknowledge the permission granted to reproduce the copyright material in this book. Every effort has been made to trace copyright holders and to obtain their permission for the use of copyright material. The publishers will gladly receive any information enabling them to rectify any error or omission at the first opportunity.

Authors: Shoba Marsha Gayah and Meritta Hyacinth
Reviewers: Dennise Bascom and Farah Christian
Publishers: Catherine Martin and Elaine Higgleton
Product manager: Saaleh Patel
Project manager: Julianna Dunn
Copy editor: Megan La Barre
Proofreader: Catherine Dakin
Illustrator: Siliconchips Services Ltd
Typesetter: Siliconchips Services Ltd
Cover designer: Gordon MacGilp
Production controller: Alhady Ali

Printed and bound by Ashford Colour Ltd.

MIX
Paper | Supporting responsible forestry
FSC™ C007454

This book contains FSC™ certified paper and other controlled sources to ensure responsible forest management.

For more information visit: www.harpercollins.co.uk/green

Contents

Getting the best from the book   v

Section A: Individual, Family and Society

(i) Individual and the Family

1 Family   1
   Definitions and functions of family   2
   Family types, relations and unions in the Caribbean and the world   12

2 Family: Roles and Responsibilities   18
   The roles and responsibilities of adults and children of a Caribbean family   19
   Changes in the roles and responsibilities of family members in Caribbean society   26
   Factors in preparing for parenthood   31

3 Social Issues   35
   Contemporary social issues   36
   Proposed solutions to problems faced by the family   44

4 Culture and Heritage   57
   The cultural diversity of the Caribbean region   58
   Global influences and cultural imperialism   79

(ii) Society and Governance

5 Social Groups   88
   Types of social groups and their characteristics   89
   Group cohesion and social control   100
   Social interaction in and between groups   106

6 Institutions and Government   113
   Types of institutions and their characteristics   114
   Government   122
   The relationships between citizens and governments as stated in the Constitution   136

7 Elections and Democracy   144
   Electoral processes and systems   145
   Preparation for elections   154
   Decision-making process and outcomes of elections   160
   Data analysis based on election processes and results   167

Section B: Sustainable Development and Use of Resources

(i) Development and Use of Resources

8 Population   175
   Characteristics of population   176
   Sources and use of population statistics   184
   Planning for development with the use of population statistics   188
   Population distribution and density   191
   Population change   198

9 Migration   205
   Causes and consequences of migration   206

10 Human Resources   221
   Developing human resources   222
   Employment, unemployment and underemployment   233

11 Natural and Physical Resources   246
   Major natural resources in the Caribbean   247
   Climate change   265

(ii) Regional Development

12 Development in the Caribbean   273
   Different groupings of territories in the Caribbean   275
   Measuring development   281
   The transformational impact of information and communication technology on Caribbean industries   296

13 Challenges to Caribbean Development   301
   Addressing the major challenges faced by the Caribbean   306
   Justification of strategies   312

14	Regional Integration	319	
	Factors that promote regional integration	320	
	Major attempts at regional integration	337	
	Objectives of the Caribbean regional organisations	340	
	The benefits and successes of regional integration	344	
	Factors that hinder the attempts at regional integration	347	
	Integration process in the Caribbean	351	
15	Tourism and Integration	355	
	The ways in which tourism can be used to promote regional integration	356	

16	The School-Based Assessment	374
	What is the SBA?	375
	Managing the project	375
	Choosing a topic	375
	Planning and executing your SBA	377
	SBA mark scheme	382
	Examples of possible SBA topics	384
	Sample Social Studies SBA	385

Index 391

Acknowledgements 402

Getting the best from the book

Welcome to *CSEC*® Social Studies

This textbook has been written as a comprehensive course designed to help you to achieve **maximum success** in your CXC® CSEC® Social Studies examination. Facts, information, explanation and theories are presented in an easily understandable way, using **simple** and **clear language**. Various formats are used, including diagrams and tables, to make the syllabus content easy to **understand** and **learn**. Colour **photographs** are also included to enliven and enrich your learning.

Important definitions are explained at the beginning of each section and are highlighted in **bold** type the first time they are used. No information is given in boxes to the side, which can be easily missed. All the information needed to fully cover the syllabus is given within the text, and only the required information is given.

Just as the CSEC® Social Studies syllabus is divided into four sections, the sixteen chapters of this book are divided into the same **four sections**. These are **colour-coded** for clarity, and each chapter covers a particular topic in the syllabus.

- **Chapters 1** to **4** cover topics in Section A(i); **Individual, Family and Society: Individual and the Family**
- **Chapters 5** to **7** cover topics in Section A(ii); **Individual, Family and Society: Society and Governance**
- **Chapters 8** to **11** cover topics in Section B(i); **Sustainable Development and Use of Resources: Development and Use of Resources**
- **Chapters 12** to **15** cover topics in Section B(ii); **Sustainable Development and Use of Resources: Regional Development**
- **Chapter 16** covers **The School-Based Assessment**

The chapters are broken down into sub-sections to split the information into manageable chunks. Each sub-section starts with **learning objectives** which relate fully to the **specific objectives** given in the syllabus.

Each sub-section ends with a series of **differentiated practice exercises** which are designed to help you test your **knowledge** and **comprehension**, and to help you to improve your ability to **use your knowledge** by developing your **thinking**, **investigative** and **analytical skills**. The exercises are **colour-coded** for clarity.

- **Knowledge and comprehension** – These exercises are designed to help you assess your ability to recall facts and define terms and concepts; use appropriate terms, concepts and principles in describing social issues and stating apparent causes and consequences of these issues; and, recognise the nature of techniques and procedures normally used in investigating social problems and phenomena.
- **Use of knowledge** – These exercises are designed to help you to organise, analyse and integrate information collected from a variety of sources to develop an informed position on social issues and problems, and to make decisions; propose solutions to social issues and problems based on concepts and principles for guiding behaviour and motivating responsible participation within social groups and communities; and, explain and support reasoned decisions and conclusions, and to evaluate the reasonableness of decisions.
- **SBA skills** – These questions help you to prepare for the School-Based Assessment. They do not feature in every section.

At the end of each chapter you will find **End of chapter questions** which will help you check what you have learned, and a **Summary**.

Introduction

If you **study** each chapter in turn and **answer all the End of chapter questions** that follow, you can then visit www.collins.co.uk/caribbeanschools to find the **correct answers**. This will enable you to assess your knowledge, help you to develop your thinking, investigative and analytical skills, and put you on the right path to achieve **maximum success** in your examination.

Key features of the book

Learning objectives inform you of what you are expected to **learn** ▶

Learning objectives
- Identify key historical factors influencing Caribbean cultural diversity, from indigenous roots to colonial history.
- Evaluate how family, groups, media and institutions shape Caribbean cultural heritage, and understand how traditions evolve.
- Explore the concepts of indigenous roots, creolisation, syncretism, indentureship and migration to understand their roles in forming the Caribbean's unique cultural identity and heritage.
- Examine how Caribbean music, literature, art, sports, festivals and more impact the world, considering both positive aspects and challenges.
- Discover how Caribbean culture travels worldwide, influencing societies and starting global discussions.
- Apply understanding to real-world challenges, suggesting sustainable strategies for preserving Caribbean culture, considering cultural sustainability and cultural entrepreneurship.

Important definitions of key terms are given at the beginning of each section, and the key terms are highlighted in **bold** the first time they appear in the text ▶

Important definitions
Floating voter – an elector who is not a consistent supporter of one particular party and may only decide late in the campaign.
Libel – the use of false written statements about a person.
Slander – the use of false spoken statements about a person.
Voter apathy – where voters do not feel inclined to participate in elections due to lack of interest.

Diagrams, charts and graphs help explain the content clearly ▶

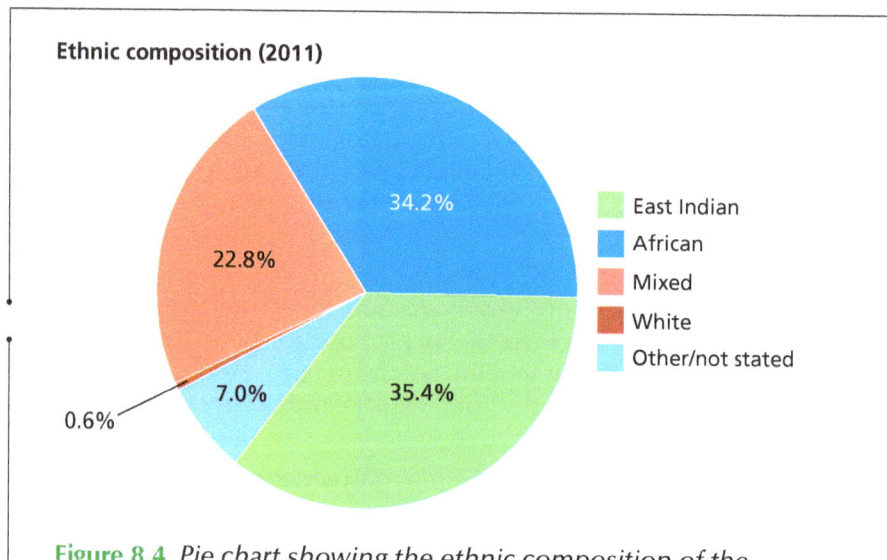

Figure 8.4 Pie chart showing the ethnic composition of the population of Trinidad and Tobago from the 2011 census

Multiple choice questions help you to prepare for Paper 1 of the exam ▶

Multiple choice

1. What is one of the primary functions of the family related to procreation and continuity?
   a) To ensure financial stability for future generations
   b) To bear and raise offspring
   c) To provide education to society at large
   d) To manage household chores

2. How does socialisation primarily occur within the family?
   a) Through formal education systems
   b) By learning values, norms, and behaviours
   c) Through peer interactions outside the home
   d) By following legal and governmental structures

3. What does economic provisioning by the family typically include?
   a) Investment in business ventures
   b) Creation of social policies
   c) Providing for basic needs like food, shelter, and education
   d) Establishing governmental institutions

4. Which of the following is a way families contribute to emotional and psychological support?
   a) By enforcing strict rules and regulations
   b) Providing love, care, and support
   c) By offering professional career guidance
   d) Conducting scientific research

5. Generational wealth in the context of family refers to what?
   a) The knowledge passed down through family traditions
   b) The physical strength and health inherited from ancestors
   c) Assets and resources passed down from one generation to the next
   d) The family's reputation and social standing in the community

Knowledge and comprehension questions help you to assess your ability to recall facts and define terms and concepts ▶

Knowledge and comprehension

1. Define the following terms.
   a) Fertility rate
   b) Migration
   c) Mortality rate

2. Describe TWO strategies to address rising birth rates in a country.

3. Describe TWO strategies to address rising death rates in a country.

4. a) Define 'internal migration'.
   b) State TWO reasons for the increase in internal migration from rural to urban areas.

5. List TWO countries that are attractive destinations to Caribbean migrants looking to move away from the region.

Introduction

Use of knowledge questions test your application of concepts and principles to analyse and propose solutions to social issues ▶

Use of knowledge

4. Discuss the following statement with the class.
   'The Office of the Ombudsman caters to those who cannot get swift justice.'

5. Prepare a comic strip using appropriate dialogue to demonstrate the dos and don'ts of being a good citizen. The strip should comprise 10 slides.

6. Create a poem or spoken word piece which highlights the major characteristics of good governance.

7. Alejandro is a Venezuelan unregistered migrant living in Tobago. He is currently unemployed and suffers because there is a language barrier.
   a) What TWO actions can be taken by individuals to assist Alejandro in improving his standard of living?
   b) Explain how EACH action suggested in (a) is likely to be successful.

SBA skills questions help you prepare for the School-Based Assessment ▶

SBA skills

You are invited to the Ombudsman's Office as a student representative to conduct an interview. What are some questions that you would ask? Some have already been added to help you. Complete the list of questions and ask your teacher if you can visit your local Ombudsman's Office to conduct the interview.

INTERVIEW SCHEDULE

Interview date:

Interviewee: The Ombudsman

Topic: Role of the Ombudsman

Interview recorded: (*Video or written report*)

Questions	Responses
1) Who is an ombudsman?	
2) How does his/her office help the general public	
3) What issues/situations does the ombudsman assist with currently?	

End of chapter questions help you check that you have understood what you have learned. ▶

End of chapter questions

1. a) Define the term 'gerrymandering'. (2 marks)
   b) Outline TWO advantages of the first-past-the post system of government in the Commonwealth Caribbean. (4 marks)
   c) In an upcoming parliamentary election, a political party would like to attract more votes from the younger section of the population.
      (i) Suggest TWO strategies the political party may take to attract younger voters. (4 marks)
      (ii) Explain why EACH strategy suggested in (c)(i) is likely to be successful. (4 marks)
      TOTAL 14 MARKS

2. a) Define the term 'manifesto'. (2 marks)
   b) Describe TWO ways in which political parties can use propaganda to attract votes. (4 marks)
   c) Over the past few years, reports have surfaced that voter apathy has been on the increase.
      (i) Suggest TWO activities that political parties can engage in to improve voter apathy. (4 marks)
      (ii) Explain how EACH activity suggested in (c) (i) is likely to be successful. (4 marks)
      TOTAL 14 MARKS

Introduction

The **Summary** at the end of each chapter helps you consolidate your understanding of the topic ▶

Summary

This chapter discusses the significance of the family unit in society, its various definitions, structures, and the roles it plays in socialisation, economic support, and emotional wellbeing. It explains the diversity of family forms, from nuclear and extended to non-traditional arrangements, and examines how cultural, legal, and sociological perspectives shape our understanding of family. It also addresses the impact of globalisation on family dynamics, and the need for respect and tolerance towards different family types to build inclusive communities. The chapter discusses kinship, marriage, and the functions families serve, to gain an understanding of the family's foundational role in societal **cohesion** and individual identity formation.

Key themes and concepts:

– Family dynamics: There are various family structures (nuclear, extended, blended) and they all play roles in procreation, socialisation, economic responsibilities, and providing emotional and psychological support.

– Cultural identity and diversity: Cultural identity shapes family structures and dynamics, creating diversity. It is important to understand and respect diverse family forms to build social cohesion.

– Societal attitudes and tolerance: Societal attitudes towards different family types and unions influence individual and collective wellbeing and we must take an inclusive approach to understanding family diversity.

Section A: Individual, Family and Society
(i) Individual and the Family
1 Family

The topics covered in this chapter are:

- evaluating different sources to determine a definition of the family
- the major functions of the family
- different family types, relations, unions and forms of marriage in the Caribbean and the wider world
- demonstrating respect and tolerance of others from different family types and unions

An introduction to individual and family

As individuals, we possess a set of behaviours which are nurtured throughout our life. Many individuals inspire us, motivate us and shape our immediate reality. We operate as an individual but at the same time, we have to learn to operate with others in groups. Creating a bond makes us human and gives us a sense of self.

We not only cater to our local needs but have to learn to navigate through national, regional and even global connections. In learning a particular way of life, we as individuals have to appreciate differences and develop patterns of behaviour to respect the diverse situations.

This chapter explores the relationships that connect individuals, families and broader communities on a local, national and global scale.

Developing an attitude that embraces tolerance, respect, and a deep appreciation for the diverse family patterns among us is crucial. In the Caribbean, the importance of the family as an institution cannot be underestimated.

Definitions and functions of family

Learning objectives

- Identify how families contribute to the socialisation of individuals.
- Explain the role of families in procreation.
- Outline the economic responsibilities of families, including budgeting and financial transactions.
- Discuss the importance of families in meeting emotional and psychological needs.
- Analyse different family definitions across sources.
- Assess the accuracy and authority of sources on family definitions.
- Evaluate the currency, objectivity, and relevance of information on families.

Important definitions

Culture – the shared beliefs, values, practices, and traditions that characterise a particular group.

Norms – socially accepted standards of behaviour and conduct that guide individuals' actions within a society.

Social institutions – established structures that regulate various aspects of society, such as education, government, and religion.

Socialisation – the process by which individuals learn and internalise societal norms, values, and behaviours.

Nuclear family – a type of family structure composed of parents and their children.

Extended family – a more extensive family setup that goes beyond just parents and children, often covering several generations and involving relatives beyond the immediate household.

Kinship – the intricate web of connections established through blood relations, marriage, or adoption. These connections collectively shape the structure of a family.

Roles – the tasks and duties every family member takes on within the family unit.

Cohesion – the emotional closeness and interconnectedness among family members.

The family is the basic unit of society. It is where children are born and raised and where they learn the values and **norms** of their **culture**. The family also provides economic support, emotional security, and love and care for its members. Families are the cornerstone for various essential purposes that underscore their significance within societies. The family is often considered the foundation of society, though its definition varies.

- Definition A: focuses on the family as a group connected by blood, marriage, or legal ties, living together and providing emotional and financial support.
- Definition B: emphasises the family as a key societal institution, responsible for socialising children, offering emotional stability, and ensuring economic well-being.
Both definitions highlight the family's essential roles but place slightly different emphasis on its social and economic functions. Together, they provide a fuller picture of the family's importance.

These functions include:

- procreation and continuity
- **socialisation** and nurturing
- economic provision
- emotional and psychological support.

Procreation and continuity

One of the primary functions of the family is procreation – the bearing and raising of offspring. Families are integral to the continuation of the human species. They also play a role in transmitting cultural values and traditions from one generation to the next.

Figure 1.1 *Procreation and continuity is a primary function of the family*

The procreation function of the family is not limited to biological reproduction. Families can also be formed through adoption or other means. Most importantly, children should be raised in a loving and supportive environment, regardless of their family structure.

Here are some of the specific ways in which families carry out this function:

- providing a safe and nurturing environment for pregnancy and childbirth
- providing emotional and financial support to parents
- helping parents to learn about child development and parenting skills
- providing avenues for children to learn and grow
- transmitting cultural values and traditions to children
- providing love, care, and support to children.

Socialisation and nurturing

Socialisation is the process by which children learn the values, norms, and beliefs of their culture. The family is the primary agent of socialisation and nurturing for children. It is through the family that children first learn about the world around them and how to interact with others. Families teach children how to behave, how to communicate, and how to think about themselves and others. They also teach children about the importance of things like honesty, respect, and responsibility.

Nurturing is the process of providing love, care, and support to children. It is through nurturing that children develop a sense of security and belonging. Nurturing also helps children to develop their emotional intelligence and how to manage stress and difficult emotions.

Section A(i) Individual, Family and Society

The family is not the only agent of socialisation. Children also learn from their peers, their teachers, and the media. However, the influence of the family is often the strongest in the early years of life.

The family's ability to socialise and nurture children is affected by a number of factors, such as the parents' parenting skills, the family's economic resources, and the family's social support network.

Here are some specific examples of how families socialise and nurture children:

Teaching children about values and norms

Families teach children about the values and norms of their culture through their words and actions. For example, a family that values honesty may tell their children to always tell the truth, and they may also model honesty in their own behaviour.

Helping children to develop social skills

Families help children to develop social skills by the continuous interaction with others. For example, families may take their children to family gatherings and religious or secular events. They may also help their children to learn how to resolve conflict and how to make friends.

Providing love and support

Families provide love and support to children by being there for them when they need them. They may offer comfort and reassurance when children are feeling sad or scared. They may also celebrate children's successes and help them to overcome challenges.

Economic provisioning

Families serve as the foundational unit of society, playing a pivotal role in the nurturing and economic stability of their members. They ensure the wellbeing of individuals from birth through all stages of life by fulfilling various critical functions. The economic provisioning function of the family is the process of providing for the basic needs of its members. These include food, shelter, clothing, education, and healthcare. The family also offers financial support to its members, such as help paying for college or starting a business. For example, parents may pay school fees.

Some families also ensure that financial stability is passed on from one generation to the next. 'Generational wealth' refers to accumulated assets, investments, and financial resources that are passed down from generation to generation within a family or lineage. It often includes real estate, businesses, investments, and financial savings that are intended to provide financial security and opportunities for future generations. Generational wealth primarily aims to provide a lasting legacy and improved socio-economic prospects for descendants.

The specific ways families provide financial provisioning vary depending on their income, assets, and needs. However, all families need to find ways to provide for their basic needs to ensure their members' wellbeing. Additionally:

- The family is only one of many sources of economic provisioning in society. Governments, businesses, and other organisations also play a role in providing for the basic needs of individuals and families.
- The family's ability to provide economic provisioning is affected by several factors, such as employment status, income, generational wealth status and the cost of living.
- The family's role in economic provisioning is changing in line with modern society. For example, more and more families rely on dual incomes to make ends meet.

Emotional and psychological support

The family's emotional and psychological support function is the process of providing love, care, and support to its members. This includes listening to them, offering comfort and reassurance, and helping them to cope with difficult emotions. The family also provides a sense of belonging and acceptance, which is essential for the emotional wellbeing of its members.

When families can provide emotional and psychological support, their members are likelier to be happy, healthy, and resilient.

Families can provide emotional and psychological support in the following ways:

Figure 1.2 *Emotional and psychological support is an important function of the family*

- Open communication: Encouraging open and honest communication within the family allows members to express their feelings, thoughts, and concerns. When family members feel heard and understood, it fosters a sense of emotional connection and support.
- Active listening: Family members can actively listen to one another without judgment or interruption. This attentiveness helps individuals feel valued and acknowledged, contributing to their emotional wellbeing.
- Empathy and understanding: Empathy involves recognising and understanding another person's emotions and experiences. Family members can empathise with each other's struggles, offering emotional support and validation.
- Conflict resolution: Families can teach conflict resolution skills, helping members navigate disagreements and disputes healthily and constructively. This reduces emotional tension and promotes psychological wellbeing.
- Physical presence: Simply being physically present for one another during challenging times or moments of distress can be a powerful form of emotional support. A hug, a reassuring touch, or sitting together can convey emotional comfort.
- Positive reinforcement: Families can provide positive reinforcement and encouragement for each other's achievements and efforts. Recognising and celebrating accomplishments boosts self-esteem and psychological resilience.
- Empowerment: Encouraging family members to set and pursue their goals, dreams, and passions promotes a sense of empowerment. Family support in achieving personal aspirations can significantly impact one's psychological outlook.
- Stress management: Teaching stress management techniques, such as mindfulness, relaxation exercises, and healthy coping strategies, can help family members better handle emotional and psychological challenges.
- Seeking professional help: In cases of severe emotional or psychological distress, families can support one another in seeking professional help, such as therapy or counselling, to address issues and develop coping strategies.
- Unconditional love: Perhaps the most fundamental form of emotional support is the unconditional love that families can provide. Knowing that one is loved and accepted by their family members can create a strong foundation for emotional and psychological wellbeing.

The family's emotional and psychological support function is complex and ever-changing. The specific ways families provide emotional and psychological support vary depending on the family's culture, values, and beliefs. However, all families must find ways to provide emotional and psychological support to their members to ensure their wellbeing.

Questions

Multiple choice

1 What is one of the primary functions of the family related to procreation and continuity?
   a) To ensure financial stability for future generations
   b) To bear and raise offspring
   c) To provide education to society at large
   d) To manage household chores

2 How does socialisation primarily occur within the family?
   a) Through formal education systems
   b) By learning values, norms, and behaviours
   c) Through peer interactions outside the home
   d) By following legal and governmental structures

3 What does economic provisioning by the family typically include?
   a) Investment in business ventures
   b) Creation of social policies
   c) Providing for basic needs like food, shelter, and education
   d) Establishing governmental institutions

4 Which of the following is a way families contribute to emotional and psychological support?
   a) By enforcing strict rules and regulations
   b) Providing love, care, and support
   c) By offering professional career guidance
   d) Conducting scientific research

5 Generational wealth in the context of family refers to what?
   a) The knowledge passed down through family traditions
   b) The physical strength and health inherited from ancestors
   c) Assets and resources passed down from one generation to the next
   d) The family's reputation and social standing in the community

Knowledge and comprehension

6 Define socialisation and describe how the process is used in the family setting.

Use of knowledge

7 How might societal structures and functions evolve if the family's traditional role of procreation and raising children declines significantly?

8 Imagine a family that doesn't have much money and how it might affect the way they raise and teach their children.

   a) What kind of challenges might these children face as they grow?

   b) What are some ways we can help these families and children?

Some important aspects of families

Kinship and blood relations: Families are often structured around kinship ties, and relationships formed through blood connections. These relationships dictate **roles**, responsibilities, and inheritance patterns within the family unit.

Marriage and partnership: Marriage forms the basis of many families, creating a legally recognised bond between spouses. Partnerships involve shared responsibilities, cooperation, and a division of labour, contributing to the family's functionality.

Socialisation: Families are primary agents of socialisation, transmitting cultural norms, values, and behaviours to children. The process of socialisation equips individuals with the tools to navigate societal expectations.

Figure 1.3 *Communication technologies influence family dynamics*

Roles and responsibilities: Families have members with distinct roles and responsibilities. These roles are often influenced by gender, age, and cultural norms, contributing to the equilibrium of the family unit.

Economic functions: Families often fulfil financial functions by pooling resources, sharing expenses, and contributing to the wellbeing of their members. Economic interdependence within families can extend to wider social networks.

Emotional support and intimacy: Families provide emotional support and a sense of belonging to their members. Close relationships within families are a safe space for individuals to express their emotions.

Transitions and life stages: Families evolve through various life stages, such as marriage, childbirth, child-rearing, and ageing. Each stage brings new challenges and adaptations, shaping the family's structure and dynamics.

Cultural and historical variability: Families exhibit diversity across cultures and historical periods. Cultural norms, societal values, and historical contexts influence family structures, roles, and functions.

Family diversity: In modern society, family forms are more diverse and varied than the traditional **nuclear family**. Single-parent families, stepfamilies, and households with non-biological relationships are examples of this diversity.

Globalisation and family dynamics: Globalisation influences family dynamics through migration, communication technologies, and cross-cultural interactions. These factors impact family connections, roles, and the transmission of cultural values.

Exploring various definitions of the family

A definition of the family can vary depending on cultural, legal, and sociological perspectives. In a broad sense, the family can be defined as a social unit composed of individuals linked by blood, marriage, adoption, or other forms of social connections. This unit typically involves shared living arrangements, mutual support and emotional bonds, and often includes the raising and socialisation of children. However, it is essential to recognise that family definitions can be culturally and contextually specific, evolving and reflecting the diversity of family structures and relationships in different societies and eras.

Sources for the definition of the family

A source is a place, item or person from which information, used by a researcher in the conduct of their work, originate. It is important to ensure that the source of any information used by researchers is authentic and reliable.

In order to garner a thorough evaluation of the family as a social group and how to define it, nine criteria are outlined below which will be analysed.

Accuracy
Since families take diverse forms and vary based on societies, there is no single accurate definition of the family. This is especially so when it comes to the general public. In most cases, it is defined in relation to family type and structure (for example, nuclear versus extended families), but there have been tendencies to consider features linked to race, social class and sexuality in some definitions.

Authority
Authority refers to the credibility and expertise of the source providing the definition of the family. A source with high authority is one produced by experts, such as social scientists, who have conducted extensive research and have specialised knowledge on family structures and dynamics within different societies.

The ideological approach
This approach to defining the family is influenced by a set of ideals about the family. The approach situates a family resembling a nuclear family with a married heterosexual couple and their dependent children. The husband's primary role is devoted to the financial support of the group while the wife's role is typically homemaking. This ideal however has changed somewhat due to employment, recognition of women's rights and globalisation.

The sociological approach
The sociological approach views the family as a key social institution that shapes individuals and society. It examines functions like procreation, socialisation, and emotional support, while recognising that family structures vary across cultures. Sociologists define family based on relationships (e.g., blood, adoption, marriage) and how societies sanction these bonds, which can include same-sex couples in some definitions.

Key theories like functionalism, conflict theory, symbolic interactionism, and feminist theory offer diverse insights into family dynamics and their societal impacts.

Family as household
This definition suggests that family members 'constitute a single household'. For our purposes in the Caribbean, this observation may not be applicable as family members span across households, and in many cases, families may be transnational, meaning they cut across national borders.

Currency
This refers to the value that society places on the institution as it exists today. In the past, there was a clear push towards marriage and child bearing. Marriage took many forms: monogamy, bigamy and polygamy. Today however, many individuals opt for common-law relationships.

Objectivity

Ideally, sources should be reliable and portray a level of fairness and neutrality. Researchers can lose sight of the immediate goals and allow their personal values to skew the observations. It is quite easy, especially when dealing with family, to pass judgement based on personal experiences.

Coverage

Different forms of literature refer to family forms in particular ways. In many pieces of literature, the nuclear family is portrayed as the 'ideal' and 'universal' or even 'typical' form. Anything outside of this is often portrayed as inappropriate or unacceptable. Defining family should cater to the differences on a regional and global scale.

Relevance

Definitions have a history; they were invented to explain a past phenomenon. However, as time passes, definitions must change and adapt to current situations. The definition of the family also has to be modified to speak to current situations.

Cultural perspectives

Nuclear family (Western perspective): In many Western cultures, the nuclear family is common, consisting of two parents and their biological or adopted children living together as a single household.

Extended family (many non-Western cultures): In contrast, some non-Western cultures prioritise the extended family, which includes not only parents and children but also grandparents, uncles, aunts and close relatives living together or in close proximity.

Extended family (during Caribbean enslavement and indentureship): During the period of Caribbean enslavement, which lasted for centuries and involved the forced labour of African people on plantations, the extended family concept was impacted and reshaped. The history of extended families in Caribbean enslavement is one of disruption, adaptation, and resilience. Enslaved individuals faced the traumatic separation of their nuclear families but formed new, extended family networks that played a crucial role in their survival and resistance. This history has left a lasting impact on contemporary Caribbean family structures and social dynamics. During indentureship, East Indians came to the Caribbean on a working contract, so their form of extended family has been maintained and has survived into the present day. Joint families are also prevalent, where each small family develops their own home but often within the same compound as their relatives.

- **Separation and disruption:** Enslaved individuals were often forcibly separated from their immediate families as they were bought and sold as commodities. This led to a profound disruption of traditional family structures. Husbands, wives, parents, and children could be separated, sold to different owners, or even sent to different plantations. This separation had profound psychological and emotional consequences, as it tore apart the bonds of the nuclear family.

- **Formation of new family bonds:** In response to this traumatic disruption, enslaved individuals often formed new family bonds within their communities. These bonds extended beyond blood relations and encompassed 'fictive kinship' – people who became like family through shared experiences and support networks. This extended family provided emotional support, protection, and a sense of belonging in the absence of the nuclear family. This was also made possible due to space and movement limitations, as the enslaved lived in the same small area.

- **Legacy and contemporary impact:** The legacy of Caribbean enslavement still affects family structures and dynamics in the region today. Many Caribbean nations have diverse and complex family systems that reflect both the historical **trauma** of enslavement and the resilience of extended family networks. Family bonds remain strong, and the importance of community and extended family support continues to shape Caribbean culture.

Legal perspectives

Nuclear family (legal definition): Many legal systems define the family based on legally recognised marriages and blood or adoptive relationships. This often aligns with the nuclear family model.

Same-sex marriage (legal recognition): In countries that recognise same-sex marriage, legal definitions of the family have expanded to include families headed by same-sex couples with legal parental rights.

Cohabiting couples (common-law marriages): In some places, **cohabiting** couples who have lived together for a certain period may be legally recognised as a family, even without formal marriage.

Questions

Multiple choice

1. How does the nuclear family contribute to the socialisation of children?
   a) By teaching values, norms, and behaviours
   b) By establishing national laws
   c) By running community organisations
   d) By managing financial investments

2. What is a key difference between extended families and nuclear families?
   a) Extended families consist only of parents and their children
   b) Extended families often include relatives beyond the immediate family, such as grandparents and aunts
   c) Extended families are typically smaller than nuclear families
   d) Extended families do not maintain strong relationships across generations

3. What role does kinship play in family structures?
   a) It dictates the financial contributions of each member
   b) It determines the social status of family members
   c) It establishes the connections and responsibilities among family members
   d) It has no significant impact on family dynamics

4. How does the family contribute to a child's development through socialisation?
   a) By teaching them cultural values and acceptable behaviours
   b) By ensuring they inherit family property
   c) By managing their financial accounts
   d) By organising community service projects for them

5 Which of the following best describes the impact of globalisation on family dynamics?
   a) It has led to more uniform family structures worldwide
   b) It has reduced communication between family members
   c) It has influenced family structures and relationships through factors like migration and technology
   d) It has had no significant effect on families

Knowledge and comprehension

6 a) What is a family as defined in the chapter?
   b) Provide at least two key functions of the family as discussed in the chapter.

7 a) Explain the importance of family as a social institution within society.
   b) Give an example of how the family contributes to the socialisation of individuals.

8 a) Define the term 'kinship' and explain its importance in the family structure.
   b) Provide an example of how kinship affects family roles and relationships.

9 a) How is the family defined in the chapter based on cultural and social perspectives?
   b) Describe how different family structures, such as nuclear and extended families, fit into this definition.

10 Define the term 'family' and explain TWO criteria that should be reflected on in the definition.

Use of knowledge

11 a) Provide an example that illustrates how family structure can influence an individual's values or behaviours.
   b) Provide an example from your own life that illustrates how cultural identity can influence an individual's beliefs or behaviours.

12 a) Analyse how the concept of family has evolved in response to globalisation.
   b) Discuss the effects of this evolution on family roles and structures in a specific cultural or national context.

13 a) Considering the various definitions of family, evaluate how socialisation and nurturing contribute to its role in society.
   b) Propose strategies that families might use to effectively support the socialisation and nurturing of their children.

Family types, relations and unions in the Caribbean and the world

Learning objectives
- Distinguish family types and dynamics using family trees.
- Compare unions, including legal, civil, and informal arrangements.
- Analyse marriage forms, focusing on Caribbean and global variations.

> **Important definitions**
>
> *Personality* – a unique set of characteristics, behaviours and qualities that distinguish one person from another.
>
> *Identity* – the sense of who a person is, encompassing personal characteristics, cultural affiliations, and self-perception.
>
> *Autonomy* – the ability to make independent choices and decisions, reflecting self-governance and self-determination.
>
> *Self-esteem* – the level of self-worth and confidence an individual holds about themselves.

The family is a fundamental unit of society, and its structure and function vary widely across cultures and over time. There are various family types, relations, and unions in the Caribbean.

The nuclear family is the most common family type in the Caribbean. It consists of a married couple and their children living together. However, there are also many single-parent, extended, and blended families. The nuclear family structure reflects a traditional and widely accepted family model. It provides a stable and closely-knit unit for raising children and sharing familial responsibilities.

Extended families are typical in the Caribbean, especially in rural areas. They comprise a nuclear family and other relatives, such as grandparents, aunts, uncles, and cousins. Extended families often provide financial and emotional support to their members. It is one of the family units influenced by the period of enslavement and indentureship. They served as a source of resilience and cultural preservation, as they passed down traditions, languages, and customs.

Figure 1.4 *Extended families are typical in the Caribbean*

Blended families or reconstituted families are formed when two people marry and each has children from a previous relationship. Blended families can be challenging, but they can also be rewarding. Members of a blended family are sometimes referred to as step-mother, step-father, step-sister or step-brother.

Reorganised families have dynamic structures that have experienced significant changes. These changes often stem from divorce, separation, or the remarriage of one or both parents. It can also occur due to new custody arrangements or the addition of new family members through adoption or fostering. Such transformations require adjustments in roles, relationships, and living arrangements, creating a new family dynamic.

Visiting unions are common in some Caribbean countries, such as Jamaica. In a visiting union, a man and a woman have a sexual relationship but do not live together and they may or may not have children together.

Common-law unions are also common in some Caribbean countries. In a common-law union, a man and a woman live together and have children together, but they are not legally married. In Jamaica, persons in a common-law union have certain rights under The Property (Rights of Spouses) Act once they have been cohabiting for five years or more.

Promoting respect and tolerance for diverse family types and unions

In today's increasingly diverse society, it is essential to foster an environment of respect and tolerance for various family types and unions. Families are all different, showing how people and their lives can be very unique and interesting. To create inclusive and harmonious communities, it is important to acknowledge and embrace this diversity.

Table 1.1 shows diverse family types.

Family type	Description
Nuclear families *value: Recognising their importance should not diminish the value of other family types.*	Traditional nuclear families, consisting of married couples and their children, are just one of many family structures.
Single-parent families *value: These families deserve support and understanding as they navigate the unique challenges of solo parenting.*	Single-parent families, often headed by mothers or fathers, play a vital role in raising children.
Extended families *value: Offer a strong support network and a sense of belonging to a larger community.*	Extended families, which encompass multiple generations and relatives.
Blended families *value: These families require patience, understanding, and empathy as they navigate the complexities of forming new bonds.*	Blended families arise when two individuals with children from previous relationships come together.

Table 1.1

Family trees

A family tree is a visual representation showing the position and relationship of members in the family.

The diagrams on the following page show two different family types with different numbers of people and we can see the relationships between and among the generations.

Diagram (a): Nuclear family

We see there are two generations with a woman and a man joined typically through marriage with their five children (three boys and two girls). 1 and 2 are spouses while 3, 4, 5, 6 and 7 are siblings.

Diagram (b): Extended family

We see there are three generations with grandparents, their adult children and their children (grandchildren). There are married and unmarried adults and so this would give rise to aunts, uncles, sisters-in-law and brothers-in-law.

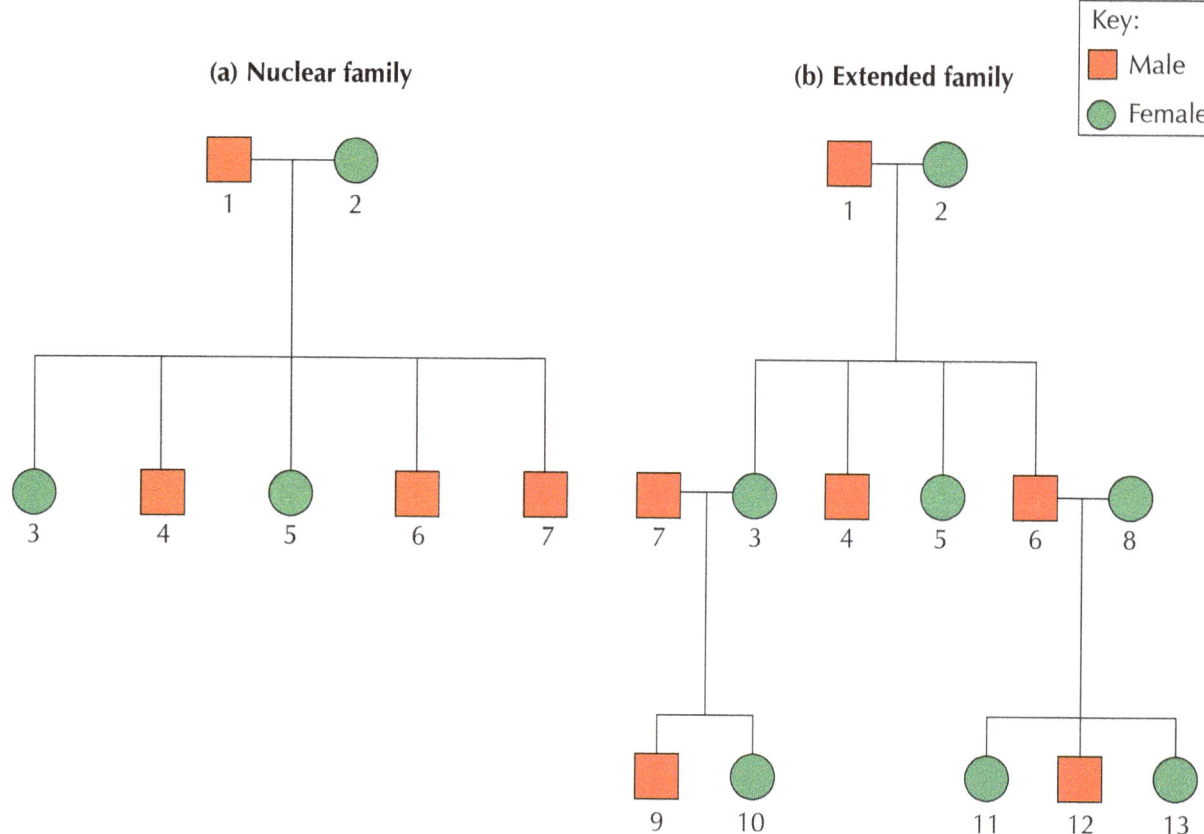

Figure 1.5 *Two different family trees*

Promoting respect and tolerance

In a diverse world, the ability to demonstrate respect and tolerance for individuals from different family types and unions is very important. There are many ways in which we can cultivate a culture of inclusivity and understanding. By acknowledging the unique experiences and challenges faced by people from various family backgrounds, we can create a more empathetic and harmonious society. The diagram on the following page should help us to reflect on our own perceptions and attitudes, and learn strategies for embracing and celebrating the diversity that defines the human experience.

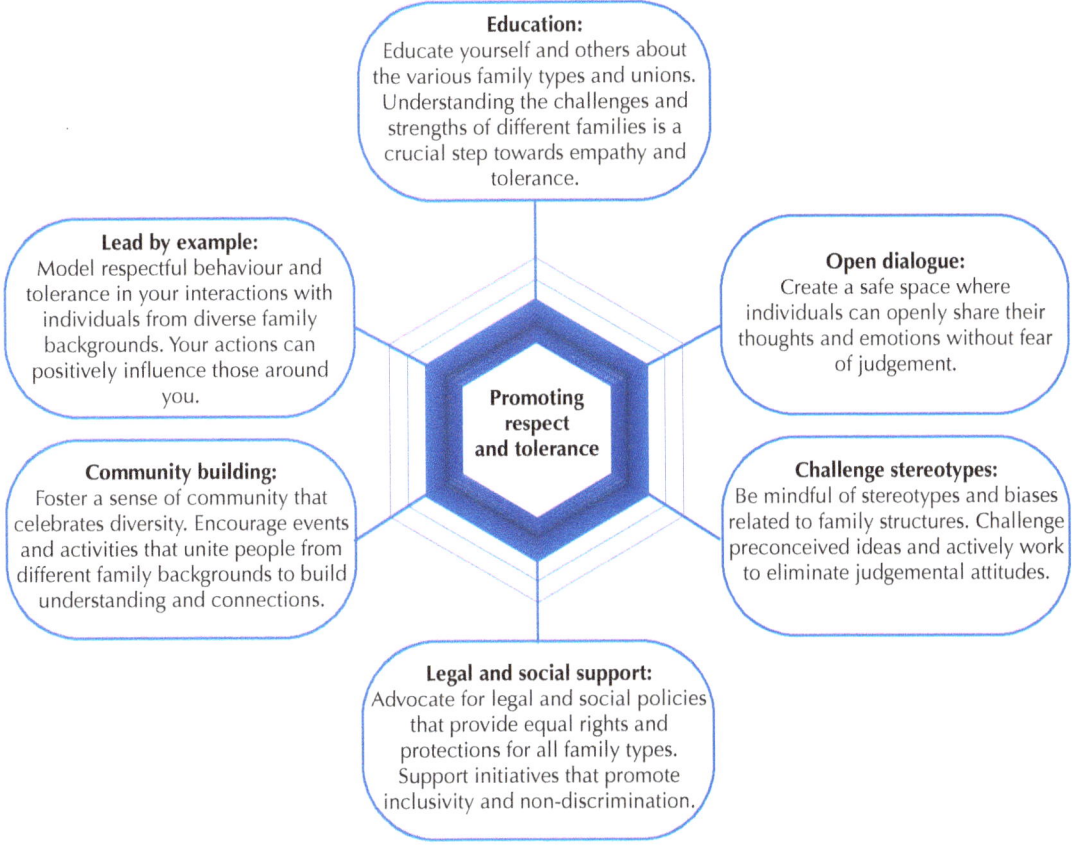

Figure 1.6 *Promoting respect and tolerance*

End of chapter questions

1. a) Describe the difference between a nuclear family and an extended family. (3 marks)
   b) How might the dynamics and roles within these two family types vary? (4 marks)

2. a) What are the key functions of the family? List at least three. (3 marks)
   b) Explain how each function contributes to societal stability and individual development. (9 marks)

3. a) What is meant by 'family diversity' in the context of the chapter? (4 marks)
   b) List different forms of family diversity and describe how each form contributes to the fabric of society. (8 marks)

4. a) What is the role of family in the economic provisioning of its members? (4 marks)
   b) Identify and explain two ways in which families contribute to the economic wellbeing of their members. (6 marks)

5. a) Describe the process of socialisation within the family. (3 marks)
   b) How do families transmit cultural norms and values to the next generation? (6 marks)

Section A(i)   Individual, Family and Society

6. Study the diagram below and answer the questions that follow.

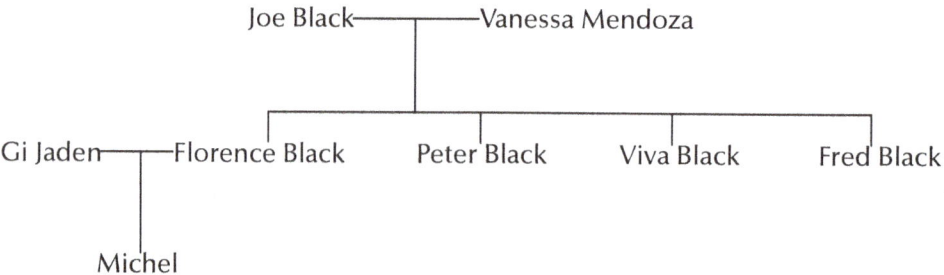

   a) Name the family type shown above. (1 mark)
   b) How many generations can be seen in this family? (1 mark)
   c) What is Michel's surname? (1 mark)
   d) What is the relationship of Vanessa Mendoza to Gi Jaden? (1 mark)
   e) How many siblings does Fred have? (1 mark)

7. Based on your understanding of cultural identity, describe how your cultural background has shaped your beliefs and behaviours. Provide specific examples from your life.
   - Description: (6 marks)
   - Examples: (6 marks)

   TOTAL: (12 marks)

8. Imagine you are a social worker. How would you apply the concept of 'tolerance' in your interactions with diverse clients and families? Provide practical strategies or scenarios.
   - Explanation and strategies/scenarios: (12 marks)

   TOTAL: (12 marks)

9. Consider a family you know well, either your own or a friend's. Analyse the roles and responsibilities of each family member within the unit. How do these roles contribute to the family's functioning?
   - Analysis: (12 marks)

   TOTAL: (12 marks)

SBA skills

Explore and understand the various family types in your school or community and how they affect students' lives.

Explanation:

The topic 'Understanding different family types in my school or community' aims to help us learn about the different kinds of families our classmates come from and how these family types affect our daily lives and interactions at school. We want to find out what types of families exist (like nuclear families with just parents and children, extended families with more relatives, and single-parent families), how these family types influence our behaviour and relationships and how we feel about other family types. To do this, we can use easy research methods like questionnaires, interviews, and observations. This project will help us understand and appreciate the diversity of families in our school, making it easier to relate to and support each other.

Guided questions

Introduction:

1. What is the purpose of this project?
2. Why is it important to learn about different family types?

Research questions:

3. What are the main types of families we have in our school or community?
4. How do these different family types influence students' daily lives at school?
5. What are the students' attitudes towards the different family types?

Methodology:

6. How will you collect information about the family types in your school/community?
7. What questions will you include in your questionnaire?
8. How will you ensure the information you collect is accurate and respectful?

Data analysis:

9. How will you analyse the data collected from the questionnaires and interviews?
10. What conclusions can you draw from your findings?

Conclusion:

11. What did you learn from this project about family diversity?
12. How can this knowledge help improve the school community?
13. What are the next steps for applying what you've learned?

Summary

This chapter discusses the significance of the family unit in society, its various definitions, structures, and the roles it plays in socialisation, economic support, and emotional wellbeing. It explains the diversity of family forms, from nuclear and extended to non-traditional arrangements, and examines how cultural, legal, and sociological perspectives shape our understanding of family. It also addresses the impact of globalisation on family dynamics, and the need for respect and tolerance towards different family types to build inclusive communities. The chapter discusses kinship, marriage, and the functions families serve, to gain an understanding of the family's foundational role in societal **cohesion** and individual identity formation.

Key themes and concepts:

- Family dynamics: There are various family structures (nuclear, extended, blended) and they all play roles in procreation, socialisation, economic responsibilities, and providing emotional and psychological support.
- Cultural identity and diversity: Cultural identity shapes family structures and dynamics, creating diversity. It is important to understand and respect diverse family forms to build social cohesion.
- Societal attitudes and tolerance: Societal attitudes towards different family types and unions influence individual and collective wellbeing and we must take an inclusive approach to understanding family diversity.

Section A: Individual, Family and Society
(i) Individual and the Family
2 Family: Roles and Responsibilities

The topics covered in this chapter are:

- the roles and responsibilities of adults and children of a Caribbean family
- the causes and effects of the changes in the roles and responsibilities of family members in Caribbean society
- formulating questions to guide information search
- factors which assist in the preparation for parenthood
- designing simple questionnaires to gather information about the family
- examining the qualities of an effective parent

The roles and responsibilities of adults and children of a Caribbean family

In Caribbean society, the family is a vibrant and essential part of life where everyone plays a significant role. Both adults and children have important responsibilities that have evolved over time. One major aspect of family life is the role of being a parent, which requires preparation through education, emotional readiness, and financial stability.

Good parenting involves being good at communicating, understanding, being consistent, patient, and flexible. These traits are important for raising happy and healthy children. Looking at the roles and duties in Caribbean families helps us understand more about their culture, community, and sense of identity.

Learning objective

- Understand the diverse roles and responsibilities of adults and children within Caribbean families.

Important definitions

Family roles – the expected and often culturally defined behaviours, tasks, and responsibilities that each family member is assigned or assumes within the family unit.

Family responsibilities – the specific duties and obligations that individuals within a family are expected to fulfil, which can include caregiving, household chores, financial contributions, and emotional support.

Interdependence – the concept that family members rely on each other for their needs, both practical and emotional, and that the wellbeing of one member is connected with that of the entire family.

Historical context – the circumstances, events, and cultural influences of the past that shape the roles and responsibilities of family members in the present.

Information literacy – the ability to critically assess information sources for accuracy, authority, currency, objectivity, coverage, and relevance, which is essential for effective research and decision-making.

Family identity – the sense of belonging and identification that individuals have within their family as a primary group, often influenced by shared values, traditions, experiences, and dependencies. This includes the collective identity formed through common backgrounds, practices, and the mutual support system within the family unit.

Transnational families – families whose members are dispersed across different countries or regions due to factors like migration, work opportunities, or education. These families maintain connections and relationships across borders, often through communication technologies, and navigate the challenges of distance and cross-cultural experiences.

Provider – an individual who assumes the responsibility for supplying the family with resources, including financial support, food, shelter and safety. This role traditionally involves ensuring that all material needs are met to maintain the wellbeing and stability of the family unit.

Nurturer – someone who offers emotional support, care, love and guidance to family members. This role involves fostering a supportive and nurturing environment that encourages the emotional, physical, and psychological development of individuals within the family. Nurturers are key in creating a sense of security, belonging and emotional wellbeing among family members.

Understanding family dynamics

The Caribbean family is a unique and tightly knit social unit with distinct roles and responsibilities assigned to each member. These roles are deeply embedded in the Caribbean culture, influenced by historical legacies, societal norms and practical needs.

To understand the Caribbean family we must acknowledge the impact of its historical roots. The legacy of enslavement, indentureship and colonialism has left a lasting imprint on family structures. The forced separation of family members during enslavement had profound consequences, and it reshaped the traditional nuclear family model. It gave rise to extended family networks, where kinship ties expanded beyond biological relations to create strong support systems. The historical trauma of enslavement, indentureship and colonialism and the resilience of these extended family networks continue to influence contemporary Caribbean family dynamics.

The Caribbean's cultural diversity is reflected in its family structures. With many different races, ethnicities, and religions, Caribbean families contain a wide range of traditions and practices. These cultural influences shape the roles and responsibilities within families and contribute to the region's rich diversity.

External influences, particularly from North America, have made their mark on Caribbean family life. Globalisation, migration and the spread of Western values have introduced new dynamics and expectations within Caribbean families.

Adult roles and responsibilities

The adult roles and responsibilities include being **providers** and **nurturers**.

Adults as providers: Caribbean adults, especially fathers, have historically been the primary breadwinners of the family. They often bear the responsibility of working to ensure the economic stability of the household. This includes providing for essential needs such as food, shelter and education for their children.

Single-parent dynamics: The Caribbean family landscape has evolved, and single-parent households are increasingly common. In these families, one adult shoulders the responsibilities typically shared by two parents. Single parents, whether mothers or fathers, must balance the roles of provider, caregiver and emotional support system. This can often mean working long hours to bring in enough money for the family, and relying on friends or extended family to help with daily life such as taking children to school. This dynamic reflects the resilience and adaptability of Caribbean families.

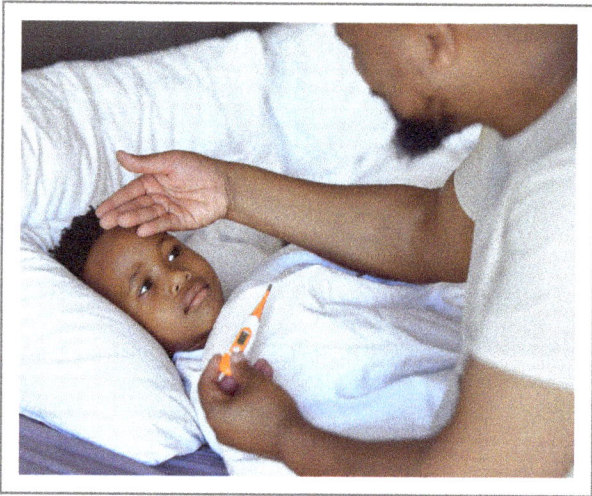

Figure 2.1 *Single parents may have to take time off work if their children are ill*

Extended family dynamics: Caribbean extended families often involve multiple generations living together or in close proximity. In such family structures, responsibilities may be shared among several adults. Grandparents, aunts, uncles, and older siblings often play vital roles in caregiving, mentorship and emotional support.

For example, in a Caribbean extended family, you might find an elderly grandmother. While she may not be the primary breadwinner, she plays a crucial role in nurturing and educating the younger generation. She shares wisdom, cultural traditions and provides emotional support. This extended family structure allows for a division of responsibilities, ensuring the wellbeing of all family members.

Nuclear family dynamics: Nuclear families consist of parents and their children, living together. Traditionally, fathers have been regarded as primary breadwinners, bringing in money for the household, while mothers typically oversee domestic affairs and child-rearing. However, this gender-based division of labour is evolving in response to changing societal dynamics, with increasing numbers of women pursuing careers outside the home.

For example, consider a Caribbean family where the father works as a schoolteacher, and the mother is employed as a nurse. While the father contributes to the family income through his teaching position, the mother's nursing profession also plays a crucial role in contributing to household finances. This is a departure from gender roles of the past, demonstrating how Caribbean nuclear families adapt to contemporary realities. Despite evolving roles, these families maintain close emotional bonds, shared responsibilities and a commitment to the wellbeing and development of all family members.

Adults as nurturers: In Caribbean families both parents are important in nurturing their children, challenging the traditional notion that sees mothers as the main nurturers. Beyond meeting material needs, their nurturing roles include offering emotional support, caring for the children and building a caring and compassionate home environment. These duties highlight the importance of developing strong emotional connections, instilling values, and encouraging the social and psychological growth of children. Additionally, mothers and fathers can provide emotional support through active listening, affirming their children's feelings and being present and engaged in their daily lives.

It is important to distinguish between nurturing and providing in the context of various family types in the Caribbean. In nuclear families, for instance, both parents typically share nurturing responsibilities, with fathers actively engaging in childcare and emotional support. Extended families, on the other hand, often involve a broader network of nurturers, including grandparents, aunts, uncles, and older siblings. These structures show how nurturing roles can be distributed among multiple family members, providing important emotional support and guidance that contributes to the development of children. Regardless of family type, nurturing remains a central component of Caribbean family dynamics, emphasising the value of emotional connections and the wellbeing of all family members.

Child abuse: It is important to note that while adults have critical roles and responsibilities within Caribbean families, these responsibilities must always be carried out with love, care, and respect for children. Child abuse in any form, whether physical, emotional, or psychological, should be unacceptable. Caribbean societies are increasingly committed to protecting the rights and wellbeing of children, recognising that their upbringing should be nurturing and free from harm. Ensuring the safety and healthy development of children is a collective responsibility that encompasses the broader community and society.

Legal roles and responsibilities of parents

In the Caribbean, as in many other regions, parents have distinct legal roles and responsibilities concerning the wellbeing and upbringing of their children. These legal obligations are outlined in various family and child welfare laws. Here are some of the fundamental legal roles and responsibilities of parents in the Caribbean, using the story of the Williams family:

Case study

The Williams family lives in a Caribbean community, known for its close-knit families and rich cultural traditions. Kevin and Kendra Williams, the parents of three children aged 3 months, 5 and 10 years, must fulfil their legal roles and responsibilities towards their children.

Providing financial support: Parents are legally obligated to provide financial support for their children. This includes covering essential expenses such as food, clothing, housing, education and healthcare. Failure to meet this responsibility can lead to legal consequences, including child support orders issued by the court.

Figure 2.2 *The Williams family*

Scenario

Kevin, a fisherman, and Kendra, a schoolteacher, aim to ensure their children's needs for food, clothing, housing and healthcare are met. Despite occasional financial hardships, especially during the off-season for fishing, they prioritise their children's wellbeing, aware that failure to provide could result in legal repercussions.

Ensuring education: Parents are legally required to ensure that their children receive an education. This may involve enrolling them in school and ensuring regular attendance. In some Caribbean countries, there are compulsory education laws that dictate the minimum level of schooling required.

Scenario

The Williams' ensure their children attend school regularly, understanding the importance of education for their future. The eldest, Deanna, shows promise in her studies and wants to attend university. Her parents are determined to support her ambitions.

Child protection: Parents are legally responsible for the safety and protection of their children. This involves safeguarding them from harm, abuse and neglect. If a parent is found to be endangering their child's welfare, legal authorities may intervene to ensure the child's safety.

Scenario

In their community, child safety is paramount. The Williams' always aim to protect their children from harm, aware of the legal obligations to safeguard them from abuse and neglect. Their involvement in community safety programmes shows their commitment to not only their children's welfare but also that of their neighbours'.

Healthcare decisions: Parents have the legal authority to make healthcare decisions on behalf of their children. This includes decisions about medical treatments, vaccinations and other healthcare matters. However, in cases where there is a dispute or concerns about a child's medical care, legal authorities may become involved to make decisions in the child's best interest.

Scenario

When their youngest, David, required surgery, Kevin and Kendra had to make informed healthcare decisions. Their legal right to decide on medical treatments reinforced the significance of their roles in ensuring their children's health and wellbeing.

Custody and visitation: In cases of separation or divorce, parents may have legal responsibilities regarding child custody and visitation arrangements. These legal agreements determine which parent has primary custody, visitation schedules and other parental rights and responsibilities.

Scenario

The Williams family has friends who have gone through separations. Witnessing these situations has made Kevin and Kendra aware of the complexities of custody, visitation and the legal framework that governs these arrangements. They value the importance of both parents playing an active role in their children's lives, regardless of marital status.

Legal consent: Parents often need to provide legal consent for various activities involving their children, such as travel, participation in certain sports, or obtaining passports.

Scenario

Kendra recently provided legal consent for their middle child, Darius, to participate in an international school sports event. This experience highlighted the parental role in enabling their children's participation in this kind of activity while adhering to legal requirements.

Moral and ethical guidance: While not always codified in law, parents are typically regarded as the primary influencers of their children's moral and ethical development. They are expected to instil values, beliefs and cultural practices within their children.

Scenario

Beyond their legal obligations, Kevin and Kendra cherish their role in guiding their children's moral and ethical development. They instil values such as respect, integrity and community spirit, hoping to see these traits reflected in their children's actions and interactions

Guardianship: In cases where parents are unable to fulfil their parental responsibilities due to factors like illness, legal authorities may appoint a guardian to assume these responsibilities temporarily.

Scenario

After Kevin had a health scare, the couple considered the legal provisions for guardianship. They had conversations about who would assume parental responsibilities if they were unable to do so, ensuring their children's continuity of care and support.

Children's roles and responsibilities

In Caribbean families, children are taught from an early age to have respect for their elders and to actively contribute to the family's overall wellbeing. While their main role involves learning and personal growth, children are also entrusted with specific responsibilities, such as assisting with household chores and supporting younger siblings.

Obedience holds an important place in the roles and responsibilities of Caribbean children. They are expected to follow the guidance and wisdom given by their parents and other elder family members. This emphasis on respect and obedience helps with the transmission of generational knowledge and the preservation of cultural traditions. It ensures that valuable insights and traditions are passed down from one generation to the next, safeguarding our rich Caribbean heritage.

Caribbean children are encouraged to take their educational opportunities seriously, recognising the importance of acquiring knowledge and skills not only for their personal development but also to contribute to their families and communities. This commitment to education reflects the value placed on learning and personal growth within Caribbean society.

The mind map below explains the roles and responsibilities of children within Caribbean families, highlighting the essential contributions they make towards their family's wellbeing and the preservation of cultural heritage. We can see the expectations placed upon children and the pivotal roles they play in maintaining and nurturing the rich traditions and values that define Caribbean society.

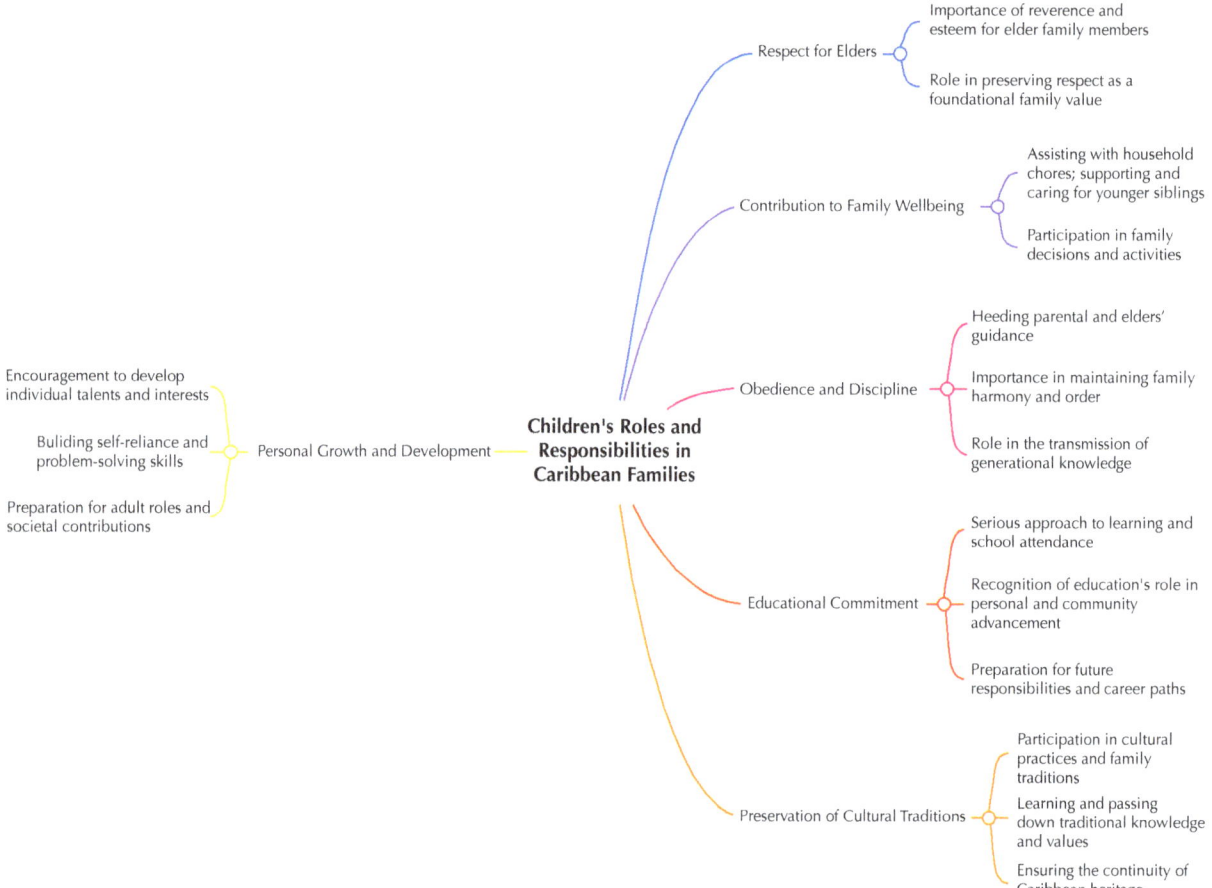

Figure 2.3 *Children's roles and responsibilities in Caribbean families*

UNICEF, the United Nations International Children's Emergency Fund, is a prominent global organisation dedicated to advocating for and protecting the rights and wellbeing of children worldwide. UNICEF recognises that children have both rights and responsibilities, and it works to ensure that children's roles and responsibilities are respected and supported.

Children's rights and responsibilities according to UNICEF:

Right to survival: UNICEF emphasises that every child has the right to survive and thrive. This includes access to healthcare, clean water and proper nutrition. While children are not legally responsible for their survival, societies and governments are responsible for ensuring that children have the conditions necessary to grow and develop.

Right to education: UNICEF is a strong advocate for the right to education for all children. Education is seen as both a right and a responsibility. Children have the responsibility to attend school and engage in their learning to the best of their abilities. At the same time, governments and societies have a responsibility to provide access to quality education.

Protection from harm: UNICEF recognises children's responsibility to be safe and protected from harm. This includes protection from violence, abuse, exploitation and conflict. It is the duty of adults, including parents, caregivers, and communities to ensure children's safety and provide environments where they can thrive.

Participation and expression: UNICEF emphasises that children have the right to express their views on matters that affect them and have those views taken seriously. While this is a right, it also carries a responsibility for children to learn to express themselves respectfully and responsibly. Adults, including parents and governments, have a responsibility to listen to children's voices and involve them in decisions that affect their lives.

Rights in emergencies: In times of emergency, such as natural disasters or conflicts, children's roles and responsibilities may become even more critical. UNICEF recognises the resilience and strength of children and their ability to contribute to their communities even in difficult circumstances.

Ending child labour: UNICEF is committed to ending child labour, recognising that children should not be engaged in work that jeopardises their health, education, or wellbeing. While children should not be employed in harmful labour, they also have a responsibility to focus on their education and personal development.

Questions

Knowledge and comprehension

1 a) Define 'family roles' and 'family responsibilities' in the context of Caribbean families.
   b) How do these roles and responsibilities contribute to the family's overall wellbeing?
   c) What is meant by 'interdependence' within Caribbean families, and why is it important?

2 a) Describe how the concept of 'effective parenting' is applied in Caribbean families.
   b) Using the concept of 'historical context', explain how Caribbean family roles and responsibilities have evolved over time.

3 a) What techniques are commonly used to investigate social issues related to family dynamics in the Caribbean?
   b) Provide an example of how these might be applied to study the impact of transnational families.

Use of knowledge

4 Analyse how the roles of 'provider' and 'nurturer' within Caribbean families have changed due to societal shifts.

5 Considering the definitions and examples provided, propose a solution to address the challenges faced by single-parent households in the Caribbean in balancing the roles of provider and nurturer.

6 Evaluate the importance of legal roles and responsibilities of parents in the Caribbean, as illustrated by the Williams family case study. How do these legal obligations support the physical, emotional and psychological wellbeing of children?

7 Discuss the impact of societal expectations on the roles and responsibilities of children in Caribbean families, especially concerning education and obedience. How do these expectations shape the children's personal development and contribution to family wellbeing?

Changes in the roles and responsibilities of family members in Caribbean society

Learning objective
- Analyse the historical, cultural, and societal factors that have led to changes in family roles and responsibilities and their consequences.

> **Important definitions**
>
> **Role evolution** – the process through which traditional family roles and responsibilities change over time due to cultural shifts, social developments, and economic factors. Factors contributing to role evolution include technological advancements, changes in the labour market, educational opportunities, and shifts in societal values and norms.
>
> **Societal expectations** – the norms and values within a given society that define what roles and responsibilities are expected of family members, including gender-specific expectations.

Changes in roles and responsibilities

Caribbean society has witnessed substantial changes in family dynamics over the years, reflecting shifts in societal norms, economic structures and cultural values. To understand these changes, it is helpful to contrast them with the family dynamics of the past.

Table 2.1 shows past and present aspects of family dynamics.

Aspect of family dynamics	Past	Present
Family structure	Extended family structures were common, including multiple generations living together.	Emphasis on nuclear family structures, consisting of parents and their children.
Gender roles	Traditional gender roles were prominent, with men as primary breadwinners and women primarily responsible for domestic duties.	Evolving gender roles, with more women entering the workforce, challenging traditional roles.
Economy	Agricultural economy where families often worked together on farms.	Diverse economic activities, including service sectors and increased urbanisation.
Religious and cultural practices	Strong influence of religious and cultural traditions in family life.	Ongoing influence of religion and culture, but with increased diversity and acceptance of different belief systems.
Education and mobility	Limited access to education for some; focus on practical skills.	Expanded educational opportunities and encouragement of higher education and career goals. Increased mobility.
Globalisation	Limited international mobility and interaction.	Greater globalisation, with diaspora communities and international migration.

Aspect of family dynamics	Past	Present
Changing values	Traditional values and norms strongly upheld.	Shifting values, increased acceptance of diverse family structures, and evolving societal norms.
Technology and communication	Limited access to technology; primarily face-to-face communication.	Widespread access to technology, enabling digital communication and connectivity across distances.
Economic challenges	Economic disparities, with many families facing financial instability and poverty.	Persistent economic challenges, emphasising the importance of social support networks within families.

Table 2.1

Causes of changes

Gender equality: As gender roles evolve, women increasingly participate in the workforce. This shift has led to shared responsibilities for providing and nurturing within families.

Figure 2.4 *More women are taking up traditionally male roles, such as engineering*

Figure 2.5 *More people are attending universities*

Education: Access to education has empowered individuals, encouraging them to pursue careers and personal goals before starting families.

Urbanisation: The migration of individuals from rural to urban areas has led to changes in family structures and lifestyles. Urban centres offer different economic opportunities and often require different family arrangements.

Globalisation: Greater connectivity to the global economy and the influence of global culture have impacted family values, norms, and practices. Exposure to diverse perspectives can lead to shifts in traditional roles and expectations.

Figure 2.6 *More people are migrating to urban areas*

Section A(i)   Individual, Family and Society

Figure 2.7 *Television exposes people to global culture*

Figure 2.8 *Regular employment leads to financial security*

Economic challenges: Economic disparities, unemployment, and underemployment have forced families to adapt to changing financial circumstances. This can result in more family members seeking employment to make ends meet.

Migration: Caribbean countries often experience significant emigration, with family members relocating abroad for work or educational opportunities. This can create transnational families and alter family dynamics.

Figure 2.9 *Many family members move abroad for work or education*

Figure 2.10 *The law can influence family structures and responsibilities*

Legislation and legal changes: Changes in laws related to marriage, divorce, and child custody have influenced family structures and responsibilities. Legal reforms can encourage or require more equitable division of responsibilities.

Healthcare advances: Improved healthcare has resulted in longer life expectancy and changes in generational relationships. Extended families may care for elderly members or adapt to changing healthcare needs. Family decisions are sometimes made about care for sick relatives; this includes living arrangements.

Social movements: Social and civil rights movements have promoted equality, tolerance and diversity. These movements influence societal attitudes towards family structures and gender roles.

Figure 2.11 *Improved healthcare has meant people live longer*

Figure 2.12 *Social and civil rights movements have influenced societal attitudes*

Figure 2.13 *Changes in religion can impact family dynamics*

Religious changes: Shifts in religious practices and affiliations can impact family dynamics, especially when religious institutions advocate different family values and roles.

Generational differences: Younger generations often have different perspectives on family life, influenced by their exposure to changing societal norms and opportunities.

Effects of changes

Dual-income households: With more women entering the workforce, Caribbean families increasingly rely on dual incomes to meet their financial needs. This shift has altered the traditional provider role within families.

Role flexibility: Modern Caribbean families exhibit greater role flexibility. Family members are more adaptable and versatile in their responsibilities, enabling them to adjust to evolving circumstances and expectations.

Delayed parenthood: Changes in family dynamics have led to delayed parenthood. Many Caribbean couples are choosing to start families later in life, often after establishing their careers and pursuing personal goals.

Smaller family sizes: The trend towards smaller family sizes is becoming more prevalent in Caribbean society. Couples are opting to have fewer children, influenced by factors such as financial considerations and changing societal norms, including starting their families later.

Figure 2.14 *Young people may grow up to have different perspectives on family life to their parents*

Increased divorce rates: As family dynamics evolve, there has been an increase in divorce rates in Caribbean countries. This can result in more complex family structures, with children often living in single-parent or blended households.

Shift in generational roles: Changes in family dynamics have shifted generational roles. In some cases, grandparents are taking on more significant caregiving roles for their grandchildren due to parents' work commitments.

Transnational families: The phenomenon of transnational families has emerged, where family members live in different countries. This can result in challenges related to maintaining family connections and providing emotional support over long distances.

Cultural adaptation: The changing dynamics have necessitated cultural adaptation within Caribbean families. Younger generations may embrace more globalised values and norms, while older generations may hold onto traditional cultural practices, creating generational and cultural gaps.

Questions

Knowledge and comprehension

1. a) Define 'role evolution' and explain how it has impacted Caribbean family dynamics.
   b) What are 'societal expectations', and how do they influence the roles within Caribbean families?

2. Discuss how technological advancements and urbanisation have contributed to changes in family roles and responsibilities in Caribbean societies.

3. Explain the apparent causes and consequences of increased gender equality within Caribbean families.

Use of knowledge

4. Analyse the effects of economic challenges and migration on the traditional Caribbean family structure. Use examples from Table 2.1 on page 26 comparing past and present aspects of family dynamics.

5. Read this case study and answer the questions which follow.

Case study

Background:

The Marshall family lives in a Caribbean city, balancing work and parenting. Michael and Lisa both work full-time, sharing financial, domestic, and childcare responsibilities for their children, Sofia (8) and Jason (12). With demanding jobs and limited family support, they face challenges in maintaining family harmony and supporting their children's educational and emotional needs.

Complications:

- Sofia is struggling academically
- Jason, entering adolescence, needs more guidance
- Lisa's work-related travel is causing family strain

a) Analyse how the Marshall family's dynamics are affected by societal expectations and the evolution of family roles.

b) Discuss the impact on the children's development and suggest solutions for the family to manage their challenges, focusing on dual-income household adaptation, role flexibility, and enhancing emotional support and communication.

Factors in preparing for parenthood

Preparing for parenthood involves a holistic approach that encompasses education, emotional readiness and financial planning. It is about equipping oneself with the knowledge and skills needed to provide a nurturing and supportive environment for a child's physical, emotional, and financial wellbeing.

Learning objective

- Explore the qualities and attributes that contribute to effective parenting within Caribbean families.

> **Important definitions**
>
> *Parenthood preparation* – *the process of acquiring the knowledge, skills, and resources necessary for individuals or couples to become responsible and effective parents.*
>
> *Effective parenting* – *the ability of parents to provide physical, emotional, and psychological support to their children, fostering their healthy development and wellbeing.*

Preparing for parenthood

Parenthood is a profound and life-altering responsibility within the context of family life. Below are the factors individuals need to consider when preparing for parenthood.

Education

Gaining knowledge about child development, parenting techniques, and child safety is crucial. Parents must understand the various stages of a child's physical, emotional, and cognitive development to provide appropriate care and support. This includes knowing how to create a safe environment, how to foster healthy attachments, and how to address the changing needs of a growing child.

Education can be obtained through formal parenting classes, reading parenting books, attending workshops, or seeking advice from experienced parents and professionals.

Continuous learning is essential, as parenting strategies and child development research evolve over time.

Emotional and psychological readiness

Being emotionally prepared to be a parent is vital. Parents need to be emotionally equipped to handle the joys and challenges that come with raising a child. This includes nurturing, guiding, and providing emotional support.

Emotional readiness involves being patient, empathetic, and resilient. It is about understanding that parenthood often involves sleepless nights, tantrums, and various other stressful things, but it also brings immense joy, love, and fulfilment. Being emotionally ready means having the capacity to handle both the ups and downs of parenting with grace and care.

Parents also need to be psychologically ready to raise a child. This means ensuring they are ready, willing and able to put the child or children first above their own needs. The stressful aspects of parenting can put strain on a person's mental health, so prospective parents must make sure they are prepared for this.

Financial planning:

Figure 2.15 *Families need to plan for the financial needs of their children*

Preparing for the financial demands of raising a child is a practical necessity. Parenthood often comes with significant financial responsibilities, including:

- Education: Parents need to plan for their child's education, which can include saving for college or other educational expenses.
- Healthcare: Medical expenses, including routine check-ups, vaccinations, and unforeseen health issues, must be considered.
- Day-to-day expenses: Providing for a child's daily needs, such as food, clothing, shelter and recreational activities, requires financial planning.

Creating a budget, setting financial goals, and saving for unexpected expenses are all part of responsible financial planning for parenthood.

Qualities of an effective parent

Effective parenting is the bedrock upon which strong families and a healthier society are built. The qualities of an effective parent are integral to fostering strong families and contributing positively to society. These qualities, such as communication, empathy, consistency, patience and adaptability, create a supportive and nurturing family environment. Effective parenting is not related to social status, highlighting that any parent, regardless of their background, can excel in raising well-adjusted and responsible individuals who enrich our communities and contribute to societal progress.

We can use the acronym P.E.A.C.E to rate the qualities of an effective parent.

Patience: Parenting comes with its share of challenges. Having patience is vital for navigating these difficulties with grace. Patient parents can guide their children through various life stages, imparting valuable life skills and problem-solving techniques without resorting to anger or punishment.

Empathy: The ability to understand a child's feelings and needs is fundamental. Empathetic parents can respond to their child's emotional and developmental requirements with sensitivity and compassion. This, in turn, contributes to a family environment where emotional wellbeing is prioritised.

Adaptability: Recognising that each child is unique and may require different approaches is essential. Adaptable parents tailor their guidance and support to meet the specific needs of their children. This quality promotes individual growth within the family and nurtures a harmonious family dynamic.

Communication: Open and honest communication within a family fosters trust, empathy, and understanding. When parents and children can freely express themselves, it strengthens their bond. This trust and connection contribute to a family where members feel heard and valued.

Equity: Establishing clear rules and boundaries provides predictability and stability for children. Equity in enforcing these guidelines fosters a sense of security within the family. Children who know what to expect are more likely to thrive academically and socially, contributing to a harmonious family.

End of chapter questions

1. What are the traditional roles of adults in Caribbean families, particularly with regards to providing for the family?
2. Explain the concept of transnational families within the context of Caribbean society.
3. How has delayed parenthood become a noticeable trend in Caribbean family dynamics?
4. What are the potential impacts of increased divorce rates on family dynamics in Caribbean countries?
5. Describe the effects of the changing roles of women on Caribbean family dynamics in the context of:
   a) Dual-income households
   b) Single-mother households
6. a) How has the concept of role flexibility influenced Caribbean families?
   b) Provide examples of how role flexibility benefits family members.
7. a) Explain the cultural adaptation that has become necessary within Caribbean families due to changing dynamics.
   b) What are the challenges associated with this adaptation?
8. Discuss the role of grandparents in Caribbean families and how it has evolved as a result of changes in generational roles.

SBA skills

To what extent have changing gender roles influenced the roles and responsibilities of adults within your community? Support your response with local examples.

1. **Statement of the problem**
   What are you trying to find out?
2. **Reason(s) for selecting the topic**
   Why did you choose this topic?
3. **Method of investigation**
   How will you find the information you need?
4. **Design of the instrument used to collect data**
   What questions will you ask, and how?
5. **Procedures used to collect data**
   How will you gather the information?
6. **Presentation of data**
   How will you show the information you collected?
7. **Analysis and interpretation of data**
   What do the numbers and answers mean?
8. **Statement of findings**
   What did you find out?
9. **Recommendations and implementation strategy**
   What should be done about your findings?

Summary

Roles and responsibilities within Caribbean families are constantly evolving, emphasising the importance of family dynamics in cultural identity. These roles are shaped by historical context. Both adults and children contribute to the family's wellbeing, and there should be a balance between providing material needs and nurturing emotional development. The impact of transnational families, legal obligations, and children's contributions to family and cultural preservation should be understood, along with the challenges and joys of parenting and the shift towards more equitable gender roles and responsibilities.

Key themes and concepts:

- Historical context: Caribbean family roles have evolved due to historical influences, including colonialism, enslavement and indentureship, impacting family structure and dynamics.
- Family dynamics: Both adults and children play crucial roles in the family, contributing to its overall wellbeing and stability.
- Material vs. emotional support: Families balance providing material needs with nurturing emotional bonds and support, crucial for healthy development.
- Transnational families: Migration has led to families living across countries, affecting emotional ties and financial support dynamics.
- Legal obligations: Laws influence family responsibilities, including childcare and support for elderly members.
- Children's contributions: Children participate in cultural preservation and family support, showing the intergenerational nature of roles.
- Parenting challenges and joys: Parenting in the Caribbean is marked by unique challenges and rewards, reflecting cultural values and societal expectations.
- Gender roles: There's a shift towards more equitable gender roles within families, challenging traditional expectations and responsibilities.

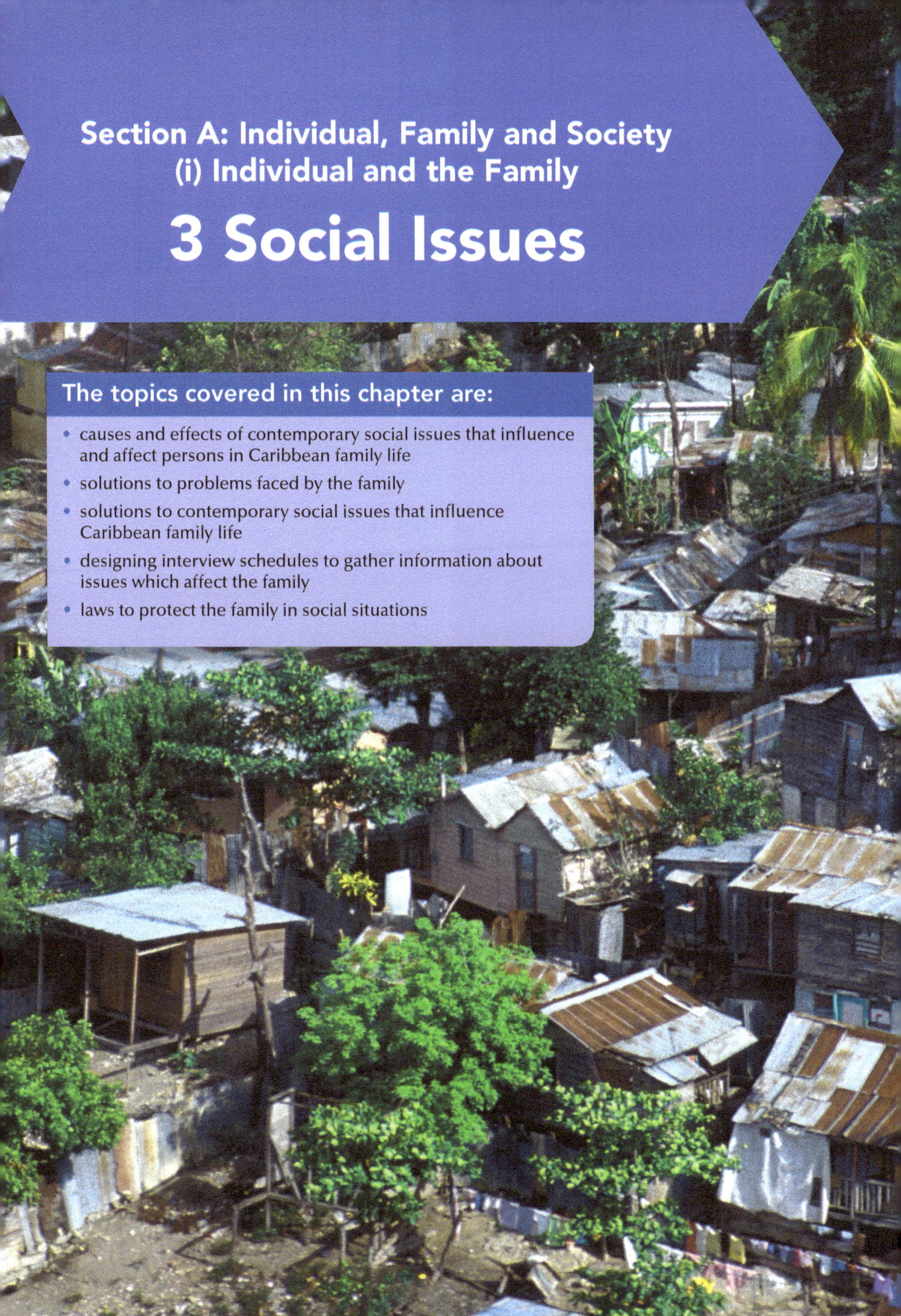

Section A: Individual, Family and Society
(i) Individual and the Family
3 Social Issues

The topics covered in this chapter are:

- causes and effects of contemporary social issues that influence and affect persons in Caribbean family life
- solutions to problems faced by the family
- solutions to contemporary social issues that influence Caribbean family life
- designing interview schedules to gather information about issues which affect the family
- laws to protect the family in social situations

Introduction to social issues

In the Caribbean, the concept of **family** is deeply rooted within social issues that significantly influence its functioning and wellbeing. For example: economic instability, education access, healthcare access, housing, nutrition, relationship stress and poverty cycle. These **social issues** not only shape the dynamics within the family but also have a profound impact on the broader society. Exploring the **relationship** between these issues and Caribbean family life allows for a comprehensive understanding of the unique challenges and complexities faced by families in the region. By delving into these issues, we aim to uncover the underlying factors and propose effective solutions that cater to the specific cultural nuances and social dynamics of the Caribbean, fostering stronger and more resilient families within the fabric of the society.

Contemporary social issues

Learning objectives

- Analyse causes and effects of social issues within Caribbean family life.
- Justify solutions to contemporary social issues in the Caribbean context.
- Design effective interview schedules to assess family issues.
- Describe laws protecting families in various social situations within your country and the wider Caribbean.

Important definitions

Social issues – *concerns or problems that affect individuals and communities within a society. They often encompass issues related to equity, justice, and wellbeing.*

Contemporary – *refers to current or modern issues and ideas.*

Family life – *the daily experiences, interactions, and relationships within a family unit, including both nuclear and extended family members.*

Causes – *factors or influences that contribute to the existence or development of a particular issue or problem.*

Effects – *consequences or outcomes resulting from the presence or persistence of social issues within the family.*

Solutions – *strategies, interventions or actions designed to address and resolve existing problems or challenges.*

Cycle of poverty – *a self-reinforcing pattern where limited access to education, healthcare, and jobs keeps families in poverty across generations.*

Quality education – *an inclusive system that fosters critical skills, enabling individuals to improve their socioeconomic status and contribute to society.*

Laws – *regulations or legal provisions established by the government to protect and regulate the rights and responsibilities of individuals within the family and broader social context.*

What are social issues?

Social issues are problems in society that affect many people. These issues can impact various aspects of people's lives, including their wellbeing, relationships, and overall quality of life. Social issues are often rooted in societal structures, cultural norms, economic systems, or political frameworks and can manifest in different forms, such as inequality, discrimination, poverty, crime, or access to resources. They may arise from a combination of factors, including historical legacies, systemic injustices, and **contemporary** challenges. Solving social issues usually means everyone needs to work together on a large scale to tackle the root problems and make things fairer and better for all.

Social issues can be diverse and multifaceted, encompassing various challenges and concerns within a society. Some common types of social issues include:

Poverty and economic inequality: The unequal distribution of wealth, resources and limited access to basic requirements such as education and employment opportunities contribute to poverty and economic disparities within a society.

Discrimination and social injustice: Prejudice, bias, and discrimination based on factors such as race, ethnicity, gender, sexual orientation, or religion can lead to social marginalisation and systemic inequalities.

Access to education and healthcare: Unequal access to **quality education** and healthcare services can hinder individuals' opportunities for personal development and overall wellbeing, contributing to broader social challenges.

Crime and violence: Issues related to crime, violence, and community safety can negatively impact individuals and communities, creating an environment of fear and instability.

Environmental concerns: Environmental degradation, pollution, and climate change pose significant challenges to societies, affecting the health and livelihoods of communities and future generations.

Mental health and wellbeing: Challenges related to mental health, including stigmatisation, lack of resources, and limited access to support services can impact individuals' overall wellbeing and social functioning.

Family dynamics and relationships: Issues within family units, such as domestic violence, divorce, and child welfare, can influence individuals' emotional and psychological wellbeing and contribute to broader societal challenges.

Teenage pregnancy: This is a major social issue with a variety of **causes** and consequences. Some of the most common causes include lack of access to sex education and contraception, poverty, and peer pressure. Teenage pregnancy can have many negative consequences for both the mother and the child, including increased risk of health complications, lower educational attainment and economic hardship. There is a need to promote sexual education in schools to assist in the understanding of sexual maturity.

Child abandonment: A variety of factors, including poverty, domestic violence and mental illness can cause child abandonment. Abandonment can have a devastating impact on children, leading to emotional trauma, neglect, and abuse.

Divorce and separation: Children are often the most affected by divorce and may experience a range of emotions, including sadness, anger and confusion. It is important for parents to support their children during this challenging time and to provide them with a safe and stable environment.

Generation gap: This is the difference in values, attitudes, and behaviours between different generations. It can be a source of conflict in families, as older and younger generations may have different views on parenting, technology and social norms.

Substance abuse: This is a serious social problem that can have a devastating impact on individuals, families, and communities. It can lead to a range of health problems including addiction, overdose and mental health issues. Substance abuse can also damage relationships and lead to financial difficulties.

Juvenile delinquency: This is criminal behaviour by young people. A variety of factors including poverty, lack of parental supervision and gang involvement can cause it. Juvenile delinquency can have a number of negative consequences for young people including detention, expulsion from school and involvement in the criminal justice system.

Contemporary social issues in Caribbean family life

Contemporary social issues in Caribbean **family life** are linked to the region's cultural, economic and political setting. Economic disparities and poverty restrict access to essential resources and opportunities. The rich diversity of Caribbean culture, while a source of pride, can also create rifts, leading to cultural identity struggles and marginalisation within families. Gender inequalities and limited access to quality healthcare and education compound the existing hurdles, posing barriers to the holistic development of family members, particularly women and children. These social issues underscore the critical need to address systemic challenges and foster inclusive, sustainable development across Caribbean communities.

Figure 3.1 *Graffiti*

Causes of social issues in Caribbean families

Caribbean families face a range of social issues that deeply affect their lives and communities. These include:

– economic disparities and poverty
– historical and cultural influences
– sociopolitical factors
– globalisation and modernisation.

Social issues in Caribbean families are caused by many reasons and affect both families and their communities. A big reason is poverty, meaning many families don't have enough money for basic needs, education, or good jobs, making it hard for them to get ahead.

In many Caribbean communities, families often struggle to find steady, well-paying jobs due to limited opportunities and low wages. This makes it tough for them to afford basic needs like a home, food and school. As a result, families face a lot of stress, which can lead to arguments and mental health issues. It is a cycle where being poor makes it hard to get a good job, and without a good job, persons remain poor, making family life even more challenging.

Key labour market statistics

Below are the main labour indicators for the Caribbean region, highlighting the recovery to pre-pandemic levels in 2022.

The statistics help to better understand some of the economic factors that underlie the social issues experienced in the region. For example, the youth unemployment rate of 18.2% means that there are approximately 3 million people up to age 24 who are unemployed and another 4 million, approximately, living below $2.15 per day. Table 3.1, on page 40, shows how these figures have been calculated.

Case study

The Thompson family lives in a small community in the Caribbean. Like many families in their area, they face several challenges rooted in broader social issues that impact their daily lives and wellbeing.

Economic disparities and poverty:

Mr Thompson works in agriculture, a sector that is often affected by natural disasters, economic changes and poor market prices, while Mrs Thompson is a part-time teacher. Their combined income barely covers their basic needs, reflecting the economic disparities in the region. Their situation is complicated by the lack of stable employment opportunities, which keeps them in a cycle of poverty.

Figure 3.2 The Thompson family

Limited access to resources, educational opportunities, and stable employment perpetuate cycles of poverty, creating significant barriers for families trying to improve their socioeconomic standing.

Historical and cultural influences:

The Thompsons' community still feels the effects of historical events, such as colonialism, which have shaped current social and economic structures. Cultural norms also influence their roles within the family and community, with Mr Thompson feeling the pressure to be the primary breadwinner, despite the limited job opportunities.

Legacies of colonialism, cultural conflicts and generational trauma shape family dynamics, leading to cultural identity conflicts and marginalisation within families.

Sociopolitical factors:

Local governance and policies have a direct impact on the Thompson family's access to healthcare, education, and social services. The lack of investment in local infrastructure and social programmes means their children attend schools with limited resources, and accessing quality healthcare is a challenge.

Government inefficiency, political upheaval and social unrest contribute to an environment of uncertainty, making it challenging for families to access essential services and support and hindering the implementation of effective social policies.

Globalisation and modernisation:

The influx of foreign goods and the pressure to keep up with modern standards of living have introduced new challenges for the Thompson family. While globalisation has brought some benefits, such as increased access to information technology, it has also led to cultural shifts and increased competition for jobs, further complicating their economic situation.

Indicator	Value (2022)	Description
Labour participation rate	63.5%	Percentage of the working-age population that is either employed or actively seeking work.
Unemployment rate	7.9%	Percentage of the labour force that is unemployed and actively seeking employment.
Employment rate	58.5%	Percentage of the working-age population that is employed.
Informal employment	47.2%	Percentage of the employed population working in the informal sector.
Youth unemployment rate	18.2%	Unemployment rate for individuals aged 15–24.
Gender participation gap	14.3%	Difference in labour force participation rates between men and women.
Real average wage growth	0.2%	Year-over-year percentage change in average wages, adjusted for inflation.
Labour productivity	Decline by 1.5%	Year-over-year percentage change in output per labour hour.
Economic growth rate	6.3% (regional average)	Annual growth rate of GDP for the Caribbean region.
Poverty headcount ratio	25% (including Latin America)	Percentage of the population living below $2.15 a day (2017 PPP).

Table 3.1

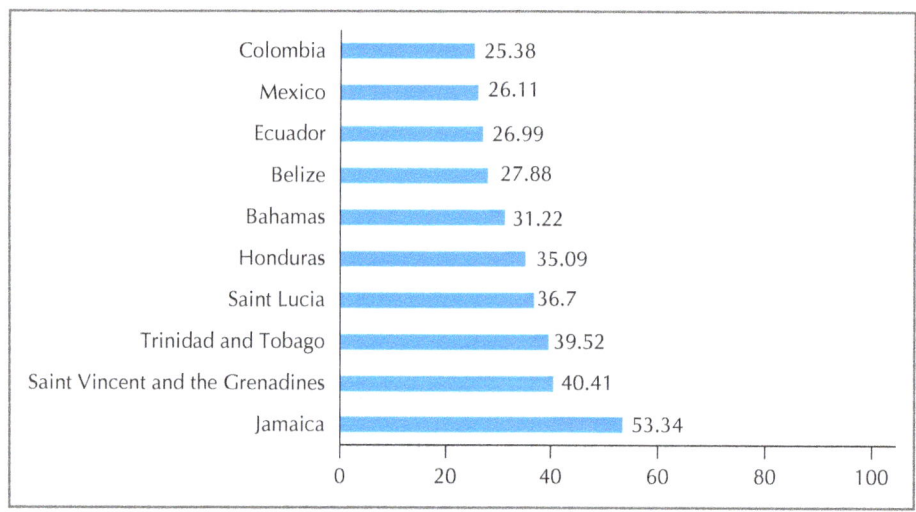

Figure 3.3 *Countries with highest murder rates 2022*

High unemployment rates often create social issues, including crime, within Caribbean families. When individuals within a family unit experience unemployment or underemployment, it can lead to financial instability and increased stress. The strain of financial pressure can contribute to conflict, anxiety, and a sense of hopelessness, which can negatively affect the wellbeing and dynamics of the family. Limited employment opportunities can cause individuals to resort to criminal activities for income, increasing crime levels within communities. The associated risks of criminal involvement can further disrupt family dynamics, leading to strained relationships, emotional turmoil, and a breakdown in trust among family members.

The history and culture of Caribbean families are deeply connected to the past, including times of enslavement and the ongoing challenges of native groups like the Kalinago people. The lasting effects of colonialism and enslavement have left a significant imprint on the cultural identity and family dynamics of many Caribbean communities. This has led to cultural conflict, identity crises, and generational trauma.

Poor governance and social unrest add to the challenges families face. Issues related to government inefficiency, political upheaval, and social unrest cause uncertainty, making it hard for families to access essential services and support. As a result, implementing effective social policies becomes increasingly difficult, making progress toward social cohesion and stability difficult.

Sociopolitical factors and economic challenges significantly impact family stability, particularly in regions such as Haiti. Political instability, with frequent changes in leadership and inefficient government, has led to uncertainty and a lack of confidence in the nation's institutions. This has made it challenging for families to access essential services and support, which contributes to increased social and economic issues. High unemployment rates, limited job opportunities and widespread poverty put further strain on families, making it difficult for them to meet their basic needs and maintain a decent standard of living. These interconnected sociopolitical and economic challenges create a number of difficulties that families in must navigate on a daily basis.

Globalisation and modernisation cause rapid changes that challenge traditional family structures and values within Caribbean communities. Globalised ideals and practices can prompt a shift in family roles and expectations, leading to shifts in societal norms and cultural dynamics. These changes can cause conflict within families, as generational gaps and differences in social values become more distinct, impacting family relationships.

Emerging social issues

In the Caribbean and globally, rising issues like scamming and human trafficking are driven by underlying challenges such as unemployment, poverty and economic disparities, which leave many vulnerable.

Scamming, particularly through internet fraud and identity theft, stems from economic hardship and high unemployment, with individuals resorting to fraudulent activities for survival. This not only damages personal trust but also tarnishes the reputation of regions known for scamming. A lack of job opportunities, especially among youth, fuels this problem.

Similarly, **human trafficking** preys on vulnerable populations facing economic instability, unemployment, and lack of education. Traffickers exploit these conditions, often deceiving victims with false promises of employment, leading them into forced labor or exploitation. Poverty-driven desperation makes it easier for traffickers to manipulate individuals into exploitative situations.

Addressing both scamming and human trafficking requires structural **solutions**, including creating employment opportunities, improving quality education, and reducing economic inequalities that push individuals into these risky circumstances.

Effects of social issues on Caribbean family life

Social issues are complex and often interconnected, and they can have a significant impact on all aspects of life, including family life.

The effects of social issues on Caribbean family life fall into the following key areas:

- Disrupted family dynamics
- Psychological and emotional impact
- Interpersonal relationships
- Educational and occupational limitations
- Health and wellbeing

- Gender roles
- Cultural identity
- Policy and advocacy

The effects can be far-reaching, impacting various aspects of an individual's wellbeing and overall family dynamics. These effects can include disrupted family dynamics, leading to strained relationships and challenges in maintaining family cohesion. The psychological and emotional impact can manifest in increased stress, anxiety and mental health struggles among family members.

Social issues can limit educational and occupational opportunities, making making promotions based on merit and economic stability more difficult. This can perpetuate poverty cycles and halt an individual's growth and development within the Caribbean family context.

Disrupted family dynamics

Disrupted family dynamics are breakdowns in the functions of a family unit, leading to challenges in maintaining healthy relationships and fulfilling familial roles. For example, in a family affected by substance abuse, the addicted family member's behaviour may lead to strained relationships, financial instability and emotional distress among other family members. The addiction could disrupt traditional family roles, with other members taking on additional responsibilities or withdrawing emotionally from the affected individual, causing a breakdown in communication and trust within the family. Such disruption can have a huge impact on the overall wellbeing and stability of the family.

Psychological and emotional impact

Psychological and emotional impacts are the negative effects on an individual's mental wellbeing and emotional stability, caused by various social issues. For example, in domestic abuse cases within Caribbean families, individuals, particularly children, may experience emotional trauma, fear and a lack of security. Witnessing or experiencing abuse can lead to long-term psychological and emotional consequences such as anxiety, depression and post-traumatic stress disorder. Additionally, victims may struggle with low self-esteem and a sense of helplessness, which can significantly impact their overall mental health and emotional resilience. These psychological and emotional impacts can affect an individual's ability to form healthy relationships and engage in positive interactions.

Figure 3.4 *Emotional trauma*

Interpersonal relationships

Interpersonal relationships are the connections and interactions between individuals within the family and their broader social circles. For example, in Caribbean families, social issues such as economic problems can strain relationships, leading to increased tension, conflict and misunderstandings among family members. Financial stress or limited resources can create a competitive or hostile atmosphere within the family, affecting how individuals communicate and relate to one another. Social issues like cultural conflict or historical trauma can lead to a breakdown of trust and empathy, further weakening interpersonal relationships within the family.

Educational and occupational limitations

Educational and occupational limitations are the constraints and challenges individuals within Caribbean families face in accessing **quality education** and employment opportunities. For example, many individuals may struggle to afford further education, limiting access to skill development. Limited employment opportunities due to a lack of economic development or job market saturation can result in high unemployment rates or overemployment in low-paying, insecure, or exploitative jobs. This can perpetuate **cycles of poverty** and limit the socioeconomic mobility, wellbeing and progress of Caribbean families.

Health and wellbeing

Children growing up in families affected by social issues such as poverty, crime and violence often face challenges to their health and wellbeing. Lack of access to nutritious food, healthcare and a safe living environment leads to increased rates of malnutrition and chronic health conditions among young people. Crime and violence in the community exposes children to traumatic experiences that can have lasting effects on their psychological and emotional development. The resulting stress, anxiety and insecurity can manifest as mental health issues, with long-term consequences for their overall wellbeing.

Child development

Children living in environments affected by social issues often face disruptions in their development, with long term impacts on their overall wellbeing. Chaotic or stressful family environments, domestic violence, substance abuse or poverty can hinder a child's cognitive, emotional and social development. These experiences may contribute to developmental delays, behavioural issues and learning difficulties, affecting their academic performance and social interactions. Lack of stable and nurturing relationships with caregivers can halt the formation of secure attachments, which are important for healthy emotional development, positive self-esteem and resilience.

Gender roles

Social issues within Caribbean families can significantly influence traditional gender roles by promoting existing inequalities and imposing constraints on the roles and responsibilities of family members. In areas of poverty and limited resources, traditional gender roles tend to be reinforced, with men assuming the role of primary breadwinners and women taking on the roles of primary caregivers.

This can limit women's opportunities for education and employment. As a result, these circumstances can perpetuate gender disparities, limit women's participation in the workforce and restrict their ability to follow their ambitions, affecting the overall dynamics and wellbeing of Caribbean families.

Cultural identity

Cultural identity is often deeply intertwined with social issues, posing challenges to the preservation and transmission of cultural heritage within Caribbean families. Globalisation and increased migration can introduce different cultural influences and practices that may dilute traditional values and customs. Family members, particularly the younger generation, may experience disconnection from their cultural roots and struggle to identify with their ancestral heritage. This can create a cultural gap between generations, making it challenging for parents to pass down their cultural knowledge and traditions to their children.

Policy and advocacy

Policy and advocacy play a vital role in addressing the effects of social issues on Caribbean family life, offering sustainable solutions and fostering community support. Investing in social programmes to support families, such as early childhood education initiatives, affordable housing projects and accessible healthcare services can help limit the impact of social issues on family wellbeing. Advocating for policies that tackle the root causes of social issues, including poverty, inequality and discrimination, is crucial for fostering a more equitable and inclusive environment for Caribbean families.

Questions

Knowledge and comprehension

1. Define 'economic disparities' and explain how they contribute to social issues within Caribbean families.

2. Describe the impact of historical and cultural influences on Caribbean family dynamics.

3. Identify two sociopolitical factors that affect family stability in the Caribbean.

Use of knowledge

4. Analyse how globalisation and modernisation have changed traditional family roles in the Caribbean.

5. Propose solutions to mitigate the impact of economic disparities on Caribbean families.

6. Evaluate the effectiveness of current educational and healthcare access in supporting family wellbeing in your country

SBA skills

1. Design a simple survey to assess the impact of crime and violence in your community on safety and family life in your area.
2. Create a school awareness campaign proposal that addresses environmental concerns affecting Caribbean families.
3. Discuss how cultural identity conflicts can be addressed within your school to promote unity and understanding.

Proposed solutions to problems faced by the family

Learning objectives

- Propose culturally sensitive solutions for family-related problems.
- Find and evaluate local resources that can help improve families' lives.
- Learn effective ways to solve conflict and communicate better within families.
- Discuss how education can help individuals move up socially and economically, reducing family poverty.

Important definitions

Community resources – Services and programmes available within a community designed to support the needs of its members, including families facing social issues. These resources range from educational programmes to healthcare services and emergency assistance.

Conflict resolution – the process of resolving a dispute or disagreement through effective communication, negotiation and compromise to achieve a peaceful and mutually satisfactory outcome.

Financial literacy – the ability to understand and use various financial skills, including personal financial management, budgeting and investing, which are essential for making informed financial decisions.

Social mobility – the ability of individuals or families to move up social levels or improve their social status, often through education, employment or changes in income.

Policy advocacy – actively seeking to influence public policy and resource allocation decisions within political, economic and social systems and institutions, to bring about positive changes in society.

Caribbean families face a variety of social issues including poverty, crime, violence and gender inequality. These issues can have a negative impact on family dynamics, child development and overall wellbeing.

There are several solutions to address the problems faced by Caribbean families. These involve community-based support systems, counselling services, educational initiatives and policy advocacy. It is important to use culturally sensitive and practical approaches that can be implemented at individual and societal levels.

Case study

The Programme of Advancement Through Health and Education (PATH) in Jamaica

Background

The Programme of Advancement Through Health and Education (PATH), launched in Jamaica in 2001, is a conditional cash transfer programme designed to support vulnerable groups, including poor families with children, the elderly, people with disabilities, pregnant women, and unemployed adults. PATH was established to streamline three existing programmes—Food Stamp, Outdoor Poor Relief, and Public Assistance—in order to reduce duplication, improve efficiency, and deliver more effective aid to those in need.

Objectives

The programme's key objectives include:

- increasing educational attainment and improving health outcomes by requiring children to attend school and receive regular healthcare

- reducing child labour by ensuring children stay in school
- alleviating poverty by providing financial transfers to poor households
- serving as a safety net to prevent families from falling deeper into poverty.

Programme features

PATH provides cash transfers to qualifying households, alongside benefits like free school lunches and health services.

An educational grant was introduced in 2008 to support students moving from secondary to higher education.

During the COVID-19 pandemic, PATH increased its cash transfers by 50% and provided students with internet data plans and devices to support virtual learning.

Impact

PATH has successfully increased school attendance and healthcare access for vulnerable families, while offering critical financial support to help alleviate poverty. During the pandemic, the programme played a vital role in keeping students engaged in education and maintaining household stability through increased financial support.

Challenges

Despite its successes, PATH faces challenges, including ensuring compliance with programme conditions in rural areas and addressing long-term dependency on cash transfers.

Conclusion

The PATH programme has proven to be an essential safety net for Jamaica's most vulnerable populations, improving education and health outcomes while providing much-needed financial support to break the cycle of poverty.

Community-based support systems

Community-based support systems can play a vital role in strengthening families and helping them to cope with social challenges. Some of these systems are:

Parenting education and support: Parenting education programmes can teach parents important skills for raising healthy and happy children. Support groups can provide parents with a place to share their experiences and receive support.

After-school programmes and summer camps: After-school programmes and summer camps can provide children with safe and enriching activities outside of school hours. This can reduce their risk of exposure to crime and violence, and help them to develop new skills and interests.

Mentoring programmes: Mentoring programmes can match young people with caring adults who can provide them with guidance and support. Mentors can help them stay on track in school, develop positive goals and make healthy choices.

Counselling and therapy services: Community-based counselling and therapy services offer support for families facing various challenges, such as mental health issues, relationship conflicts, or coping with trauma. These services provide a safe and confidential space for individuals and families to address their emotional and psychological needs.

Substance abuse prevention and treatment programmes: Community-based programmes focused on preventing and treating substance abuse can offer support to families dealing with addiction issues. These programmes may include education, counselling and rehabilitation services to help individuals and families navigate addiction and recovery.

Emergency assistance programmes: Community-based emergency assistance programmes can provide immediate support to families facing crises such as natural disasters, homelessness, or financial instability. These programmes may offer temporary housing, food assistance and financial aid to help families stabilise during challenging times.

Family resource centres: Family resource centres offer various support services including childcare, parenting classes, job training and educational programmes. These centres can provide families with access to a wide range of resources that support their overall wellbeing and development.

Legal aid and advocacy services: Community-based legal aid and advocacy services can offer support to families dealing with legal issues, including access to affordable legal representation, guidance on navigating the legal system and advocacy for issues such as housing rights, immigration, and domestic violence.

Religion

Churches and other religious institutions play a vital role in supporting and nurturing family life within communities. Acting as hubs for a variety of services, these organisations extend their support far beyond spiritual guidance, deeply influencing families.

- Youth and family ministries: Churches often have dedicated youth and family ministries that provide support, mentorship and spiritual guidance to children, adolescents and their families. These ministries offer a range of activities, such as youth groups, family retreats and parenting seminars, to foster spiritual growth and strengthen family bonds.
- Marriage enrichment programmes: Churches frequently organise marriage enrichment programmes that aim to support and strengthen these relationships. They may include premarital counselling, marriage seminars and workshops focused on communication, conflict resolution and building healthy relationships.

Educational initiatives

Educational initiatives can play an important role in addressing the root causes of social issues that affect Caribbean families. Early childhood education Programmes can help to prepare children for success in school and life. For example, the OECS Programme for Educational Advancement and Relevant Learning (OECS PEARL) is a four year programme aimed at improving equal access to quality education for every learner in the OECS countries.

Financial literacy programmes can help adults to manage their finances more effectively and avoid debt. Job training programmes can help adults to develop the skills they need to obtain and maintain employment, for example the Ministry of Energy and Business' National Financial Literacy Expansion Programme in Barbados.

Policy advocacy

Policy advocacy can help to create social and economic conditions that are more supportive of families. For example, advocates can work to increase the availability of affordable housing, quality childcare and healthcare. They can also work to promote policies that support family-friendly workplaces and reduce poverty.

Cooperation and interaction

Cooperation and interaction are essential for addressing the problems faced by Caribbean families. Cooperation requires working together and sharing responsibility. Interaction requires maintaining positive relationships within the family.

At the individual level, family members can cooperate to support each other and overcome challenges. For example, parents can share childcare responsibilities, and children can help with household chores. Family members can also interact with each other in positive ways by spending time together, communicating openly, and resolving conflict peacefully.

At the societal level, cooperation and interaction are essential for building strong communities that support families. For example, community organisations can work together to provide families with access to essential resources and services.

Questions

Knowledge and comprehension

a) What are 'community resources', and how can they support Caribbean families facing social issues?

b) Define 'conflict resolution' and explain its importance in family dynamics.

a) Discuss how economic disparities contribute to social issues within Caribbean families. Use the concept of 'financial literacy' in your explanation.

b) How do sociopolitical factors influence the wellbeing of Caribbean families? Provide examples.

Identify techniques used in policy advocacy that could address social issues affecting Caribbean families.

Use of knowledge

a) Analyse the role of educational initiatives in enhancing social mobility within Caribbean societies.

b) How can these initiatives reduce family poverty?

a) Based on the concept of social mobility, propose a culturally sensitive solution to improve the economic status of Caribbean families.

b) Suggest ways community-based support systems can address the challenges of globalisation and modernisation on Caribbean family structures.

SBA skills

1. Developing research questions (C):
   Formulate a research question that investigates the impact of historical and cultural influences on the roles and responsibilities of family members in your community.

2. Designing surveys/questionnaires (C):
   Design a simple questionnaire to gather information on the effectiveness of after-school programmes in reducing youth involvement in crime within your community.

Justify solutions to contemporary social issues that influence Caribbean family life

Effective solutions that are justifiable, practical and culturally sensitive are important to tackle various contemporary social issues in the Caribbean. Solutions to address these social challenges should include education and training, financial support, increased employment opportunities, counselling, law enforcement, social services and family support.

The concepts of conflict management, development, interaction and cooperation, interdependence, freedom of choice, justice and integration, each have a crucial role in a cohesive approach to addressing social issues in the Caribbean.

Education and training

Accessible education and training is important to build a knowledgeable and skilled workforce, contributing to the economic and social development of the region. By investing in educational initiatives that are tailored to the cultural and social needs of Caribbean families, we can promote lifelong learning, critical thinking and creative problem-solving skills among individuals, empowering them to overcome various social challenges. By prioritising education and training, we can build empowerment and self-reliance within families, enabling them to actively participate in the region's socioeconomic progress and development.

Here are some of the educational initiatives across the region:

Jamaica

The Jamaican government has implemented a number of initiatives to improve education quality, including the introduction of the Primary Exit Profile (PEP) exam, which assesses students' literacy and numeracy skills at the end of primary school. The government has also invested in teacher training and the development of new school curricula. The curricula involves students looking at some of the social issues impacting families to help them better under these issues and how best to deal with them. Students are also engaged in a variety of school activities such as conflict management, healthy lifestyle practices and protection of self.

Trinidad and Tobago

The Trinidadian government has introduced the Universal Secondary Education Programme (USEP), which provides free secondary education to all citizens. The government has also invested in the construction of new schools and the expansion of existing ones.

Barbados

The Barbadian government has introduced the Barbados Secondary Schools Entrance Examination (BSSEE), which assesses students' readiness for secondary school. The government has also invested in teacher training and the development of new school curricula.

Dominica

The Dominican government has invested in Technical and Vocational Education and Training (TVET) programmes to train students in skills that are in demand in the country. The government is also working to develop apprenticeship programmes to provide students with hands-on experience.

Financial support

Providing comprehensive financial support to families in need is essential to build economic stability and reduce the impact of poverty on Caribbean communities. Through sustainable financial support programmes and initiatives, income inequality, limited access to resources, and financial insecurity among vulnerable individuals and families can be addressed. By promoting financial literacy and inclusive financial services, families can be empowered to make informed financial decisions, build assets and secure their financial future, contributing to the overall wellbeing and prosperity of the region.

Here are some examples of financial support programs and initiatives in the Caribbean.

Conditional Cash Transfer (CCT) programmes

CCT programmes provide regular cash payments to families in need, providing they meet certain requirements, such as school-attendance or regular medical checkups. CCT programs have been shown to be effective in reducing poverty and improving health and education outcomes. The Programme of Advancement Through Health and Education (PATH) in Jamaica is an example of a CCT programme.

Microfinance programmes

Microfinance programmes are like stepping stones for entrepreneurs and small business owners in the Caribbean, especially for those who might not get loans from big banks. These programmes can give people the boost needed to start or grow their business, leading to more job opportunities and better living standards for everyone involved. Some examples of financial agencies that offer microfinance options across the Caribbean are Courts, Unicomer, Axcel Finance and Fast Cash.

In Dominica, the Dominica Small Business Development Centre (DSBDC) provides microfinance loans to entrepreneurs and small businesses. It has helped to start and grow businesses in Dominica.

Social safety nets

Social safety nets provide financial assistance to vulnerable individuals and families, such as the elderly, the disabled and single-parent households. Social safety nets can help to reduce poverty and inequality, and they can also provide a safety net for people who fall on hard times. For example, in Trinidad and Tobago the government's National Insurance Board (NIB) provides social safety net benefits to the elderly, the disabled and single-parent households. The NIB helps to reduce poverty and inequality in Trinidad and Tobago. In Jamaica, the government implemented the Social Pension Programme for persons over 75 years who were without a pension and who were not benefiting from any other financial programme such as the PATH.

Increased employment opportunities

Employment opportunities are vital to foster economic growth, reduce unemployment rates, and promote social mobility within the Caribbean region. Initiatives like the Caribbean Single Market and Economy (CSME), which allows for the free movement of skilled Caribbean nationals to find jobs within the region, significantly improve employment opportunities. This not only improves job availability but also encourages a more integrated economic environment across the Caribbean nations.

Through job creation projects, skill development programmes and labour market reforms, issues related to unemployment, underemployment, and income disparities can be addressed. This provides families with stable and sustainable employment opportunities. Prioritising gender equality and promoting equal access to employment builds a more inclusive and diverse workforce. This reflects the region's rich cultural and social diversity and steers society towards greater equality and justice, making the most of the opportunities that the CSME presents.

Law enforcement

Effective law enforcement practices and policies ensure the safety and security of Caribbean families and communities. Community-based policing, legal reforms, and the implementation of culturally-sensitive law enforcement strategies can address issues related to domestic violence, substance abuse and criminal activities within the region. Through a culture of accountability and transparency, stakeholders can promote trust and cooperation between law enforcement agencies and communities, leading to a safer and more secure environment for families to live in.

Social services and institutions

Accessible and inclusive social services and institutions are important to address the diverse needs of Caribbean families and communities. Community-based social service programmes, healthcare facilities and social welfare initiatives can help address issues of healthcare access, social support, and community development within the region. Through the integration of social services and institutions, stakeholders can foster collaboration and cooperation, contributing to a more cohesive and supportive social infrastructure that meets the needs of Caribbean families and communities.

To better understand the cycle of poverty and the impact of quality education, let's look at a fictitious example of Sunshine Town, a small Caribbean community facing serious challenges in healthcare, social support, and community development. In Sunshine Town, local stakeholders established the Hope Community Centre to address these issues. This centre became a pivotal hub, offering healthcare services, social support programmes and community development initiatives through a collaborative effort involving local government, NGOs, healthcare professionals and volunteers.

Its integrated approach significantly improved the community's wellbeing, providing residents with access to medical care, support services, and opportunities for personal and community growth. The success of the Hope Community Centre highlights the importance and impact of creating accessible, inclusive social services and institutions through stakeholder collaboration, serving as a model for enhancing community support structures in the Caribbean.

Family support

Robust and inclusive family support programmes are vital to build familial resilience, unity and wellbeing within the Caribbean. Family support initiatives that promote positive parenting, family engagement and community participation can address issues related to family breakdown, intergenerational conflicts and social isolation. Through a culture of mutual support and understanding, stakeholders can promote the creation of strong and resilient family units that can effectively navigate various social challenges, to create a more cohesive and supportive community.

Describe the laws to protect the family in social situations

The Caribbean region is home to a range of cultures and societies, each with its own unique family structures and traditions. However, despite these differences, there are a number of common challenges that Caribbean families face, such as domestic violence, child abuse, and poverty.

A robust legal system should protect families from these challenges and promote their wellbeing. Caribbean countries have made significant progress in developing legal frameworks to protect families in social situations. However, there are still some gaps in the law and challenges in implementation.

Domestic violence

Domestic violence poses a significant issue in the Caribbean. Studies have found that many women in the region experience violence from a partner at some point in their lives.

Domestic violence can cause physical injuries, emotional trauma and financial difficulties for the victims. Caribbean nations have established laws to combat domestic violence, ranging from criminalising the act to offering specific victim protections like shelter access and restraining orders.

Despite these legal frameworks, challenges persist in law enforcement and victim support. Reluctance among police to address domestic violence cases and fear of retaliation among victims can stop proper implementation of these laws, so ongoing efforts are required to enhance protection and support for those affected.

Child protection

Child abuse and neglect are also serious problems in the Caribbean. Child abuse can have an impact on children's physical and mental health, development and education.

All Caribbean countries have laws that criminalise child abuse and neglect. Some countries have also enacted laws that provide specific protection for children at risk of abuse or neglect, such as child welfare laws and foster-care programs and some of these include The Children's Act (2012) in Trinidad and Tobago; The Child Care and Protection Act (2004, amended 2018) in Jamaica; and The Children and Young Persons Act (2001) St. Lucia.

However, there are still some challenges in implementing these laws. For example, in some countries, there may be a lack of resources to investigate and prosecute child abuse cases. Additionally, some cultures may be reluctant to report child abuse or neglect, due to stigma or fear of family shame.

Insights from organisations like the United Nations Office on Drugs and Crime, the Pan-American Health Organisation and CARICOM stress the importance of regional collaboration and dedicated resources to address child abuse and neglect effectively. Their findings call for a united approach in the region to protect children's rights and ensure their wellbeing.

Family rights

Caribbean families have a number of important rights, including the right to privacy, the right to education and the right to access healthcare. These rights are enshrined in both international and domestic law.

International law such as the United Nations *Convention on the Rights of the Child* and the *Convention on the Elimination of All Forms of Discrimination Against Women* provide important protections for families. Domestic law in Caribbean countries also includes a number of protections for the rights of families.

However, there are still some challenges. For example, in some countries, there may be a lack of awareness of family rights. Additionally, some families may face discrimination in accessing services and opportunities.

A legal system protects families from social challenges and promotes their wellbeing. Caribbean countries have made significant progress in developing legal frameworks to protect families in social situations. However, there are still some gaps in the law and challenges in implementation.

It is important to continue strengthening legal protections for Caribbean families. This can be done by:

- enacting and enforcing laws that specifically address domestic violence, child abuse, and other social challenges that families face
- raising awareness of family rights and providing families with the support they need to access their rights
- addressing discrimination and other barriers that families face in accessing services and opportunities.

Questions

Multiple choice

1. Which of the following social issues is noted for significantly impacting Caribbean family life due to economic instability?

a) Environmental pollution

b) Access to healthcare

c) Cybersecurity threats

d) Technological advancements

2. What does the term 'social mobility' refer to in the context of Caribbean societies?

a) The ability to move freely between different physical locations

b) The ability of families to improve their social status through education or employment

c) The societal shift towards more modern forms of communication

d) Changes in social media usage patterns

3. Which of the following is NOT listed as a cause of social issues within Caribbean families?

a) Economic disparities and poverty

b) Historical and cultural influences

c) Globalisation and modernisation

d) Universal healthcare coverage

4. How are community-based support systems proposed to help Caribbean families facing social challenges?

a) By providing luxury housing options

b) By offering parenting education, after-school programmes, and counselling services

c) By promoting overseas employment exclusively

d) By ensuring all family members have access to personal electronic devices

5. What role does policy advocacy play in addressing the effects of social issues on Caribbean family life?

a) It focuses on creating private investment opportunities for families

b) It aims to influence public policy and resource allocation to support families

c) It encourages families to become self-reliant without external support

d) It is primarily concerned with international trade agreements

End of chapter questions

1. a) Define the term 'social issue'. (2 marks)
   b) Outline TWO social issues which impact members of a Caribbean family. (4 marks)
   c) Young people today are consumed with the use of mobile phones which is affecting their roles in the family.
      (i) Suggest TWO ways that parents can address this concern. (4 marks)
      (ii) Explain why EACH way suggested in (c)(i) is likely to be successful. (4 marks)

2. What are some of the contemporary social challenges discussed in the chapter that significantly impact Caribbean families? (3 marks)

3. Name THREE specific solutions proposed in the chapter to address the economic disparities and poverty in the Caribbean region. (3 marks)

4. How does the chapter emphasise the importance of education and training as a solution for empowering Caribbean families? (3 marks)

5. In the context of job creation and skill development, provide one example of an initiative discussed in the chapter that aims to create sustainable employment opportunities for Caribbean families. (3 marks)

6. What role does counselling play in the proposed solutions, and how is it tailored to meet the emotional and psychological needs of Caribbean families? (3 marks)

7. Explain the significance of strengthened law enforcement and legal protection in the context of protecting the rights and dignity of Caribbean families. (3 marks)

8. Name one initiative outlined in the chapter focused on enhancing social services and community outreach to address the diverse social needs of Caribbean families. (3 marks)

Essay questions

1. Investigate the effects of globalisation on Caribbean family life. Discuss how global interconnectedness and cultural shifts are influencing family dynamics, identities and the preservation of cultural heritage.

2. Assess the impact of economic disparities on social issues affecting Caribbean families. Examine the relationship between poverty, unemployment, and limited access to resources, and suggest strategies to address these issues within the Caribbean context.

3. Explore how historical and cultural legacies have shaped family structures and relationships in the Caribbean. Analyse the impact of colonialism, cultural conflicts and generational trauma on social issues, and recommend culturally sensitive approaches to enhance familial wellbeing.

SBA skills

Explore the impact of one contemporary social issue (e.g. poverty, unemployment, domestic violence, drug abuse) on family life in your community. Your project should include:

Introduction: Define the social issue and justify its significance for Caribbean family life.

Objectives: Outline what your study aims to discover or understand about the impact of this issue on family structures, dynamics, and wellbeing.

Methodology: Describe how you will collect data (e.g. surveys, interviews, observation) and the rationale for your chosen methods.

Analysis: Explain how you will analyse the data collected to draw conclusions about the issue's impact.

Conclusion and Recommendations: Summarise your findings and propose actions or policies to mitigate the negative impacts of the social issue on families.

SoloCast: tackling Caribbean social issues

In this individual project, students will create a podcast episode addressing a contemporary social issue affecting Caribbean family life. The episode will focus on a specific issue, providing a well-researched discussion and proposing creative solutions grounded in cultural sensitivity.

Instructions

Selecting a topic:
- Choose a contemporary social issue from a provided list.
- Issues may include teenage pregnancy, generational gap, substance abuse, etc.

Research and scripting:
- Conduct thorough research on your chosen issue, considering cultural and historical contexts.
- Prepare a scripted podcast episode (10–15 minutes) discussing the causes, effects and potential solutions.

Podcast elements:
- Be creative in your presentation, including interviews, storytelling and sound effects.
- Integrate Caribbean music or traditional elements relevant to your chosen topic.

Cultural sensitivity reflection:
- Include a segment in your episode reflecting on the cultural sensitivity of proposed solutions.
- Discuss how historical and cultural influences impact the chosen social issue.

Recording and editing:
- Use provided resources for podcast recording and basic editing.
- Emphasise clear and engaging communication, considering your target audience.

Presentation:
- Present your podcast episode to the class.
- Engage in a Q&A session to encourage critical thinking and discussion.

Summary

We have explored the relationship between social issues and family life in the Caribbean, highlighting the impact of economic instability, access to education and healthcare, housing, nutrition, relationship stress and the poverty cycle on family dynamics and societal wellbeing. We looked at the causes, effects and solutions to these issues, all while emphasising the need for culturally sensitive approaches tailored to the Caribbean context.

The chapter outlines social issues such as poverty, discrimination, crime, environmental concerns and family dynamics and their impact on Caribbean families. It also touches on specific challenges like teenage pregnancy, child abandonment, and substance abuse.

Solutions include community-based support systems, educational initiatives, policy advocacy, and the importance of legal protection for families. These strategies highlight the need for cooperation, interaction and a comprehensive approach to fostering family resilience.

Key themes and concepts:

Social issues and Caribbean family life

Causes and effects: Examination of the causes (economic disparities, historical and cultural influences, sociopolitical factors, globalisation) and effects (disrupted family dynamics, psychological impact, educational and occupational limitations) of contemporary social issues on Caribbean family life.

Specific issues: Focus on key social issues such as teenage pregnancy, substance abuse, child abandonment, domestic violence, generational gaps and juvenile delinquency.

Solutions to social issues

Cultural sensitivity: Emphasis on culturally sensitive solutions that respect the unique cultural and historical context of the Caribbean.

Community-based support: Importance of community-based support systems, including parenting education, after-school programmes, mentoring, counselling, substance abuse prevention, emergency assistance and family resource centres.

Educational initiatives: Role of education in promoting social mobility and reducing family poverty, with examples of specific programmes (e.g. OECS PEARL, TVET).

Policy advocacy: Advocacy for policies that support families, reduce poverty and promote access to resources and opportunities.

Employment opportunities: Efforts to create sustainable employment opportunities through job creation projects and labour market reforms.

Law enforcement and legal protection: Strengthening legal protections for families against domestic violence, child abuse and other social issues.

Cultural and historical context

Historical legacies: Impact of colonialism, cultural conflicts and generational trauma on family dynamics and social issues.

Cultural identity: Challenges to preserving cultural identity in the face of globalisation and modernisation.

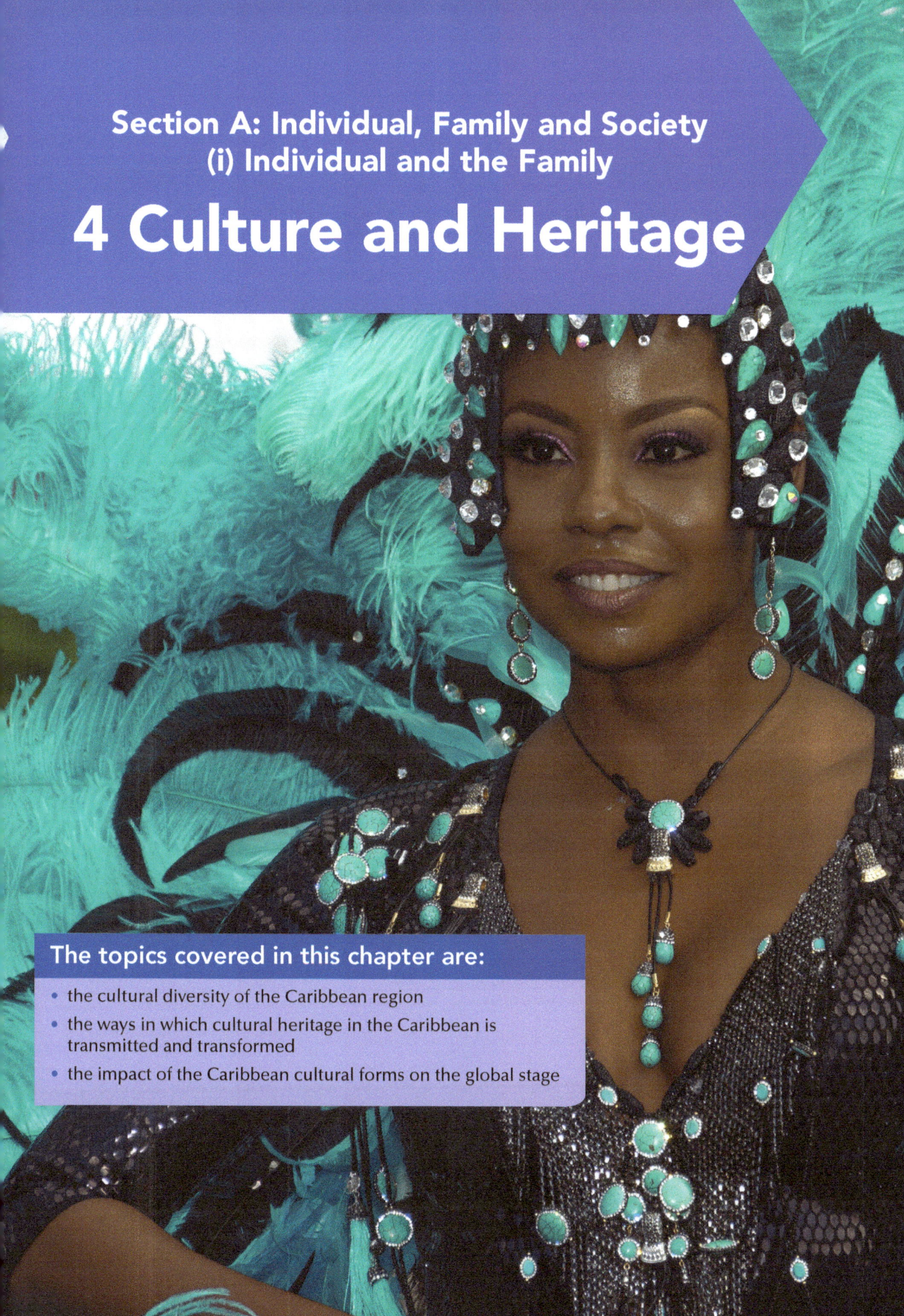

Cultural diversity

The Caribbean is like a giant mixing bowl where different cultures blend together, creating something unique and vibrant. It is well-known for its stunning beaches with crystal clear water and lush green forests. But what really makes the Caribbean special is its mix of music, food and traditions that come from its diverse history.

To begin with, there were the rich cultural roots of the indigenous peoples who first called these islands home. Then came the Europeans, who took control of the islands and brought Africans as enslaved people to work on plantations. Over time, people from all over the world migrated to the Caribbean, each group adding its own flavours to the local culture.

The Caribbean story is one of different people coming together, sometimes through difficult and painful circumstances, but ultimately creating a community that stands out for its diversity and creativity. It's a place where the past and present merge, showing us how different cultures can come together to make something beautiful.

The cultural diversity of the Caribbean region

Learning objectives

- Identify key historical factors influencing Caribbean cultural diversity, from indigenous roots to colonial history.
- Evaluate how family, groups, media and institutions shape Caribbean cultural heritage, and understand how traditions evolve.
- Explore the concepts of indigenous roots, creolisation, syncretism, indentureship and migration to understand their roles in forming the Caribbean's unique cultural identity and heritage.
- Examine how Caribbean music, literature, art, sports, festivals and more impact the world, considering both positive aspects and challenges.
- Discover how Caribbean culture travels worldwide, influencing societies and starting global discussions.
- Apply understanding to real-world challenges, suggesting sustainable strategies for preserving Caribbean culture, considering cultural sustainability and cultural entrepreneurship.

Important definitions

Indigenous people – *the original inhabitants of a specific region, often with distinct languages, customs and traditions that predate the arrival of external influences.*

Creolisation – *the process of cultural blending and fusion, often resulting in the creation of new cultural elements, expressions, or identities.*

Syncretism – *the merging or reconciliation of different cultural elements, often in the realm of religious beliefs, resulting in a new, integrated form.*

Indentureship – *a system in which individuals were contracted to work for a specified period in exchange for passage, food, and shelter, often associated with the migration of labourers from Asia.*

Migration – *the movement of people from one place to another, often with the intention of establishing a new permanent residence.*

Cultural exchange – *the mutual sharing and interaction of cultural elements between different groups or societies, leading to the enrichment of each.*

> *Mass media* – various forms of communication designed to reach a large audience, including newspapers, radio, television and social media.
>
> *Global influences* – external factors, such as media and travel, that impact and shape local cultures by introducing new ideas, trends, or practices.
>
> *Intangible cultural heritage* – aspects of cultural heritage that cannot be touched but are nevertheless important, including oral traditions, rituals and expressions.
>
> *Cultural identity* – the sense of belonging and identification with a particular cultural group, encompassing shared values, beliefs and practices.

Reasons for cultural diversity

Indigenous people

The Caribbean region's cultural pool begins with its **indigenous peoples**, each contributing unique customs, languages and art forms. These communities have given the region a treasure trove of distinctive customs, languages and art forms, shaping the very essence of Caribbean culture. In countries such as Dominica and St. Vincent, where the descendants of these groups live today, we can see a narrative of the Caribbean's rich history, highlighting the indigenous peoples who originally inhabited the region. From their profound connection to the land to their detailed artistic expressions, the indigenous peoples laid the groundwork for the vibrant cultural heritage that continues to this day in the Caribbean.

Pre-indigenous peoples of the Caribbean

Ciboney: The earliest known inhabitants of the Caribbean, arriving around 15,000 years ago. They were a nomadic hunter-gatherer people who left behind

Figure 4.1 *Carnival in Trinidad and Tobago*

Figure 4.2 *An engraving of a Kalinago man*

Section A(i) Individual, Family and Society

little archaeological evidence, but their presence can be seen in rock art and other artifacts found throughout the region.

Saladoids: Arrived in the Caribbean around 500 BC and brought with them a more advanced culture, including agriculture, pottery and weaving. The Saladoids built large settlements and ceremonial centres, and their influence can be seen in the cultures of the later Taíno and Kalinago peoples.

Otoroids: Lived in the Lesser Antilles, and were known for their distinctive pottery and stone carvings.

Casimoroids: Lived in the Greater Antilles, and were known for their skill in shell-working and bone-carving.

As archaeological research continues, additional groups are being identified. Some of these groups remain relatively obscure, and our knowledge about them is limited. The extent of our understanding will, to a large extent, depend on the findings of future research. For example;

Guanahatabey: A nomadic hunter-gatherer people who lived in Cuba.

Arcaico: A pre-ceramic people who lived in the Dominican Republic.

Igneri: An Arawak people who lived in the Lesser Antilles.

Sub-Taíno: A group of Arawak peoples who lived in the Greater Antilles and the Bahamas.

These groups are not as well-known because they left behind less archaeological evidence and were often displaced or assimilated by the larger and more powerful Taíno and Kalinago peoples. However, they still played an important role in shaping the cultural pool of the Caribbean region.

For example, the Igneri are credited with developing the cultivation of cassava, a staple crop in the Caribbean.

The Taíno and Kalinago

Taíno: An Arawak people who lived in the Greater Antilles and the northern Bahamas. They were a non-combatant and egalitarian society, and were skilled farmers, fishermen and artisans.

Kalinago: The Kalinago lived in the Lesser Antilles and the southern Bahamas. They were a more military society than the Taíno, and were skilled warriors and navigators.

Indigenous peoples and the Maroons

The Caribbean's cultural history was also influenced through the indigenous people's interactions with Maroon communities. The Caribbean's culture today comes from a mix of different traditions blending together. A great example is how the indigenous peoples and Maroons (escaped enslaved peoples who created their own communities) shared their ways of living. They combined their knowledge of farming, languages and religious practices, creating a unique mix that influenced the culture of the region. It shows us how our past connections shape who we are today.

The Maroons were runaway enslaved peoples who escaped from European plantations and established their own communities in the mountains and forests of the Caribbean. They were a diverse group, but shared a common culture and language. They were skilled warriors and hunters, and fought fiercely to defend their freedom.

The indigenous peoples of the Caribbean interacted with each other and with the Maroons

Figure 4.3 *The Maroons lived in the mountains and forests of the Caribbean*

in a variety of ways. They traded goods, intermarried and shared cultural knowledge. For example, the Taíno and Kalinago both learned from the Saladoids in terms of agriculture and pottery.

The Maroons also learned from the indigenous peoples. For example, they learned how to survive in the harsh Caribbean environment and how to cultivate crops.

The interaction between the indigenous peoples and the Maroons led to a rich and diverse culture. This culture is still reflected in the music, food and art of many Caribbean islands today.

Here are some specific examples of integration and learning between the indigenous peoples of the Caribbean and the Maroons:

- The Maroons learned how to cultivate cassava, a staple crop in the Caribbean, from the Taíno.
- The Taíno learned how to use guerilla warfare tactics to resist European colonisation from the Maroons.
- The Kalinago learned how to navigate the Caribbean Sea in small boats from the Maroons.
- The Maroons learned how to make baskets and other crafts from natural materials from the Kalinago.
- The Taíno and Kalinago both learned how to speak a common language from the Maroons, which is now the basis for many Caribbean creole languages.

The integration and learning from each other between the indigenous peoples and the Maroons shows the resilience and adaptability of both groups. It is also a reminder that the Caribbean region's cultural pool is a rich and diverse one, shaped by the contributions of many different peoples.

Figure 4.4 *Nanny of the Maroons*

Table 4.1 below shows the arrival times of the Indigenous groups in the Caribbean.

Group	Time period	Culture	Location
Guanahatabey	15,000–500 BC	Nomadic hunter-gatherers	Cuba
Arcaico	15,000–500 BC	Pre-ceramic agriculturalists	Dominican Republic
Ciboney	15,000–500 BC	Nomadic hunter-gatherers	Throughout the Caribbean
Saladoids	500 BC–200 AD	Agriculturalists and potters	Greater Antilles
Otoroids	200 AD–present	Agriculturalists, potters, and stone carvers	Lesser Antilles
Casimoroids	200 AD–present	Agriculturalists, potters, and bone carvers	Greater Antilles
Igneri	500 BC–1400 AD	Agriculturalists and potters	Lesser Antilles
Sub-Taíno	700 AD–present	Agriculturalists and potters	Greater Antilles and Bahamas

Table 4.1

European colonisation

The impact of European colonisation on the Caribbean is a pivotal chapter in the region's history. The introduction of new languages, religions and traditions left an indelible mark on the Caribbean's cultural landscape.

Linguistic transformations

Introduction of European languages

The arrival of European colonisers in the Caribbean in the 15th century marked the beginning of a linguistic transformation in the region. As European powers established their dominance, they brought with them their own languages, which gradually replaced or coexisted with the indigenous languages of the Caribbean.

English: English was introduced to the Caribbean by the British, who colonised the islands throughout the 17th and 18th centuries. Today, English is the official language of several Caribbean countries, including Antigua and Barbuda, Barbados, Dominica, St. Lucia, St. Vincent, Grenada, Guyana, Jamaica, Monserrat and Trinidad and Tobago.

French: France colonised in the 17th century. Today, French is the official language of several Caribbean countries, including Haiti, Martinique and Guadeloupe.

Spanish: The Spanish were the first to colonise the Greater Antilles, including Cuba, the Dominican Republic and Puerto Rico, in the 16th century. Spanish is still the official language of these countries today.

Dutch: The Dutch colonised Aruba, Curaçao and Sint Maarten in the 17th century. Today, Dutch is an official language of these countries.

Portuguese: The Portuguese colonised Brazil in the 16th century. The influence of Portuguese can be seen in some Caribbean Creole languages, such as Papiamento, which is spoken in Aruba, Curaçao, and Bonaire.

The introduction of European languages had a profound impact on the linguistic landscape of the Caribbean. In some cases, European languages completely replaced indigenous languages, such as on the island of Dominica, where the indigenous Kalinago language is now only spoken on a small scale. In other cases, European languages coexisted with indigenous languages, the languages of the African enslaved people and other people during the plantation era and post plantation era, leading to the development of mixed languages or Creole languages.

Creolisation

Creolisation is the formation of a new language by merging elements from two or more existing languages. It occurs when people from different linguistic backgrounds interact and exchange linguistic elements. Creolisation can lead to the creation of entirely new languages with unique grammatical structures, vocabularies and sound systems.

Creole languages are characterised by a number of features, including:

- Simplified grammar: Creole languages typically have a simpler grammar than the source languages.
- Lexical borrowing: Creole languages borrow words from a variety of source languages, including European languages, African languages and indigenous languages.
- Unique phonology: Creole languages often have their own unique sound systems, which are distinct from the sound systems of the source languages.

Here are some examples of Creole languages spoken in the Caribbean:

- French Creole – based on French and spoken by over 10 million people in Haiti, Dominica, St. Lucia, Seychelles, Reunion Island, Guadeloupe, Marie Galante and Martinique.
- English Creole – based on English and spoken by people in Jamaica, Dominica (Kokoy), Grenada, Montserrat and Antigua.

- Spanish Creole – based on Spanish and is spoken by people in Cuba, Haiti, Dominican Republic and Puerto Rico.
- Papiamento – a Portuguese-based Creole language spoken by over 300,000 people in Aruba, Curaçao and Bonaire.

Religious influences

Spread of Christianity

The arrival of European colonisers in the Caribbean in the 15th century marked the beginning of a religious transformation in the region. As European powers established their dominance, they brought with them their own Christian beliefs and practices, which gradually replaced or coexisted with the indigenous religious systems of the Caribbean.

Catholicism

Catholicism was the first Christian denomination to take root in the Caribbean, introduced by Spanish missionaries who accompanied the conquistadors. The Spanish established Catholic missions throughout the Greater Antilles. Catholicism was also introduced to the Lesser Antilles by French missionaries in the 17th century. Catholicism had a profound impact on the Caribbean, becoming the dominant denomination in many parts of the region.

Protestantism

Protestantism arrived in the Caribbean in the 17th century through British and Dutch colonisers. Protestant denominations, such as the Moravians, Methodists and Baptists, established missions in various Caribbean islands. Protestantism gained popularity among enslaved Africans and their descendants, as many protestants supported the humanitarian mission; Protestant churches also played an important role in education and social activism, particularly in the fight against enslavement and colonialism.

Religious syncretism: positives and negatives

The introduction of Christianity to the Caribbean led to the development of **syncretic** religious practices, which blended elements of Christian beliefs with indigenous and African traditions. These syncretic religions often incorporated rituals, deities and beliefs from multiple sources, reflecting the complex cultural interactions in the region. This allowed the persons of African and Indigenous heritage to be open to the European religions as they saw aspects of their cultural experience incorporated.

The introduction of Christianity to the Caribbean during colonisation led to the blending of Christian beliefs with African and indigenous traditions. This religious syncretism produced practices such as Vodou (Haiti), Santería (Cuba), Obeah (Caribbean), and Rastafarianism (Jamaica), combining Christian rituals with African deities and indigenous beliefs.

Positives:

Cultural Preservation: Syncretism allowed enslaved Africans and indigenous peoples to retain elements of their traditions, blending them with Christianity. Spiritual Resilience: It provided a spiritual outlet to cope with the trauma of colonisation. Unity and Identity: Syncretic religions helped build a collective identity among oppressed groups. Flexibility: It made Christianity more relatable by incorporating familiar rituals.

Negatives:

Dilution: African and indigenous traditions were often diluted by Christian elements. Loss of Authenticity: Critics argue syncretism weakened both sets of spiritual practices. Cultural Conflict: Syncretic religions faced persecution from mainstream Christianity. Misunderstanding: These religions, like Vodou, were often misunderstood and stigmatised.

However, the impact of European religious culture on indigenous cultures in the Caribbean was complex and often devastating. As European colonisers asserted their dominance over the region, they imposed their own religious beliefs and practices on indigenous peoples and persons of African descent. This process of religious conversion was often accompanied by violence, coercion and cultural suppression.

One of the most significant impacts of European religious culture was the displacement of indigenous and African religious practices and beliefs. Many indigenous religious sites were destroyed, and indigenous spiritual leaders were persecuted. Indigenous people were often forced to convert to Christianity, and their traditional rituals and ceremonies were suppressed.

These rituals were seen as a threat to the social order of the plantation as they provided enslaved Africans with a source of **cultural identity** and spiritual comfort. Planters prohibited the use of drums and other musical instruments, banned gatherings of enslaved Africans, destroyed African religious artifacts, and forced enslaved Africans to attend Christian services. Despite the suppression, enslaved Africans found ways to preserve their traditional practices.

The arrival of European religious culture also had a profound impact on Indigenous and African social structures and cultural identity. Christianity introduced new concepts of gender roles, family structures and morality, which challenged traditional indigenous and African values. In some cases, this led to the breakdown of traditional social structures and the loss of cultural identity.

Table 4.2 shows some specific examples of the negative and positive impacts of European religious culture on indigenous and African cultures in the Caribbean.

Impact	Example
Negative impacts	
Displacement of indigenous religious practices and beliefs	Destruction of indigenous religious sites, persecution of indigenous spiritual leaders, forced conversion of indigenous people to Christianity, suppression of indigenous rituals and ceremonies
Erosion of indigenous languages and traditions	Standardisation and simplification of indigenous languages, loss of indigenous languages
Suppression of African traditional rituals and ceremonies	Prohibition of the use of drums and other musical instruments, banning of gatherings of enslaved Africans, destruction of African religious artifacts, forced attendance at Christian services
Positive impacts	
Incorporation of elements of indigenous spirituality into Christian practices	Creation of syncretic religious traditions that blend elements of both European and indigenous beliefs
Introduction of new forms of education and social organisation	Establishment of schools and missions, promotion of literacy and numeracy, development of social welfare programs
Promotion of interfaith dialogue and understanding	Efforts to bridge the gap between different religious communities, fostering mutual respect and tolerance

Table 4.2

Figure 4.5 *Today, Haitians reclaim and celebrate Vodou as a vital part of their identity*

Traditions and cultural practices

Table 4.3 shows some terms that are useful to understand.

Term	Definition	Example
European powers	Countries in Europe that had strong military and economic strength and could control other countries.	Britain, France, and Spain, which established colonies in the Caribbean.
Dominance	Having power and influence over others.	European countries controlled the Caribbean, making their culture, language and laws the standard.
Assimilated	To absorb and integrate into a wider society or culture.	Caribbean culture includes European traditions, like wearing suits to formal events, which comes from European dress codes.
Social customs	The traditional ways that a society behaves and operates.	Greeting someone with a handshake is a social custom influenced by Europeans.
Etiquette	The formal manners and rules that are followed in social and professional settings.	Using 'please' and 'thank you', or eating with certain utensils, reflects European etiquette.
Culinary practices	The methods and traditions related to cooking and eating.	The use of European ingredients like wheat flour and cooking techniques such as baking in the Caribbean.

Section A(i)   Individual, Family and Society

Term	Definition	Example
Reparations	Compensation given for loss or harm suffered.	Discussions on providing financial aid or support to the Caribbean for the damages caused by European colonisation.
Colonialism	The policy or practice of acquiring full or partial political control over another country, occupying it with settlers, and exploiting it economically.	European countries establishing colonies in the Caribbean and using its resources.
Economic and social disadvantage	Conditions that make it more difficult for certain groups of people to succeed financially and socially.	The lasting impact of enslavement and colonialism that has contributed to higher rates of poverty and fewer educational opportunities in some Caribbean communities.
Equitable development	Fair and impartial opportunities for development that consider the needs of all members of society.	Creating programmes that provide equal access to education and healthcare in the Caribbean, aiming to reduce inequality.
Restorative justice	A system of criminal justice that focuses on the rehabilitation of offenders through reconciliation with victims and the community at large.	A programme where former colonisers and Caribbean communities work together on projects that benefit the latter, acknowledging past wrongs and working towards healing.
Forced labour	Work that people are compelled to do against their will under threat of punishment.	Enslaved Africans being forced to work on plantations in the Caribbean without pay or freedom; a practice used by European colonisers.

Table 4.3

European powers, primarily Britain, France and Spain, established their dominance in the Caribbean from the 15th century, bringing with them their languages, religions and cultural practices. This has had a profound impact on the daily lives of Caribbean people, shaping their social customs, etiquette, culinary practices, dress, dance, type of music and can be seen in Caribbean culture in various aspects of daily life. Social customs such as the use of titles, dress code and table etiquette reflect European etiquette norms. Culinary practices have also been transformed by the introduction of European ingredients and cooking techniques, giving rise to a unique Caribbean cuisine that blends indigenous, African, Indian, Asian and European influences. Similarly, European fashion trends have significantly impacted Caribbean clothing styles, with traditional garments worn alongside modern European-inspired designs.

The presence of European cultural elements in the Caribbean has raised discussions about reparations, a movement advocating for compensation and restorative justice for the harms inflicted by colonialism. Campaigners for reparations argue that the centuries of European exploitation, including enslavement of the indigenous and African population, forced labour and land dispossession, have left a lasting legacy of economic and social disadvantage in the Caribbean. They argue that reparations are necessary to address the enduring effects of colonialism and assist with equal development in the region.

Opponents of reparations often point to the complexities of historical events and the challenges of assigning blame and determining appropriate compensation. They argue that focusing on the past may hinder progress and that efforts should be directed towards addressing current issues and fostering economic growth in the Caribbean.

The debate over reparations reflects the ongoing reckoning with the legacy of colonialism in the Caribbean. While the cultural assimilation of European traditions has undoubtedly shaped the region's identity, it is essential to acknowledge, address and correct the historical injustices that have contributed to inequalities and underdevelopment in the Caribbean. The discussions surrounding reparations are a crucial step in fostering a more equitable and just future for the Caribbean people.

Table 4.4 shows how European influences have impacted Caribbean culture.

Aspect of Caribbean culture	European influence	Impact on family structure
Social customs and etiquette	European social customs and etiquette emphasise reserved thinking, proper table manners and have helped to shape class identity with certain behaviours ascribed to certain classes	Reinforcement of hierarchical structures within families, along with the certain norms and practices within the family
Culinary practices	Introduction of European ingredients and cooking techniques	Diversification of family meals and culinary traditions
Dress	Adoption of European attire, particularly among the elite and middle classes	Influence on family fashion choices and expressions of status
Architecture	Building forts, grand plantation houses, and charming colonial towns and cities	Shaping of family living spaces and sense of community
Political system (Westminster)	Emphasis on a constitutional monarchy, a bicameral legislature, and an executive led by a prime minister	Influence on family participation in democratic processes and governance

Table 4.4

Economic impacts

The European impact on the Caribbean has resulted in periods of growth and prosperity, yet the region has also been subject to exploitation, dependency and inequality. The colonial rule, with its focus on plantation economies and extraction of resources, laid the foundation for many of the economic challenges the Caribbean faces today.

The reliance on a few export crops, the exploitation of enslaved labour and the concentration of wealth in the hands of European planters left the region vulnerable to fluctuations in global market prices and limited its ability to develop diversified and self-sustaining economies. The decline of the Banana industry in many of the Windward Island countries is a typical example of this.

The legacy of colonialism continues to be felt in the Caribbean's trade patterns, wealth distribution and socioeconomic disparities. The region remains heavily reliant on exports to developed countries and yet heavily dependent on imports from these same countries and as small nations, operate with a narrow range of economic activities. This dependency has made it difficult for Caribbean nations to break free from the cycle of poverty and inequality that has plagued them for centuries.

Table 4.5 shows the economic impacts of European colonialism in the Caribbean.

Ideology	Definition	Example of European impact in the Caribbean	Family impact
Mercantilism	Economic theory emphasising wealth accumulation through trade and colonisation	Plantation economies and exploitation of enslaved labour	Separation of families due to forced labour and relocation, disruption of traditional family structures and roles

Ideology	Definition	Example of European impact in the Caribbean	Family impact
Capitalism	Economic system based on private ownership and profit	Application of capitalist principles to plantation economies, maximising profits through export crops and labour exploitation	Prioritising economic pursuits over family life, erosion of traditional family values and support networks
Social Darwinism	Ideology applying natural selection principles to human societies	Justification of European colonialism and exploitation of non-European populations, dehumanisation of enslaved Africans	Promotion of racial hierarchies and discrimination, undermining of family unity and cohesion
Neocolonialism	Indirect colonialism through economic and political dominance	Maintenance of economic dependencies established during colonial rule between the Caribbean and developed countries	Limited economic opportunities for families, perpetuation of poverty and inequality, hindering family wellbeing and social mobility

Table 4.5

African enslavement in the Caribbean

The forced **migration** of Africans to the Caribbean during the era of enslavement is a pivotal chapter in the region's history. During this immense suffering, a cultural transformation unfolded as enslaved Africans brought with them languages, religions, fashion, culinary and musical styles. These elements, though often suppressed and distorted under enslavement, proved resilient and enduring, and formed part of Caribbean society. The traumatic period of enslavement laid the foundation for the rich and vibrant cultural identity that characterises the Caribbean today.

Linguistic legacy – keeping African roots alive in the Caribbean

Even though there was a time when African languages were not allowed to be spoken during enslavement, the Caribbean still shows strong signs of its African heritage through the way people talk today. Here is how African roots have stayed alive in the Caribbean:

Figure 4.6 *Enslaved Africans brought their own fashions with them to the Caribbean*

Borrowed words: Lots of words in Caribbean Creole come from African languages. For example, 'doudou', which means 'sweetheart' in French Creole, comes from the Yoruba language.

How sentences are built: The way sentences are structured in Creole languages can be traced back to African languages. A lot of the time, the order of words in a sentence in Creole is the same as in West African languages.

The rhythm of speech: The way Creole languages sound, with their unique rhythms and patterns, also points back to African roots. This gives Creole speech a special musical quality.

These African influences show that, despite efforts to erase them, the languages of Africa have left a lasting mark on the Caribbean. Families have been key in keeping these linguistic traditions alive, passing them down from generation to generation.

Language evolution

The way people speak in the Caribbean uses a unique mix of African and European elements. This blend comes from the history of enslaved Africans, European colonisers and the original inhabitants of the Caribbean.

Creole languages: The emergence of Creole languages represents a remarkable fusion of African and European linguistic elements. These languages, while distinct from their European and African sources, embody the unique cultural identity of the Caribbean.

Pidgins: Pidgins, simplified languages that emerge from contact between speakers of different languages, also played a significant role in Caribbean linguistic history. Pidgins are basic languages that pop up when people who speak different languages need to talk to each other, often for trading or other types of communication. In the Caribbean, these simple languages were developed by the enslaved and were an important step in creating the more complex Creole languages we hear today.

Oral tradition: Oral tradition, which means sharing stories and cultural knowledge by talking rather than writing, has played a big part in how Caribbean languages have developed. This way of passing on information has helped keep African language features alive and has made the Caribbean known for its rich storytelling traditions.

The following story teaches the importance of unity and cooperation in facing and overcoming challenges.

In the heart of Africa, where the earth sings with the rhythm of nature, there existed a lush valley, filled with a myriad of flowers, each whispering the secrets of the natural world. In this valley roamed Sisserou, a vibrant bird with feathers as colourful as the blossoms below, and Koulév, a wise snake whose scales shimmered like the dew at dawn. They were guardians of the valley, tasked with preserving the delicate balance of nature.

One year, a great drought threatened the valley, wilting flowers and dimming the vibrant hues that once painted the landscape. Sisserou and Koulév noticed the despair settling over their home and decided to act. Sisserou, with her melodious voice, sang to the skies, pleading for rain, while Koulév whispered to the earth, urging it to hold tight to every drop of moisture. Moved by their unity and love for their home, the spirits of nature conspired to bring a gentle rain, reviving the valley.

Figure 4.7 *Sisserou and Koulév*

The flowers bloomed like never before, serving as a reminder of the resilience of nature and the importance of harmony between all living beings. From then on, the valley flourished, protected by the bond between bird and snake, and the flowers whispered tales of their guardians to anyone who would listen, teaching the importance of respecting and nurturing the natural world.

The story highlights how different beings, like the Sisserou bird and Koulév the snake, can work together for a common good, emphasising the lesson that diverse strengths and perspectives can create powerful solutions.

Additionally, it underscores the significance of respecting and caring for nature, showing that the wellbeing of our environment is crucial for the survival and prosperity of all its inhabitants.

It also carries the language as Koulév is 'snake' in Haitian Creole and Sisserou is a bird found in Dominica.

Religious syncretism

During the period of African enslavement, which lasted from the late 15th century to the 19th century, millions of Africans were forcibly taken from their homelands and brought to the Caribbean and the Americas to work on plantations. This era is marked by extreme hardship and brutal treatment of enslaved Africans by European colonisers and plantation owners.

The suppression they faced was not just physical but also cultural and spiritual. Enslaved Africans were often prohibited from practising their religions and were forced to convert to Christianity. Their spiritual symbols, rituals and ceremonies were banned, and gatherings for worship were often met with punishment.

Despite this, African spiritual beliefs didn't just survive; they adapted and flourished, blending with elements of Christianity and indigenous practices to form new, syncretic religions like Vodou in Haiti, Santería in Cuba and Candomblé in Brazil.

These religions are a testament to the resilience of the human spirit and the desire to maintain a connection to one's heritage and identity, even in the face of harsh suppression. This resilience of African spirituality can be attributed to several factors, including:

Secrecy and camouflage: Enslaved Africans adopted strategies of secrecy and camouflage to preserve their traditional practices, blending them with Christian rituals to avoid detection and punishment.

Symbolic representations: African spiritual concepts were often represented through symbols and objects that held dual meanings, allowing practitioners to maintain their beliefs without explicitly contradicting Christian teachings.

Community solidarity: Enslaved communities maintained their heritage and found solace through storytelling, drumming and celebrations, fostering unity and resilience. These practices helped preserve their African roots and strengthened communal bonds, offering a sense of belonging amidst adversity.

Family bonds: Families became vital conduits for passing down ancestral knowledge, ensuring the transmission of spiritual practices from one generation to the next. The family unit, through its shared beliefs and rituals, became a sanctuary of cultural preservation, contributing significantly to the resilience of African spirituality in the Caribbean.

Table 4.6 shows African religions that have impacted the Caribbean.

African religion	Origin	Impact in the Caribbean
Yoruba religion	West Africa (Yoruba people in Nigeria)	• **Santería (Cuba):** Syncretised with Catholicism, Orishas worshipped as saints.
		• **Vodou:** Influence seen in the veneration of lwa, incorporating Dahomey mythology.
Vodun (Voodoo)	West Africa (Fon and Ewe people)	• **Vodou (Haiti):** Retains West African elements, deeply embedded in Haitian culture.
		• **Candomblé (Brazil):** Rooted in Yoruba and Fon traditions, worshipping Orishas.

African religion	Origin	Impact in the Caribbean
Kongo religion	Central Africa (Kongo people)	• **Palo (Cuba):** Draws from Kongo spiritual traditions, involving the veneration of spirits.
Myal and Kumina	Akan people (Myal) and Bantu people (Kumina)	• **Jamaican folk religions:** Myal focuses on healing rituals, while Kumina involves drumming and dance.
Islam	North and West Africa	• **Islamic influences:** Some enslaved Africans brought Islamic practices, influencing cultural expressions.

Table 4.6

Musical expressions

The rhythmic and percussive foundations of Caribbean music are deeply rooted in African traditions; the pulse of the Caribbean. Enslaved Africans brought with them a rich musical heritage characterised by complex polyrhythms, syncopation and the use of a variety of percussion instruments. These African elements have had a profound and lasting influence on the development of Caribbean music genres.

Polyrhythms: Polyrhythms, the layering of multiple rhythmic patterns, are a hallmark of African music and have become a defining feature of Caribbean genres. For instance, the rhythmic complexity of reggae is derived from the interplay of the bass line, drumbeat and guitar riffs.

Figure 4.8 *Calypso uses percussion instruments and syncopated beats*

Syncopation: Syncopation, where the emphasis is on the off-beats, is another prevalent element in African music and is evident in many Caribbean genres. The syncopated rhythms of calypso, for example, create a distinctive and infectious musical style.

Percussion instruments: African percussion instruments, such as drums, shakers and bells, have played a central role in shaping the soundscape of Caribbean music. These instruments provide the rhythmic backbone and add a layer of energy and excitement to various genres.

Traditional into the modern

Traditional Caribbean genres, including mento, tuk band, gwo ka, zouk, cadence, soca and bouyon, bear the direct influence of African music. These genres, characterised by call-and-response patterns, cool layered rhythms and traditional African percussion instruments, have not only preserved their cultural roots but also evolved into diverse and modern musical expressions.

– Blend of African and European:

Mento: Mento is a traditional Jamaican music genre, characterised by its rhythmic blend of African and European influences, featuring acoustic instruments and reflecting the cultural heritage of the Caribbean.

Figure 4.9 *Bob Marley popularised reggae around the world*

Ska: Mento laid the foundation for ska, a Jamaican genre that emerged in the late 1950s. Ska combines mento's upbeat rhythms with elements of jazz, rhythm and blues, and African-Caribbean music.

Reggae: Reggae, influenced by mento, emerged in the late 1960s. Bob Marley's early works showcase the rhythmic and melodic influence of mento, contributing to reggae's global recognition.

Caribbean music, rich with African influences, has left its mark on music worldwide. For example, reggae, known for its distinctive rhythm and vibe, has significantly influenced hip-hop. Hip-hop artists often sample reggae beats and adopt its storytelling style, showing how the Caribbean's musical heritage has shaped and enriched global music genres. Another genre influenced by Caribbean music is jazz, especially in its use of rhythms and improvisation. Caribbean music brought vibrant rhythms and unique beats to jazz, helping to create a lively, dynamic sound. This fusion shows how Caribbean music's influence extends far beyond its own borders, enriching other music styles around the world.

– Call and response to percussion:

Tuk Band: Tuk Band is a traditional Barbadian music ensemble known for its lively and rhythmic performances, incorporating African-derived percussion instruments and call-and-response patterns.

Spouge: Originating in Barbados in the 1960s, spouge is a fusion of tuk band rhythms with influences from calypso, jazz and soul. It features lively rhythms and danceable beats.

Modern Calypso and **Soca music**, with their roots in Calypso rhythms, have become the heartbeat of Caribbean carnival celebrations. These genres fuse traditional beats with contemporary sounds, producing an irresistibly lively and energetic vibe that captures the essence of Caribbean joy and festivity. The rhythms of modern calypso are catchy and upbeat, inviting everyone to dance and celebrate, while soca music, with its fast-paced beats and pulsating rhythms, turns any gathering into a vibrant party. These musical styles not only keep the spirit of Caribbean culture alive but also encourage unity and happiness, as people of all ages come together to dance, sing and celebrate their heritage. The colourful costumes, dynamic dance moves and the sheer exuberance of the crowds at carnival time are a testament to the powerful influence of modern calypso and soca music, making them an integral part of the Caribbean's musical legacy and its joyful expression of life.

Figure 4.10 *Bands entertain the crowds at carnival time*

– Modern evolution:

Zouk: Gwo ka rhythms have significantly influenced zouk, a genre that emerged in the French Caribbean in the late 1970s. Zouk blends traditional gwo ka drumming with elements of funk, disco and Latin music.

Global Fusion: The polyrhythmic and percussive elements of gwo ka have found resonance in various global music genres, contributing to the broader fusion of world music.

Figure 4.11 *Kassav are one of the most famous zouk bands*

Kizomba: Zouk has influenced the development of kizomba, a genre that originated in Angola. Kizomba incorporates zouk's romantic melodies and danceable rhythms, evolving into a popular genre in the global dance scene.

Soca: Derived from 'soul of calypso', is a vibrant and energetic genre of Caribbean music that originated in Trinidad and Tobago. It blends elements of calypso, African rhythms, and East Indian musical traditions, characterised by a fast tempo, catchy melodies, and lyrics often focused on celebration, carnival, and social commentary.

Cadence: Cadence is a genre of music originating from Dominica in the Eastern Caribbean. Also known as Cadence-lypso, it is a fusion of traditional Dominican and African rhythms with influences from Haitian kompa and calypso. Cadence is characterised by its lively beats, use of modern instrumentation and often French Creole lyrics.

Iron Band: Iron Band music, also known as Steel Band or Steel Pan music, is a genre born out of the innovative use of steel drums, or pans, in Trinidad and Tobago. These drums, originally oil barrels, are tuned to create melodic and harmonic sounds. Iron Band music encompasses various styles, from traditional calypsos to contemporary popular music.

Bouyon: Born in Dominica during the 1980s, Bouyon mixes Caribbean vibes like jing ping and cadence with cool sounds from reggae, calypso, and even hip-hop. It's all about fast beats, deep bass, and getting everyone to dance. The content in a Bouyon song varies, the main goal is to make beats that are impossible not to move to.

Cultural practices and customs

The cultural landscape of the Caribbean is deeply mixed with African social customs and rituals. These practices, passed down through generations, have shaped interpersonal relationships, celebrations and daily life in Caribbean communities.

Greetings and hospitality: African greetings, characterised by warmth and nonverbal cues, such as handshakes, embraces, and even facial expressions used to communicate feelings or thoughts, remain prevalent in Caribbean cultures. Hospitality is also highly valued, with guests being welcomed and offered food and drink as a sign of respect.

Figure 4.12 *A carnival participant playing a soucouyant – a sorcerer from Caribbean folklore*

Rites of passage: African traditions influence life cycle celebrations, such as births, weddings, and funerals. These ceremonies often involve music, dance and rituals that reflect African customs. For instance, the pouring of libations – the offering of drinks to ancestors or spirits is a common practice in many Caribbean cultures.

Community spirit: African traditions emphasise communalism and a strong sense of community. This is evident in Caribbean practices such as communal gatherings, cooperative work projects and the sharing of resources within extended families and neighbourhoods.

Cooking techniques: African cooking techniques such as frying, stewing and smoking, are widely used in Caribbean cuisine. These techniques impart rich flavours and textures to dishes, often using local ingredients.

African ingredients, such as plantain, okra and yam, have become staples in Caribbean cuisine. These versatile ingredients are often combined with locally sourced seafood, meats and spices to create diverse and flavourful dishes.

Communal dining: Communal dining is a central aspect of Caribbean culture, reflecting African traditions of sharing meals and fostering a sense of community. These gatherings often involve family, friends, and neighbours, providing opportunities for socialising, storytelling and cultural expression.

Dance: African dances have played a significant role in shaping the diverse and vibrant dance traditions of the Caribbean. These dances, characterised by their energy, rhythm, and expressive movements, continue to be performed and celebrated throughout the region. For example, Bèlè, a traditional dance known for its intricate footwork, call-and-response patterns and use of drums and gourds is often performed during celebrations and community gatherings.

Folklore and storytelling: African folklore and storytelling traditions have enriched the cultural heritage of the Caribbean. These tales, often passed down orally, convey moral lessons, historical narratives and cultural values. For example, the Anansi stories, featuring the trickster spider Anansi, are popular throughout the Caribbean. These tales entertain and educate, often teaching lessons about morality, resourcefulness, and the importance of community.

The continued presence of African social customs, culinary influences, traditional dances and folklore in the Caribbean demonstrate the resilience and adaptability of African cultural heritage. These practices, deeply intertwined with the region's identity, continue to shape the vibrant and diverse cultural landscape of the Caribbean.

Resistance and cultural retention

Table 4.7 shows how Caribbean communities have sought to maintain their traditions.

Aspect	Description	Role of the family
Maroon communities	Maroon communities emerged as havens of resistance and cultural preservation for enslaved Africans who escaped to remote areas and established independent societies. These communities served as crucibles for the preservation of African traditions, languages and social structures.	Maroon families played a central role in transmitting cultural knowledge and practices across generations. They nurtured the cultural identity of Maroon communities, ensuring the survival of African traditions amidst the harsh realities of enslavement.
Cultural resilience	Enslaved Africans demonstrated remarkable cultural resilience, finding creative ways to maintain and transmit their cultural practices despite the oppressive conditions of enslavement. They adapted their traditions to fit their new environment, blending them with local customs to create unique cultural expressions.	Families served as the primary custodians of cultural practices, transmitting them through storytelling, music, dance, and everyday interactions. They instilled in their children a sense of cultural pride and identity, ensuring the continuity of African heritage.
Assimilation	Assimilation, the process of adopting the cultural norms and practices of a dominant group, occurred in varying degrees among enslaved Africans. Some individuals and families embraced aspects of European culture, such as language and religion, while others actively resisted assimilation and maintained their African identities.	The family played a crucial role in shaping the assimilation process. Families who chose to assimilate often did so in an effort to improve their social and economic standing. However, families also avoided assimilation, preserving cultural traditions and fostering a sense of identity within the enslaved community.

Table 4.7

Indentureship and migration after indentureship

Indentureship was the system of bonded labour that brought millions of people from Asia and India to the Caribbean between the 19th and early 20th centuries It had a profound and multifaceted impact on the region's cultural landscape.

The arrival of indentured labourers marked a significant turning point in the Caribbean's cultural evolution. These newcomers brought with them traditions, languages and beliefs that intermingled with the existing cultural elements of the region.

Linguistic diversity

The introduction of Indian languages such as Hindi, Tamil and Bhojpuri, added to the linguistic diversity of the Caribbean, creating multilingual communities with unique linguistic identities.

Figure 4.13 *A Maroon family passing on cultural knowledge to their children*

Despite the challenges of assimilation and the pressures of the colonial system, Indian languages have exhibited remarkable resilience in the Caribbean. These languages have been preserved through various means, including:

Family transmission: Families played a crucial role in transmitting Indian languages across generations. Parents and grandparents passed down their linguistic heritage through everyday interactions, storytelling, and cultural practices.

Community institutions: Religious institutions, social organisations, and cultural centres served as important hubs for language preservation. These institutions provided opportunities for language instruction, community gatherings and cultural events that fostered the use and appreciation of Indian languages.

Linguistic adaptations: Indian languages adapted to the Caribbean context, incorporating local words and linguistic features. This process of adaptation created unique linguistic variations that reflected the cultural fusion of Indian and Caribbean influences.

Linguistic creolisation: In some Caribbean regions, the interaction between Indian languages and the prevailing languages such as English, French and Spanish, led to the emergence of creole languages. These creoles incorporated elements from both Indian and European languages, resulting in unique linguistic systems that reflected the cultural and linguistic diversity of the region, for example Indo-Trinidadian Creole and Sarnami Hindustani

The introduction of Indian languages to the Caribbean has undoubtedly enriched the region's linguistic landscape. The retention and adaptation of these languages, along with the emergence of creole languages, have created a unique and vibrant linguistic tapestry that reflects the cultural diversity and historical dynamics of the region.

Culinary fusion

Indian culinary traditions, characterised by the use of spices and aromatic ingredients, blended with existing Caribbean culinary practices, resulting in a diverse and flavoursome cuisine that continues today.

- Roti – a staple in Caribbean cuisine, directly derived from Indian flatbreads like paratha. It is often served with a variety of curries, stews and vegetable dishes.
- Dhalpuri – a variation of roti, filled with a savoury mixture of split peas, spices and herbs.
- Doubles – a popular Trinidadian street food, doubles consists of two baras, a deep-fried bread similar to the Indian puri, filled with curried chickpeas and chutney. It exemplifies the blending of Indian and Caribbean culinary elements.
- Pelau – a rice dish which combines Indian and Caribbean influences. It features rice cooked with pigeon peas, meat and a blend of spices, reflecting the fusion of culinary traditions.
- Spice blends – Caribbean spice blends, such as curry powder and garam masala, often incorporate a mix of Indian and local spices, reflecting the fusion of culinary traditions. These blends add layers of flavour and complexity to Caribbean dishes.
- Patty – the Jamaican patty is a semi-circular pastry containing a spiced beef filling, which came about as a fusion of pastries from Cornwall in the UK, and spices from Indian indentured labourers, together with enslaved Africans.

Musical enrichment

Indian musical traditions, including the use of tablas, sitars and harmoniums, entered the region's music scene, introducing new rhythms, melodies and instruments that enriched the Caribbean's musical landscape.

The introduction of Indian musical traditions has led to a dynamic fusion of musical styles in the Caribbean. Indian instruments, rhythms and melodies have blended with existing Caribbean musical elements, creating new genres and enriching the region's musical heritage.

Figure 4.14 *Trinidad doubles*

Figure 4.15 *Jamaican patty*

Figure 4.16 *Machel Montano – a Trinidadian Soca artist*

- Chutney – a vibrant music genre that exemplifies the fusion of Indian and Caribbean musical traditions. Its rhythmic patterns draw inspiration from Indian folk music, while its melodies incorporate elements of both Indian and Caribbean music.
- Parang – a genre associated with the Indo-Trinidadian community that combines Indian musical elements with Spanish Christmas carols. Its songs feature the use of tablas, harmoniums and guitars, showcasing the cultural fusion that has shaped Caribbean music.
- Soca – the energetic and danceable music of Trinidad and Tobago which has also been influenced by Indian rhythms and melodies. The use of the dholak, a drum similar to the tabla, and the incorporation of Indian musical scales have contributed to the unique sound of soca.

Post-indentureship migration and cultural exchange

Even after the formal end of indentureship in the early 20th century, migration continued to shape the Caribbean's cultural landscape. Both internal migration within the Caribbean islands, and external migration to other parts of the world, contributed to the ongoing exchange and blending of cultural elements.

Internal migration and cultural vitality

The movement of people from rural areas to urban centres led to the diffusion of cultural traditions, fostering a dynamic exchange of customs, languages, and artistic expressions.

Ongoing cultural evolution and the Caribbean identity

The Caribbean's cultural identity is a testament to the enduring impact of indentureship and migration. The region's cultural landscape continues to evolve, shaped by the dynamic interplay of its diverse heritage and the ongoing exchange of cultural elements through internal and external migration.

Cultural festivals and celebrations: The Caribbean is renowned for its vibrant cultural festivals and celebrations, such as carnivals, Diwali and Hosay, which serve as platforms for the expression and preservation of cultural traditions.

Artistic expressions: Caribbean art, music, literature, and dance reflect the region's rich cultural heritage, showcasing the fusion of African, Indian, European and indigenous influences.

Cultural tourism: The Caribbean's cultural diversity has become a significant draw for tourists, offering a unique and enriching experience that celebrates the region's rich heritage and vibrant traditions.

Table 4.8 shows a timeline of migratory history in the Caribbean.

Period	Key events	Impact on Caribbean migration
15th century	Arrival of European colonisers	Initiates the movement of people to the Caribbean from Europe, setting the stage for future migration patterns.
16th century	Transatlantic Slave Trade	Forcibly transports millions of Africans to the Caribbean, shaping the region's demographic and cultural landscape.
17th century	Establishment of European colonies and growth of the sugar trade	Attracts European settlers and labourers from various backgrounds, contributing to the Caribbean's multicultural society.
18th century	Maroon Wars and continued Slave Trade	The Maroon Wars indicate resistance to colonial rule, while the Slave Trade further intensifies the movement of enslaved people to the Caribbean.

Period	Key events	Impact on Caribbean migration
19th century	Abolition of enslavement and introduction of indentured labour	The abolition of enslavement leads to migration of freed enslaved people within the Caribbean and to other parts of the world, while indentured labour from India adds a new dimension to the region's migration patterns.
20th century	Economic decline, political unrest, and migration to North America, Europe and other regions	Economic challenges and political instability drive migration from the Caribbean to various countries, seeking better opportunities and freedom from oppression.
21st century	Caribbean diaspora's continued impact and cultural preservation efforts	Caribbean migrants remain influential in their host countries, while the diaspora plays a crucial role in preserving and promoting Caribbean heritage.

Table 4.8

Questions

Knowledge and comprehension

1. What are the main groups that have contributed to the cultural diversity of the Caribbean?

2. Define 'creolisation' and explain its significance in the context of Caribbean cultural history.

3. Discuss the impact of European colonisation on the indigenous languages and traditions in the Caribbean.

Use of knowledge

4. Analyse how the blend of African, European and indigenous influences has shaped the Caribbean's musical traditions.

5. Based on the concept of cultural sustainability, suggest strategies to preserve the linguistic diversity of the Caribbean.

6. Assess the role of family and community in the transmission of Caribbean cultural heritage.

SBA skills

1. Conduct a small study on the influence of Indian culinary practices on Caribbean cuisine, illustrating the concept of cultural fusion.
2. Develop a community-based project proposal that aims to promote and celebrate the diverse cultural heritage of your community.
3. Critique the effects of globalisation on the preservation of **intangible cultural heritage** in your community, providing reasoned conclusions.

Global influences and cultural imperialism

In our globalised world, different cultures are mixing more than ever. One just needs to look at global fast-food chains popping up in the Caribbean. Thanks to better travel and communication, we're seeing a mix of influences everywhere. While this can bring in new styles and ideas, it can also lead to cultural imperialism, where the big, global brands overshadow our local Caribbean flavours and traditions.

Learning objectives

- Understand how globalisation affects Caribbean culture, leading to cultural exchange and imperialism.
- Explore how media shapes and spreads Caribbean culture, and its potential to homogenise traditions.
- Assess the influence of tourism on authentic Caribbean cultural practices and traditions.
- Study the blending of diverse cultural influences in the Caribbean to form unique cultural identities.
- Examine the worldwide impact of Caribbean music, dance and other cultural expressions.

Important definitions

Globalisation – increased interconnectedness and interaction between people, companies and governments worldwide, often leading to cultural exchange and influence.

Cultural imperialism – the dominance of one culture over another, often resulting in the imposition of its values, practices, and beliefs, which can overshadow or replace the local culture.

Commodification – the process of turning something into a product that can be bought and sold, often referring to cultural elements being marketed for profit.

Creolisation – the blending of different cultures to create a new, unique culture, often seen in places where diverse groups have interacted, like the Caribbean.

Commercialisation – the process of exploiting something for financial gain, often at the expense of its original value or purpose.

Authenticity – being genuine or true to the original form, often used in cultural contexts to refer to traditions that are preserved without significant alteration.

Soca music – a style of Caribbean music originating in Trinidad and Tobago, combining elements of calypso with Indian rhythms and beats.

Mas Domnik – the unique Carnival celebration in Dominica, known for its traditional and cultural elements.

Vodou – a syncretic religion practiced chiefly in Haiti and the Haitian diaspora, blending elements of West African, Native Caribbean, and Christian (particularly Roman Catholic) practices.

Wakes – social gatherings or ceremonies held in some Caribbean communities following the death of a person, featuring music, storytelling and food, reflecting the community's cultural beliefs and practices about death and the afterlife.

Basket weaving – a traditional craft in the Caribbean, creating functional and decorative items from natural materials like vines, grasses and strips of wood.

Global musical landscape – the international reach and influence of music genres and styles, showcasing how music from one region can impact and shape the musical culture globally.

The media

The influence of media, particularly television, the internet and social media, has transformed the landscape of cultural exchange. While these mediums provide wider access to different cultures and perspectives, they can also inadvertently promote **cultural imperialism** by reinforcing Western values and lifestyles.

The Caribbean media landscape is shaped by both local and international influences, with Western media often dominating. This exposure broadens perspectives but risks overshadowing Caribbean culture, challenging the balance between global influence and local heritage preservation.

Figure 4.17 Stranger Things *is a popular show from the USA*

Travel

Travel encourages cross-cultural understanding and appreciation but can also contribute to cultural imperialism. Mass tourism often leads to the **commercialisation** of local cultures, transforming traditional practices into spectacles for foreign visitors. This **commodification** can distort the **authenticity** of cultural heritage, eroding local traditions and prioritising the expectations of tourists over the preservation of customs.

The Caribbean's tourism industry plays a pivotal role in the region's economy. However, the influx of foreign visitors can also pose challenges to the preservation of authentic cultural heritage. Mass tourism often leads to the commercialisation of local customs and tradition.

For example:

- The commodification of Carnival: Carnival celebrations, a hallmark of Caribbean culture, have become increasingly commercialised in some parts of the region. Large-scale carnival events often cater to the expectations of foreign tourists, emphasising elaborate costumes, extravagant performances and sanitised versions of traditional customs. This can overshadow the authentic and community-based aspects of Carnival, diminishing its significance as a cultural expression of Caribbean identity.
- The transformation of traditional crafts: Traditional arts and crafts, such as **basket weaving**, pottery, and woodworking, have long been an integral part of Caribbean culture. However, the demand from tourists for souvenirs and handicrafts has led to the mass production of these items, often compromising their quality and authenticity. This commercialisation can erode the traditional value and significance of these crafts, reducing them to commodities.

> In some Caribbean places, spiritual traditions like **vodou** and **wakes** are turned into tourist attractions. This can twist how they are traditionally practiced and upset locals who value these rituals. Some Caribbean regions might alter their culture so it looks the same as everywhere else – as that is what some tourists expect. This can make the unique and exciting parts of Caribbean life seem less special.

Agents of transmission

The Caribbean region boasts a rich cultural heritage that reflects the unique tapestry of its diverse ethnic groups. This heritage, including traditions, customs and expressions, has been transmitted and transformed through a complex process that has been shaped by various factors. These agents of transmission also act as sources of preservation of the cultural heritage.

Families
Families play a central role in transmitting cultural heritage across generations, sharing stories, folklore, traditional skills, and values. This transmission ensures the continuity of customs, festivals, and celebrations, while also allowing for adaptation and evolution over time, incorporating new elements from other cultures.

Artist
Artists, including musicians, dancers, writers, and visual artists, draw inspiration from traditional forms of expression and incorporate them into their contemporary works. This creative process not only preserves cultural heritage but also showcases it to a global audience, contributing to its recognition and appreciation.

Mass media
Mass media, including social media, plays a significant role in disseminating cultural content, reaching a wide audience and influencing perceptions and preferences. While this exposure can promote cultural exchange and understanding, it also raises concerns about potential homogenisation and misrepresentation of cultural heritage.

Cultural groups
Cultural groups, such as dance troupes, music ensembles, and community organisations, actively promote and preserve cultural heritage through events, education, and advocacy. These groups foster cultural exchange among different ethnic groups, leading to the fusion of cultural elements and the creation of new forms of expression.

Institutions
Institutions, such as museums, libraries, cultural centres, educational institutions, and government agencies, play a crucial role in preserving and promoting cultural heritage. Through exhibitions, educational programmes, and cultural initiatives, these institutions safeguard artifacts, promote cultural understanding, and support cultural preservation efforts.

Figure 4.18 *Agents of transmission*

It is important not just to keep traditions alive, but to make them vibrant and relevant today. Families gather to cook and share recipes passed down through generations, blending old flavours with new twists. Dance troupes take folktales and turn them into electrifying performances, while musicians fuse traditional beats with modern sounds, creating hits that travel worldwide.

Artists are not just preserving the past; they are redefining what Caribbean culture means, making it fresh and exciting. Through social media, they share this dynamic culture far and wide, challenging stereotypes and inviting everyone to explore its depth and diversity.

Museums and cultural centres do more than preserve artifacts; they are vibrant hubs of activity that bring history to life. Schools and libraries often collaborate by hosting workshops where elders share traditional crafts and stories, ensuring that the rich Caribbean heritage continues to influence and inspire future generations.

Caribbean culture is always changing, mixing tradition with new influences. Although global trends can make cultures seem the same, the energy of families, artists and cultural organisations keep Caribbean culture alive and exciting. By valuing our heritage and staying open to new ideas, Caribbean culture will keep flourishing and inspiring others.

Transformation

Think about the lively scene of Trinidad's Carnival, famous for its energetic celebration, where the streets come alive with music and colour. Then, shift to Dominica's distinct Carnival, known for its traditional **Mas Domnik** – a unique blend of French, African and Carib influences, showcasing colourful costumes, 'bwa bwa', and the 'sensay' outfits.

Creolisation in Trinidad is evident in its language and music, with Soca blending Indian rhythms and African beats, creating a sound that is all its own. Meanwhile, in Dominica, creolisation is seen in the culinary fusion of Creole dishes, where African, French and Kalinago flavours combine, creating hearty and aromatic meals like the national dish, Callaloo.

Both islands face the challenge of commercialisation, as their cultural festivals and traditions attract tourists. In Trinidad, Carnival has become a global attraction, while in Dominica, the unique aspects of Mas Domnik are marketed to tourists seeking authentic experiences, risking the over-simplification of these deep-rooted traditions.

In Trinidad and Dominica, we can see two vibrant examples of how Caribbean cultures adapt and evolve, blending heritage with modern influences, all the while navigating the complexities of preserving authenticity in a globalised world.

The impact of Caribbean cultural forms on the global stage

The Caribbean region is a cultural melting pot where diverse influences have converged to create a rich heritage. This amalgamation is often seen on the global stage through the mediums of music and dance.

Globalisation has helped spread Caribbean culture worldwide. Thanks to better technology and easier travel, Caribbean music and dance have gained fans everywhere. While this shows how powerful globalisation is, it is not a one-way street. The Caribbean also picks up influences from around the world, showing the give-and-take relationship in global culture sharing. This exchange keeps Caribbean culture lively and evolving, influencing and being influenced by the wider world.

Figure 4.19 *Slinger Francisco, known as Mighty Sparrow*

While we celebrate the global impact of our region, we must also consider its authenticity and commodification. The tension between preserving the value of Caribbean cultural forms and catering to global tastes involves navigating a delicate balance. As Caribbean cultural forms become part of the global entertainment industry, an understanding of the relationship between globalisation and cultural identity is important.

The global reach of Caribbean cultural forms clearly shows the interconnectedness caused by globalisation. From reggae's rhythmic beats to Shelly-Ann Fraser-Pryce crossing the finish line at the Olympics, the Caribbean has left a mark on the world's cultural stage. However it is important to reflect on the implications of globalisation for the authenticity and preservation of Caribbean cultural heritage.

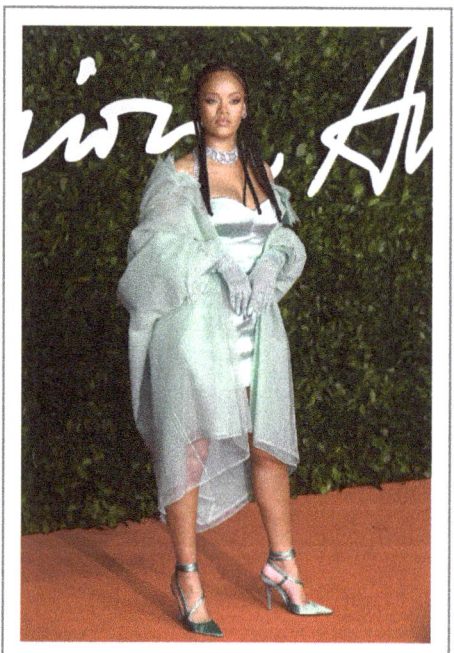

Music

Caribbean music, with its infectious rhythms, soulful melodies and rich storytelling traditions, has captivated audiences worldwide, becoming an integral part of the **global musical landscape.** Genres like reggae, calypso, soca and salsa have transcended borders, reaching the top of international charts and influencing popular music across

Figure 4.20 *Rihanna*

the globe. Artists like Bob Marley, Jimmy Cliff and Celia Cruz have become global icons, their music resonating with themes of social justice, love and the beauty of the Caribbean spirit.

Rihanna, a Barbadian singer, has become one of the most successful pop stars in the world, blending Caribbean influences with contemporary pop and R&B. Her music has topped charts worldwide, and she has won numerous awards, including nine Grammy Awards. Rihanna's success has helped to popularise Caribbean music and culture on a global scale

Dance

Caribbean dances have ignited dance floors around the world, with their sensual movements, infectious energy and unique cultural expressions. Salsa, merengue and bachata have become popular social dances, while traditional Caribbean dances like limbo have gained international recognition for their cultural significance and artistic beauty. These dances embody the vibrant spirit of the Caribbean, captivating audiences with their rhythmic allure and expressions of cultural identity.

Literature

Caribbean writers have enriched the global literary landscape with their unique storytelling traditions, vivid imagery and exploration of themes ranging from social and political issues to the complexities of Caribbean identity. Authors like Derek Walcott, V.S. Naipaul and Jamaica Kincaid have earned international acclaim, and their works have been celebrated for their literary merit and cultural insights. Through their writing, Caribbean authors have provided a window into the Caribbean soul, offering insights into the region's history, culture and the complexities of the human experience.

Figure 4.21 Derek Walcott

The contributions of historical writers like Hilary Beckles, C.L.R. James, Walter Rodney and Eric Williams have helped shape the discourse on Caribbean history, identity and the legacy of colonialism. Hilary Beckles, a historian from Barbados, has contributed significantly to the understanding of Caribbean history, particularly focusing on the impact of enslavement. C.L.R. James, a Trinidadian intellectual, authored influential works that explored the intersections of race, class and colonialism. Walter Rodney, a Guyanese scholar and activist wrote critical perspectives on the African diaspora and the history of the Caribbean. Eric Williams, the first Prime Minister of Trinidad and Tobago, authored *Capitalism and Slavery*, a seminal work that examined the economic foundations of Caribbean enslavement.

Fashion

Caribbean fashion has influenced the global fashion scene with its vibrant colours, bold patterns and eclectic mix of influences. Traditional garments like dashikis and sarongs have become fashion staples, while designers from the Caribbean are increasingly gaining recognition for their innovative designs and celebration of Caribbean style. Caribbean fashion has moved beyond the boundaries of the region, becoming a source of inspiration for designers worldwide, showcasing the creativity and cultural heritage of the Caribbean.

Cuisine

Caribbean cuisine has tantalised taste buds worldwide with its rich flavours, diverse ingredients and unique fusion of culinary traditions. Dishes like jerk chicken, roti, and plantain have become popular favourites, while Caribbean cooking techniques and ingredients have enriched the cuisine of many countries. Caribbean cuisine reflects the region's history and cultural diversity, blending influences from Africa, Europe and Asia.

Sport

Sport in the Caribbean is not merely a pastime; it is an important part of the region's cultural identity, uniting nations and igniting a collective pride that crosses borders. The Caribbean has emerged as a powerhouse in track and field, particularly through unparalleled achievements in Olympic competitions. The iconic figure of Usain Bolt from Jamaica is a testament to the Caribbean's dominance in sprinting. Bolt's electrifying speed, charisma, and record-breaking performances not only elevated him to legendary status but also turned the global spotlight onto the Caribbean's ability in athletics.

Figure 4.22 *The West Indies one-day international cricket team in 2023*

Cricket is a cultural phenomenon in the Caribbean. The West Indies cricket team, a formidable force with a long history, has been a source of immense pride and collective identity. The team's successes in the early years, marked by the likes of Sir Vivian Richards, Clive Lloyd and Malcolm Marshall, were symbolic of the Caribbean's resilience and determination. The West Indies' dominance in international cricket during the late 20th century not only showcased sporting excellence but also became a source of inspiration for a region navigating complex socio-political landscapes.

Questoins

Multiple choice

1. What is the term for the process of blending different cultures to create a new, unique culture in the Caribbean?

    a) Assimilation

    b) Creolisation

    c) Commodification

    d) Globalisation

2. Which European power was the first to colonise parts of the Caribbean?

    a) Britain

    b) Spain

    c) France

    d) Netherlands

3. What is the name of the traditional dance known for its intricate footwork and drumming?

    a) Soca

    b) Bèlè

    c) Zouk

    d) Reggae

4 Which Caribbean celebration is known for its elaborate costumes and vibrant music?
   a) Diwali
   b) Carnival
   c) Hosay
   d) Christmas

5 What is the main impact of cultural imperialism in the Caribbean?
   a) Preservation of local traditions
   b) Enhancement of cultural diversity
   c) Overshadowing of local culture by dominant cultures
   d) Increase in cultural exchange

6 In what language is the Creole spoken in Haiti primarily based?
   a) English
   b) French
   c) Spanish
   d) Dutch

7 Who is a famous Caribbean singer known for blending Caribbean influences with contemporary pop and R&B?
   a) Bob Marley
   b) Rihanna
   c) Jimmy Cliff
   d) Celia Cruz

8 What is the practice of turning cultural elements into marketable products known as?
   a) Cultural exchange
   b) Creolisation
   c) Commodification
   d) Assimilation

9 What Caribbean dish is known for its combination of flatbread and curry?
   a) Roti
   b) Doubles
   c) Pelau
   d) Jerk chicken

10 Which concept refers to the global interconnectedness that influences cultural exchange?
   a) Creolisation
   b) Globalisation
   c) Cultural imperialism
   d) Assimilation

11 What is the traditional Caribbean instrument made from steel drums called?
   a) Djembe
   b) Sitar
   c) Steelpan
   d) Tabla

12 What genre of music from Trinidad is known for its fast tempo and energetic beats?
   a) Reggae
   b) Calypso
   c) Soca
   d) Zouk

13 Which of the following is a significant theme in Caribbean literature?
   a) Technological advancements
   b) Fantasy worlds
   c) Social and political issues
   d) Space exploration

14 What is the Caribbean festival that includes music, dance, and costumes to celebrate before Lent in some countries?
   a) Easter
   b) Carnival
   c) Thanksgiving
   d) Independence Day

15 How has the Caribbean's cuisine been influenced by its history of colonisation and migration?
   a) By maintaining traditional indigenous diets
   b) By blending African, European, Indian and indigenous flavours
   c) By adopting fast food as the primary diet
   d) By resisting foreign culinary influences

End of chapter questions

1. a) List TWO potential threats to Caribbean cultural heritage based on historical factors, globalisation, and external influences. (2 marks)
   b) Explain how each threat could impact specific aspects of Caribbean culture. (2 marks)
2. Devise a cultural sustainability plan outlining measures to safeguard key elements of Caribbean culture.
   Consider strategies for preserving indigenous languages, customs, and traditions against modern challenges. (5 marks)

3. Explore the concept of cultural entrepreneurship as a means to sustain Caribbean heritage.

   Suggest some entrepreneurial ideas that leverage and promote Caribbean cultural elements, providing economic opportunities for the local communities. (3 marks)
4. How has the historical interplay of indigenous, European, African and indentured labourer influences shaped the unique cultural mosaic of the Caribbean region? (5 marks)
5. In what ways has migration, both forced and voluntary, contributed to the diverse cultural expressions found in the Caribbean diaspora? (3 marks)
6. How do families serve as agents of cultural transmission, and what role do cultural groups and institutions play in preserving and passing on Caribbean cultural heritage? (3 marks)
7. Discuss the impact of globalisation and cultural imperialism on traditional Caribbean cultural forms, considering factors such as media and international travel. (4 marks)

Technology-based assessment

Create a podcast or video presentation discussing the role of a specific cultural form in the Caribbean. Incorporate interviews, music samples, or visual elements to enhance your presentation.

SBA skills

Investigate the extent to which families practice and preserve specific cultural forms or traditions within the community.

Summary

Culture is a way of life of a group of people. It is not only learned but has to be shared among societal members. In the Caribbean, we possess a range of cultural groups due to a colonial past, a period of enslavement and indentureship, as well as a result of globalisation.

There have been significant influences to traditional cultural practices in terms of religion, food, rituals, dress and social customs. Original culture therefore may not exist in its truest sense but Caribbean culture today is an amalgamation of all of the influences of the past as well as the present.

The festivals and music are just two examples of ways in which the Caribbean culture is recognised globally. Each cultural group has unique demonstrations of their culture which can be identified by other cultural groups.

Although some cultural practices have been lost due to historical processes, there is a drive towards retention and resilience. The world as we know it is changing quickly due to the increase in the use of technology. Culture is being transported quite fiercely around the globe to facilitate a number of processes: cultural imperialism, commodification, commercialisation and appropriation.

Let's do our part to become cultural experts and entrepreneurs so that Caribbean culture remains viable.

Section A: Individual, Family and Society
(ii) Society and Governance
5 Social Groups

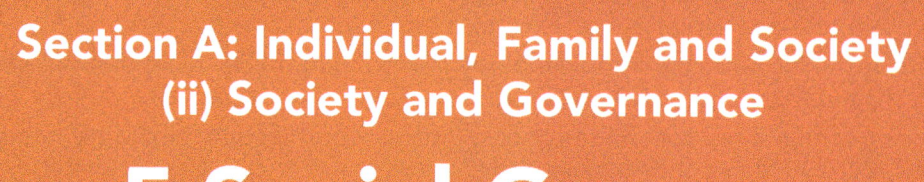

The topics covered in this chapter are:

- types of social groups and their characteristics
- the requirements for cohesion in groups and institutions
- the ways in which social control is achieved in groups
- the different aspects of interaction within and among social groups
- showing respect for differences within and among groups
- designing observation checklists to gather information about social groups

People need interaction with others to feel good about themselves, to have a sense of purpose and to learn values such as kindness and compassion. The saying 'No man is an island' means that we need interaction with other people to be happy and healthy. In an earlier section, you will have been introduced to the many facets of the family, which provide a starting point to learn the basics of group formation, functions and features.

Types of social groups and their characteristics

Learning objectives

- Identify the different types of social groups found in the Caribbean and describe their characteristics.
- Distinguish between the different types of social groups found in the Caribbean.

Important definitions

Social group – a collection of people who interact with one another to achieve common goals.

Hierarchy – a system where individuals are placed in different ranks depending on their level of authority.

Structure – the framework that guides/describes how a social group operates.

Rules – guidelines that allow for the proper functioning of the social group.

Sanction – a reward or a punishment for behaviour within a social group.

Leader – an individual who has the responsibility to guide members and make decisions within the group.

Peer pressure – the positive or negative influence your social group can have on your behaviour.

Regulations – rules which maintain a degree of order among members of a group.

Constitution – the set of rules and laws used to govern a group or country.

Emblem – an icon, logo or symbol which is used to represent or identify a group.

Types of social groups

A group comprises of people who may just be sharing a common space for a particular time. Examples include spectators at a sporting event or even all females within a community. A **social group** has a stronger level of connection which can take many forms. Groups based on size:

- Primary groups
- Secondary groups
- In-groups
- Out-groups
- Reference groups

Figure 5.1 *Family is an example of a primary social group*

Section A(ii)   Individual, Family and Society

- Formal groups
- Informal groups
- Voluntary groups
- Involuntary groups

Primary group

A primary group is a small group of people who know each other well and interact with each other regularly. The members of a primary **social group** are usually close friends or family members. The two important elements of this group are the size of the group and the level of closeness among its members. A primary group is usually small, with about 5 to 15 members. The members of a primary group are also close to each other. They interact with each other regularly and have deep, personal connections with individual members.

Secondary group

This is a group with a large collection of members. The large size prevents regular communication, interaction and even closeness. Some popular examples of secondary groups include a political party, a sports team, an online support group, a religious congregation, a club or organisation or an established music fan group.

Figure 5.2 *The Trinidad & Tobago Red Cross Society is an example of a secondary social group*

Groups based on structure:

Formal group

This is a highly structured group which is governed by a visible **hierarchy** or organisational **structure**. The group itself may have a long-standing presence in the community with well-known written **rules** and accompanying **sanctions**. The group can be identified quite easily as it possesses a recognised symbol or **emblem**. There is an official method of entry to the group as well as elected **leaders**. Since rules are written and relied upon, order is maintained among the members. Formal groups tend to be long lasting due to their highly structured nature. A school community or even CARICOM are good examples of formal groups.

Informal group

This group consists of a collection of members who operate using unwritten rules or an invisible code of conduct and have limited sanctions, if any. The goal of the group, albeit temporary, is achieved through mutual understanding, and order is maintained under an unofficial leader.

Figure 5.3 *CARICOM is an example of a formal social group*

Groups based on membership:

Voluntary group

These groups allow members to join and withdraw whenever they choose to achieve a goal. People join groups for different reasons, such as sharing interests, making friends or networking and helping others through humanitarian work. Cooperative Societies, which are prevalent in Jamaica, encourage persons to take part in a business venture by being able to participate and contribute to the organisation themselves. These Societies are well structured and offer education and training to their members. They also share information with the public.

Figure 5.4 *A school study group is an example of an informal group*

Involuntary group

This is a group that people join without their consent. This can be because they are born into the group, such as in a family, or because they are forced to join such as in a military draft.

Groups based on special attributes:

Figure 5.5 *An organised beach clean-up group is an example of a voluntary group*

Figure 5.6 *In South Korea people are conscripted into the military. This is an example of an involuntary group*

Peer group

This group comprises of members of similar ages and possibly from similar backgrounds. The group can be easily formed in a class within a school community since students are of similar ages. Peer groups are important as they provide members with a sense of self and belonging, and foster a high level of loyalty. Each member in the group directly influences others to behave in particular ways. **Peer pressure** exists, which can be beneficial if it encourages things like revising for a test or negative if it encourages members to engage in bad behaviour, for example, experimenting with illegal substances.

Figure 5.7 *Peer groups can be negative if they encourage bad behaviour*

Section A(ii) Individual, Family and Society

Interest group

The goal of interest groups is to effect change to improve the wellbeing of members of society. This includes pressure groups who lobby for legislative reforms from government agencies. Interest groups can operate in the interest of workers through unions, as well as for the general public. Some examples of interest groups include the Digicel Foundation in Jamaica which aims to create a level of sustainability among the population and enrich lives, while Pan Trinbago (Trinidad and Tobago) strives to preserve the interests of national and international steelpan players while encouraging the promotion and development of the steelpan on a national and international scale. Interest groups can be a powerful force for good in society.

Figure 5.8 *Pan Trinbago is an example of an interest group*

As groups have varying attributes, it is important to note that social groups can fall into a number of types. For instance, a family is considered to be an involuntary group while at the same time is considered a primary and informal group. The school community is also seen as both a formal group as well as a secondary group.

Groups – Distinguishing social groups from aggregates and categories

Understanding different types of groups is essential for grasping how human behaviour is structured. Not all groups are considered social groups and the distinction is key when looking at formations like social aggregates and social categories.

A social aggregate refers to a collection of individuals who are in the same location but don't interact meaningfully. Picture a crowded train station during rush hour. Everyone is physically together, but they aren't forming any lasting relationships. People are just moving through the space, likely focused on their own destinations. Even though they share the same space for a time, there's no bond or shared identity that makes them a group in the social sense.

In contrast, a social category includes people who share a certain characteristic, but they don't necessarily interact. For instance, think of all the teachers in a city. They belong to a social category due to their profession, but this doesn't mean they all know each other or form relationships based on this trait. Their commonality groups them statistically but not socially, making them a category rather than a social group.

Interestingly, even groups that carry a negative image, like gangs or mobs, still meet the criteria for being social groups. These groups engage in regular interaction, have a shared identity, and often possess strong internal dynamics. Whether voluntary or coerced, membership in these groups creates a sense of belonging. Despite their unlawful or destructive actions, they function with defined codes of conduct, demonstrating the complex ways social structures manifest, even in darker settings.

Understanding these distinctions helps to explore the diverse and sometimes unexpected ways people come together or remain separate, all while navigating social structures in everyday life.

Characteristics of social groups

In order to compare social groups, we can look at their key features. These include structure, marks of identity, values, established patterns of behaviour and goals.

Structure

When a social group has a structure, this suggests that the group has a set of rules, written or unwritten, that are followed. Formal groups tend to function under a rigid hierarchical structure with specific roles and rules. A written document, a **constitution**, outlining the operations may govern the affairs of the group while a leader may be needed to make decisions.

Informal groups operate with less structure while still able to attain their specific goal.

Table 5.1 gives a comparison of formal and informal groups.

Formal group	Informal group
 **Figure 5.9**	 **Figure 5.10**
This group has a clear structure where each member has a role to perform. This is a top down design where decisions are made at the top and executed at the lower levels.	This group does not seem to have a formality attached as the boys, who are the same age, are casually having some outdoor fun.

Common goals

Generally, in voluntary groups there is agreement among members about the established goal of the group. As members join the group, they commit to a recognised goal, as in a formal setting, or they might very well be part of securing the goal as in an informal group. Often, the reason individuals are attracted to group membership is because they see that a shared interest can lead to goal achievement. The group comes into being because the members have a similar aim to fulfil.

Cooperation

In the natural world, ants and bees work together to achieve their goals. So too, in the social world, people require teamwork, listening, communication and **leadership** skills to achieve the groups' goal.

Membership

People join groups willingly (voluntarily) or unwillingly (involuntarily). They can decide to join a particular group based on their own choice and free will, as in a membership club. Others are forced to join a group, for example performing community service as a punishment.

Figure 5.11 *Road builders work together on the Mandela Highway in Kingston, Jamaica*

Section A(ii) Individual, Family and Society

Advocacy groups consist of individuals who offer their time, money, expertise and talent to a legitimate cause to assist the disadvantaged. Not all advocacy groups function in the same way which shows that all groups have a unique dynamic.

Voluntary membership	Involuntary membership
 Figure 5.12	 Figure 5.13

Marks of identity

Common identifiers such as a badge, uniform, flag, crest, shared colour (as in school house), tattoo or even a surname can unite individuals from different economic, racial, educational, and even differently abled backgrounds. They foster a sense of belonging, loyalty and pride among the members. Group members who adopt these marks of identity are therefore responsible for conducting themselves in an appropriate manner as they are representing the core values of the group.

Figure 5.14 *School uniform is a mark of identity*

Common needs, interests and values

People will always be looking to belong and fit in with society. Maslow's hierarchy of needs shows us that humans have different needs, like food, water, safety, love and a sense of belonging. We all need to work together in groups to produce adequate supplies to live, thrive and provide for our shared needs. As members of sub-groups such as clubs, teams and even religious organisations within society, we benefit from collaborating with others to increase our potential and to share our core values and talents.

Figure 5.15 *Maslow's hierarchy of needs*

Rules and regulations

In order for a group to continue, guidelines need to exist to ensure order is maintained. Some groups, such as formal groups, have written rules and sanctions while others, such as informal groups, may function using unwritten rules. All groups

Figure 5.16 *Pool rules*

should work to preserve the communication and interaction among members, so it is important that guidelines be employed to maintain normal behaviour.

Sanctions

These rewards or punishments are necessary to encourage acceptable behaviour and deter poor behaviour in the group. It is very important to the group that members appreciate and understand the need to enforce the rules.

Established patterns of behaviour

Every social group has an ethos, the character of the group that is learned and shared through communication, so that the members follow the expected and acceptable behaviour. Things like asking for permission or waiting your turn to share/speak show that you understand the rules and are conforming to the **norms** of the group.

Figure 5.17–18 *Rules and sanctions are important to keep the group functioning*

Diversity and inclusion

Exploring the nature of social groups involves understanding their composition, objectives and member dynamics, which are influenced by diversity and inclusiveness. The distinct features of social groups, including their structure, purposes and membership, can differ widely across cultural environments.

Regarding structure, social groups can be anywhere from highly formal and structured to more informal and loosely organised. Caribbean cultural organisations, for example, often display a semi-formal framework. They might have official leadership and structured committees similar to formal entities but operate with greater flexibility and community focus, mirroring the communal and collective values of Caribbean society. This is in stark contrast to the more rigid and hierarchical setup prevalent in Western corporate entities.

As for the goals, these are shaped by the group's cultural, societal and political backdrop. Caribbean environmental groups, for instance, typically aim to safeguard local ecosystems, encourage sustainable tourism, and raise awareness about how climate change affects island communities. These objectives are specifically designed to address the unique environmental and socio-economic challenges of the region, which is a departure from the broader, often more national-focused goals of environmental groups in more developed nations.

Membership dynamics within social groups also reflect cultural specificities. In the Caribbean, local initiatives like neighbourhood watches or artisans' collectives usually have members who share geographical closeness, heritage and economic interests, fostering a strong community bond and shared identity important in smaller, interconnected societies. Conversely, in more individualistic cultures, participation in similar groups might hinge on personal or professional interests, with less emphasis on communal connection.

For example, in Caribbean disability advocacy groups, the influence of cultural context on structure, objectives and membership is evident. These organisations typically adopt a community-oriented approach, making decisions through collective input and underscoring communal values. Their objectives often focus on improving local accessibility and inclusivity, vital in regions where infrastructure might not be fully disability-friendly. Membership extends beyond individuals with disabilities to include their families, caregivers and community supporters, highlighting the collaborative nature of advocacy and assistance in these societies.

Technological impact

The use of technology today has greatly aided in group formation where online social exchanges have intensified. The internet has given users the ability to participate in virtual seminars, workshops and join social networking sites. Fandoms, support groups and friendship networks are heavily subscribed locally, regionally and internationally. There is a high level of flexibility within these groups as the virtual contact can regulate participation and involvement. Most virtual groups are voluntary and as with regular social groups, some may be formal or informal and they may or may not have established rules and a leader.

Questions

Knowledge and comprehension

 Choose the BEST match from the type of group on the left with the statements on the right. Remember that the characteristics of groups do overlap.

Type of group	Statement
Formal group	The homeless people outside the church have a language of their own.
Interest group	There is a routine in my household: my mum cooks, my dad and the kids eat, then my dad cleans up.
Primary group	I visited the local Red Cross Society in my country and learned that there were other Red Cross Societies all around the Caribbean.
Informal group	Going to the movies with my best friends dressed like Barbie look-a-likes was crazy but we did it!
Secondary group	The leader of my youth club is always on time to meetings and ensures we say our pledge at every meeting.
Peer group	The turtles return to our shores every year like clockwork to lay their eggs and poachers are always ready to slaughter them for their eggs, meat and shells. How can we help stop this?

2. Identify TWO characteristics of formal groups and TWO characteristics of informal groups.

3. List TWO groups that you are part of in school and TWO groups that you are part of out of school. Identify the personal value of being part of these groups.

4. Read the article below and answer the questions that follow.

> Otto Carrington
> Senior Reporter
>
> A faction within the Public Services Association (PSA) is pressuring its president Leroy Baptiste to accept the Government's four per cent wage offer.
>
> Yesterday, members, including some from the union's general council, staged a protest outside the PSA head office in Port-of-Spain.
>
> Over 20 PSA members gathered were in favour of settling for the Government's offer.
>
> Last month, Baptiste agreed to seek advice from Senior Counsel Douglas Mendes for a judicial review of the Special Tribunal's decision to impose a ten-year settlement on the PSA.
>
> In a media release, the union leader stated that the decision to challenge the ruling came after a general council vote.
>
> However, opposing the union leader's decision, former PSA general secretary Oral Saunders stated, "During the special general council meeting on June 22, myself and comrade Jude participated virtually.
>
> The mood of the meeting and the direction of the conversation indicated that the members believed the PSA's negotiating position had been compromised.
>
> Other unions have accepted the four per cent wage offer and, to make matters worse, President Leroy Baptiste was adamant about seeking a judicial review."
>
> Saunders said members have been contacting them non-stop to express their dissatisfaction with this course of action.
>
> "They are not happy with the four per cent offer, but considering the current circumstances, they believe it is better to accept the four per cent like the other unions and continue fighting for the collective period of 2020–2022."
>
> Jennifer Fredericks, a General Council member, emphasised that a precedent has been set.
>
> She said, "We cannot afford to sit idly by while the matter is brought before the High Courts, Privy Council, or Court of Appeal, leaving us with salaries from 2013. The police have accepted it, as have the Prison Officers Association, TTUTA, Amalgamated Workers Union, and Fire Services Association."
>
> Union member Jude Davidson called for a return to in-person general council meetings.

> Speaking to Guardian Media, Davidson said, "Our meetings must take place within the PSA. We should have the ability to vote accordingly and abstain if necessary. We no longer want to rely on Zoom meetings, as they can be manipulated by administrators who handle the vote."
>
> Davidson further questioned the accountability regarding legal fees. "We have no information about the lawyers' costs and what we have paid them. When will it end? How much more can public servants endure? How much are we asking for? We have had enough. It's time to say enough is enough."
>
> *Adapted from article in the* Trinidad Guardian

   a) What types of groups are mentioned in the article?

   b) What were some of the characteristics that you were able to identify?

5 Define the following terms:

   a) Formal group

   b) Interest group

   c) Sanction

   d) Emblem

6 Identify the following types of groups. Remember groups can be classified as more than one type. List all that apply.

Example of group	Type of group
Online support group	
Friend group	

7 Copy and complete this table in your books. Insert examples of groups in your community or country that fit the characteristics. The first row is completed for you.

Primary group	Students on the same bus travelling to school	Workers in a small clothing store	Maths study group
Formal group			
Voluntary group			
Interest group			

Use of knowledge

8 **(a)** Define the term 'hierarchy'.

   (b) Describe the hierarchy in a restaurant kitchen structure.

9 Imagine that you are the leader of a youth club in your community. List THREE rules that would help the club to function properly. Explain why you chose TWO of these rules.

10 Interest groups are considered to be special groups.

You are a member of the environmental group known as 'Protect the Scarlet Ibis'. This is the national bird of Trinidad.

a) Describe THREE activities the group should carry out to help meet the goals of the group.

b) Explain why each activity in (a) above would be appropriate and successful.

SBA skills

Work in groups to complete the table below, identifying how each of the characteristics are present for each type of social group. The first one is done for you.

Book club		
Structure	Regular meetings Informal arrangement	No fixed leader Flexible/unwritten rules
School community		
Common goals		
Government		
Membership		
Street gang		
Marks of identity		
Commercial bank		
Common needs		
Basketball team		
Rules		
Study group		
Established patterns of behaviour		
Tug of war team		
Cooperation		
Police force		
Sanctions		

Group cohesion and social control

Group members are kept together by practices and shared interactions which create a sense of togetherness. Group **cohesion** can be described as the glue that keeps the group together and motivates members to stay involved.

Learning objectives

- Outline the requirements for cohesion in groups.
- Evaluate the different types of leadership styles and authority.
- Examine the various methods of social control within the group.

Important definitions

Cohesion – the 'glue' that keeps group members together.

Leadership – the ability to guide, inspire and motivate individuals in a social group.

Socialisation – how an individual learns to behave appropriately in society. Primary socialisation occurs in the family while secondary socialisation occurs via the school community, places of worship, peer groups and the media.

Authority – the right to influence or be in charge of the social group.

Social control – methods stopping individuals from breaking socially approved rules.

Folkways – parts of the culture of a group that do not carry any consequences if broken.

Norms – accepted rules of a society which allow for socially acceptable behaviour.

Mores – these are norms with a moral basis which control human behaviour.

Laws – these are official rules that govern the affairs of the state/nation. There are strict punishments if these are broken.

Requirements for group cohesion

While social groups have a number of key features that distinguish one from the other, each group has unique dynamics which help the groups' goal.

Leadership

Normally, all groups have a leader who uses a variety of skills to motivate, listen, offer advice and resolve conflict among members and to delegate responsibilities. They often need special skills to cope with many different scenarios during their leadership. Some qualities of a good leader are resilience, honesty, reliability, transparency and humility.

Figure 5.19 Working together is essential for group cohesion

There are three main types of leadership style. However, in a group setting, some situations might need alternative styles to complete the task. Table 5.1 below shows the different features of these leadership styles.

	LEADERSHIP STYLES		
	Autocratic/Authoritarian	**Democratic/Participative**	**Laissez-faire**
Group involvement	The leader issues instructions to members, and they are expected to follow them.	Members are encouraged to be creative and use their initiative to achieve goals.	Role of leader is minimal so members have to be almost entirely self-motivated.
Decision-making	Leader does not readily involve members in the decision-making process.	Leader ensures everyone is part of the decision-making.	Group members take responsibility for decision-making with no guidance.
Approach to guidance	Little to no guidance offered to members, which can impact morale.	Guidance and support are freely given which encourages productivity.	No guidance offered as such, but does offer autonomy to members.
Personal traits	Bossy, dictatorial, strict, egotistical, harsh	Good communicator, motivating, supportive	Whimsical, undependable, hands-off
Potential motto	'Listen to me or else'	'How can we solve this?'	'I believe you all can fix this'

Table 5.1

Control

Leadership can mean control of group members with the use of sanctions, rules and the agents (family members) and/or agencies (family, educational institution) of **socialisation**. Members are expected to follow the rules and standards which allow the group to function well.

In formal groups, behaviour is governed with rules and sanctions. Members feel a sense of fair treatment when leaders use their **authority** to stop negative behaviour within the social group. Within informal groups where rules are largely unwritten, members might use their own sense of right or wrong to influence behaviour. This is learned from their social environment and guides their general behaviour including the way they work with others.

Table 5.2 depicts certain values which might be shared in various groups.

In the family	In the community	In the school community	In the place of worship
Respect for others, including their property, their time and their differences of opinion	Cooperation to complete community projects and communicate respectfully	Recognise and respect of different financial background and even social status	Respect for all religions and people
Tolerance of differences among people, including their religion and their appearance	Appreciation of various religious and cultural celebrations	Receive and appreciate religious/cultural differences; not making fun of 'strange' practices	Good treatment of others, no matter their social standing or background

Table 5.2

Cooperation

In order for groups to operate like a well-oiled machine, members need to work together. This level of cooperation can lead to increased participation, passion and motivation among group members, which can help them to complete tasks more successfully. Individuals from different classes, educational and religious backgrounds, racial and ethnic origins, gender and those who possess disabilities can work in harmony to achieve the end goal. Each individual is seen as possessing special skills and talents to benefit the group.

Authority

In a family, parents have more authority than children. This is due to the age of the parent, the dependence of the child and the influence that the parent has over their life decisions. In most groups, authority is not as clear. There are three types of authority. Table 5.3 below demonstrates the types of authority and some distinguishing descriptors.

	Authority Types		
	Traditional	Rational-Legal	Charismatic
Origin of authority	Based on custom and practice Passed down the generations	Based on the occupation of a certain position. Once individuals are appointed to the position, their authority is accepted	Based on the personality of the individual Individuals are able to charm, convince and persuade followers of their ability to lead
Example	The Royal family	Head of State	Politicians, religious leaders
Weakness	The qualities of the individual are not considered	The individual may have a poor track record	Extreme behaviours can be engaged in by their followers due to their persuasive personality

Table 5.3

Commitment

Social groups foster deep ties among members and with the group. Members spend quality time to improve and enhance the group to reap the rewards later. This dedication encourages the group to continue to work together.

Loyalty

Members hold a feeling of faithfulness and pride in the group. Once individuals join groups, they can become so much a part of it that they are able to attract more members. Conversely, individuals can become disenchanted and lose interest in the group if the goals are not being met.

Social control

Social control regulates the behaviours of members and maintains order. Socialisation, which speaks to instilling the approved values and socially accepted behaviours in individuals, is a key mechanism in social control.

Figure 5.20–23 *Different forms of social control*

Laws

These are official guidelines outlined in a written document known as the Constitution. Formal groups tend to have a constitution comprising of a number of key areas such as the conduct of elections, entry of new members to the group and procedures to change existing **laws**. When laws are upheld rewards (positive reinforcements) can be given to individuals while punishments (negative reinforcements) are used to encourage people to conform to the laws. These are known as sanctions.

Rules

These exist largely in formal groups to maintain order within the group and to control the members. They contribute significantly to the stability and balance of more structured groups. Unwritten rules exist in informal settings too; these lack the power of written rules but still help stop unwanted behaviour.

Folkways

These are useful to encourage culturally acceptable behaviour in a setting. In a social group, members normally aim to be on time (punctual) and to follow the recognised rules. Additionally, in the Caribbean, many people address elders or people they have just met with the title of Miss, Mrs, or Mr. **Folkways** are not enforced as strictly as rules, but it can be seen as impolite if they are not followed.

Norms

Norms possess a bit more 'structure' than folkways; every social group has a set of expected behaviour – its 'norms'. The Caribbean has a number of norms, which differ from one country to the next. It is the norm to respect elders, greet individuals in their cultural manner as well as to offer/serve food to your houseguests. Individuals need to learn the norms. If these norms are not learned, there is no significant penalty attached. Norms exist to maintain a certain degree of order and acceptable behaviour, but also a feeling of community cohesion.

Mores

These are socially developed constructs that operate using a moral code of conduct. Individuals' personal values inform what they consider to be right and wrong. In formal groups, rules exist which are quite clear and specific. **Mores**, or unwritten ethical norms, direct behaviour within these groups. For example, taking office supplies for personal use is considered theft and a violation of workplace mores.

Questions

Knowledge and comprehension

a) State ONE difference between leadership and authority.

b) Define the term 'group cohesion'.

c) Outline ONE factor which can significantly assist in cultivating group cohesion in a social group.

Read the editorial below and answer the questions that follow.

> IN the not so distant past, about three decades ago, Guyana could have boasted about the highest behavioural standards and social norms. Fast-forward to current times, the driver of the bus belonging to a high-profile church body discards an empty water bottle on the parapet of the road; a grandmother and grandson abuse each other in the most profane language; a teacher allows a delinquent student to provoke him into violence, and in response, the parents of the child retaliate by kicking two male teachers and punching a female teacher in the face inside the school building.
>
> Students from high schools, tech voc schools, and even from private schools, which indicates some degree of solvency, are caught hijacking taxis, robbing persons while armed, ganging up to beat up on their peers, among other criminal activities.
>
> One teenaged schoolboy visited the National Park with some other friends for some innocent fun, only to be confronted by some other teenagers who picked a fight with the schoolboy, who attempted to walk away from the bullies, but was chopped to the bone – for no reason that anyone can fathom except that this was one of the innumerable instances of bullyism often perpetrated on the more decent and peace-loving children in schools.
>
> One woman allows her yard to be taken over by grass while she spends her days gossiping, then, when her industrious neighbour, a single mother who works long hours to earn her living, plants a kitchen garden, she sends her relatives to jump the woman's fence and pick all her vegetables and fruits, and even steal her tools and anything else they can lay their hands on.
>
> A tenant, while moving out of the home of a poor old woman, strips off all the electrical fittings and other moveable material, and then slinks off in the night without paying a large backlog of rent.

> A widow's grown children trick her into signing a Power-of-Attorney for her property and then they deposit her in an old folks' home.
>
> Such stories as the foregoing can fill volumes. However, there are also the wonderful stories of humane actions emanating from the most unlikely sources.
>
> The high social standards, of yesteryear that were the norm seem to be in descent while in direct correlation bestial tendencies seem to be overwhelming the psyche of the nation.
>
> Adapted from article in the *Guyana Chronicle*

a) List some of the social norms identified.
b) Describe some of the reasons for the breakdown of these social norms.

Use of knowledge

 a) Suggest THREE actions an organisation may take to develop group cohesion among its members.

b) Explain how EACH action suggested is likely to be successful.

 Christian, a Form 3 student, has heard Paul, another boy in his year group, make malicious comments about members of his class.

a) Discuss TWO steps Christian can take to try and stop Paul's behaviour.

b) Explain how EACH step suggested is likely to be successful.

SBA skills

Use the interview schedule below to gather information from the elders in your family about certain folkways, norms and mores. An interview schedule on food is used as an example. You should create your own interview using another topic/area of interest.

INTERVIEW SCHEDULE

Interview date:

Interviewee: *Grandparent/Great aunt*

Topic: *Food*

Interview recorded: *Video/written report*

Questions	Response
1) What foods were prepared in the past that you think young people are not eating now?	
2) How was the dish prepared?	
3) Who taught you to prepare the dish?	

Questions	Response
4) Why do you think it is not being prepared as frequently?	
5) Do you think you are able to teach the young people to make it?	

Social interaction in and between groups

Learning objective
- Explain the interactions between and within social groups.

> **Important definitions**
>
> **Intergroup** – a collection of groups where members from each group can interact.
>
> **Intragroup** – individuals who belong to the same group.
>
> **Group dynamics** – the interactions between members of the group.
>
> **Conflict resolution** – finding ways to mitigate issues between members through dialogue, negotiation and discourse.
>
> **Mediation** – when two disputing parties seek assistance from an impartial third party who aims to end the conflict and negotiate a solution that everyone is happy with.
>
> **Arbitration** – where two parties submit their disagreements to a separate body of independent arbitrators to make a final, binding decision.

Social interaction in and between groups

Individuals associate with members in their group which create **intragroup** relations. When two groups interact, they experience **intergroup** relations. These relations can result in healthy competition, cohesiveness and help the group reach their goal.

Competition

Competition can be a good thing because it can make you work harder and do your best. Although healthy competition can be a good thing, it can make some group members feel inadequate and therefore group leaders must ensure it does not get out of hand.

Intergroup competition can highlight the different strengths of the groups and demonstrate teamwork in action. For example, if a team or group places second in a sporting competition, they may then think about the changes that need to be made to place first next time.

Conflict

Conflict can occur in any group, especially when people have different backgrounds or experiences. For example, someone from a wealthy background might see an increase in a fee as nominal, whereas a poorer member might find the increase unjustifiable. This can lead to arguments and disagreements which can distract from the group's goals. The key rests in **conflict resolution** which allows members to communicate openly and honestly. In a formal setting, **mediation** and sometimes **arbitration** are important steps to end conflict.

Intergroup conflict can impact on the function of both groups. Mediation and arbitration can also be used effectively to resolve intergroup conflict.

Creativity and problem solving

Members of social groups today possess a range of 21st century learning skills which help groups adapt to new situations, using innovative thinking and productivity. Within a group, problem solving is crucial to the survival of the group and members need to be prepared to 'think outside of the box'.

Collaborating between groups can improve and increase levels of creativity and problem-solving skills. As a society, we need to find the best way to work smarter. Established practices can be adapted to suit the needs of the group.

Cooperation and collaboration

A social group functions better when members are able to work as a team to deliver a goal. Teamwork is important because everyone has something to contribute. When people work together, they can accomplish more than they could ever do on their own.

Intergroup cooperation is beneficial for all groups involved; advice and guidance can be shared across group borders at all levels, even at national, regional and international level. Modern technology offers us the ability to work efficiently with others from a diverse range of backgrounds and in very different locations.

Compromise

Members of social groups are storehouses of ideas and skills learned from individual experiences. They may not agree on every topic but are willing to meet in the middle in order to achieve something. Compromising does not mean giving up or giving in, but instead negotiating with all parties to settle on something that benefits everyone.

Intergroup compromise is also important to keep the group moving forward otherwise feelings of disagreement and competition may become entrenched, interrupting progress.

Questions

Knowledge and comprehension

 List TWO ways students in a particular school house can show support for the house during an inter-house competition.

 Outline the difference between mediation and arbitration.

Use of knowledge

3 Read the article below and answer the questions that follow.

> **USC second year student participates in National Youth Parliament**
>
> On Monday 11th November, 2019 the 17th National Youth Parliament of the Republic of Trinidad and Tobago was held at Tower D, Waterfront Complex. It began at 10:00 a.m. This event gave young people from across the country the opportunity to explore an important issue affecting the nation, and serve, for a day, as members of the House of Representatives in various capacities.
>
> Students from various secondary schools, youth organisations and tertiary institutions participated in the debate.
>
> The USC representative for the debate was David Gomez, a second-year Social Studies major. David attended weeks of training in oratory and debating skills, dress and etiquette, and the use of parliamentary Standing Orders.
>
> His portfolio for debate day was on the government bench as Minister of Finance and Member for Diego Martin North East. This year's motion was the compelling debate "Should parents be held accountable for their children's social media activities?" This government motion, presented by the Minister of Public Administration, sought to bring legislation to ensure parents' liability for their children's inappropriate use of social media platforms.
>
> David, in his contribution to the debate, gave his own experience of being cyberbullied. He also encouraged the opposition bench to take note of the monies being budgeted in the 2019/2020 fiscal year for training in ICT for all citizens, thus ensuring that parents can become knowledgeable and better monitor their children's social media activities and behaviour.
>
> Adapted from article on the website of the University of the Southern Caribbean

a) Suggest some of the ways David and his colleagues would have prepared for the debate as a group.

b) Explain the interactions between David's group and the opposition bench while preparing for the debate.

4 Plan a sporting tournament between two schools in your community. Discuss the steps involved during the social interaction among the major stakeholders which would allow for the tournament to be successful.

5 What informal groups lack in structure, they make up in influencing societal norms. Discuss.

6 Peer pressure in adolescent social groups is prevalent. Discuss the potential negative effects on the members.

SBA skills

In order to gather data, a researcher can use a number of tools and techniques. As researchers, we need to be mindful that not all social interactions or social groups are researchable due to privacy. These include some family groups and government groups.

An observation checklist helps the researcher to record what is being observed using specific headings and areas. In any setting, the researcher will gather a lot of qualitative data (descriptive data) and need to pin-point the key areas which they will concentrate on; the checklist helps them organise their information.

Checklists should have a number of key elements. Students should:

- use clear language; statements and descriptors should be specific and observable
- use a layout that makes the checklist easy to read, with allocated space to comment and add additional information
- make the checklist simple to complete as the user may not have much time to complete the investigation
- make sure the statements and descriptors appear in the right order to suit the needs of the research.

PICTURE THIS!

A two-vehicle accident occurred in the middle of a major intersection. Four nearby schools had just dismissed their students for the day. The rain was falling heavily for half an hour before the accident, and then eased to a slight drizzle.

You can well imagine the scene.

Students filtering out of their schools, some with umbrellas, parents on the roadways waiting to receive their children in vehicles or standing with umbrellas, traffic piling up in each direction unable to pass the accident, police and traffic wardens making their way to the accident area. There is genuine chaos.

As a researcher, we need to develop the skills to zoom in to our particular subject matter and reduce the need to document the whole scenario.

From this situation, we are able to gather a number of themes/subtopics which will aid in creating observation checklists. In this particular context, social groups will be highlighted.

Theme 1	Theme 2	Theme 3
Student preparedness for weather conditions	Response of authorities in emergencies	Drivers and road safety
Possible sub-themes	Possible sub-themes	Possible sub-themes
Students were dressed for the weather conditions	Time the accident occurred to when the first authority presented themselves	What make of vehicles were involved in the accident
Students' ability to have umbrellas, raincoats and any other protective gear	What interactions occurred between drivers involved immediately after the accident	What frame of mind were the drivers in (stressed, intoxicated, emotional) at the time of the accident

Theme 1	Theme 2	Theme 3
Student preparedness for weather conditions	Response of authorities in emergencies	Drivers and road safety
How many students had EACH type of protective gear for the weather condition	What interactions occurred between drivers involved after the accident when the authorities arrived on the scene	What were the conditions of the roads at the time of the accident
Students who chose to walk in the drizzle	What was the interaction between the drivers and the authorities	Were the drivers observing road safety practices

Activity 1

Students can use any ONE of the Themes above to create their personalised observation checklists.

SAMPLE 1

THEME 1: Student preparedness for weather conditions

No.	Descriptors / Criteria	Yes	No	Sometimes	Additional notes
1.	DATE / TIME				2:33 p.m. 21/09/23
2.	Students were dressed for the weather conditions at dismissal in School 1				
	Students were dressed for the weather conditions at dismissal in School 2				
	Students were dressed for the weather conditions at dismissal in School 3				
	Students were dressed for the weather conditions at dismissal in School 4				
3.	Students used protective gear such as umbrellas, raincoats etc. at School 1, 2, 3, 4				
4.	Students used umbrellas more than raincoats at School 1, 2, 3, 4				
5.	Students used raincoats more than umbrellas at School 1, 2, 3, 4				
6.	Students walked in the drizzle without protective gear at School 1, 2, 3, 4				

Activity 2

Students are asked to create an observation checklist to be used in a place of worship with specific reference to attendance.

SAMPLE 2

No.	Descriptors / Criteria	Yes	No	Sometimes	Additional notes
1.	DATE /TIME				17.09.23/8:00 a.m.
2.	Parishioners were punctual to the service				
3.	The place of worship was at full capacity				
4.	There were more men than women in attendance				
5.	There were more women than men in attendance				
6	There were children in attendance				
7.	There were more female than male young people				
8.	There were older persons in attendance				
9.	Parishioners left during the service				
10.	Parishioners left promptly after the service				

End of chapter questions

1. a) State TWO features of a formal social group. (2 marks)
   b) Social cohesion is necessary for the proper functioning of a group. Describe TWO other requirements which are necessary for a group's survival. (4 marks)
   c) Formal groups usually use a symbol or emblem to represent the group.
      (i) Suggest TWO strategies that a named formal group can use to ensure that all members recognise and uphold this symbol/emblem of the group. (4 marks)
      (ii) Explain why EACH strategy suggested in (c) (i) is likely to be successful. (4 marks)
      TOTAL 14 MARKS

2. Social groups vary in size, structure and membership.
   a) List TWO types of groups which vary in size. (2 marks)
   b) Describe TWO types of leadership styles used in social groups. (4 marks)
   c) A new security firm is targeting home owners to offer their 24/7 security services to the neighbourhood for a reduced rate if all the residents in the area agree to accept the service.
      (i) What TWO actions could the security firm take to ensure all the neighbours agree to accept the service? (4 marks)
      (ii) Explain why EACH action suggested in (c) (i) is likely to be successful. (4 marks)
      TOTAL 14 MARKS

Summary

A social group is a set of people who come together to achieve a specific goal. Groups vary in terms of size, structure and membership. Groups are also categorised based on special attributes.

A social group can be defined as many different types of group depending on the combination of characteristics it presents. A family is an involuntary, informal and primary group.

Social groups possess a number of characteristics which include:

- structure
- common goals, needs, interest, values
- membership (voluntary or involuntary)
- an identifier such as a uniform or a badge
- mechanisms to control behaviour with accompanying sanctions
- established customary behavioural patterns
- cooperation.

There are a number of elements that need to be present for social groups to be functioning units. Social cohesion can be described as what keeps the group together while **social control** allows for the group to continue to exist because there are devices in place to regulate behaviour among members. The table below is useful to recognise the differences.

Social cohesion	Social control
Leadership and authority	Folkways and mores
Control	Norms and socialisation
Cooperation and Commitment	Rules and laws
Loyalty	Sanctions

Social groups function not as individual things but among and within other social groups. **Group dynamics** shape interactions between members and with those in other groups. These interactions can be based on competition, conflict, compromise, collaboration and problem solving through creativity.

**Section A: Individual, Family and Society
(ii) Society and Governance**

6 Institutions and Government

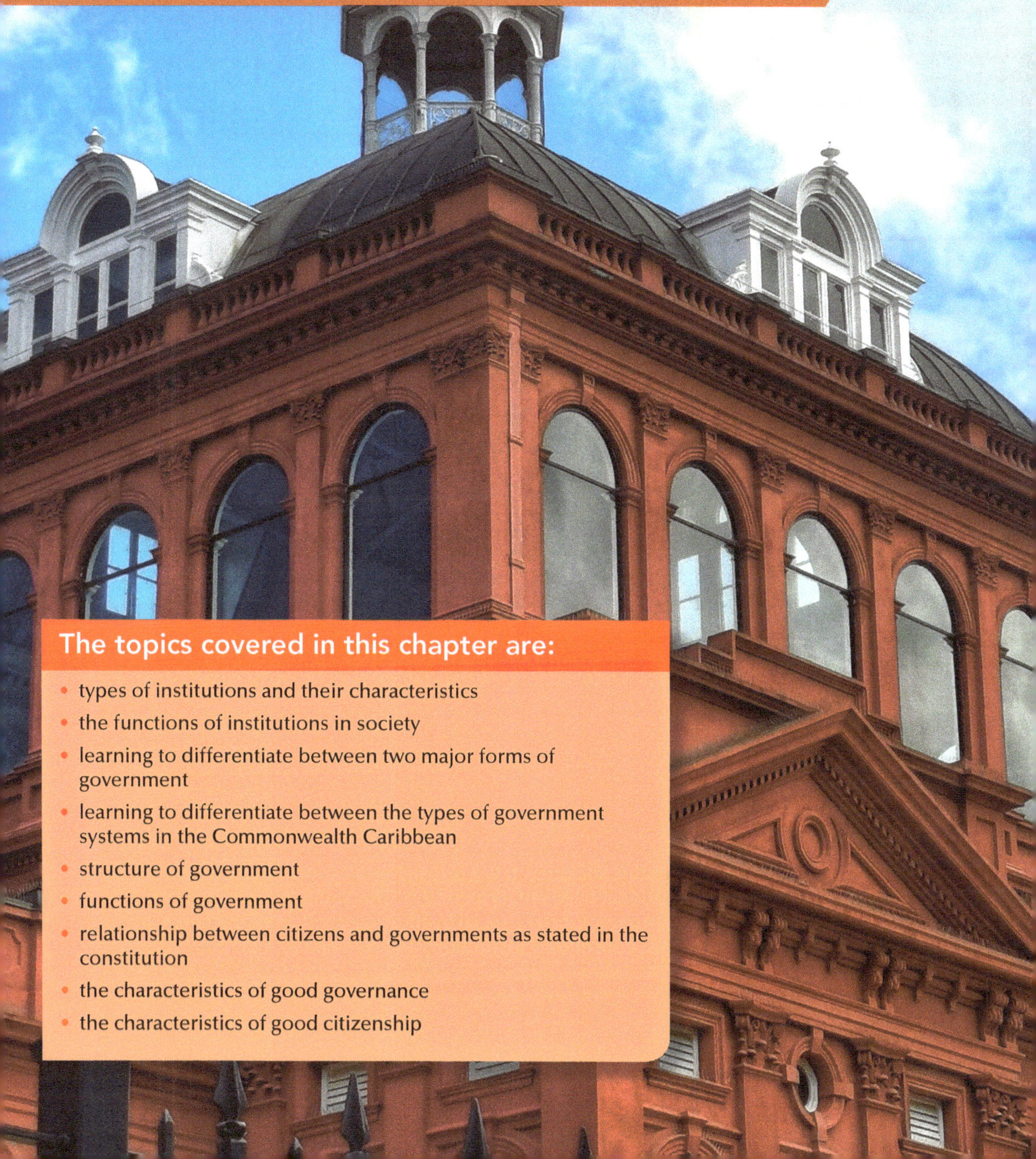

The topics covered in this chapter are:

- types of institutions and their characteristics
- the functions of institutions in society
- learning to differentiate between two major forms of government
- learning to differentiate between the types of government systems in the Commonwealth Caribbean
- structure of government
- functions of government
- relationship between citizens and governments as stated in the constitution
- the characteristics of good governance
- the characteristics of good citizenship

Institutions are important because they help to organise our society and make it work. They provide structured ways to serve individual members. The Caribbean region has a long history of colonisation, enslavement, emancipation, indentureship, independence, and republicanism. At each stage, different institutions were created to meet the needs of the people. Some of these institutions still exist today, while others have changed or been forgotten.

Types of institutions and their characteristics

Learning objectives

- Outline the types of institutions and their characteristics.
- Evaluate the functions of the institutions in society.

> **Important definitions**
>
> *Institution* – a formal establishment serving a specific purpose. It can also be a social mechanism used to understand how ideas, values and beliefs affect people's choices.
>
> *Function* – an established role that an institution, a norm or practice plays in meeting specific needs in society.
>
> *Formal education* – skills and knowledge shared in a school setting. Both technical and transferable skills are taught.
>
> *Hidden curriculum* – within the school system, students learn non-academic behaviour which adds to their overall knowledge.
>
> *Informal education* – skills shared among family, clan or tribe members mainly through oral means.
>
> *Quality education* – a Sustainable Development goal (SDG 4) aimed at enhancing the relationship between school, home, community and policy environments.
>
> *Social solidarity* – group togetherness, which creates appreciation and respect for the members of a group.
>
> *Denomination* – a large religious group with the same name and beliefs.
>
> *Values* – personal beliefs which guide an individual's actions and behaviour.
>
> *Primary socialisation* – the process where an individual is taught the culture of society from their immediate family members.

Types of institutions

Social institutions

The family is a basic **institution** in many societies. It is a primary unit of social organisation and provides for the physical and emotional needs of its members. The family plays an important role in the socialisation process. Other important social institutions apart from the family include governments, religious institutions, educational institutions and the media.

Educational institutions

In the Caribbean, educational institutions deliver **formal education** to students from pre-school to tertiary level. Education is the acquisition of knowledge and skills to be used in the future. Trained teachers instruct students using a shared curriculum. Students aim to learn the material and are assessed using tests and exams, after which they can move up to the next level. At each level, different skills are taught to match the current curriculum and the age of the child.

Figures 6.1–6.4 *Students attend different educational institutions according to their age*

Table 6.1 shows the different levels of educational institutions that exist and some supporting details.

Educational institution	Method of entry	Age	Skills taught	Result
Pre-primary/ Kindergarten/Pre-school	Registration	Usually 3–5 years old	Gross and fine motor skills, basic numeracy and literacy	Graduate from pre-school
Primary	Application/ registration	5–12 years old	Mathematics, Science, Social Studies and Language	National assessment/exit exam
Secondary	Assigned to secondary school based on results of the national assessment/exit exam	12–17/19 years old	Broad range of subjects to choose from	CSEC and CAPE exams

Educational institution	Method of entry	Age	Skills taught	Result
Skills training	Registration	17 years old and above	Broad range of technical skills and training	Diploma, apprenticeship
Tertiary	Application	19 years old and above	Specific area of study	First degree, diploma

Table 6.1

Functions of educational institutions

Educational institutions are where knowledge and skills are taught. Students can learn many different traditional and non-traditional disciplines such as mathematics, technology education, modern languages, visual and performing arts, as well as physical education. Gaining skills in a range of subjects should lead to better job opportunities in the future. Educational institutions also play a role in the socialisation of children. They play a part in the secondary socialisation while the family carry out the **primary socialisation**. These institutions are significant in the transmission of culture within a society. The school system also teaches respect, punctuality, appreciation of hierarchical structures and ways of communicating via the **hidden curriculum**. Students are given opportunities to succeed in the modern age with the use of the 21st century skills like collaboration, critical thinking, communication and creativity.

Religious institutions

Religion is a system of beliefs, practices, rituals and customs that are shared among members. In the Caribbean there are a number of different religions due to our rich heritage. The different religions have different practices and rules, which can give believers a sense of belonging and provide a guide on how to live their life.

Figure 6.5 *The Hindu Temple in the Sea, Carapichaima, Trinidad*

Figure 6.6 *Sunday Mass at a Catholic church in Jamaica*

Functions of religious institutions

Religious institutions in the Caribbean are intertwined with the culture of the region. Each country is known for their famous places of worship, which have a long history and established standards of behaviour. Practices and symbols are used to unite followers and bring a sense of **social solidarity**. Religious institutions still do have a solid presence in the Caribbean but evidence shows that while some **denominations** are growing due to an increase in cultural diversity, there has been a decline in the social significance of religion. This is called **secularisation**; when institutions use alternative teachings rather than religious affiliations.

Figure 6.7 *A mosque in New Amsterdam, Guyana*

Figure 6.8 *A Rastafari man in Jamaica*

Economic institutions

Economic institutions include banks, but also more traditional saving mechanisms such as 'The Gift Club' in Bermuda, 'Partner' in Jamaica and 'Sou-Sou' in Trinidad. These systems help poor people save by allocating a fixed amount to each member over an agreed period. Each individual collects the monies from all the members at a time. It is a circular system and is completed when everyone has received a full amount.

The economy relates to the trade, production and consumption of goods. Economic institutions range from privately owned establishments to state owned institutions and can be categorised according to the type of economic activity they work with, such as agriculture or business.

Figure 6.9 *A credit union in Grenada*

Figure 6.10 *ACB Caribbean, Antigua*

Section A(ii)   Individual, Family and Society

Functions of economic institutions

Commercial banks provide a number of services. One such service is to keep your money safe, and to use your money deposits to grant loans to those who need it. The central bank of a country, which is maintained by the government, issues money, sets interest rates and ensures that the banking sector is stable. The Caribbean Development Bank, located in Barbados, is a regional financial institution that assists with economic development and the growth of CARICOM member states.

Recreational institutions

Many countries have adopted the premise that a 'healthy nation is a wealthy nation'. Health does not only mean free of diseases but also includes the mental and social wellbeing of an individual. Different forms of recreation are provided by the government and private organisations to encourage better health practices.

Functions of recreational institutions

The Caribbean is known as a destination for sports tourism. People visit for golfing, surfing, snorkeling, sailing, athletics, football and cricket, but these also play an important role in keeping local people healthy. Community centres give young people the opportunity to discover sport and encourage the goal of pursuing sports as a career option.

Figure 6.11 *The Caribbean Development Bank logo*

Figure 6.12 *Apes Hill Golf Club, Barbados*

Figure 6.13 *National Stadium, Kingston, Jamaica*

Figure 6.14 *Sir Vivian Richards Stadium, Antigua*

Political institutions

Political institutions are governments, political parties and political organisations. Their job is to govern the country, looking after the interests of their citizens and the property, land and natural resources which belong to the country.

Functions of political institutions

Governments are political institutions that have the responsibility of governing in a way which benefits society through law making and policies. Trade unions are also seen as political institutions, because they fight to secure the rights of workers.

Figure 6.15 *Supporters of the PNM, a political party in Trinidad and Tobago*

Characteristics of institutions

Institutions contain a number of unifying features that can help us to categorise them. These features are as follows:

1. **Social control**
   Institutions use norms, mores, folkways, rules and laws to keep things orderly and predictable. Rules and sanctions help to maintain order in the institution, but the rules should not infringe on members' rights and freedoms. Sometimes a dress code is used in religious and educational institutions. These dress codes help to create a sense of order and respect for the institution.

2. **Value system**
   Institutions develop a certain way of behaving, which is then adopted by new members. These value systems are rooted in tradition and become a fixture in the organisation.

3. **Longevity**
   If the service that institutions provide benefit their members, this tends to suggest that their presence is worthwhile and they remain part of society for a long time.

4. **Adapt to change**
   Institutions must always be able to move with the times and adapt to changes in society. Over time, industry and mechanisation have taken over from agriculture as the cornerstone of the economy and institutions have adapted to suit that. More recently, technology and the internet age have changed the world again. While all institutions must be prepared to change in some way, that change can be slower in some more than others.

5. **Serve a societal need**
   Institutions exist so that society can operate efficiently, and achieve progress.

6. **Hierarchical structure**
   Institutions have a clear structure, where individuals occupy roles ranked one above the other in terms of authority and status. The important decisions are made at the top and filter down to those at lower levels.

7. **Specific function**
   Each institution has a specific function, or role, to play in society. For example, the family is responsible for the physical, emotional and economic needs of its members, while the government is responsible for maintaining law and order in society.

8. **Symbols, emblems or logos**
   Institutions adopt symbols as a mark of identity and to encourage members to feel pride and a sense of belonging.

9. **Rituals**
Many institutions have particular actions which form part of the regular business of the institution. For example, religious institutions have many rituals, such as the specific process for praying or for mourning after a death.

Questions

Knowledge and comprehension

1. Conduct research to identify TWO marriage customs or childcare customs followed in a family found anywhere in the world.

2. Work in groups of four to conduct research on skills training institutions in your country. What are the benefits of these institutions to young people?

   Here are a few examples:

   Grenada National Training Agency

   Barbados Vocational Training Board

   National Energy Skills Center – Trinidad

   Human Employment and Resource Training Trust – Jamaica

3. Identify the benefits of joining recreational institutions. Use the headings given.

Social benefits	
Emotional benefits	
Psychological benefits	
Physical benefits	

4. Identify the values found in each of the institutions outlined.

Institutions	Values
Social (family)	
Educational	
Religious	
Economic	
Recreational	
Political	

5. Work in groups of four to deliver a slide presentation on a named institution in your country. You can include details such as:
   - Name of the institution
   - Brief history, including vision, mission, motto (if any)
   - Hierarchical structure with the names of the current management
   - Symbol / emblem / logo of the institution
   - Governing laws and rules
   - A recent article relating to the institution.

6 a) Government is seen as an institution. State ONE reason why government is an institution.

b) Identify ONE example of EACH of the following types of institutions.
   i) Economic institution
   ii) Political institution

Use of knowledge

7 Some schools around the globe have opted for a 'no homework' policy as part of a mission to deliver **quality education**. This is one of the Sustainable Development Goals (SDG 4).

Discuss whether this would work in our educational institutions in the Caribbean. Would teachers and parents be happy with this approach?

8 Examine the statement below and discuss it in groups.

'Co-educational schools provide a more well-rounded representation of society than single-sex schools.' You can use a debate format, discussing ideas about student enrolment, subjects offered, success rates, personal development, etc.

9 'Marriage is seen as an institution.' Discuss this statement using the characteristics of an institution we looked at earlier.

SBA skills

Take an opinion poll from older persons and young adults in your community about how religious they feel. You can include one or all of these variables.

Target sample: *Insert the number of people you are likely to survey*

Members	Older persons			Young adults		
Questions	Yes	No	Total	Yes	No	Total
Do you believe in a god?						
Are you knowledgeable about a particular religion?						
Do you engage in religious rituals?						
Do you feel emotional when engaged in religious practice?						
Do you incorporate religion in your everyday life?						

Analyse your results by answering the question below, and constructing a bar graph to show the results.

Did more older persons feel religious than the young adults? Justify your response by making a statement about your findings.

Government

Governments have been part of all known civilisations and societies in some form, throughout history. Today, our world is so structured and complex that political institutions need to exist to work in the interests of the masses.

Learning objectives

- Differentiate between two forms of government and the government systems in the Commonwealth Caribbean.
- Outline the structure of government.
- Evaluate the functions of government.
- Evaluate the relationship between citizens and governments as stated in the Constitution.
- Identify the characteristics of good governance and good citizenship.

Figure 6.16 *An election rally in Trinidad*

Important definitions

Commonwealth Caribbean – countries in the Caribbean who were once part of the British Empire.

Government – a regulatory and official body that has the power to direct the affairs of a country.

Electorate – all individuals above the age of 18 who are legally allowed to vote.

Referendum – a vote taken by the whole electorate to make a decision about a proposal or law.

Constitution – a written document that outlines the fundamental laws governing a country.

Separation of powers – different, distinct authorities perform independent, separate roles; such as the legislature, the judiciary and the executive.

Collective responsibility – a principle used in Cabinet to ensure that all decisions are supported by all members.

Bill – a proposal for a new law.

Universal adult suffrage – the right given to all individuals over the age of 18 to vote no matter their social or economic status.

Forms of government

Government is the system by which a country or group of people is controlled. Governments make decisions about things like laws, taxes and how to spend money. **Democracy** is a form of government where the people have a choice about who makes the decisions. This is usually done through free and fair elections, where people vote from a list of candidates to become representatives. The word *democracy* comes from the Greek words *demos* (citizens) and *kratos* (power) which translates as 'power to the people'.

In certain parts of the world, **direct democracy** or **pure democracy** is practised where all the citizens are part of the law-making process. Switzerland and Uruguay are two countries where direct democracy has been used to ask the **electorate** to vote on significant issues. A **referendum** is conducted which becomes binding.

Indirect democracy or **representative democracy** is more widely practised in the Caribbean, where individuals are voted into office by the electorate as representatives of the people. These representatives have a moral duty to serve the people; including those that did not vote for them. This form of democracy is more practical as it is logistically difficult to ensure that every person in a country is available to vote for every proposal in Parliament.

Figure 6.17 *Democracy*

An **autocracy** is a government system where an individual holds supreme power, making single-handedly decisions for the rest of society. Historically, autocracies were common under kings, queens and emperors. Today, they can be seen in absolute monarchies and dictatorships. In these regimes, the people have no say in the law-making process while the leader declares laws, punishes wrongdoings and suppresses individuality.

Table 6.2 compares the two forms of government.

Descriptors	Democracy	Autocracy
How government is selected	The people vote in elections which are free and fair	Position is passed down from one family member to the other or power is seized through military means
Control of the masses	By the use of laws and other agencies	By indoctrination, propaganda and threat of punishment
Accountability	Members of government are accountable to the people who put them in office	No accountability
Ways of voicing grievances	Through the media, meeting with representatives	Protest actions, but with the risk of punishment

Table 6.2

Section A(ii) Individual, Family and Society

Figure 6.18 *Autocracy*

Types of government systems

Crown Colony

This system of government was introduced by the British when they colonised the Caribbean nations. A governor was appointed by the British Empire to oversee the political affairs of the colony and it functioned with a legislative and executive council chosen by the governor. Today, countries under this system are known as British Overseas Territories. They are the British Virgin Islands, the Cayman Islands, Montserrat, Anguilla and Turks and Caicos.

Constitutional Monarchy

In this system of government, the monarch (King or Queen) maintains the position of head of state but the country has gained political independence, and the monarch no longer has the ability to make or pass laws. The **constitution** reflects the separate and distinct relationship between the head of state and the head of government or Prime Minister. In the Caribbean, a Governor General, who occupies a ceremonial position, represents the monarch.

Republic

In the **Commonwealth Caribbean**, Barbados, Dominica, Co-operative Republic of Guyana and Trinidad and Tobago have all become Republics. This means that the head of state, the President, is an approved citizen of the country. He or she replaces the Governor-General who served the interests of the Monarch. The country operates under a new constitution with complete autonomy. The most recent country in the Commonwealth Caribbean to convert into a Republic from a Constitutional Monarchy was Barbados on November 30th, 2021.

Table 6.3 below displays the types of government systems in the Caribbean.

Commonwealth countries			British overseas territories
Antigua and Barbuda	**Dominica**	St. Kitts and Nevis	Anguilla
The Bahamas	Grenada	St. Lucia	British Virgin Islands
Barbados	**Co-operative Republic of Guyana**	St. Vincent and the Grenadines	Cayman Islands
Belize	Jamaica	**Trinidad and Tobago**	Montserrat
			Turks and Caicos

KEY

■	Republic
■	Constitutional Monarchy

Table 6.3

There are two types of Republic in the Commonwealth Caribbean: Parliamentary Republic and Executive Republic. Table 6.4 explains the differences.

	Parliamentary Republic	Executive Republic
Election of President	The president is elected by the Electoral College	The president is elected by a vote of the electorate
Tenure	5 years	5 years
Executive power of President	Only ceremonial and therefore power is limited. The Prime Minister has executive power	President is head of state and head of Government, so has full executive power
Examples	Trinidad, Barbados, Dominica	Co-operative Republic of Guyana

Table 6.4

Structure of government

The Commonwealth Caribbean countries share a British legacy and this is reflected in their governance. Countries have followed the Westminster system since independence. Governments function with a bicameral legislature, a cabinet who possesses executive power, a titular head of state, **separation of powers**, an official opposition to the ruling party and general elections held every five years.

The Westminster system has faced criticism in the Commonwealth Caribbean as it is seen to lead to corruption as the Prime Minister has almost all power. In some cases this has created a crisis with increasing crime rates due to poor enforcement of laws, and where poverty and debt are common. However, these issues are influenced by a complex interplay of factors, not solely the governance model.

Separation of powers

There are three branches of government which work independently to reduce the power of the state. Pure separation of powers means that the functions of each branch, the individuals who comprise the branch and the branch itself should not overlap or interfere with each other. This however might not be practical. In order for governments to function efficiently and expeditiously, there needs to be some overlap and cooperation among the branches.

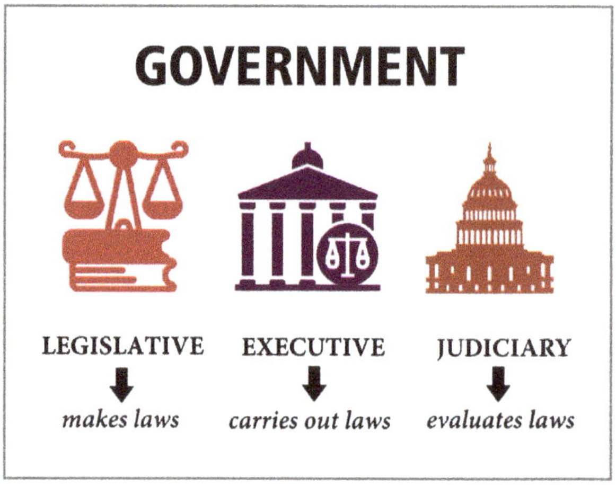

Figure 6.19 *The three branches of government*

Legislature

This branch consists of the head of state and a unilateral (one house) or bilateral legislature (two houses) and is responsible for enacting, amending and repealing laws. Dominica, Co-operative Republic of Guyana, St. Kitts-Nevis and St. Vincent and the Grenadines all have a unilateral legislature.

Unilateral legislature

The parliament is known as the House of Assembly (Dominica, St. Vincent and the Grenadines) or the National Assembly (St. Kitts-Nevis, Co-operative Republic of Guyana) and is made up of directly elected members of parliament and appointed senators who serve a five-year term.

Co-operative Republic of Guyana

The Co-operative Republic of Guyana has a slightly different structure to other unilateral legislatures. The National Assembly has 65 members. 53 are elected through General Elections under **Proportional Representation** (See Chapter 7), 10 representatives come from each of the 10 regional democratic councils and 2 elected representatives come from the National Congress of Local Democratic Organs.

Bicameral legislature

This legislature, known as Parliament, has two Houses: The Lower House (House of Representatives or House of Assembly) and the Upper House (Senate).

The Lower House consists of elected representatives, known as Members of Parliament, who represent the voice of the electorate and are presided over by the Speaker of the House. The Upper House consists of nominated members, known as Senators, who are appointed by the Head of State. A President of the Senate is the presiding officer who monitors the conduct of the House.

Table 6.5 gives an overview of the function of each House.

Lower House (House of Representatives/ House of Assembly)	Upper House (Senate)
Conducts debates on proposals for new laws and repeals existing laws	Reviews and debates bills received from the Lower House and approves proposals
Imposes taxation	Examines all financial actions thoroughly
Creates an opportunity for government and opposition ministers to discuss national issues	Explores and inspects the administration of laws for accountability purposes from the various ministries

Lower House (House of Representatives/ House of Assembly)	Upper House (Senate)
Approves the national budget	Questions government policies to hold the government to account
Allows the government to issue funds from the treasury	Introduces non-financial legislation as the need arises

Table 6.5

Steps in making laws

Commonwealth Caribbean countries follow these general guidelines when making laws. Laws govern all countries and need to be created and revised to suit an ever-changing society. Table 6.6 gives the broad process.

Step	Description	Debates
An idea/proposal starts the process	This might be done by concerned citizens or members of parliament	
Legal preparation	The Cabinet approves the proposal, requests that the legal departments draft the **bill** after which Cabinet accepts the proposal and advises the Office of the Attorney General to draft the legislation	
Introduction to the Lower House	Member of Parliament in the Lower House introduces the bill. Public consultation can occur at this stage	
Second reading	The bill is debated by all members of Parliament and a vote is taken	First
Committee examination	A special Committee is selected to review the bill and present a report to the Lower House	
Third reading	The revised draft bill is presented to the Lower House for debate and vote	Second
Passed to Senate	The Senate receives the revised draft bill to approach the process in a similar way as in the Lower House. There is a debate and eventual vote	Third
Assent from Head of State	Once the Senate approves the bill, the Head of State signs it, which declares the bill as an Act of Parliament. The Head of State can also 'withhold their assent' which is referred to as veto power.	

Table 6.6

The role of the Opposition

Opposing groups in society are 'normally' perceived as having differing opinions on everything presented to them. However, in a democracy, opposition parties play a crucial role in forming and outlining policies by weeding out any issues through responsible debate. This leads to **good governance**. Opposition parties can also help to stop corrupt behaviour in government by holding them to account to ensure that they are serving the population they represent. They aim to build relationships with the electorate to understand their issues, and also in the hope of being elected at the next opportunity.

The role of the Head of State

Depending on the government system followed in the Commonwealth Caribbean, there are variations in the functions and their titles. Table 6.7 is useful to see these differences.

Republic	Constitutional Monarchy
President	Governor-General
Executive President (Co-operative Republic of Guyana)	

Table 6.7

In a Republic, the role of the President can be divided into three main strands. Table 6.8 reflects the three components.

Constitutional	Ceremonial	Community Services
Appoints individuals in key positions on advice given from Prime Minister/Leader of the Opposition	Commander in Chief of the Armed forces	Advocates for equal rights
Gives assent to Bills		Hosting of National Awards function
Dissolves Parliament when the need arises (upcoming elections) on the advice of the Prime Minister		Accommodates visits from nationals and non-nationals on special occasions
Selection of some senators		

Table 6.8

Office of the President

- The President can be nominated for the position only if they are a citizen of the country, are at least 35 years old, and have been resident in the country for more than 10 years before being nominated.
- The President is elected by an Electoral College comprising of the Lower House, Senate and the Speaker of the House in a secret ballot.
- They hold office for a five-year term.

In an Executive Republic, the President has supreme Executive Authority managing a range of duties. These include:

- appointing Cabinet members
- determining how State land can be used
- pardoning individuals for criminal offences
- acting as Commander in Chief of the Armed Forces.

In a Constitutional Monarchy, the role of the Governor-General is largely ceremonial; they represent the monarch at ceremonial events such as parades or the opening of Parliament. Constitutionally, they have some authority to appoint officers, grant pardons to individuals serving a life sentence on behalf of the monarch and on the advice of the Privy Council and allow the government to pass laws by signing parliamentary bills.

Executive

This branch runs the administration of the country; the Cabinet headed by the Prime Minister (Parliamentary Republic) or the President (Executive Republic). Its responsibilities include:

- constructing and implementing national policies and programmes
- enforcing laws accepted in the Legislature
- offering advice about the control and methods of government
- upholding the principle of **collective responsibility**.

The Cabinet includes the head of government and the ministers named by the head of government, who are appointed by the head of state and given assigned portfolios managing a Ministry or Department. These portfolios can be reshuffled at any time, in accordance with the Constitution.

The Cabinet meets weekly, or in special circumstances, to discuss government, any national or on-going concerns. Updates are presented by various ministries and departments and special committees can be formed if needed. Cabinet policy decisions are then presented to Parliament (Legislature) to be endorsed before they can be implemented. This is one example of the separation of powers. However, it should be noted that members of the Cabinet can also be members of the Legislative arm.

Role of Civil/Public Service

The Civil Service falls under the Executive arm of government, and is responsible for implementing the decisions of the government. Historically, independence brought with it many changes. One such change was the way in which matters were dealt with concerning public administration. Methodical approaches were needed to hire, appoint, promote, transfer and even discipline civil servants who implement the decisions of the government.

When newly appointed Cabinet members receive their instruments of appointment, they are assigned Permanent Secretaries who assist the Cabinet Ministers in their particular Ministry or Department. These public officers have a number of responsibilities which include:

- the administration of the Ministry
- accounting for the money allocated to the Ministry
- serving as principal advisor to the Minister
- monitoring the policies implemented.

The administration of the civil service is one of the pillars of good governance. Permanent secretaries and civil servants look after the interests of the Ministry to which they are attached and are independent of any political party.

Judiciary

The third branch of government, the judiciary, consists of a responsible court system for the interpretation and application of the laws created in the legislature. It should be an independent arm so that all case judgements are fair and handled in a timely manner.

The judiciary is headed by a Chief Justice in most territories and in Co-operative Republic of Guyana, the Chancellor of the High Court. This individual is appointed by the head of state based on a recommendation from the Prime Minister after consultation with the Opposition party leader. The Chief Justice is seen as a judge of the courts who should display impeccable standards in the execution of justice and

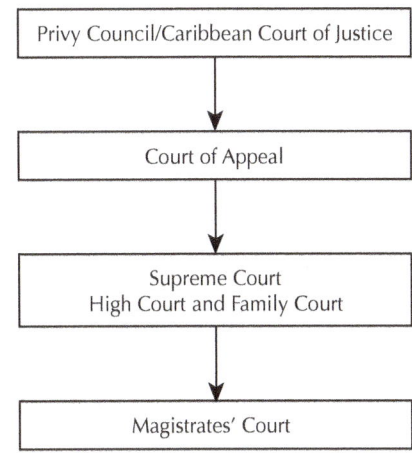

Figure 6.20 *Structure of the judiciary*

should be able to voice concerns from the judges, magistrates and other personnel who he or she leads.

The judiciary follows a tiered structure of judges or magistrates hearing various civil and criminal matters.

The current government structure in the Commonwealth of Dominica.

President	first female and first indigenous individual, Her Excellency Sylvanie Burton
Prime Minister	Honourable Roosevelt Skeritt (2004–2022)
Ruling Party	Dominica Labour Party
Opposition	Independent Candidate, Jesma Paul-Victor/ Anthony Charles
Number of constituencies	21
House	Unicameral, House of Assembly
Composition of House	21 representatives, 9 senators (appointed by President where 5 members are on the advice from the Prime Minister and 4 on the advice of the opposition)
Executive	President, Prime Ministers and Cabinet ministers
Legislature	the government and the House of Assembly

Case study

Look at the current government structure of a specific Caribbean country to highlight specific details such as:

– the current size of the executive (number of ministries and examples of some of the names)
– the size of the legislature (number of seats in the lower house and upper house, number of senators nominated by the PM and number by the opposition)

Table 6.9 identifies the functions of EACH level of the judicature.

Type of Court	Function	
Magistrates' Court presided over by a Magistrate	– Handles summary criminal offences; common offences such as assault, disorderly conduct and minor criminal damage to property – Hears preliminary inquiries concerning major criminal violations such as murder/manslaughter, rape and armed robbery before it is referred for trial in the High Court	
Supreme Court presided over by Judges with a jury	– Hears civil matters such as family issues of divorce and custody as well as civil issues such as debt recovery	– Hears criminal matters accepted from the Magistrates' court
Court of Appeal presided over by Justices and the Chief Justice	– Reviews cases on appeal where decisions can be upheld, be overturned or have a differing judgement imposed in the lower court. A new trial can be ordered	
Judicial Committee of the Privy Council/Caribbean Court of Justice	– Final appeal court which handles review of cases based on certain monetary value or of exceptional public significance.	

Table 6.9

6 Institutions and Government

Table 6.10 looks at the final Court of Appeal for the Commonwealth Caribbean countries. The Privy Council is located in London while the Caribbean Court of Justice is headquartered in Trinidad.

Commonwealth countries in the Caribbean			British Overseas Territory
Antigua and Barbuda	**Dominica**	St. Kitts and Nevis	Anguilla
The Bahamas	Grenada	St. Lucia	British Virgin Islands
Barbados	**Co-operative Republic of Guyana**	St. Vincent and the Grenadines	Cayman Islands
Belize	Jamaica	Trinidad and Tobago	Montserrat
			Turks and Caicos

Key

	Privy Council
(green)	CCJ

Table 6.10

Role of the Director of Public Prosecutions

A prosecutor is a state elected official who is responsible for the investigation, laying of charges and the prosecution of citizens who break the law. The role of the Director of Public Prosecutions as head of the criminal justice division is contained in the Constitution and is an independent position, free of any political affiliation. Other duties of the department include prosecuting criminal cases in the Appeal courts, formulating policies for the prosecution and communicating regularly with the various security systems.

Role of security systems

Police service

The official law enforcement body of a country is the police service. They work in tandem with the courts to preserve justice by:

- conducting investigations when an offence has been committed
- making initial arrests and charging the accused person or persons
- escorting the offenders to court where judgements can be made based on evidence
- executing warrants issued to individuals by the courts
- providing protection for witnesses who have been requested to supply evidence in a trial.

Prison system

When rulings are made by the courts, individuals can either be set free or sentenced. The type of sentence depends on the type and severity of the crime, the harm that was caused to the victim, the individual's past criminal activity as well as their mental state at the time of the offence. A sentence can be community service, a fine, a curfew or a prison sentence.

A prison sentence is the most severe and is used to directly punish the perpetrator, reduce their criminal activity and remove them from society as well as to deter others from the same behaviour. Prisons aim to rehabilitate and reform prisoners to reduce similar crimes in the future, while at the same time protecting the public.

Local government

Local governments exist in most Commonwealth Caribbean countries to provide services to citizens and manage resources. These officials from Constituency/District/Village/Town and City Councils are usually elected, but can be appointed in some cases, as happens sometimes in Barbados and Dominica. They work with the central government to get funding and support. Members usually serve for three years and are responsible for a variety of services, including:

- Health and sanitation. Local governments provide garbage collection, sewage treatment and other services to keep communities healthy.
- Community and cultural heritage. Local governments preserve historical sites and promote cultural activities.
- Road maintenance, street lighting and street signage. Local governments maintain secondary roads, install street lights and put up signs to keep communities safe.

Functions of government

Governments have many administrative powers, which help them to control the day-to-day affairs of a country. Each government is guided by their Constitution, which recognises and protects the fundamental human rights and freedoms of the people. The government serves in many different capacities.

Figure 6.21 *Construction workers in Ocho Rios, Jamaica*

- Welfare: Vulnerable citizens who are unable to provide for themselves due to lack of money, disabilities or sickness can access social welfare. They are given financial and social assistance to help them until they can provide for themselves.
- Employment opportunities: Citizens are the human capital of a country and should be able to find a job suited to their education subject and level. In developing countries skilled people often leave because they cannot find appropriate employment, a phenomenon known as 'brain drain'. To avoid this, it is important that governments recognise the issue and put in place systems such as entrepreneurial incentives, agricultural industries, tourism industries and public sector employment to retain skilled labour.
- Health: Governments are responsible for the general wellbeing of the population, which is important for the economy as a healthy workforce generates a high level of productivity. As well as ensuring healthcare is available (either private or public) this also includes ensuring that the public are educated about their health. This was particularly important during the COVID-19 pandemic.

Figure 6.22 *Prime Minister Holness of Jamaica shakes hands with Prime Minister Trudeau of Canada*

- Education: Education is vital to any population so that resources can be used efficiently. Educational infrastructure should be provided by the government to develop the next generation of the population.

- Revenue generation: In order to complete important projects, governments need to find ways to raise money (revenue). Citizens pay various taxes to generate this revenue. Taxes fall into two categories: direct and indirect. Direct taxation is when persons or companies pay money directly to the government. Indirect taxation occurs when manufacturers or shops pay tax to the government and pass this cost onto consumers through the price of goods and services.

Table 6.11 gives some useful examples.

Direct Tax: paid directly to the government	**Indirect tax:** consumers pay this through the goods and services they use
Income tax	V.A.T
Property tax	Excise tax
Corporate tax	Service tax
Stamp duty	Sales tax

Table 6.11

- International relations: As most countries in our region are relatively small, there is heavy reliance on trade from outside the region. Governments must form alliances and sign treaties with foreign countries to maintain trade relationships.

- Law and order: Citizens should feel safe. Governments should aim to reduce crime such as domestic violence, drug abuse, child abuse and corruption. The police force and the judiciary help to enforce the laws and should be given the investment and equipment they need to do so.

- Infrastructure and utilities: Governments should work to build and maintain infrastructure such as airports, government buildings and recreational areas, business areas and transportation networks, and also utility networks such as water, sewage, electricity and gas.

- National security: Governments are expected to maintain armed forces to protect the interests of the country, and also border force agencies to help keep the country safe.

Figure 6.23 *Passengers boarding a bus in Bridgetown, Barbados*

Figure 6.24 *Members of the Trinidad and Tobago Defence Force*

- Manage a budget: Just like a household, the government needs to practice good money management in terms of money spent and money earned. Revenue is generated from exports, licences, fines, customs and duties as well as taxes and money is spent on infrastructure, salaries, imports, welfare, pensions, health and education. Governments seek advice from professional economists about how different policies will impact the economy.

- Supervisory and regulatory functions: governments must regulate and set controls on the operation of private businesses and public utilities. They set rates and regulations in the form of tax relief, grants and duty exemptions. Regulatory bodies also oversee the operations of the media to ensure rights and freedoms are not infringed while at the same time maintaining standards. However, in a true democracy the media should remain impartial.

Questions

Knowledge and comprehension

Read the case study below and answer the questions which follow.

Case study

Republican movement

A movement for Barbados to become a republic began more than two decades ago. In 1996 a Constitution Review Commission was mandated to explore the appropriateness of maintaining Barbados' link with the Crown. In 1998 it recommended that Barbados become a parliamentary republic.

In 2005, the country replaced the London-based Judicial Committee of the Privy Council as its final court of appeal with the Caribbean Court of Justice in Trinidad and Tobago. A referendum on becoming a republic was planned in 2008 but never took place. Finally, on 15 September 2020, the Government of Barbados announced its intention to cease being a constitutional monarchy, therefore removing the Queen as its head of state.

Figure 6.25 *The Presidential Inauguration Ceremony, Bridgetown, Barbados*

In a Throne Speech (the Barbados equivalent of the Queen's Speech), the current Governor-General, Dame Sandra Mason, said the time had come for Barbados "to fully leave our colonial past behind". "Barbadians want a Barbadian head of state," Dame Sandra added. "This is the ultimate statement of confidence in who we are and what we are capable of achieving."

Amending the constitution to become a republic

In order to become a republic, the Barbados Parliament had to amend the Barbados Independence Order 1966, something that required a two-thirds majority. Although some questioned whether this was possible, as an independent country Barbados could amend or repeal any part of its statute book, including acts and orders passed by the UK Parliament before 1966.

The Constitution (Amendment) (No. 2) Bill, 2021 was introduced to the Barbados Parliament on 20 September and was passed unanimously on 6 October. This effectively transferred the responsibilities of the Governor-General to a new position of President, elected by Parliament. It meant that the oath of allegiance would be to the state of Barbados rather than to the Queen.

On 12 October 2021, Dame Sandra Mason was jointly nominated by the Prime Minister and the Leader of the Opposition as the first President of Barbados. She was elected by the Barbados Parliament on 20 October and will formally be sworn in today (30 November).

Role of the UK Parliament

As an independent country since 1966, Barbados did not need the UK's authorisation to become a republic. However, Westminster will have to pass consequential legislation to avoid any confusion in its domestic law. The UK Government hasn't yet introduced legislation in relation to Barbados, and there is not necessarily any urgency to do so.

The Commonwealth

Barbados has chosen to remain a member of the Commonwealth, which already includes several republics. Before 2007, a Commonwealth Realm transitioning to a republic had to reapply for membership. This is no longer the case and Barbados will become the first country to remain a member having ceased to be a constitutional monarchy.

1. Define the following terms from the above article.
   a) Constitution
   b) Referendum
   c) Republicanism

2. a) Define 'separation of powers'.
   b) Discuss TWO reasons for the 'separation of powers'.

3. Outline the role of Local Government.

4. List the differences among the three arms of government.

Use of knowledge

5. Create a debate between Melissa (student 1) and David (student 2) where Melissa argues that an autocratic government is the best fit for society. David must explain some of the drawbacks of an autocracy and recommend the benefits of alternative forms of governance.

6. Caribbean authors have commented that republicanism is on the rise in the region. Discuss the benefits and drawbacks of Caribbean territories gaining republican status.

7. Use the checklist below to record your answers concerning the structure of government.

	Legislature	Executive	Judiciary
Which arm interprets the law?			
Which arm passes or vetoes a bill which becomes law?			
Which arm decides on court cases?			
Which arm formulates the budget?			

	Legislature	Executive	Judiciary
The Chief Justice belongs to this arm.			
To which arm does the Speaker of the House belong?			
The Attorney General primarily belongs to this arm.			
Which arm adopts the collective responsibility principle?			
There are senators in this arm.			
The police force and the prisons assist this arm in the execution of its duties.			

8. View a pre-recorded session from either the Lower House or the Senate in your country and examine the subject matter, the language used and any other prominent facts. Present your findings to the class.

9. Examine the statement below, and debate it with your classmates.

    'The adoption of the CCJ as the final appeal court is important for regionalism.'

10. Take one of the functions of government and write 3–5 sentences to argue that the function of government is being accomplished. Use evidence from newspaper articles to support your argument.

11. Rank the functions of the government in terms of your personal preference. Justify your response.

The relationships between citizens and governments as stated in the Constitution

Important definitions

Fundamental human rights – rights outlined in the Constitution which citizens should be guaranteed.

Freedom – an individual has the power to behave as they wish, according to the law.

Human dignity – the ability to be valued and treated respectfully.

Constitutional reform – amendments made to the existing constitution to bring about new and improved legislation.

Governance – the framework of an organisation; its decision-making processes, hierarchies and control mechanisms.

Secondary socialisation – the process where individuals are taught the culture and acceptable behaviour from agencies outside of the family. These include school community, place of worship, sports club, the government and even the media.

Transparency – being open and clear about what you are doing, disclosing relevant information for scrutiny.

> *Accountability* – decision-makers take responsibility for their behaviour and acknowledge their actions.
>
> *Rule of law* – this principle identifies that no one individual is above the law.
>
> *Greening* – using sustainable approaches to meet the needs of the nation while protecting the environment.

The Constitution outlines the recognition of citizens of a country through birth or descent or by registration (nationals of Commonwealth countries) or naturalisation (nationals of non-Commonwealth countries). The protection of **fundamental human rights** and **freedoms** are prioritised in the Constitution of every Commonwealth Caribbean country. Citizens are guaranteed these human rights and freedoms no matter their race, place of origin, colour, creed, sex, political opinions or religion. **Human dignity** is satisfied when individuals are valued as social beings rather than by any 'perceived' social differences.

Table 6.12 offers some examples of protections, fundamental rights and freedoms.

Protections	Fundamental Rights	Freedoms
of right to life	work	movement
of right to personal liberty and protection from forced labour	education	assembly and association
of the law	equality before the law	speech and expression
from deprivation of property	to join political parties and to express political opinions	conscience (thought, religion)
from discrimination	of security	of the press

Table 6.12

These rights and freedoms can be suspended during a period of public crisis if a head of state declares a state of emergency. The declaration of a state of emergency can be due to the possibility of war between the home country and a foreign power, natural disasters including the outbreak of an infectious disease as well as threat to public safety.

According to Indira Gandhi, third Prime Minister of India, 'people tend to forget their duties but remember their rights'. All rights should have corresponding responsibilities which both the government and citizens should recognise.

Table 6.13 highlights some of these responsibilities.

Responsibilities of the government	Responsibilities of citizens
protect citizens' rights and freedoms	obey laws
investigate infringements of rights	pay taxes
	assist law enforcement in their duties
	partake in civic duties (jury service, voting)
	preserve the environment

Table 6.13

When citizens feel their fundamental rights and freedoms are being infringed or violated, they are free and within their rights to go to the High Court to determine whether the government is acting in accordance with the constitution. This can result in **constitutional reform** to suit the needs of a modern society.

Table 6.14 lists some 'first generation' (human) rights violations and ways to seek redress.

Human rights violation	Remedies for victims
police brutality	public protest action, constitutional complaint
inaction by the state to protect individuals or groups	public protest action
discrimination in the workplace	involvement of the media, warnings, constitutional complaint
segregating students in the education system	public protest action, involvement of the media

Table 6.14

Many regulatory authorities are available in each Caribbean country to deal with complaints about consumer protection, police misconduct and corruption and even to regulate the administration of healthcare facilities and old-aged homes. One such regulatory authority is the Office of the Ombudsman.

What do we do for countries without this?

Citizens are able to access guidance when their rights conflict with particular policies. The ombudsman acts as impartial intermediary, offering both investigative and advisory assistance where claims of mismanagement by government departments can be addressed. For claims and complaints to be pursued by the ombudsman, they should be linked directly to a government department. The decisions of the ombudsman, which should be done in a simple, quick and reasonable manner need to be acceptable to the victims as well as protect the department from speculative claims.

The ombudsman reports directly to the Parliament on a yearly basis giving full statistical analysis of claims investigated and the departments involved, claims discontinued and not justified as well as claims still in action.

Characteristics of good governance

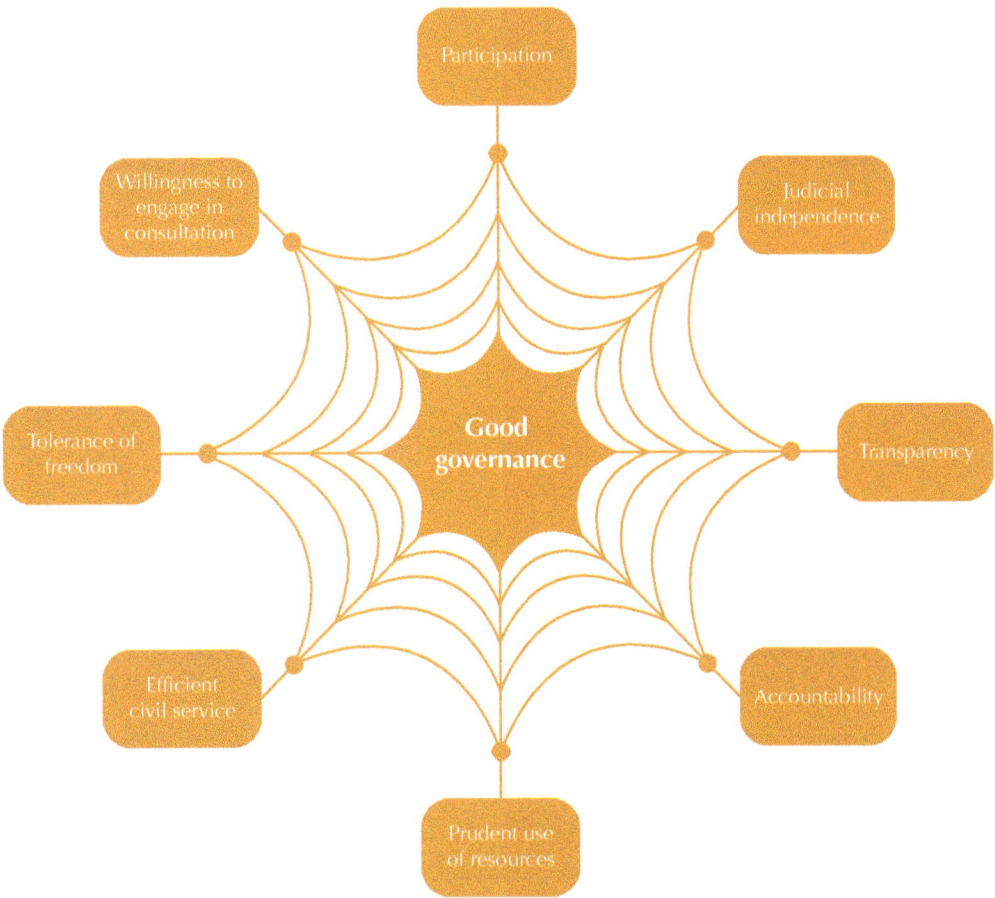

Figure 6.26 *The characteristics of good governance*

Good governance

A country full of people with no money
A city devastated by lack of solidarity
Towns ruined by law breakers who,
Continue to deconstruct the fabric by coup

We need a system
To rule the nation
To work with the rich and the poor
So we have a better tomorrow for sure
Well-oiled mechanisms to check efficiency
And personnel who, prides itself on accountability
Checks and balances reveal transparency
So the citizens are free in their creativity,
To use resources effectively
So that profits can grow exponentially

Society depends on a number of themes
Institutions, services and innovative schemes
To build, to develop, to prosper and exist
Standing side by side with leaders and strategists

Power to the people, power of the pen
Let us work together and hopefully then
The nation will reach maximum performance
While embracing, good governance

M. Gayah

Good governance means adhering to high standards while managing the affairs of a country and should be aspired to by all nations. Countries should move to embrace Sustainable Development Goal 16 which identifies peace, justice and strong institutions as its core principles. Government representatives oversee numerous functions and have various responsibilities for which they are accountable to the people. Good governance can be 'measured' by the use of a number of indicators. They are:

- **Level of participation and inclusivity among citizens.** Members of society are encouraged to become change agents in their communities, promoting networking, responsibility and proactive thinking. This is helpful to governments who genuinely want individuals to appreciate the democratic way of life, to become knowledgeable about issues which affect them and to recognise their fundamental rights and freedoms. They are able to cast their votes during an election to participate in the democratic process while at the same time recognising the need for political change.

- **Judicial independence and rule of law.** Constitutions outline the function of the judiciary which should operate to interpret and enforce the laws in an independent manner. It is governed by the rule of law which seeks to limit the power of this branch.
- **Transparency.** All public business should follow recognised regulations and rules and disclose information freely to the public. This helps limit corruption.
- **Accountability.** Government agencies are responsible for their decisions.
- **Prudent use of resources.** In the era of '**greening**', governments have to be mindful about the future. They should always be mindful of sustainability and protection of the environment, and ensure that human capital is also used with care.
- **Efficient civil service which is responsive to citizens' needs.** These agencies are instrumental in providing services which meet the needs of the public effectively. The public expect and require fair laws and justice, timely services and safe conditions.
- **Tolerance of freedom.** Good governance can work when the voice of the people matters. The population should be free to expose factual information, raise issues and seek answers from their government.
- **Willingness to engage in consultation.** Governments should be open to receiving respectful and constructive feedback and suggestions from the public. This helps to put the public at the centre of decision - making by listening and learning.

Characteristics of good citizenship

Citizens have a duty to their country. They are governed by laws which control their behaviour. The governing laws encourage conformity, uniformity and respectability. Different social institutions encourage citizens to demonstrate good citizenship. It starts in the family where members instil values such as healthy living and lifestyle practices, respect for laws as well as respect for others. In the school system and other **secondary socialisation** agencies, the individual develops these ideas further and learns to be an active, social participant in society. Patriotism is encouraged at all levels of the education system. As the individual becomes an adult and enters the world of work, they should take part in the country's affairs by voting, which is a civic duty, and help to recognise and protect the rights of others and make sustainable choices where the environment is concerned. There is also a good display of citizenship when we show concern for others while being knowledgeable about current affairs.

Questions

Knowledge and comprehension

1. Define 'constitutional reform'.

2. Work in groups of four to create a collage focusing on good citizenship using local artifacts.

3. Identify TWO fundamental human rights and TWO freedoms which citizens are guaranteed.

Use of knowledge

4 Discuss the following statement with the class.

'The Office of the Ombudsman caters to those who cannot get swift justice.'

5 Prepare a comic strip using appropriate dialogue to demonstrate the dos and don'ts of being a good citizen. The strip should comprise 10 slides.

6 Create a poem or spoken word piece which highlights the major characteristics of good governance.

7 Alejandro is a Venezuelan unregistered migrant living in Tobago. He is currently unemployed and suffers because there is a language barrier.

   a) What TWO actions can be taken by individuals to assist Alejandro in improving his standard of living?

   b) Explain how EACH action suggested in (a) is likely to be successful.

SBA skills

You are invited to the Ombudsman's Office as a student representative to conduct an interview. What are some questions that you would ask? Some have already been added to help you. Complete the list of questions and ask your teacher if you can visit your local Ombudsman's Office to conduct the interview.

INTERVIEW SCHEDULE

Interview date:

Interviewee: The Ombudsman

Topic: Role of the Ombudsman

Interview recorded: (*Video or written report*)

Questions	Responses
1) Who is an ombudsman?	
2) How does his/her office help the general public	
3) What issues/situations does the ombudsman assist with currently?	

End of chapter questions

1. **a)** Define 'social control'. (2 marks)
   b) Discuss TWO ways in which behaviour is regulated in the family. (4 marks)
   c) The youth arm of a political party would like to encourage more youth participation in sporting activities.
      (i) Suggest TWO proposals that the youth arm of the political party can make to the leaders of the party. (4 marks)
      (ii) Explain why EACH proposal suggested in (c) (i) is likely to be successful. (4 marks)

TOTAL 14 MARKS

2. a) Define the term 'democracy'. (2 marks)
   b) Discuss TWO functions of the government in your country. (4 marks)
   c) There has been an increase in gun violence in a country over the past few months.
      (i) Suggest TWO actions the government may take to reduce the rate of gun violence in the country. (4 marks)
      (ii) Explain why EACH action suggested in (c) (i) is likely to be successful. (4 marks)

   TOTAL 14 MARKS

Summary

Institutions are important to the proper functioning of society. Institutions can be tangible as in actual buildings serving a specific function, or intangible as in shared norms transferred from one generation or group to another. Society consists of a number of institutions which supply the needs of various groups.

Social institutions, such as the family, fulfil the social needs while educational institutions provide expert and skills training for the population.

Religious institutions focus on the moral and spiritual needs of a nation while the economic institutions provide the financial aspects of living.

Recreational institutions provide for the social and wellbeing needs and political institutions are concerned with policymaking to affect the quality of life of citizens.

These institutions have important characteristics such as mechanisms of social control, a stable value system, ability to endure over time and ability to adapt to changes in society.

One of the institutions focused on in this chapter was the Government. A government can be part of an autocracy (ruled by one) or a democracy (ruled by many).

In the Commonwealth Caribbean, there are a number of government systems which operate in very definitive ways. Crown Colony reflects the legacy of the British colonisers; Constitutional Monarchy makes a move towards democracy although British ties are still maintained and Republicanism is concerned with full autonomy.

The government is structured to ensure transparency among the three arms or branches.

- The legislature is responsible for making, amending and repealing laws.
- The executive is responsible for the daily operations of the country.
- The judiciary is responsible for interpreting and enforcing the laws.

Governments perform a number of functions which include creation of employment opportunities, ensuring citizens are safe, educating the population and taking care of their health needs as well as improving the general infrastructure by raising revenue.

Regulatory bodies seek to protect the rights of citizens who have been treated unfairly. One such body is the Office of the Ombudsman who assists in claims made against government offices.

Citizens and the government both have their role to fulfil in order to foster an understanding of laws, rights and freedoms. Governments can practice good governance through accountability, transparency, efficiency and responsiveness which can encourage good citizenship. Both can work hand in hand in partnership to promote sufficiency, sustainability and survivability.

Section A: Individual, Family and Society
(ii) Society and Governance

7 Elections and Democracy

The topics covered in this chapter are:

- the systems used to elect a government in the Commonwealth Caribbean
- how political parties prepare for elections
- learning to distinguish between facts, opinions and propaganda
- designing data collection tools to collect information on people's opinions
- learning to make informed decisions based on arguments presented
- learning to show tolerance for other people's opinions
- the factors that influence the outcomes of elections
- learning to analyse statistical data in the form of tables, graphs and charts on elections
- drawing conclusions about elections and electoral processes based on data presented

To understand how governments work, it is important to understand how they are formed. In a democracy, countries conduct elections where people vote for the persons they want to represent them. These procedures are known as **electoral processes**.

Electoral processes and systems

Learning objectives
- Describe the electoral processes in the Commonwealth Caribbean.
- Explain the electoral systems used to elect a government.
- Distinguish between the different electoral systems used in the region.

Important definitions

Electoral process – *the process followed by candidates during an election as well as the voting structures in place to conduct elections.*

General elections – *the voting process whereby individuals are selected as Members of Parliament. This usually occurs every five years.*

Elector – *an individual eligible to vote.*

Constituency – *the geographical area that a Member of Parliament represents.*

Candidate – *an individual running in an election.*

Representative – *an individual who successfully won an election and therefore occupies an official office.*

Ballot – *slip of paper containing a list of the candidates with a column to record your vote. Once completed, it is placed in the ballot box.*

Quantitative – *data that can be presented in a number format.*

Qualitative – *data that can be presented in words as a description of something.*

Franchise – *a right to vote.*

Coalition government – *a government formed by a partnership between multiple political parties.*

Electoral reform – *any changes to the electoral processes to allow for efficiency, fairness and inclusivity.*

Electoral processes

Dissolution/prorogation of parliament

Parliament is dissolved when the House stops its activities for an election. The party in power advises that the parliament is to be dissolved, and the Prime Minister informs the Head of State. The Head of State makes a public proclamation (announcement), which signals the official end of a parliamentary term and indicates that a **general election** will happen shortly. Ministerial and presidential roles are maintained during this period until new members are elected.

Case study

Antigua and Barbuda Electoral Commission (ABEC) has been in operation since 2001 with its main purpose to ensure, in an independent manner, the conduct and control of free and fair elections. They oversee the preparation of the voters' lists and execute the election protocols in each constituency while maintaining transparency.

Structure of the Electoral Commission:

Chairman (nominated by Prime Minister)

Deputy Chairman (nominated by the Opposition Leader)

5 Commissioners (2 nominated by the Prime Minister, 1 nominated by Opposition leader, 1 nominated by religious bodies and 1 nominated by financial bodies)

There are a number of key positions which include: The Chairman, Deputy Chairman, Supervisor of Elections, Public Relations Officer and an Accounts Department.

The Supervisor of Elections (SOE) acts as the Chief Executive Officer of the Commission.

Role of Elections Commission/Electoral Office

As laid out in the Constitution, each country should have an independent agency responsible for:

- supervision of the registration and verification of eligible voters
- conduct of elections in each **constituency** and/or **region**
- reviewing and adjusting the boundaries of constituencies as outlined in the constitution
- education of **electors** about the **electoral process**.

Universal adult suffrage means that every adult over the age of 18 has the right to vote. This principle is sometimes referred to as 'one man, one vote'.

Table 7.1 looks at specific duties of the Elections Commission around election time.

Figure 7.1 Election campaign posters in Antigua

Before election day	On the day of the election	After election day
Register eligible voters	Ensure polling stations are accessible to voters at 6 a.m. or 7 a.m. Assistance for disabled electors is made available.	Returning officer declares the winner for the constituency
Verify electoral lists	Check identification card and poll card	Recount if a request is made in a given constituency
Host Nomination day for candidates	Inspect finger for traces of electoral ink	Produce the list of successful candidates to be elected based on majority votes
Prepare and post poll cards	Guide voter through the voting process	Take custody of ballot boxes
Educate the public on voting procedures	Issue **ballot** with directions	

Before election day	On the day of the election	After election day
Train election officials	Provide private area to make secret ballot selection	
Prepare polling stations for voting	Ensure elector casts vote in the ballot box	
Prepare and secure ballots for voting	Seal full boxes after 6 p.m. and transport to central area to be counted	

Table 7.1

The meaning of free and fair elections

The electoral process is a specific set of procedures which should be carried out perfectly to guarantee public confidence in a fair election.

Table 7.2 gives an overview of the conduct of free and fair elections.

Elections	Adult citizens	Political parties	Elections Commission
must occur regularly	must have the right to vote based on registration and be able to stand as candidates	must represent the population satisfactorily	must prepare electoral lists which are accurate
be free of violence, intimidation and bribery which could affect results	can form political parties and attract voters through campaigning	should have equal access to the media to voice their political agendas	must secure ballots before, during and after elections and be transparent when counting ballots
	be treated fairly during the election season by the election officials, police and the courts		must allocate sufficient time for voting
	may question any component of the electoral process	should refrain from inciting any form of violence during public engagement	must maintain the 'one man one vote' policy and allow persons secrecy when voting

Table 7.2

Figure 7.2 Voters line up outside a polling station

Figure 7.3 CARICOM Election Observation Mission to Dominica, December 2022

Independent Observer Mission

According to the United Nations, election observation enhances the 'quality of elections' and includes:

- Building public confidence in the electoral process: Election observation can help people trust that the election process is fair and impartial.
- Protecting voters' rights: Election observation can help ensure that all voters have the right to vote and that their votes are counted fairly.
- Identifying problems: Election observation can help identify problems with the electoral process such as voter intimidation or fraud.
- Strengthening trust in democracy: Election observation can help strengthen democracy by encouraging transparency and accountability in the electoral process.

International observers must systematically observe the electoral processes and assess the practices involved by collecting both **quantitative** and **qualitative** data and reporting their findings. These reports should include details about whether domestic law was followed, information about any weaknesses seen and whether international standards were upheld, together with suitable recommendations for improvement.

International observers are usually invited by the host government to examine the pre- and post-election periods as well as the election day events. The observers should be knowledgeable about election administration, law, political affairs, human rights, security, media, statistics and logistics. CARICOM member states benefit from the CARICOM Election Observation Mission (CEOM), which was established in the 1990s. CEOM are able to meet with various stakeholders to understand the environment as well as to observe the readiness level for elections.

Having local observers from the country where the election is taking place can encourage public participation in the election process especially during the election day itself when polling stations can be monitored.

Role of political parties

Political parties seek to gain political power and use a number of strategies to succeed. During elections, they must inform the electorate of their plans for the country so that the voting public can make informed decisions and participate fully in the democratic process. They hold rallies, give speeches and publish pamphlets to broadcast their intentions as they want the people to know what they stand for and what they plan to do if they are elected.

They also have to select candidates to be the faces of the political party. They look for people who are intelligent, articulate and have a strong commitment to the party's values. Candidates should:

- be an adult (over 21) and a Commonwealth citizen
- be a resident in the country for a period of time leading up to the nominations.

Political parties also need to raise funds to manage the routine activities of the party and the running of campaigns. This fundraising must be disclosed.

Parties looking for support from the electorate should aim to fully represent the various sections of society in terms of race, ethnicity, age, gender, education and impairment.

Responsibility of voters

The voters are an important element in the electoral process. In some countries, there are groups of people who are not eligible to vote, such as non-citizens or people who have been convicted of certain crimes. These individuals are not considered part of the electorate.

The electorate should have the necessary tools in order to cast their votes legally and successfully. They must:

- register to vote
- check their polling card for the location of the polling station
- bring proper identification to vote
- understand the election protocols
- know the candidates who will potentially represent them
- report any problems/concerns about the voting process
- ensure the ballot is completed correctly.

Figure 7.4 *Electors listen to a campaign speech in* St. *Kitts*

Election day

Although election day is not a public holiday, some places are closed, such as schools, as they are used as polling stations. The day begins with the opening of the polling stations at 6 a.m. or 7 a.m. to give voters the opportunity to exercise their **franchise**. Everyone has their part to play during this 'decision day'.

The Elections Commission takes centre stage in the voting process. They are responsible for many processes during the day and the night immediately after the polling stations close. Below is a general illustration of the voting process at a polling station.

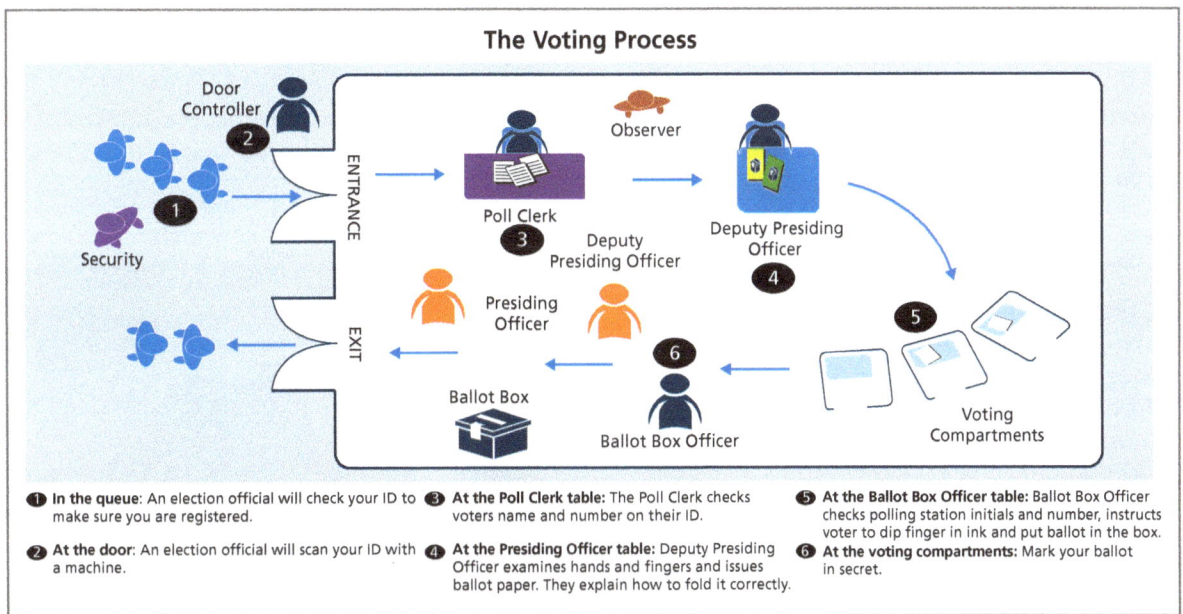

Figure 7.5 *The process inside a polling station*

When voting is finished, the officials secure all the ballot boxes from the different constituencies and take them to a central location for the votes to be counted. It can take many days for the preliminary results to be reported by the Chief Election Officer. There is a great deal of emotion, relief and anticipation during the night as political analysts and the media make predictions.

Section A(ii)   Individual, Family and Society

International and/or regional observers monitor activities at the polling stations, and assess the different roles and responsibilities of the stakeholders in order to generate a comprehensive report.

The police and law enforcement authorities monitor and patrol during the day and night to maintain law and order during the electoral process. They sometimes issue public warnings before election day to stop persons from breaking the law.

Declaration of winners

The political party and their successful candidates are formally declared on the night of elections or in the following days by a returning officer. The winning party celebrates the victory with speeches and acknowledgements. The party who comes in second may concede defeat or ask for a recount when votes are close. The declaration becomes official only after the Chairman of the Elections Commission produces their preliminary report.

Selection of Prime Minister or President

The new Prime Minister or President is usually the leader of the winning party and is appointed by the head of state or a **representative**.

Swearing in activities

Dignitaries, diplomats and officials from various agencies attend the swearing in ceremony of the new head of government or head of state. The President-Elect or Prime Minister takes an oath of office and signs their name, and is presented with the instrument of appointment. The new head of government then makes their first speech. It is an opportunity to thank all stakeholders and outline the general plans for the country during their tenure.

Electoral systems

While the electoral processes outlined the 'what' of the systems used to elect a government, the electoral system is the 'how'. In the Commonwealth Caribbean, there are two distinct electoral systems: 'First-past-the-post' or simple majority, and proportional representation which is used in the Co-operative Republic of Guyana.

First-past-the-post

In the first-past-the-post system, the country is split into constituencies by the Elections Commission. Candidates can be part of a political party or contest a constituency seat as an independent. The **candidate** who receives the most votes in a constituency will be elected into Office – they have won their seat. The political party who wins the most number of seats wins the election and so forms the government. The leader of the winning political party will serve as the Prime Minister. The Opposition is formed from the party who secured the second highest number of seats.

Figure 7.6 *Prime Minister of Jamaica, Andrew Holness, signs the Instrument of Appointment*

Table 7.3 demonstrates the advantages and disadvantages of the first-past-the-post system.

Advantages	Disadvantages
The 'contest' among the candidates is relatively simple as a clear winner is determined by the most number of votes.	A political party can gain the highest overall number of votes and still lose the election, as constituencies are different sizes. Some persons might therefore feel that their vote is wasted.
The constituents are able to have a direct relationship with the **representative** as it was their 'will' to vote for the candidate.	Gerrymandering or malapportionment can occur where the boundaries of constituencies are shifted to gain more votes for a particular political party.
Individuals who have public support and want to serve independently can make meaningful change.	Constituencies that voted for the losing party may be neglected once the ruling party gains office.

Table 7.3

Proportional Representation

This system is used in the Co-operative Republic of Guyana where the whole country is seen as one constituency. The electorate does not vote for a candidate but for a political party who supports a national list of candidates. Successful political parties win a certain proportion of the votes and are given that proportion of seats in parliament. The national list of candidates will then be used to fill the proportion of seats allocated.

Table 7.4 demonstrates the advantages and disadvantages of the Proportional Representation system.

Advantages	Disadvantages
The results reflects the views of the electorate directly and more accurately.	When political parties do not secure enough votes, political parties can form a **coalition** to have greater political sway.
This system removes gerrymandering.	Parliamentarians do not have a moral obligation to the electorate as voting occurred along party lines as opposed to constituency.
Every vote counts and this means the public can feel more involved in the electoral process.	The leader of the political party holds power over who will eventually serve as parliamentary representatives.
Parliamentary representation comes from an assortment of different political parties.	The varied political parties may have different agendas or philosophies.

Table 7.4

Electoral systems in the Commonwealth Caribbean come under great scrutiny when election results are declared. In situations of a **hung parliament**, there is no clear majority winner and the solution might be to go back to the polls or to form a coalition. This can lead to campaigns for **electoral reform** which would reduce the awkwardness of some election results.

A **national unity government** is one planned before or formed after an election with the aim of uniting principles, mandates, personalities and experiences among various political parties for the sake of the nation. The vision of this type of government is to hold power in order to keep the interests of the people in the forefront, as opposed to just working against an opposing party.

Questions

Knowledge and comprehension

1 Name TWO Commonwealth Caribbean countries where parliament was dissolved and snap elections were called before the five year parliamentary term, and state the reasons given for this, if given.

2 Imagine you are speaking to a first time voter. Outline some election protocols observed on election day.

3 Describe the election day activities for the various stakeholders.

4 Choose ONE Commonwealth Caribbean country and complete the following table.

Topic	Response
Name of country	
Date of last election	
Electoral system	
Number of constituencies	
Number of political parties	
Size of electorate	
Voter turnout	
Results	

5 Define the following terms.
   a) Constituency
   b) Candidate
   c) Corruption
   d) Coalition government

Use of knowledge

6 Explain each of these principles of universal adult suffrage.

   universal   direct   free   personal   secret   non-transferrable

7 Discuss the challenges of conducting a parliamentary election during the outbreak of an infectious disease.

8 Create an advertisement to attract potential candidates for a political party. The advertisement should include but not limited to:
   - the name of the political party
   - an accompanying symbol
   - a vision and mission statement
   - list of qualities that the candidate should possess.

9 In groups, discuss the experiences that independent candidates may face during elections. You can create a table and populate it with pros and cons.

10 Examine the election results below to determine which political party would form the new government under the first-past-the-post system. Who would form the Opposition?

Constituency	Political Parties			
	JMM	CGC	HLM	PRG
Green Cove	445	370	115	62
Marble Bay	75	156	730	457
Sky Vale	362	659	421	234
Park View	431	237	342	111
New Castle	345	212	79	340
Total Votes	1658	1634	1687	1204

SBA skills

Read the article below. Create a checklist that an election observer might use on the day of elections, to help them check whether the election is being conducted correctly.

PRELIMINARY STATEMENT – CARICOM ELECTION OBSERVATION MISSION TO THE ANTIGUA AND BARBUDA GENERAL ELECTIONS, 18 JANUARY 2023

JANUARY 19, 2023

The seven (7) member CARICOM Election Observation Mission (CEOM) which was mounted by the Caribbean Community, at the invitation of the Government of Antigua and Barbuda, observed the General Election on 18 January 2023. The CEOM visited 184 of 188 polling stations across 16 constituencies in Antigua. Due to logistical challenges polling stations in Barbuda were not visited. The Mission monitored the Election Day activities by observing the opening of the poll, the voting process, the closing of the poll, the transporting of ballot boxes and the counting of ballots.

In all stations observed, indications are that polling stations opened on time and voting started promptly at 6:00 a.m. It was observed that all polling stations were fully staffed, and that the two (2) major political parties each had political agents present at all locations. Most polling stations were conveniently located and generally accessible to the electorate including the disabled.

The CEOM observed that all materials and supplies needed were present in the required quantities. Adequate security was in place at locations observed. The officers displayed professionalism in the maintenance of law and order which contributed to the level of calm that accompanied the day's activities. The Mission observed that prior to the opening of polls, many voters were eagerly waiting to cast their vote. Throughout the day, the polling staff remained focused as they steadily carried out the required procedures, ensuring that eligible voters who turned out were able to cast their vote.

The CEOM also observed that transportation of ballot boxes from the polling stations to the counting stations was done with adequate security, in the presence of party agents. In all stations observed, the Returning Officers commenced counting of ballots promptly, upon arrival of the ballot boxes. The count of ballots was done transparently and professionally in the presence of party agents.

> While the conduct of the election is highly commendable, all stakeholders, including the main opposition party, with whom the Mission met, raised concerns about the delay in the publication of the register of elections, therefore they had no opportunity to put forward claims and objections. The Electoral Commission informed the CEOM that the date for the publication of the register was calculated based on the advice of legal counsel and, in its view, the calculation is correct.
>
> The CEOM was made aware that in 2021, persons were appointed to the Constituencies Boundaries Commission to address the disparity in the number of electors in the constituencies. While the Mission applauds the effort to address this disparity, there is urgent need to ensure that this exercise is not delayed any further, as completion is extremely necessary prior to the next general election.
>
> Stakeholders raised concerns about the lack of accountability and transparency regarding campaign financing regulations. This is indicative of the need for a framework to be put in place to deal with the issue of campaign financing.
>
> The Mission's assessment of the Election Day's activities is that the voters were able to cast their ballots without intimidation and that the General Election was free and fair, and the outcome reflects the will of the people of Antigua and Barbuda.
>
> The Mission will prepare a detailed report for submission to Her Excellency, Dr. Carla Barnett, Secretary-General of the Caribbean Community (CARICOM). This report will include recommendations and suggestions for strengthening the electoral process in Antigua and Barbuda.
>
> The Mission wishes to congratulate the staff of the Electoral Commission, the Poll Workers, the Candidates and the Security Forces for the mature way in which the elections were conducted. The level of discipline displayed throughout the entire process is highly commendable.
>
> The CARICOM Election Observation Mission wishes to thank the Leaders of the Political Parties, Independent Candidates, Civil Society Groups, Media and the wonderful people of Antigua and Barbuda for their warm hospitality and cooperation which no doubt contributed to the success of the Mission.
>
> JOSEPHINE TAMAI
> CHIEF OF MISSION
> CARICOM ELECTION OBSERVATION MISSION
> 19 JANUARY 2023

Preparation for elections

Political parties are constantly planning ways to persuade the electorate in the hope that they will vote for them in the next election.

Learning objectives

- Evaluate the election preparation done by political parties.
- Distinguish among facts, opinions and propaganda.

> **Important definitions**
>
> *Campaign* – a series of planned events leading up to an election aimed at gaining votes.
>
> *Canvassing* – candidates and other party officials meet face to face with members of the constituency to gain their support.
>
> *Marginal seats* – constituencies where the ruling party won by a small margin in the last election.
>
> *Safe seat* – a constituency which is considered to be reliably secure by a particular political party.
>
> *Manifesto* – document outlining the list of promises by political parties; the actions that they intend to make if they are elected.
>
> *Stronghold* – a constituency which has been won repeatedly by the same political party.
>
> *Objectivity* – when decisions are made without judgement or bias.
>
> *Subjectivity* – when decisions are based on someone's own personal thoughts and feelings.

Establishing party structure

A political party is a highly structured organisation with a formal name, emblem, motto, constitution and designated roles. The leader of this formal group is elected by an internal vote of the party membership. He or she is the recognisable face of the party.

Other members and officers include the deputy leader, party chairperson, secretary, treasurer, public relations officer, youth and women's affairs officers.

These individuals are responsible for making sure that the structures are in place to conduct a successful election in the constituency, for forming committees to make decisions during election preparation as well as ensuring that speeches are arranged so that candidates can address the public.

Selecting candidates

Candidates can be part of a political party or can stand as an independent. A candidate from a political party has to go through a careful screening process before being recommended by the party. They should be knowledgeable on the constitution of both the party and the nation as well as on regional and international matters. They will serve as the faces of the party as they promote their political philosophy across many different platforms.

Figure 7.7 *Jamaica Labour Party candidates on nomination day*

Section A(ii)　Individual, Family and Society

Under the first-past-the-post system, the political party must decide whether they will put up a candidate in each constituency, while under proportional representation the list of candidates is selected by senior party officials.

On nomination day, conducted by the Elections Commission, candidates register their intention to stand in the election by completing a nomination form signed by electors from the constituency. They also pay a deposit to the treasury which is non-refundable if they gain fewer than a specific number of votes.

Sourcing campaign finance

A **campaign** for any type of election is expensive. Political parties spend money on advertisements – billboards, posters, television and radio, transportation to political events, entertainment, food and drink as well as gifts for voters. Finance is mainly raised from the business community especially in cases where the political party has been in existence for a long time. Money is also raised from fundraising events.

In Barbados, for example, an annual government grant is shared among the existing political parties to offer financial support. Party membership fees and donations from the business community can also be added to the party finances but are largely unregulated compared to other countries.

Conducting campaigns

The aim of a campaign is to increase political support. Political parties or independent candidates usually have a campaign committee who plan and carry out various tasks and events.

Table 7.5 displays the various campaign activities.

Figure 7.8 *Rally by the United National Congress party in Trinidad*

Campaign activities	Frequency	Includes
Media coverage	Used heavily by the political party and candidate to communicate what they stand for	Print media such as advertisements
		Radio coverage – announcements and advertisements
		Television coverage – advertisements and live coverage of events
		Social media – advertisements, posts
		Billboards and flyers
Public meetings/ rallies/motorcades	Used generally to meet with supporters	Showcasing the candidates
		Speeches and presentation of manifesto
		Distributing memorabilia such as flags, stickers, posters and clothing
Walkabouts/ **canvassing**	Used heavily by candidates to meet with their constituents especially in **marginal seats**	Listening to the constituents' concerns
		Making promises
		Distributing memorabilia such a flags, stickers, posters and clothing

Table 7.5

In recent years political parties have tried to create pomp and pageantry on the campaign trail with a number of different election activities. Potential voters may become concerned with the heavy spending and blanket advertising. There has also been a rise in 'negative campaigning' that political parties use to highlight the errors of the other parties.

Figure 7.9 *Campaign posters and merchandise, and a car with speakers in Basseterre, St. Kitts and Nevis*

Monitoring of electoral processes

The party selects persons who will monitor the activities leading up to the elections and on the election day. They should be trained in electoral processes to offer advice on the progress of the campaign.

Commissioning opinion polls

Throughout election campaigns, political parties run opinion polls to see how well their message is going down with the electorate. Essentially, an opinion poll takes a small section of the electorate and administers a survey.

Figure 7.10 *Campaign banner in Belize*

This survey can include questions concerning:

- probable choice of political party
- popularity of candidates
- opinion of current ruling party
- which issues they feel most strongly about i.e. crime, education
- feelings about local politics
- feelings about political leaders.

Developing the manifesto

One of the main tasks of political parties in preparing for elections is to outline a proposal to address current national issues. This document is known as a **manifesto** and details the strategies and policies that the party would undertake if elected. The manifesto is usually presented at a live public rally and can operate as a convincing tool to influence supporters on election day. Other parties can then use the manifesto to hold their opponents to account, pointing out issues within the manifesto and criticising the elected government if they do not adhere to it.

Some civil society groups have developed a framework to ensure that political parties follow an ethical code of conduct. Volatile statements made on political platforms, complaints of bribery and personal insults can be reported. There is no official sanction established once the reports are made, but the aim is that the parties will behave morally.

Section A(ii) Individual, Family and Society

Facts, opinions and propaganda

Political parties and other agencies use information throughout the election preparation process. When assessing this information it is important to understand the difference between facts, opinions and propaganda.

Facts are based on evidence that can be proven. In politics, facts can be used to demonstrate the success or failure of a policy. The collection of facts helps to maintain **objectivity**. Writing a text about 'Political systems in the Commonwealth Caribbean' would be laced with facts as political systems have a history which can be traced.

Opinions are statements based on individual interpretation. An opinion gives a limited view of something because it is based on individual experiences, values and feelings. It carries a high degree of **subjectivity** where truth or falsehood cannot be proven. A letter to the editor would contain some facts depending on the subject matter but would normally include a large proportion of opinions.

Propaganda is a form of communication that deliberately presents ideas that are subjective and create misrepresentation. It has been used throughout history to encourage certain attitudes and opinions from the public. Advertisements use a number of devices such as songs, pictures, drawings and graphs to appeal to the emotions of the receivers. They also use techniques which can manipulate reality to give a particular impression of something. Propaganda is much more than discovering the 'truth' or convincing others by using persuasive language. It is a method of manipulating other people's beliefs, by only presenting one side of an argument.

Table 7.6 looks at some of the techniques in propaganda with their accompanying descriptions.

Technique	Description
The bandwagon effect	It is suggested that the majority of people are in support of an issue and encourages others to agree through a fear of being left out.
Testimonials	Well-known personalities make statements which should be the basis for your decision. If you like the personality, you might be more inclined to agree with the statements.
Bait and switch	Use of exciting words or pictures initially to catch the reader's attention, but then to switch to a less appealing focus.
Use of emotive words and repetition	Often not based on facts but used to evoke emotions.

Table 7.6

Questions

Knowledge and comprehension

1. State the difference between a candidate and a representative.

2. Describe TWO campaign activities that political parties can use to attract votes.

3. Define the following terms.
   a) Manifesto
   b) Marginal constituency
   c) Campaign
   d) Safe seat

4. Distinguish between facts, opinions and propaganda using the following statements. You can place a tick in the relevant box.

	Fact	Opinion	Propaganda
Barbados recently became a Republic.			
'After Mr X's departure from office, the murder rate increased.'			
'I do not believe any candidate visited my constituency.'			
'The People's Promise will surely win.'			
'If you want to see and experience a better tomorrow, vote for John Doe.'			

Use of knowledge

5. Discuss the reasons why a political party may choose not to contest all of the available seats under the first-past-the-post system.

6. Create a manifesto using the SMART objectives for an opportunity to lead a popular formal group at your school. The SMART objectives are:

   Specific

   Measureable

   Achievable

   Realistic

   Time specific

7. Explain the difference between opinions and propaganda.

SBA skills

Using the Likert scale questionnaire below, gather data from a sample group about the benefits of political rallies as a campaign activity. Display your results using a pie chart.

	Strongly disagree	Disagree	Neutral	Agree	Strongly agree
1. Political rallies are effective to target potential voters					
2. The speeches are well delivered and can convince an undecided voter					
3. At a political rally, the electorate can meet with their candidates					
4. I prefer to receive some memorabilia as opposed to listening to a speech					
5. The live, free 'concerts' are what will attract me to the rally					

Section A(ii)   Individual, Family and Society

Decision-making process and outcomes of elections

Decision-making is part of daily living. As consumers, members of groups and voters, we are regularly faced with a number of options from which to choose. We can adopt steps and procedures to make informed decisions.

Learning objectives

- Make informed decisions based on arguments presented.
- Outline the factors that influence the outcomes of elections.
- Describe the impact of the factors that influence the outcomes of elections.

Important definitions

Floating voter – an elector who is not a consistent supporter of one particular party and may only decide late in the campaign.

Libel – the use of false written statements about a person.

Slander – the use of false spoken statements about a person.

Voter apathy – where voters do not feel inclined to participate in elections due to lack of interest.

Decision-making process

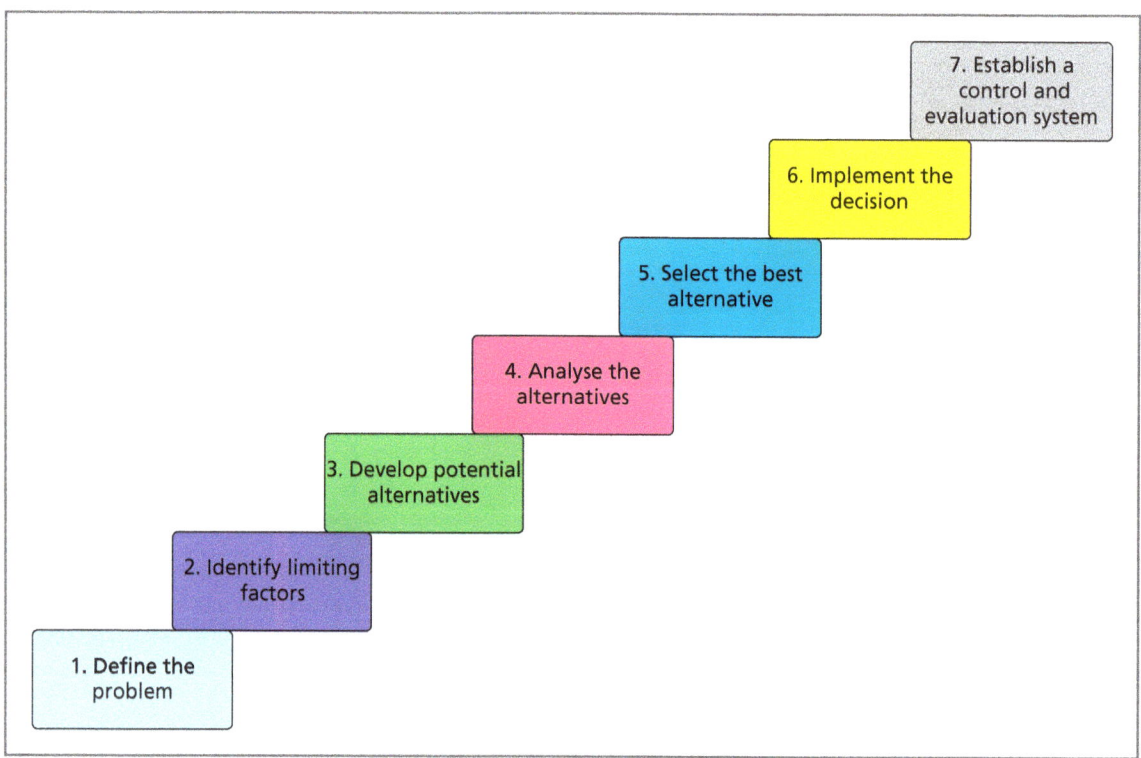

Figure 7.11 *The seven steps of decision-making*

7 Elections and Democracy

Step 1: Define the problem

Individuals have lots of problems, from the very simple to the more complex. The specific problem must be identified clearly so that it can be solved. Think about a traffic jam. The problem, when defined, is that the traffic pile up is causing you to arrive late to a function. The most effective decision will need to be made in order to solve the problem and arrive on time.

Step 2: Identify the limiting factors

Once a clear definition of the problem is found, the limiting factors should be recognised. A limiting factor is anything that prevents the achievement of the goal. In the traffic scenario above, the limiting factor might have been the limited alternate routes available to arrive at the destination on time.

Step 3: Develop potential alternatives

Brainstorming can be useful to figure out potential alternatives. Brainstorming in groups is particularly helpful because different persons might have alternative ideas.

Step 4: Analyse the alternatives

The pros and cons of each approach from the brainstorming exercise should be considered. From this group discussion, a suitable idea could be identified.

Step 5: Select the best alternative

The 'best' alternative may not be perfect, but it might be best suited to achieve the goal. This step may require creative problem solving, initiative and critical thinking skills from the group. It may even make sense to use a mixture of alternatives rather than just selecting one definitive alternative.

Step 6: Implement the decision

Having selected the best alternative, the group leader should apply the solution and carry out follow-up procedures to monitor success or failure.

Step 7: Establish a control and evaluation system

At this point, the decision should be reviewed, to check how effective it was. It might have worked perfectly, or it is possible that some changes need to be done to reach the goal.

Factors that influence the outcomes of elections

The result of an election is always highly anticipated. Political parties, independent candidates, party supporters and the media all want to feel that their efforts had an impact. They would have used a number of strategies to appeal to the various classes, races, genders and ages of the electorate.

Media coverage

Figure 7.12 *An election headline designed to grab attention*

The media is a particularly powerful institution of communication during elections, since newspapers, television, radio, magazines and the internet are all used collectively to communicate political messages.

The media captures data, details and latest developments from the political parties and candidates and filters them through to the electorate. Editorials in newspapers suggest that readers question political opinions while front-page headlines on elections grab the readers' attention. Election advertisements via the television are attention-grabbing while live coverage of election events give the population a front row seat. Talk show hosts conduct interviews with candidates and commentators who are able to influence decisions before an election, and the internet, via blogs and websites, offers educational material relevant to elections.

The media has its part to play to promote democracy and peace during the election season as they report, investigate and uncover. Sometimes, the owners of media houses may be affiliated with particular political parties and groups which means they cannot always be considered impartial. Media codes of conduct should encourage reliable reporting so that everyone is afforded equal access. The media is used extensively to sway and convince the **floating voter**, a first time voter and the 'die hard' supporters.

Digital marketing via social media has become another method of reaching the electorate as candidates use Facebook, X, Instagram and others to broadcast their achievements. Statistics show that social media platforms are heavily used and a viable alternative to the traditional forms of media. Social media was particularly useful during the pandemic as physical campaigns were not possible.

This form of media allows users to share intimate details of daily living within a political context for immediate reactions. Social media posts have the advantage of going 'viral' where a number of people can view, share and like, making it a popular post. This means it is a particularly useful way to reach younger voters.

Campaign advertising

In order for the electorate to be informed and encouraged to vote for them, political parties need to employ various advertising strategies.

Figure 7.13 *Social media has become increasingly important in election campaigns*

Different types of advertising are suitable for different voting groups. Advertising takes the biggest piece of the candidate or party's budget.

Table 7.7 gives some examples of campaign advertising.

Advertising strategies	Use of advertising
Posters (signage)	Broadcast the intentions of the candidates, the date of elections and often a slogan
Television advertisements	Introduce candidates, outline mission, appeal to voters, display candidates/political party achievements
Radio advertisements	Use catchy jingles and easy to remember slogans
Social media advertising	Promote the use of instant feedback while at the same time allow for replay and emotive features

Table 7.7

Campaign advertising has seen a move from traditional forms of media to more advanced methods using social media. Political advertising has come under scrutiny with regard to 'negative advertising'. Political parties and candidates may use rumours and allegations to try and discredit candidates. The use of **libel** and **slander** can present serious legal issues during election time as candidates use 'smear tactics' and rumour-mongering to gain support.

Public opinion polls

These surveys are used by political parties and candidates to understand the political views of the electorate and the success of their campaigns. In countries where there are two competing parties, opinion polls can encourage a party that they are succeeding, or can distort reality and influence public opinion as a result of the bandwagon effect.

Voters' ability to analyse information

Every voter is unique when it comes to making electoral decisions. Voters differ in age, gender, race, class, religion, education, and access to social media and all of these variables influence their voting tendencies. Information shared via the media, party 'faithfuls', candidates themselves and family members can direct an elector to vote a certain way or even abstain from voting altogether. The information therefore has to be accessible so that all voters, no matter their backgrounds, are able to make sound judgements.

Voter turnout/participation

Having thousands of people show up to a political rally does not guarantee that same number will turn up to vote on election day. There has been inconsistent voter turnout over election periods due to a number of factors. Members of the voting public can show a lack of interest in and knowledge about the electoral systems, they may feel disillusioned by the politicians or they could take for granted that their constituency was a **safe seat**.

Table 7.8 gives data on the most recently held parliamentary elections in the Commonwealth Caribbean countries.

Commonwealth Caribbean countries	Voter turnout in the last parliamentary elections		
	Year	Turnout %	Total votes
Antigua and Barbuda	2023	70.34	42,849
The Bahamas	2021	65	126,495

Commonwealth Caribbean countries	Voter turnout in the last parliamentary elections		
	Year	Turnout %	Total votes
Barbados	2022	41.73	111,135
Belize	2020	81.86	149,650
Dominica	2022	31.6	19,066
Grenada	2022	70.32	60,941
Jamaica	2020	37.85	724,317
Cooperative Republic of Guyana	2020	46.84	2,510,135
St. Kitts and Nevis	2022	57.98	29,554
St. Lucia	2021	51.47	89,049
St. Vincent and the Grenadines	2020	67	65,363
Trinidad and Tobago	2020	58.04	658,297

Table 7.8

Pandemic

As the table above shows, a number of countries opted to hold elections during the second half of 2020 and 2021 when the COVID-19 pandemic presented serious challenges for the region as well as the rest of the world. Countries established lockdowns, social distancing measures were in place and some individuals were in quarantine. This could account for some of the low voter turnout rates in some countries.

Age

Voting choices are based on culture, choice and change. Just like culture is passed from one generation to the next, political mindedness should

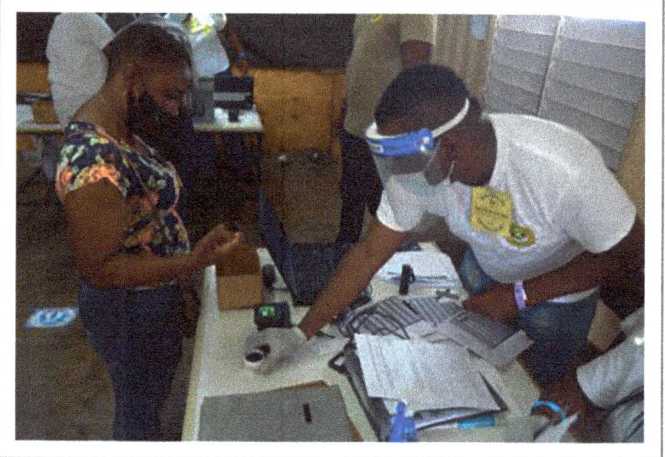

Figure 7.14 *Voters wearing facemasks during the pandemic*

also be passed down. Individuals are more inclined to vote if their parents and grandparents did. Political parties must ensure that their policies will be positive for the younger generation in order to encourage them to vote. Individuals who seek social change might be those who have been unhappy with past election results over their lifetime. These are the electors who engage with the political process.

Education

There is a direct link between voter education and the likelihood of casting a vote. When electors are knowledgeable about the election process, there is a reduction in **voter apathy**. The school curriculum is a good starting point to introduce the social, political and economic aspects of good governance. This leads to a well-informed electorate equipped with the electoral tools.

Party loyalty

Loyal supporters are the driving force behind a successful election campaign. These individuals have passion for the party's presence, performance and policies. They work in the best interests of the political party to support, inform and encourage others.

Quality of candidates

Under the first-past-the-post system, voters select from a number of candidates who are held in high esteem. Standing as a candidate means that society will look closely at their personal and political beliefs, public image and background and leadership traits. Voters base their selection on the most preferred candidate.

Voter attitude and personal motivation

If a voter is educated about the electoral processes, confident about candidates and has a desire to effect change, they might be more willing to cast their vote. However, voters who are disinterested in the process, imagine that government officials do not fulfil their manifesto goals and experience unmet needs by government policies throughout the years, might be unwilling to participate in elections.

In addition, there may be some specific issues that an individual is particularly passionate about; for example availability and cost of childcare, pension age, or business taxes. The voter may choose to vote for the party or candidate who is most likely to address their specific issue.

Economic status

An elector's economic background can impact where they place their vote. Electors suffering from unemployment and other social ills may fully support the promise of improved conditions. Political parties strive to appeal to all classes in society to attract votes. However, the majority of voters lie in the middle and lower classes.

Campaign strategy

The incumbent government is at an advantage as they can start unofficial campaigning even before parliament is dissolved for an election. The primary purpose behind the campaign is to reach a large number of people who will be driven to vote in a certain manner. The other political parties need to organise themselves efficiently to complement their opponents. Maintaining respect for the electoral process, people's opinions and voting behaviour is essential throughout the campaign as political parties and the electorate interact. In some areas, violence arises when there are differing views and loyalties, and basic human rights violations.

National issues

Citizens should be aware of matters that affect a large cross section of society. That being said, the candidates and political parties must be sure to address real, relevant, relatable and recent national issues in order to have traction with the electorate.

Campaign spending

The more advertising, promoting and souveniring that is done, the better the chances for election success. Unfortunately this can often mean that the party with the most money stands a better chance of winning.

Questions

Knowledge and comprehension

1. Identify a problem within the school community where a decision needs to be made. Use the decision-making process to reach to a decision.

2. Outline the differences between traditional forms of media and social media during the election period.

3. State the importance of campaign advertising during elections.

4. Define the term 'opinion poll' and state ONE use of an opinion poll.

5. List THREE factors that result in a high voter turnout for elections.

Use of knowledge

6. Examine the following case study and use the decision-making process from above to make an informed decision about what action should be taken.

   > A school population has 600 female students. Some students depend on the cafeteria to purchase at least one item: drinks, snacks and lunches. The cafeteria can comfortably maintain a capacity of 50 students at any given time. The students have an hour for lunch and after this period, classes resume. However, students are complaining to their Form teacher that the cafeteria is not serving the students quickly enough and they receive their items too slowly, resulting in lateness to the afternoon classes.

7. Discuss, in groups, the benefits and drawbacks of a political poster found in a newspaper as opposed to a digital poster found on a social media platform.

8. Evaluate the 'successes' of campaign advertising conducted by independent candidates and political parties.

9. A new political party has been formed. The upcoming elections are set within the coming weeks so they don't have much time to campaign. Recommend THREE factors that can boost votes for this new party.

10. Explain THREE ways political parties can increase the likelihood of success at the polls through the use of a campaign.

SBA skills

Calculate the size of the electorate for each country using Table 7.8.

Commonwealth Caribbean countries	Voter turnout in last parliamentary elections			
	Year	Turnout %	Total votes	Size of electorate
Antigua and Barbuda	2023	70.34	42,849	
The Bahamas	2021	65	126,495	

Commonwealth Caribbean countries	Voter turnout in last parliamentary elections			
	Year	Turnout %	Total votes	Size of electorate
Barbados	2022	41.73	111,135	
Belize	2020	81.86	149,650	
Dominica	2022	31.6	19,066	
Grenada	2022	70.32	60,941	
Jamaica	2020	37.85	724,317	
Cooperative Republic of Guyana	2020	46.84	2,510,135	
St. Kitts and Nevis	2022	57.98	29,554	
St. Lucia	2021	51.47	89,049	
St. Vincent and the Grenadines	2020	67	65,363	
Trinidad and Tobago	2020	58.04	658,297	

Table 7.8

Data analysis based on election processes and results

After an election, electoral agencies are tasked with counting votes. This quantitative process produces **data** which has to be processed to make sense to the public. Calculations produce **correlations** and **trends** to inform studies of voting habits.

Learning objectives

- Analyse statistical data on elections.
- Using data, draw conclusions about elections and the electoral processes.

Important definitions

Data – raw facts and figures that a researcher collects.

Information – this is processed data which can be presented in words.

Primary source – data collected directly by the researcher as in the administration of a questionnaire.

Secondary source – when data is collected by another agency and is interpreted by someone else.

Variables – something that a researcher is trying to measure.

Correlation – a relationship between two variables.

Trends – statements that can be made about the data after analysis.

Managing data

As social scientists, data collection and data analysis are key elements to understand our social world. Election processes, systems and activities are the subject matter of our scientific enquiry and produce useful **information**.

ELECTION AND BOUNDARIES COMMISSION
2020 GENERAL ELECTION RESULTS SUMMARY

DISTRICT WITH ELECTORATE	COP	DPT	ILP	IN1	IN2	IN3	IN4	MND	MSJ	NCT	NNV	NOW	OTV	PDP	PEP	PNM	PP	TDF	THC	TNP	UNC	UPP	UTP	REJECTED	Grand Total
ARIMA - 26382									95						212	9,293					3,858			30	13,488
AROUCA/MALONEY - 26673																12,697					2,768			57	15,522
BARATARIA/SAN JUAN - 25690															204	7,240					8,300			27	15,771
CARONI CENTRAL - 30107															245	6,890					11,511			31	18,677
CARONI EAST - 29031															296	4,271					12,819			30	17,416
CHAGUANAS EAST - 26923						79									143	7,882					8,968			53	17,125
CHAGUANAS WEST - 28625									138							1,878					15,502			48	17,566
COUVA NORTH - 29864	99														259	5,222					12,633			25	18,238
COUVA SOUTH - 30348																5,542			106		12,597			36	18,281
CUMUTO/MANZANILLA - 30468															158	7,557			35		10,901			51	18,702
D'ABADIE/O'MEARA - 30788								139								11,864					5,783			57	17,843
DIEGO MARTIN CENTRAL - 29609									374	120		69			404	10,627					2,693			60	14,347
DIEGO MARTIN NORTH/EAST - 29273	133								209						436	10,218					2,827			35	13,858
DIEGO MARTIN WEST - 29886									456							10,791			93		2,569			39	13,948
FYZABAD - 27447										127					143	6,888					10,850			37	18,045
LA BREA - 26008									223			71			129	9,342					5,735			71	15,571
LA HORQUETTA/TALPARO - 27528															145	9,713					7,790			30	17,678
LAVENTILLE EAST/MORVANT - 26644											39				169	10,356					1,965			39	12,568
LAVENTILLE WEST - 25586	47									31		310			126	9,310					1,324			23	11,171
LOPINOT/BON AIR WEST - 27864			3,817												123	9,608					3,587			36	17,171
MAYARO - 28834															133	7,229					10,593			81	18,036
MORUGA/TABLELAND - 29043		37		12												9,462				12	10,534			68	20,125
NAPARIMA - 27066																2,686					13,306			54	16,046
OROPOUCHE EAST - 28271																3,416					13,737			52	17,205
OROPOUCHE WEST - 25289															250	3,708					11,535			41	15,534
POINT FORTIN - 26003								545							58	9,276		20			5,761			36	15,696
POINTE-A-PIERRE - 25096								208							144	7,357					8,869			37	16,615
PORT-OF-SPAIN NORTH/ST. ANN'S WEST - 25003															385	9,475					1,705	73		47	11,685
PORT-OF-SPAIN SOUTH - 24754										145					257	8,202					1,850			26	10,480
PRINCES TOWN - 27178															209	4,708					11,280			32	16,229

ELECTION AND BOUNDARIES COMMISSION
2020 GENERAL ELECTION RESULTS SUMMARY

DISTRICT WITH ELECTORATE	COP	DPT	ILP	IN1	IN2	IN3	IN4	MND	MSJ	NCT	NNV	NOW	OTV	PDP	PEP	PNM	PP	TDF	THC	TNP	UNC	UPP	UTP	REJECTED	Grand Total
SAN FERNANDO EAST - 25008																9,864					4,689			36	14,589
SAN FERNANDO WEST - 25035															128	8,457	211			23	6,651			45	15,515
SIPARIA - 28663																3,855					13,487			56	17,398
ST. ANN'S EAST - 29454															327	10,979					3,438			46	14,790
ST. AUGUSTINE - 28094	188														235	5,264			33		11,943			43	17,706
ST. JOSEPH - 28452							217									9,354			30		8,543			49	18,193
TABAQUITE - 28832															221	5,209					11,440			50	16,920
TOBAGO EAST - 23102													80	5,866		7,127							39		13,112
TOBAGO WEST - 27686					43									4,501		9,275							40	24	13,883
TOCO/SANGRE GRANDE - 31096															166	10,698					7,313			60	18,237
TUNAPUNA - 27433															228	9,460			57		7,534			38	17,317
Grand Total	**467**	**37**	**3,817**	**12**	**43**	**79**	**217**	**1,039**	**1,223**	**234**	**493**	**310**	**80**	**10,367**	**5,933**	**322,250**	**211**	**20**	**366**	**23**	**309,188**	**73**	**40**	**1,775**	**658,297**

KEY

In the column headed "Party" the abbreviations have the following meanings:

NAME OF POLITICAL PARTY	ABBREVIATION
Congress of the People	C.O.P.
Democratic Party of Trinidad and Tobago	D.P.T.
Independent Liberal Party	I.L.P.
Independent	IN1-4
Movement for National Development	M.N.D.
Movement for Social Justice	M.S.J.
National Coalition for Transformation	N.C.T.
New National Vision	N.N.V.
National Organisation of We The People	N.O.W.
One Tobago Voice	O.T.V.
Progressive Democratic Patriots	P.D.P.
Progressive Empowerment Party	P.E.P.
People's National Movement	P.N.M.
Progressive Party	P.P.
Trinidad and Tobago Democratic Front	T.D.F.
Trinidad Humanity Campaign	T.H.C.
The National Party	T.N.P.
United National Congress	U.N.C.
Unrepresented Peoples Party	U.P.P.
Unity of The People	U.T.P.

Figure 7.15 *Preliminary results of the 2020 Parliamentary Elections in Trinidad and Tobago*

A number of general observations are visible based on the preliminary 2020 General Election results summary produced by the Elections and Boundaries Commission in Trinidad and Tobago.

Table 7.9 displays some of the general observations.

Number of political parties	Number of independent candidates	Number of constituencies	Popular parties	Election results
19	4	41	PNM, UNC	PNM 22, UNC 19

Table 7.9

Researchers have to dig deeper to uncover what lies under the surface when analysing the data. These can include:

- reasons for low voter turnout in particular constituencies
- strategies employed by political parties or candidates before the election day to attract voters
- reasons for rejected ballots.

A number of trends and patterns can be determined based on the data supplied:

- The independent candidates did not possess a presence among the electorate.
- There were two major competing political parties, the PNM and the UNC.
- There were two political parties which attempted to contend particular seats, ILP (Trinidad, Lopinot/Bon Air West) and PDP (Tobago East and West).
- The PEP had a small presence in 68% of the constituencies.
- The UNC, one of the major competing political parties, did not contest Tobago in the 2020 General Election.

These trends and patterns can help political analysts to make future predictions about election results. All the trends presented so far are quantitative, using the numerical data. The analysis can also include qualitative data, in words, to describe the journey taken by the political parties through interviews and observations leading up to elections. This adds more depth and coverage of the **variables** selected to research. An example of qualitative data can be the weather conditions on the day of elections which could have explained the voter turnout in a particular constituency.

Ballots can be rejected based on three main occurrences.

- Voter did not indicate a candidate on the ballot. The ballot was unmarked.
- Placement of the 'X' by the voter was not clear as it overlapped on another candidates' name/box.
- Voter made a mark which was not an 'X,' such as a signature.

Drawing conclusions

Conclusive statements are generally made at the end of a research or scientific enquiry. For the purpose of elections, data captured by the **secondary source** (Elections and Boundaries Commission/Department) and analysed by individuals can lead to definitive statements about the results. Conclusions help to give an outline of what was discovered when the data was analysed.

GENERAL ELECTION
OFFICIAL RESULTS
Elections and Boundaries Department
Mahogany Street Extension
11th November 2020

Electoral Divisions	Candidates	Political Party	# of Reg. Voters	Total Votes Cast	% of Voter Turnout	# of Votes	# of Votes By Party
Freetown			3782	3114	82.34%		
	Francis Fonseca	PUP				2114	67.89%
	Orson Jerome "OJ" Elrington	UDP				959	30.80%
	rejected					41	1.32%
Caribbean Shores			4363	3726	85.40%		
	Kareem David Musa	PUP				2194	58.88%
	Lee Mark Chang	UDP				1487	39.91%
	rejected					45	1.21%
Pickstock			3997	3281	82.09%		
	Anthony Robert Mahler	PUP				2570	78.33%
	Anthony "Uncle Boots" Martinez	UDP				574	17.49%
	Patrick Raymond Rogers	BPP				60	1.83%
	rejected					77	2.35%
Fort George			1876	1541	82.14%		
	Henry Charles Usher Sr.	PUP				983	63.79%
	Melvin "Mello" Hewlett	UDP				499	32.38%
	William "Wil" Maheia	BPP				34	2.21%
	rejected					25	1.62%
Albert			2886	2531	87.70%		
	Tracy Panton	UDP				1271	50.22%
	Paul Adrian Thompson	PUP				1230	48.60%
	rejected					30	1.19%
Queen's Square			2714	2431	89.57%		
	Denise "Sista B" Barrow	UDP				1351	55.57%
	Allan Pollard	PUP				1020	41.96%
	Garry Matus	BPP				23	0.95%
	rejected					37	1.52%
Mesopotamia			2277	1715	75.32%		
	Shyne Barrow	UDP				910	53.06%
	(Dr.) Candice Pitts	PUP				751	43.79%
	rejected					54	3.15%
Lake Independence			4863	3958	81.39%		
	Cordel Hyde	PUP				3539	89.41%
	Dianne "Miss D" Finnegan	UDP				359	9.07%
	rejected					60	1.52%
Collet			3732	3037	81.38%		
	Patrick Faber	UDP				1834	60.39%
	Oscar "Polo" Arnold	PUP				1142	37.60%
	rejected					61	2.01%
Port Loyola			4717	3649	77.36%		
	Gilroy Usher Sr.	PUP				2106	57.71%
	"Superman" Philip Willoughby	UDP				1313	35.98%
	"Boo Boo" Evan Thompson	BPP				152	4.17%
	rejected					78	2.14%
Belize Rural North			4721	3903	82.67%		
	Marconi Prince Leal	PUP				2238	57.34%
	Edmond "Clear The Land" Castro	UDP				1568	40.17%
	Karen Sharon Banner	BPP				52	1.33%
	rejected					45	1.15%
Belize Rural Central			7445	5956	80.00%		
	Dolores Balderamos-Garcia	PUP				3409	57.24%
	Beverly Williams	UDP				2166	36.37%
	Lion Bennett	BPP				181	3.04%
	Luz Maria Hunter	BPF				54	0.91%
	rejected					146	2.45%

Figure 7.16 *Official results of the Belize General Election in 2020*

Electoral Divisions	Candidates	Political Party	# of Reg. Voters	Total Votes Cast	% of Voter Turnout	# of Votes	# of Votes By Party
Belize Rural South			8586	6887	80.21%		
	"Andre" Perez	PUP				4336	62.96%
	Manuel Jr. Heredia	UDP				2419	35.12%
	Thomas Henry Greenwood Jr.	BPF				37	0.54%
		rejected				95	1.38%
Corozal Bay			5410	4475	82.72%		
	David "Dido" Vega	PUP				2402	53.68%
	Pablo Saul Marin	UDP				1994	44.56%
	Carlos Javier Sawers	IND				22	0.49%
		rejected				57	1.27%
Corozal North			7000	6155	87.93%		
	Hugo Patt	UDP				3479	56.52%
	David Castillo	PUP				2563	41.64%
	Alfonso Acosta	BPF				66	1.07%
		rejected				47	0.76%
Corozal South East			7012	6138	87.54%		
	Florencio Julian Marin Jr.	PUP				3413	55.60%
	Antonio "Tony" Herrera	UDP				2614	42.59%
	Eloim Ellis	BPF				57	0.93%
	Edna Doris Diaz	BPP				14	0.23%
		rejected				40	0.65%
Corozal South West			5888	5130	87.13%		
	Ramiro Ramirez	PUP				2898	56.49%
	Dr. Angel CAMPOS	UDP				2142	41.75%
	Laurencio Lucio BUL	BPF				52	1.01%
		rejected				38	0.74%
Orange Walk Central			6045	5157	85.31%		
	Johnny Briceño	PUP				2902	56.27%
	Denni Grijalva	UDP				2140	41.50%
	Antonia Cruz Sanchez	BPF				61	1.18%
		rejected				54	1.05%
Orange Walk North			7833	6785	86.62%		
	Ramon "Monchi" Cervantes	PUP				4043	59.59%
	Carlos Zetina	UDP				2628	38.73%
	Marino Assi	BPF				57	0.84%
		rejected				57	0.84%
Orange Walk East			7033	6038	85.85%		
	Kevin Bernard	PUP				3277	54.27%
	Elodio "Son of the East" Aragon Jr.	UDP				2612	43.26%
	Lorenzo Adrian 'Andy' Aldana	BPF				74	1.23%
		rejected				75	1.24%
Orange Walk South			6858	5782	84.31%		
	Jose Abelardo Mai	PUP				3499	60.52%
	Guadalupe "Lupe" Dyck Magaña	UDP				2088	36.11%
	Eber Misael Herrador	BPF				117	2.02%
		rejected				78	1.35%
Cayo North			8058	6679	82.89%		
	Michel "Micho" Chebat	PUP				3745	56.07%
	Omar Figueroa	UDP				2790	41.77%
	Kurt Mathew Lizarraga	BPF				62	0.93%
		rejected				82	1.23%
Cayo Central			8107	6219	76.71%		
	Alex Balona	PUP				3434	55.22%
	Rene Montero	UDP				2699	43.40%
		rejected				86	1.38%
Cayo West			6465	5340	82.60%		
	Jorge "Milin" Espat	PUP				2703	50.62%
	Erwin Rafael Contreras	UDP				2478	46.40%
	Eduardo Raul Ayala	BPF				68	1.27%
		rejected				91	1.70%

Figure 7.16 *Official results of the Belize General Election in 2020 - Continued*

Electoral Divisions	Candidates	Political Party	# of Reg. Voters	Total Votes Cast	% of Voter Turnout	# of Votes	# of Votes By Party
Cayo South			7069	5261	74.42%		
	Julius Espat	PUP				4071	77.38%
	Ramon Francisco Witz	UDP				1113	21.16%
	rejected					77	1.46%
Cayo North East			5706	4764	83.49%		
	Orlando "Landy" Habet	PUP				2996	62.89%
	John Francis August Jr.	UDP				1674	35.14%
	Nefretery Nancy "Nancy" Marin	BPF				59	1.24%
	rejected					35	0.73%
Belmopan			8758	6943	79.28%		
	Oscar Mira	PUP				4172	60.09%
	John Birchman Saldivar	UDP				2004	28.86%
	Anna "ABG" Banner-Guy	IND				684	9.85%
	rejected					83	1.20%
Dangriga			5482	4212	76.83%		
	"Dr. Zab" Louis Zabaneh	PUP				2600	61.73%
	Frank "Papa" Mena	UDP				1501	35.64%
	John Francis Suazo	BPF				56	1.33%
	rejected					55	1.31%
Stann Creek West			9864	7745	78.52%		
	Rodwell Stephen Ferguson	PUP				4900	63.27%
	Ivan "Junie" Williams	UDP				2509	32.40%
	Melvin Hulse	IND				179	2.31%
	Richard McCaulay	BPP				32	0.41%
	Mateo Tomas Polanco	IND				9	0.12%
	rejected					116	1.50%
Toledo East			6831	4698	68.77%		
	Michael Espat	PUP				2869	61.07%
	Dennis Garbutt	UDP				1755	37.36%
	Orlando Albert Muschamp	IND				30	0.64%
	rejected					44	0.94%
Toledo West			7437	6400	86.06%		
	Oscar Requena	PUP				3921	61.27%
	Simeon Coc	UDP				2444	38.19%
	rejected					35	0.55%

Source: Elections and Boundaries Department

SUMMARY

Total Registered Electors	182,815	100%
Total Votes Cast	149,650	81.86%
Total Votes Cast for PUP	88,040	58.83%
Total Votes Cast for UDP	57,374	38.34%
Total Votes Cast for BPP	548	0.37%
Total Votes Cast for BBF	820	0.55%
Total Votes Cast for IND	924	0.62%
Total Ballots rejected	1,944	1.30%

Figure 7.16 *Official results of the Belize General Election in 2020 - Continued*

The data in the official results revealed the following observations.

Number of political parties	Number of independent candidates	Number of constituencies	Popular parties	Election results
4	5	31	PUP, UDP	PUP 26, UDP 5

The PUP won by a wide margin of 21 seats with a general voter turnout of 81.86%. PUP received the most number of votes which amounted to 58.8% of the total votes cast.

End of chapter questions

1. a) Define the term 'gerrymandering'. (2 marks)
    b) Outline TWO advantages of the first-past-the post system of government in the Commonwealth Caribbean. (4 marks)
    c) In an upcoming parliamentary election, a political party would like to attract more votes from the younger section of the population.
    - (i) Suggest TWO strategies the political party may take to attract younger voters. (4 marks)
    - (ii) Explain why EACH strategy suggested in (c)(i) is likely to be successful. (4 marks)

    TOTAL 14 MARKS

2. a) Define the term 'manifesto'. (2 marks)
    b) Describe TWO ways in which political parties can use propaganda to attract votes. (4 marks)
    c) Over the past few years, reports have surfaced that voter apathy has been on the increase.
    - (i) Suggest TWO activities that political parties can engage in to improve voter apathy. (4 marks)
    - (ii) Explain how EACH activity suggested in (c) (i) is likely to be successful. (4 marks)

    TOTAL 14 MARKS

Summary

The electoral processes and systems symbolise our democratic procedures. There are several steps, agencies and protocols involved. From the dissolution of Parliament to the swearing in of a new head of government/head of state, all these steps have specific practices.

There are two main electoral systems in the Commonwealth Caribbean. The first-past-the-post system is widely used, where the success of political parties is based on the number of **seats** achieved. Proportional representation, alternatively, is based on the proportion of **votes** achieved reflecting the proportion of seats to be assigned in the Parliament. Although first-past-the-post is used nearly everywhere in our region, the necessity of electoral reform to improve the electoral process is a discussion being had more widely.

It is crucial for political parties to prepare appropriately for elections. They have to:

P	L	A	N
Promote themselves to the public via a campaign	Lead a slate of candidates to victory	Allocate personnel to oversee and monitor the electoral processes	Notify the public about future plans through a prepared manifesto

There is always a need to qualify statements made on public platforms, differentiating between facts, opinions and propaganda.

Facts	Opinions	Propaganda
Based on evidence which can be proved	Based on personal views which cannot be proven	Based on selective use of emotive language

All aspects of life require some form of decision making. Using a series of steps can ensure that the decision made is in the best interests of all parties.

A sound election outcome is the goal of any government when parliament is dissolved. There is interaction among many elements of society to produce this outcome. The media covers a host of events, voter participation is crucial to success and campaign strategies should be clear and focused.

Votes are the source of a win or defeat by a political party and care should be taken when handling this numerical data. Trained personnel should analyse the data focusing on trends and patterns. Past occurrences, coupled with present situations can be used to make sensible forecasts.

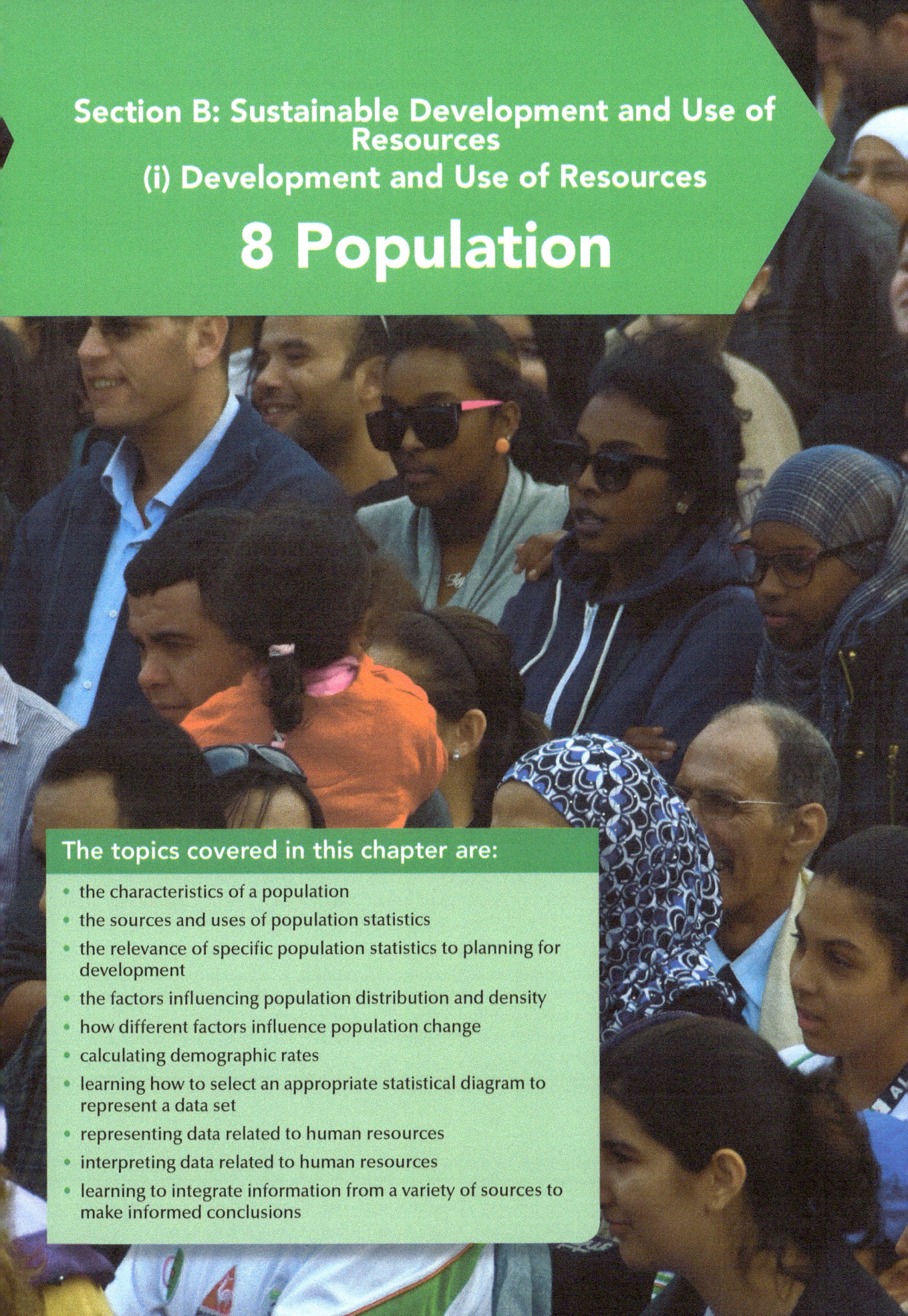

Section B: Sustainable Development and Use of Resources
(i) Development and Use of Resources
8 Population

The topics covered in this chapter are:

- the characteristics of a population
- the sources and uses of population statistics
- the relevance of specific population statistics to planning for development
- the factors influencing population distribution and density
- how different factors influence population change
- calculating demographic rates
- learning how to select an appropriate statistical diagram to represent a data set
- representing data related to human resources
- interpreting data related to human resources
- learning to integrate information from a variety of sources to make informed conclusions

Every fraction of a second, a new life begins, contributing to the global **population** that currently exceeds 8 billion people. According to the United Nations, population size is estimated to rise to 9.7 billion by 2050. Understanding these dynamics is crucial, as they directly influence sustainable development, resource distribution and long-term planning for nations around the world.

Characteristics of a population

Learning objectives

- Describe the characteristics of a population.
- Identify the sources and uses of population statistics.
- Determine the relevance of specific population statistics to planning for development.

Important definitions

Population – the number of people living in a particular geographical location.

Demography – the scientific study of the population.

Overpopulation – a situation where there are too many people for the available resources.

Birth rate – the number of live births per thousand of the population.

Death rate – the number of deaths per thousand of the population.

Natural increase – the difference between births and deaths.

Life expectancy – the average number of years a person is expected to live.

Dependency ratio – the proportion of non-economically active population to the economically active population multiplied by 100.

Age sex pyramid/Age structure diagram – visual aid used to show the age and sex of a population over a period of time.

Defining population

According to the World Health Organization (WHO), population is defined as:

'All the inhabitants of a country, territory, or geographic area, total or for a given sex and/or age group, at a specific point of time.'

Demography is the study of a population where a demographer is interested in the population to understand its composition, size, spread and structure. In looking at a population in an area or country, one can make a number of specific observations. For instance, there may be a large number of retired people or more males than females. As social scientists, we have to evaluate these characteristics to ensure inclusion, equality and the general standard of living among the members of the population in the area or country.

A population can be viewed in terms of:

Age

The population of any area or country varies based on various factors including age, which significantly influences its demographic structure. For example, in China there was a government strategy known as the 'one-child policy' between 1980 and 2016 which aimed to control birth rates and curb **overpopulation**. Overpopulation occurs when the population in a given area exceeds the available resources, such as food, housing and other essential amenities. **Birth and death rates** help us understand the structure and growth patterns of a population. The birth rate represents the number of live births per thousand people in a specific period, while the death rate, or mortality rate, indicates the number of deaths per thousand people.

By calculating the difference between the birth rate and the death rate, we can find the rate of **natural increase**. A positive natural increase signifies a growing population, while a negative natural increase indicates a declining population. An area experiencing a **natural decrease** is one where the death rate exceeds the birth rate.

Case study

Official statistics reveal a sharp decline in birth rates for Jamaica. According to the National Epidemiology Branch of the Ministry of Health and Wellness (2000–2022), live births dropped from 56,134 in 2000 to 31,276 in 2021.

In 2022, the number of deaths were 21,390 while 2021 (COVID-19) recorded 26,974 deaths.

These rates have not only social but economic and cultural implications for the future.

Figure 8.1 A mother with her baby

Gender distribution

This refers to the numbers of males and females in a country or area. Generating these statistics helps governments plan for the future. An imbalance in the population based on sex can lead to a number of social issues. Some which might include:

- unemployment in certain positions traditionally occupied by either males or females
- decrease in marriage rate and birth rate
- battle of the sexes for economic and political power.

One specific, quantifiable characteristic of a population is its size. The size of a population has a number of economic, social and environmental effects on the country.

In the study of population, **life expectancy** should always be factored in as it has effects on the overall population structure. Life expectancy is a measure of the average number of years a person is expected to live.

Table 8.1 gives an overview of the life expectancy in selected Caribbean countries for 2020.

Countries	Male life expectancy (years)	Female life expectancy (years)
Belize	71.4	77.8
Grenada	70.6	75.3
Haiti	62.5	69.4
St. Lucia	71.3	77.7
Trinidad and Tobago	72.5	79.9

Table 8.1

Section B(i) Sustainable Development and Use of Resources

Population pyramids

An **age-sex pyramid** or **age structure diagram** shows the age and sex of a population over a certain period. Trends and historical comparison can be made from population pyramids. There are THREE specific trends which can be illustrated using this diagram.

In constructing the age-sex pyramid, females are on the right of the diagram while males are on the left. The vertical axis shows the age, which increases in increments of 5 years starting at 0. The horizontal axis shows the population size.

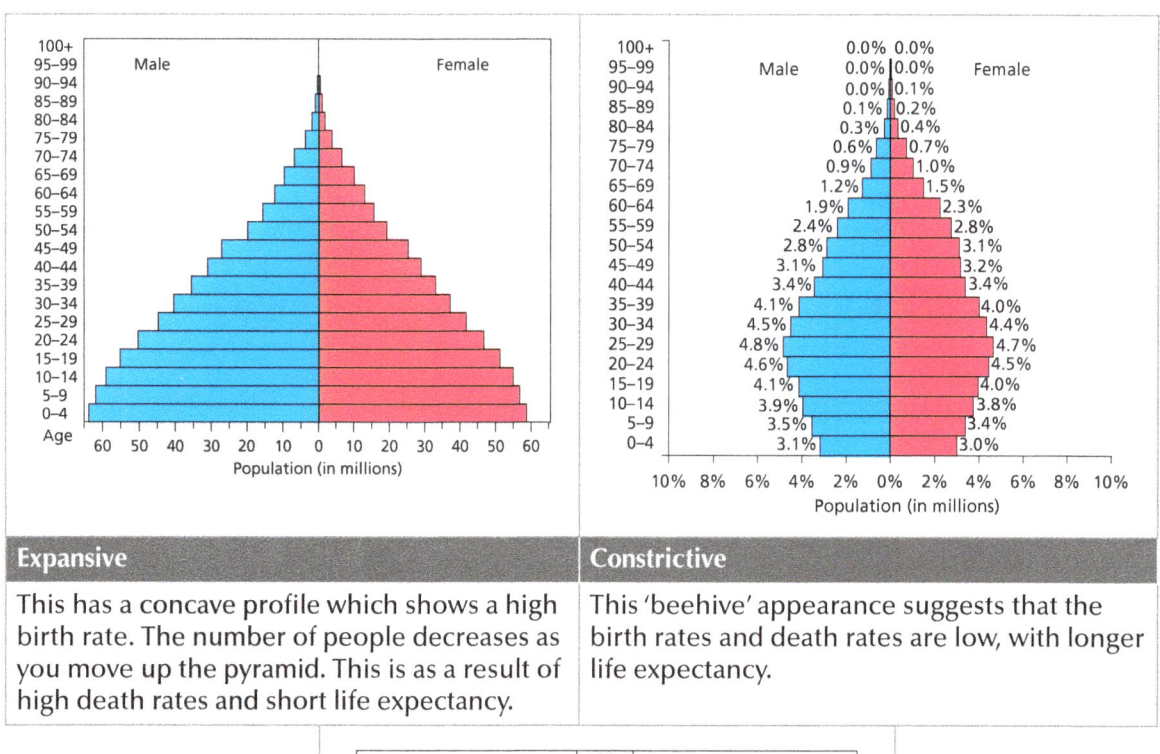

Expansive

This has a concave profile which shows a high birth rate. The number of people decreases as you move up the pyramid. This is as a result of high death rates and short life expectancy.

Constrictive

This 'beehive' appearance suggests that the birth rates and death rates are low, with longer life expectancy.

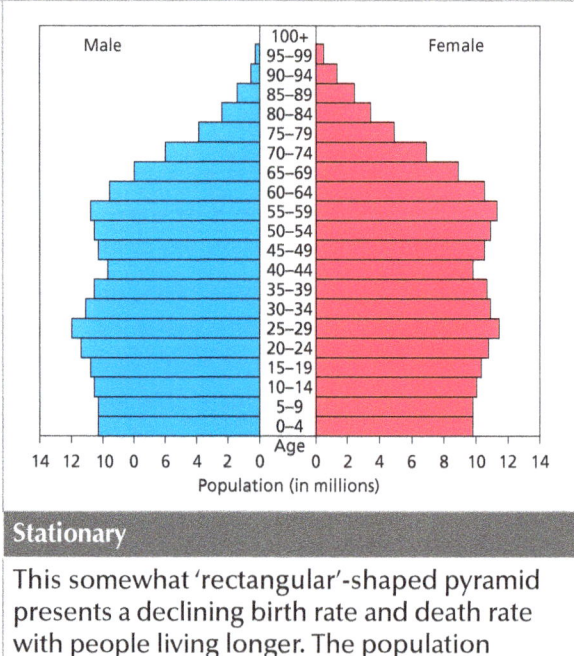

Stationary

This somewhat 'rectangular'-shaped pyramid presents a declining birth rate and death rate with people living longer. The population generally shows little growth in size.

Figure 8.2 *Three different trends which can be seen in age-sex pyramids*

We can also measure **the dependency ratio** from the diagrams above. This is the relationship between the number of children (0–14 years) and older people (over 65 years) to the number of persons of working age (15–64 years). This shows us the rate to which the non-economically active population is dependent on the economically active population. A high rate suggests a growing youthful population or growing aging population, which can place strain on social services and burden the working population.

Dependency ratios can:

- help us understand a countries' economic growth, since the size of the dependent population can be compared with the size of the working population
- indicate the rate of birth and death among the population. A rising dependency ratio may indicate an increasing birth rate or a decreasing death rate. Conversely, a falling dependency ratio could suggest a declining birth rate or an increasing death rate
- offer useful data when planning and providing for social services such as education, housing and programmes for the elderly.

Occupation

A population can be analysed based on the types of work that people do. In the past, the Caribbean population worked mainly in agriculture, with limited opportunities in other types of work. Since the 1970s, Caribbean economies have diversified and education has been tailored to meet these requirements. The range of occupational opportunities tend to fluctuate among the primary, secondary, tertiary and quaternary sectors.

The labour force or working population includes both the employed and the unemployed portion of the population.

The Guyanese data on the following pages shows different occupations across the 10 regions of the country.

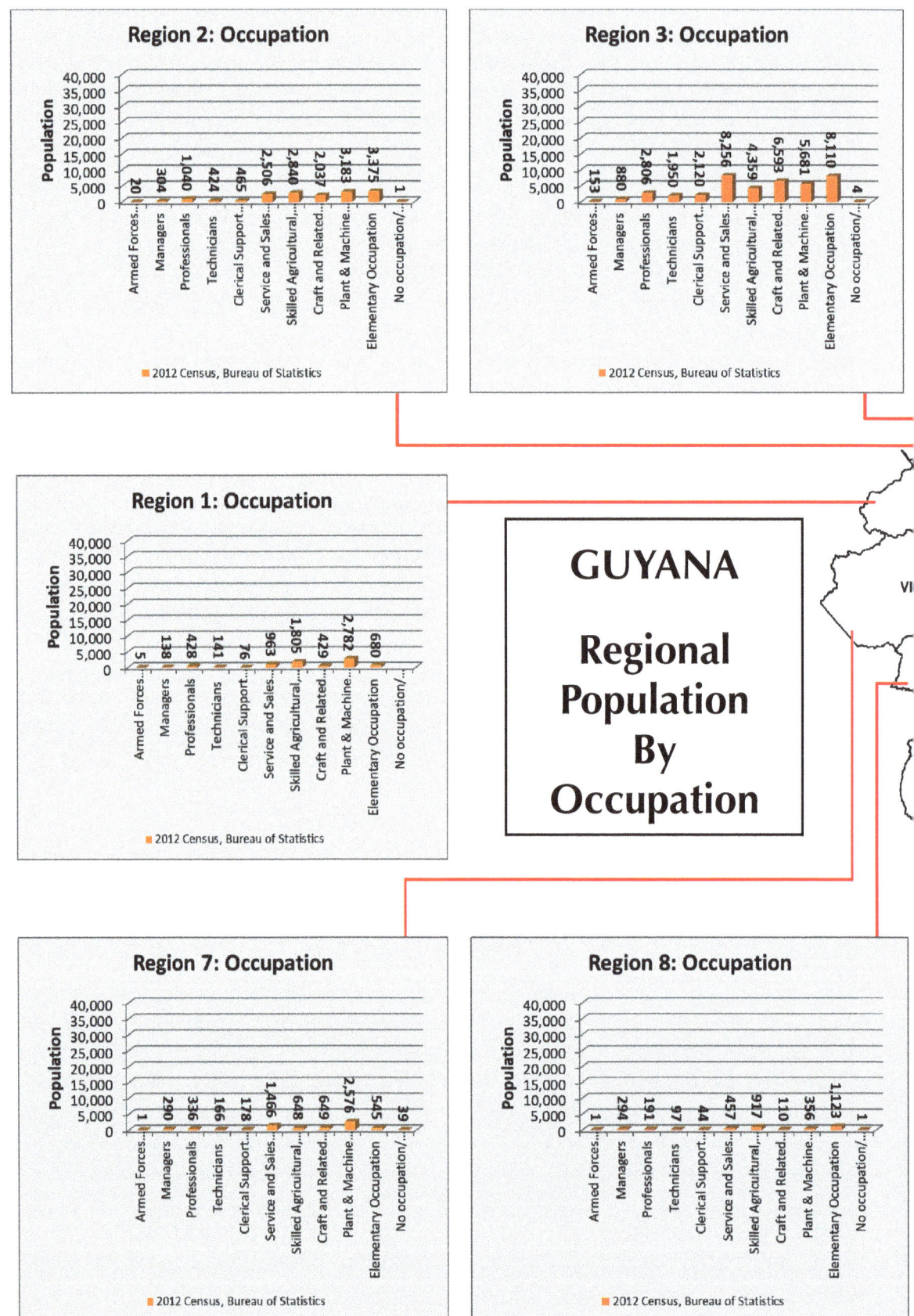

Figure 8.3 Chart showing Regional Population of Guyana by Occupation

8 Population

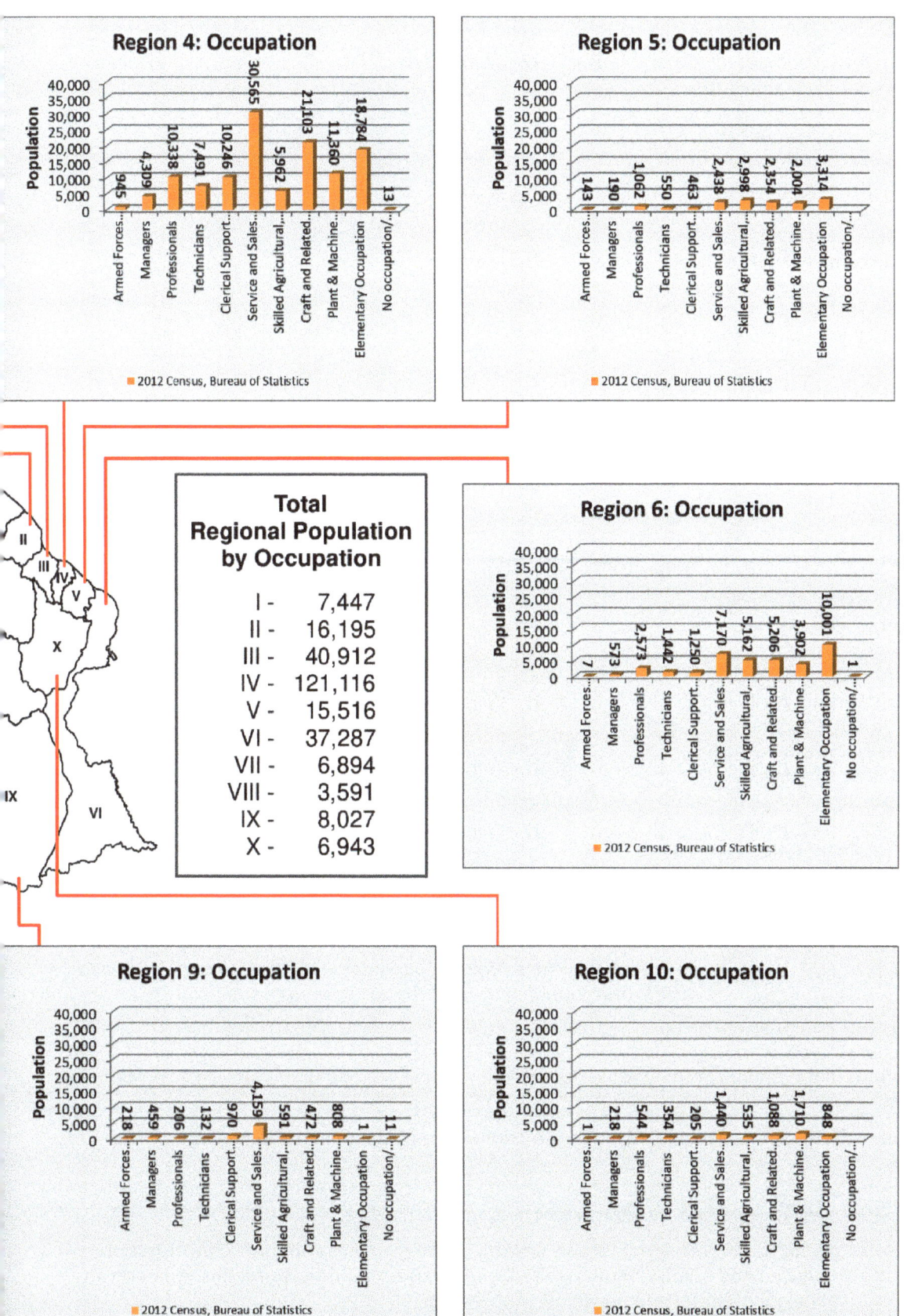

Ethnicity

Historically, the Caribbean region has always contained a mixture of various ethnic groups due to colonisation, enslavement and indentureship. The European colonisers, the African enslaved and the Indian and Chinese indentured servants all had distinct cultural traits which set them apart from each other. Today we are witnessing a real fusion of cultural practices such as in language, music and festivals. The population has diverse cultures which adds to our 'Caribbean-ness.'

The pie chart shows the ethnic composition of Trinidad and Tobago from census data in 2011.

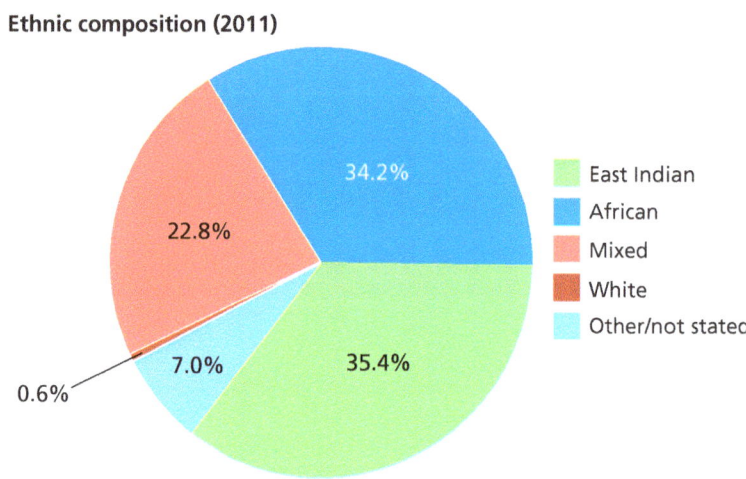

Figure 8.4 *Pie chart showing the ethnic composition of the population of Trinidad and Tobago from the 2011 census*

Religion

Religion is a useful category to consider when looking at the composition of a population. Many groups of people from various parts of the world came to the Caribbean not only bringing with them their language, food and practices but also their religions. Christianity is the predominant religion in the region, with many denominations such as Anglican and Methodist, followed by Hinduism, Islam and syncretic religions such as Voodoo, Rastafarianism and Orisha that combine African belief systems with other religions in the region. Some people do not follow a religion and that is also an important part of the data.

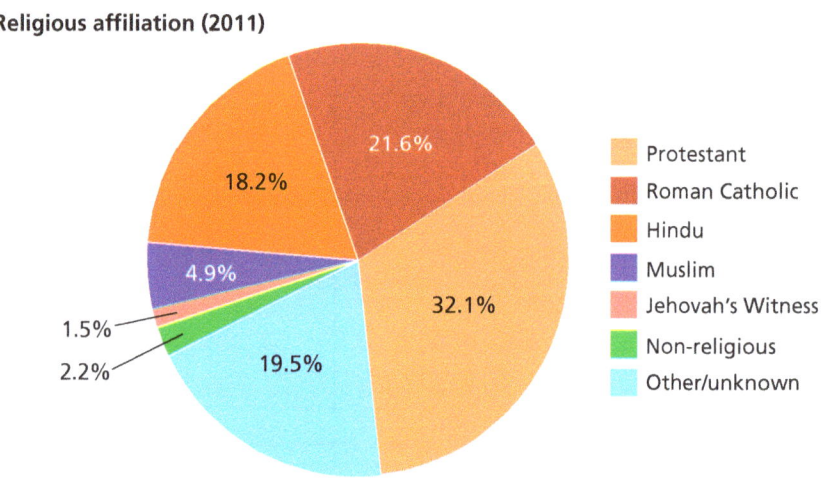

Figure 8.5 *Pie chart showing the religious affiliation of the Trinidad and Tobago population from the 2011 census*

The pie chart above shows the religions found in Trinidad and Tobago in the 2011 census.

Population density and distribution

Populations across the Caribbean are unevenly spread. There are areas with high concentrations of people, and also unused and relatively uninhabited land. In order to understand this, we need an appreciation of **population density** and **population distribution.**

In simple terms, population density describes the number of people in a given area relative to the physical size of the area in square kilometres. To calculate the density, the total population of the country/area is divided by the total area (sq. km). For example, if there are 100 people living in an area of 10 square kilometres, then the population density is 10 persons per square kilometre. This data helps governments to identify the areas of high or low concentrations of people so that essential social and economic amenities can be provided.

Population distribution, on the other hand, represents how people are spread out in an area. It describes the pattern of settlements and where people live. Historically, people tended to live near water sources, as water was essential for drinking, cooking and transportation. Today, people live in different places for many reasons, including cultural factors, economic opportunities and physical factors, like the terrain. Flat land is easier to build on than mountainous terrain, while access to good transportation is a reason people might want to live somewhere, rather than an area with poorly developed roadways.

Examples of population density and distribution

Monaco, in Western Europe, is the most densely populated country in the world with over 19,000 people per square kilometre. This is because Monaco is comparatively small, with many people occupying a small area. On the other hand, Mongolia, a country in Asia, is the least densely populated country in the world with only 2 persons per square kilometre. This is because Mongolia is very large, and there are few people living in a vast area.

In the Caribbean, Barbados is one of the most densely populated islands with over 667 people per square kilometre. This is because Barbados is a relatively small island, and many people live there. Guyana, on the other hand, is one of the least densely populated countries in South America with only 4 people per square kilometre. This is because Guyana is a very large country, and there are few people living in a vast area.

It is important to understand population density and distribution as:

- it helps governments plan for things like roads, schools, and hospitals
- it helps businesses decide where to locate their stores and factories
- it can help us understand how different cultures and economies have developed.

Health status and education

Citizens of a country depend heavily on social services such as health and education.

Table 8.2 shows the health and education standards accessed by a population.

Health	Education
Quality medical care, both physical and mental health care	Levels of primary, secondary and tertiary education
Proper nutrition	Trained personnel/educational infrastructure to improve literacy rates
Good air, water and soil quality	Quality education to reduce gender gaps

Table 8.2

Income level and employment status

These two characteristics can be used to demonstrate a variety of indicators such as level of development, access to health and education and even life expectancy. Most countries may not experience equitable distribution of wealth and as such it is wise to consolidate the data to display the social hierarchy which can exist. Data collected depicting employment status is useful to show the relationship between the non-economically active population and the working population.

Sources and use of population statistics

Learning objectives
- Identify the national sources of population statistics.
- Describe the uses of population statistics.
- Appreciate the importance of accuracy of population statistics.

> **Important definitions**
>
> *Official statistics* – secondary forms of data collected and supplied by government agencies.
>
> *Data source* – the place where data originates from.
>
> *Census* – an official head count of the population.
>
> *Sustainable development* – when development of a country takes place using good economic, social and environmental practices.

National census

In Trinidad and Tobago, as in many Caribbean territories, a national **census** is taken every 10 years. This is a formal house to house count of the population which is conducted and compiled by an official body producing largely quantitative and numerical data.

In Guyana, the census is carried out by the Bureau of Statistics, which operates under the Ministry of Finance. The President, Dr Mohammed Irfaan Ali, launched the National Population and Housing Census in September 2022 with the theme: 'We countin' We.'

Table 8.3 below shows the details of the last census taken in a few Caribbean territories.

Country	Jamaica	Grenada	Guyana	Barbados
Last held census	2022	2021	2022	2021
Population count	2,697,983	105,539	746,955	277,821
Theme	'Yuh count, mi count, all a wi count!'	'Count us'	'We countin' We'	'Our nation, our future, be counted'

Table 8.3

Before the census is carried out, those in charge must prepare the questionnaire tool, test its suitability and chart the different districts. After the census is conducted they must process the data and analyse the findings. The census data may show important changes in population size, population composition, food security and even educational access.

The collection of population data does present some challenges. The population may not trust the exercise and feel that the data collection offers no advantage to their participation. They may worry that the captured data might be used for other purposes such as tax collection exercises. There have also been instances where census-takers have been attacked by animals and angry community members. Gated communities and remote areas also pose access issues which can present inaccurate data in the long run.

Civil registration

Countries must capture vital statistics and civil registrations such as births, deaths, marriages and divorces. Documenting births helps the economy as it provides individuals with a birth certificate or identity papers to legally occupy a job and pay taxes, to hold a bank account, to apply for a passport and to obtain a driver's licence. In keeping with the SDGs, vital statistics help to improve the delivery of health care (SDG 3), quality education (SDG 4) and even decent work (SDG 8) to registered individuals.

Regional bodies such as PAHO (Pan American Health Organisation) also assist with health planning and government actions such as issue of passports, removal of deceased elector's names from voter registration or even establishing eligibility to school enrolment. Parents, guardians and medical practitioners must report births and deaths.

There is no standard international procedure for civil registrations, and this can lead to problems within the international community, affecting people's livelihoods and opportunities to travel and work abroad.

Number of Marriages by Region, Guyana: 2015 to 2022											
	TOTAL	REGION									
	MARRIAGES	1	2	3	4	5	6	7	8	9	10
2015	4,744	73	351	465	2,591	227	705	116	40	68	181
2016	4,445	101	256	445	2,493	179	632	82	14	57	186
2017	3,990	67	241	380	2,285	172	565	57	15	51	158
2018	4,008	71	227	407	2,303	166	545	76	25	35	153
2019	4,352	101	289	383	2,454	223	572	68	30	62	170
2020	3,426	92	278	343	1,853	133	444	88	14	38	140
2021	4,623	130	296	402	2,645	193	578	94	33	68	184
2022	4,090	116	257	371	2,316	181	460	67	42	89	191

Figure 8.6 *Number of marriages by region, Guyana, 2015–2022*

Records of religious institutions

Collecting data about religious affiliation can be gathered from places of worship or 'gathering places' when attendance is taken or when special events occur at these religious buildings. Houses of worship often keep lots of historical data as they have existed for a long time and can provide helpful data about the religious community.

Customs and immigration records

Caribbean Immigration departments hold administrative data on individuals who enter or leave the country at any given time. At certain times of the year, Caribbean countries welcome a large influx of tourists who visit for cultural celebrations such as Carnival: Trinidad (Feb/Mar); Barbados (Aug) and Guyana (May). Tourist boards across the region can use this data to show whether tourism is growing or declining and compare statistics over a specific time or a given country.

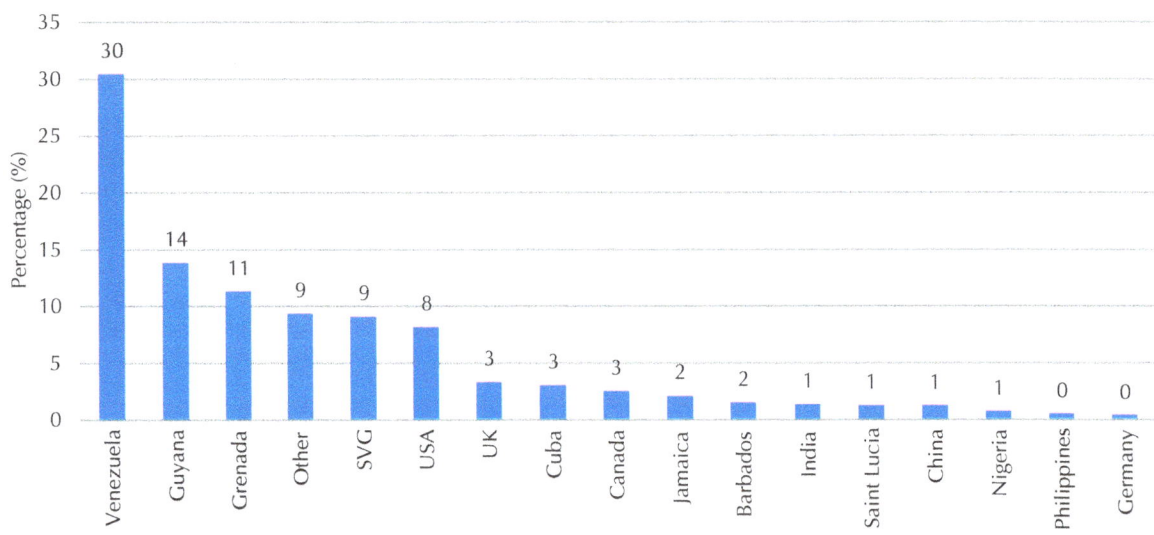

Source: UN DESA Population Division – International Migrant Stock 2020.
Note: SVG refers to St. Vincent and the Grenadines.

Figure 8.7 *Sources of immigrant populations in Trinidad and Tobago in 2020*

During the pandemic (2020–2021) when borders were closed, many individuals, especially from Venezuela, were making their way to other countries via irregular routes to seek protection. This has led to immigration divisions capturing inaccurate data about the migrant population since they would not have had any immigration documents and would therefore be undocumented.

Uses of population statistics

Handling population data requires government ministries, registrars and appointed agencies to collect, analyse and present the data in a clear and comprehensive way. This information is used by policy makers, researchers and business owners when making informed decisions.

Table 8.4 below displays some ways in which population statistics are used.

Use	Description	Example
Elections	Election officials should have an up-to-date list of persons who are eligible to vote. This allows for the elections to be free and fair.	In Grenada, the Parliamentary Elections Office was able to use these statistics to calculate the voter turnout of 70% in 2022.
Housing	Use of land to include agriculture, open spaces and locations for development. Constructing various housing developments based on the size, structure and composition of the population.	Barbados has undertaken a Planning and Development Plan to promote, conserve and protect the use of the land given the population size and growth.
Healthcare	Health information provides crucial information to improve general public health and identify the health care needs in the population.	During the COVID-19 pandemic, deaths and new infections were documented daily to give the population information about the spread and to reinforce safety protocols.
		Children in large family groups can suffer from poor nutrition due to limited resources.

Use	Description	Example
Education	Information about the non-economically active population can be helpful when planning staffing of schools, training of teachers and construction of learning institutes.	While education in the Caribbean is seen as popular and free where public access is given, in some countries there is an issue with high dropout rates among boys.
Employment	Quantitative data on the size of the labour force helps plan for the future to provide various types of employment.	2018 statistics in Antigua showed that 65.9% of the population was employed, and that more women were employed in service and sale work.
Social welfare	Demographic information about the homeless, infirm, differently abled, unemployed and those in need of assistance can help in planning social welfare investment.	The Planning Institute of Jamaica (PIOJ) created a long-term plan spanning from 2009–2030 to alter the management and delivery of services to benefit the neediest in society. A number of programmes were initiated based on census data for the youth, elderly, homeless, deportees and refugees, among others.
Infrastructure development	Population data can inform the provision of roadways, electricity, water supply and telecommunications in areas of need.	Guyana has been in the middle of an economic boom since 2022; the infrastructure must be developed to support the growing economy.
Industrial development	Population data enables the government to grow certain industries in key locations with the goal of maximising profits.	In Tobago, the Eco-Industrial Development Company, established in 2009, aimed to develop and diversify the economy using eco-industrial parks.
Population control	Governments can initiate programmes to combat overpopulation and have a level of control over population density.	In 1955, a family planning association was established in Barbados. The result was a reduction in the number of pregnancies.
Sustainable development	If population size increases due to a high birth rate and low death rate, it may cause problems for future sustainable development.	St. Lucia has adopted the 2030 Agenda for Sustainable Development with tourism, agriculture, infrastructure, healthcare, education and citizen security at its core. However, progress is needed to improve the national data collection system in order to measure progress.
Management of resources	Resources can be used effectively and efficiently if governments have accurate data about population size, density and distribution, housing and employment demands, patterns of settlement, transportation networks and even squatting data.	Caribbean countries have taken strides to monitor, control and regulate their population so that population profiles can guide planners in the provision of services.

Table 8.4

Planning for development with the use of population statistics

Learning objective
- Ascertain the relevance of specific population statistics to development planning.

> **Important definitions**
>
> **Population profile** – overview of the population inclusive of age, various rates and ratios as well as social and economic indicators.

Development planning using specific population statistics

Population data is also known as demographic data. Once analysed it is converted into statistics which are used by urban planners to help make decisions for healthcare, education and the delivery of other social services.

Demographic data must be up-to-date and accurate so that problems and needs can be addressed in a time efficient manner.

Demographic data analysis provides a number of benefits:

- The population is quantifiable so that growth or decline can be viewed over two or more specific periods (censuses). They can also demonstrate which segments of the population require particular services.
- They can allow governments to plan and organise strategies for the size and composition of the population. This will include housing, educational needs such as skills provision, health and social welfare needs, electoral list amendments and industrial and infrastructural development.
- They can target specific areas which need urgent attention. For example, if the infant mortality rate is high, the health care sector and in particular, prenatal care, will need to be addressed.
- They offer assistance and better direct the use of resources so that there is some level of sustainability.
- Demographic data plays an important role in the provision of social services needed by the vulnerable groups in society.
- Generally, governments are guided by demographic data analysis to make investments, purchases and improvements in many sectors. Two principles underlying good governance are transparency and accountability, and using statistics to make investment wisely helps governments demonstrate these.

Questions

Knowledge and comprehension

 1 Define the following terms.
  a) Population
  b) Birth rate
  c) Life expectancy

2 Describe TWO characteristics of a population.

3 Outline the role of civil registration in population statistics.

4 Read the case study below and answer the questions that follow.

> **TRINIDAD**
>
> As of December 2021, there were approximately 21 000 refugees and asylum seekers, 86% Venezuelan, registered with the Government or humanitarian organisations in Trinidad and Tobago. Numbers are unclear, given that many Venezuelans enter the country by irregular means and are not registered in the Government's databases. These estimated numbers represent the highest per capita population of Venezuelans in the Caribbean, as the islands have a total population of 1.3 million people.
>
> Public entities in Trinidad and Tobago have announced a lack of budget to provide shelter for all Venezuelan migrants and refugees. This, combined with limited regularisation plans and the economic impact of COVID-19, has led to many Venezuelans being unemployed and evicted from their homes. As a result, in July 2021, more than 700 Venezuelan migrants returned to their country on a trip arranged by the Venezuelan Government.
>
> Manifestations of xenophobia continued throughout 2020 and 2021, as migrants were blamed for COVID-19 infections. The routes used by migrants to reach Trinidad and Tobago expose them to protection risks, as some boats have shipwrecked on the way to the islands. In addition, Venezuelan migrants have denounced cases of sex and human trafficking and child labour during their journey and after arrival.
>
> On 9 April 2021, a one-month registration period for migrants in irregular status in Trinidad and Tobago ended. Several thousand Venezuelans were unable to register, as the service was only available to migrants who had registered during the migrant registration process in 2019. Since 17 June 2019, Venezuelan nationals need a visa to enter Trinidad and Tobago. This requirement is a barrier to entry that may lead migrants to seek unsafe, informal routes into the country.
>
> *ACAPS*

a) Define the term 'census'.

b) The national census provides prepared statistics for a country. Based on the above case, give some ways in which a national census might be deemed inaccurate or hide data.

c) List some of the social issues faced by the Venezuelan asylum seekers.

5 Describe the dependency ratio of a developing country.

6 State how population statistics can be used in population control.

Use of knowledge

7 Discuss the challenges a demographer would raise with a government minister concerning the population statistics in an urban centre.

8 The figure below displays the population pyramid of a Caribbean country in 2010 and 2050. Study these diagrams carefully and then answer the questions that follow.

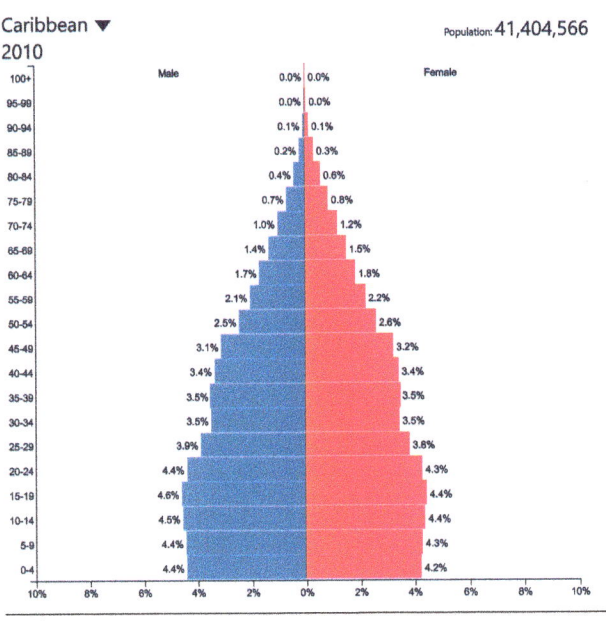

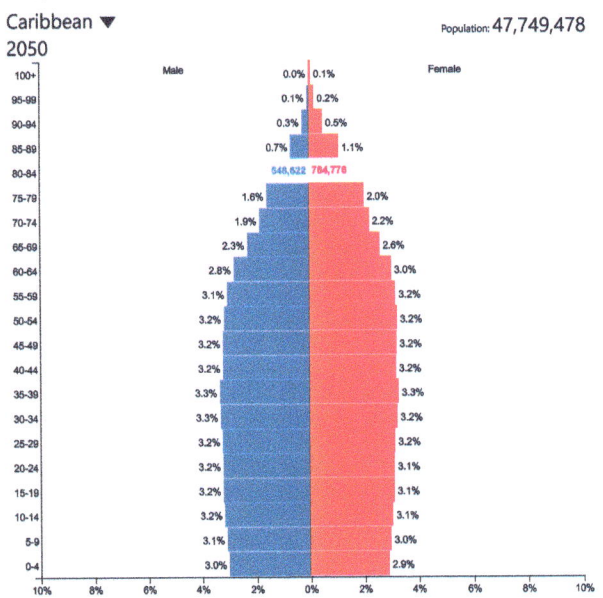

Figure 8.8 *Population pyramids for a Caribbean country in 2010 and 2050*

a) Which age group which was the largest in 2010?

b) Describe TWO ways in which the age structure of the population will change from 2010 to 2050.

c) Discuss ONE phenomenon which is likely to be examined by a demographer when analysing the diagrams.

SBA skills

Calculation of demographic rates

In order to appreciate population statistics, students are asked to contact the national statistical offices to gather raw data. This is useful to locate trends, identify growth rates and perform calculations to create a population profile.

1. Calculate the birth and death rates and natural increase for the following Caribbean countries. Remember birth rates and death rates are calculated using per thousand of the population.

Year	Country	Population size	Births	Deaths	Natural Increase
2022	Barbados	267,800	2241	3354	
2019	Guyana	743,699	15,491	5560	
2018	Trinidad	1,359,193	16,210	11564	

2. Calculate the population growth, for the period based on these selected countries.

Country	2000	2020	Population growth
Dominica	68,346	71,995	
Antigua and Barbuda	75,055	92,664	
Jamaica	2,612,205	2,820,436	

Population distribution and density

Learning objectives
- Examine the factors influencing population distribution and density.
- Interpret maps showing population distribution and density.

> **Important definitions**
>
> **Population distribution** – the spread of a population over an area.
>
> **Population density** – the number of people per square kilometre.
>
> **Choropleth map** – a shaded map with an appropriate key indicating concentrations of population used to illustrate population density.
>
> **Dot map** – a map filled in using dots with an appropriate key indicating number of people used to illustrate population distribution, where the bigger the dot, the bigger the concentration of people.

Factors influencing population density and distribution

As we learned in a previous section, **population density** is the concentration of people in a given area while **population distribution** is the spread of the population. Why do people choose to occupy certain places? Why are some areas and spaces more densely or sparsely populated than others? What attracts people in the first place?

Section B(i) Sustainable Development and Use of Resources

Physical factors

Relief or topography of the land: Early settlements were generally on flat, low lying plains with a reliable water supply. Higher ground provided safety but often meant rugged terrain where temperatures and air pressure decreased. Permanent settlements in mountainous areas is largely unconventional and unsuitable as it is inconvenient.

Climate: Settlement location also takes into account the level of rainfall, humidity levels, the length of seasons and temperature changes. In our tropical climate, we anticipate a fair degree of rainfall as we experience two seasons (dry and wet). The combination of wet, warm weather means our lands are fertile and good for growing crops. Tourists are generally attracted to our warm conditions.

Soils: There are many parts of the world where the soils are unusable such as in the Arctic and in areas where soil erosion is a problem. Soils such as sand, clay, chalk and silt are all present in the Caribbean which is good for farming.

Vegetation: Populations tend to settle in areas where crops can be grown and animals grazed, rather than forested areas or deserts.

Location of natural resources: Areas where there are lots of mineral deposits attract potential settlers. Mineral finds and energy supplies are often places where people settle which in turn can lead to industrial and urban development.

Human factors

Industry: A number of Caribbean countries are known for their industrial development. Trinidad is known for the extraction and production of petroleum and petrochemicals, Suriname for its oil and gold exports and in Guyana a discovery of an offshore oilfield in 2015 led to an increase in oil production and a subsequent improvement in the wealth of the nation.

Agriculture: Traditionally, our region depends on agricultural industries which are labour intensive. Agriculture is best placed in rural areas where there is an expanse of land. The maps of Suriname on the following page give a visual aid of the density and distribution of the population.

Accessibility of transport: Due to improvements in technology, transportation has made remote areas more accessible for citizens. Today, people are commuting using private vehicles, public transportation in the form of buses, hired vehicles and even water taxis and light aircrafts. The cities provide a transport hub and as such the population tends to be concentrated around these places where transportation networks are plentiful.

Infrastructure: This refers to structures such as roads, buildings, water and electricity supplies needed to comfortably live in a given area. These are more readily available in urban areas. As you move away from these urban areas, there is less infrastructure to support settlement so the population density is generally reduced.

Social services: People are more likely to occupy an area where more services are available. Schools, hospitals, government offices and commercial centres provide the population with assistance and job opportunities which leads to a higher population density.

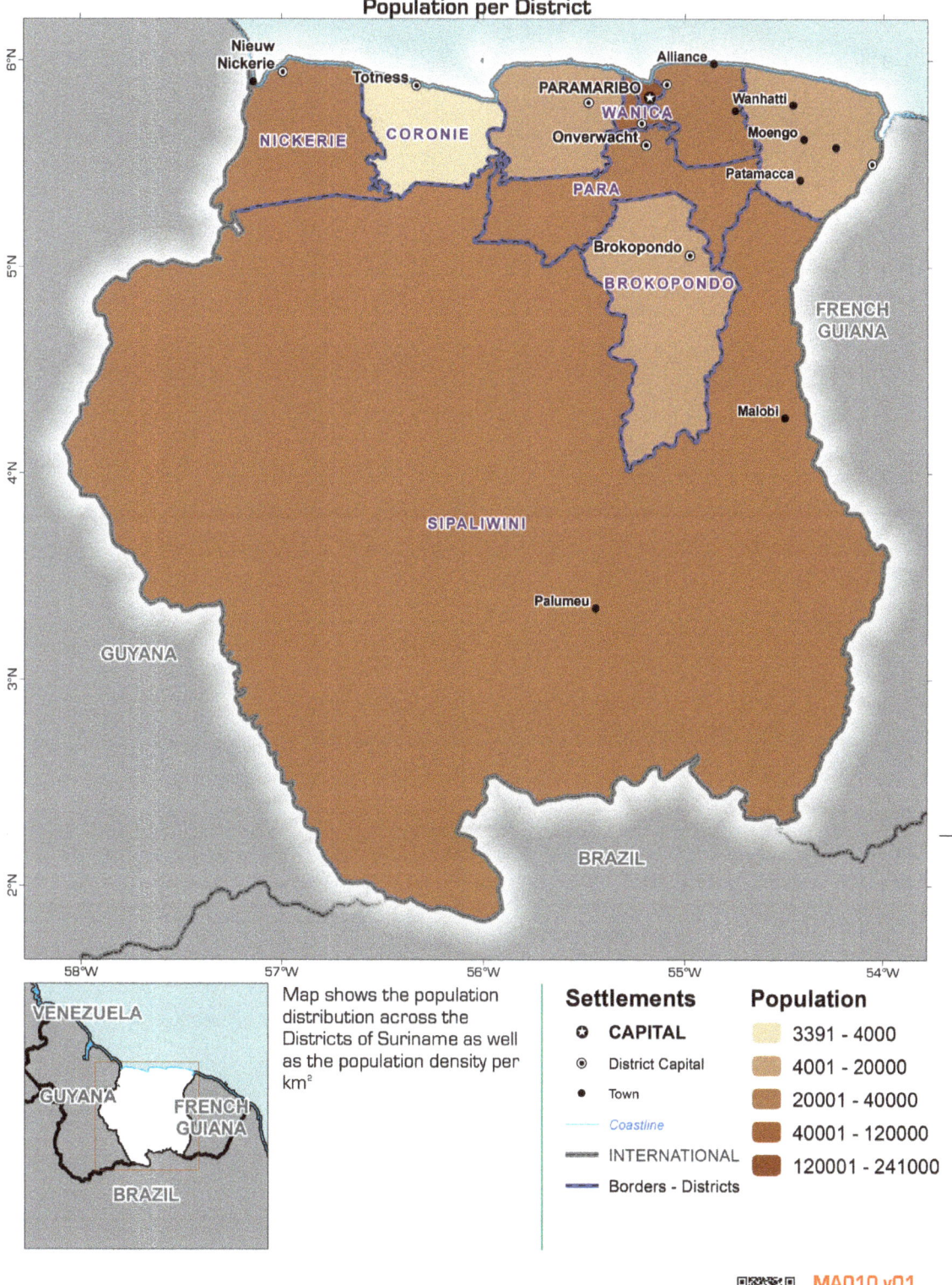

Figure 8.9 *Population distribution and density of Suriname*

Section B(i) Sustainable Development and Use of Resources

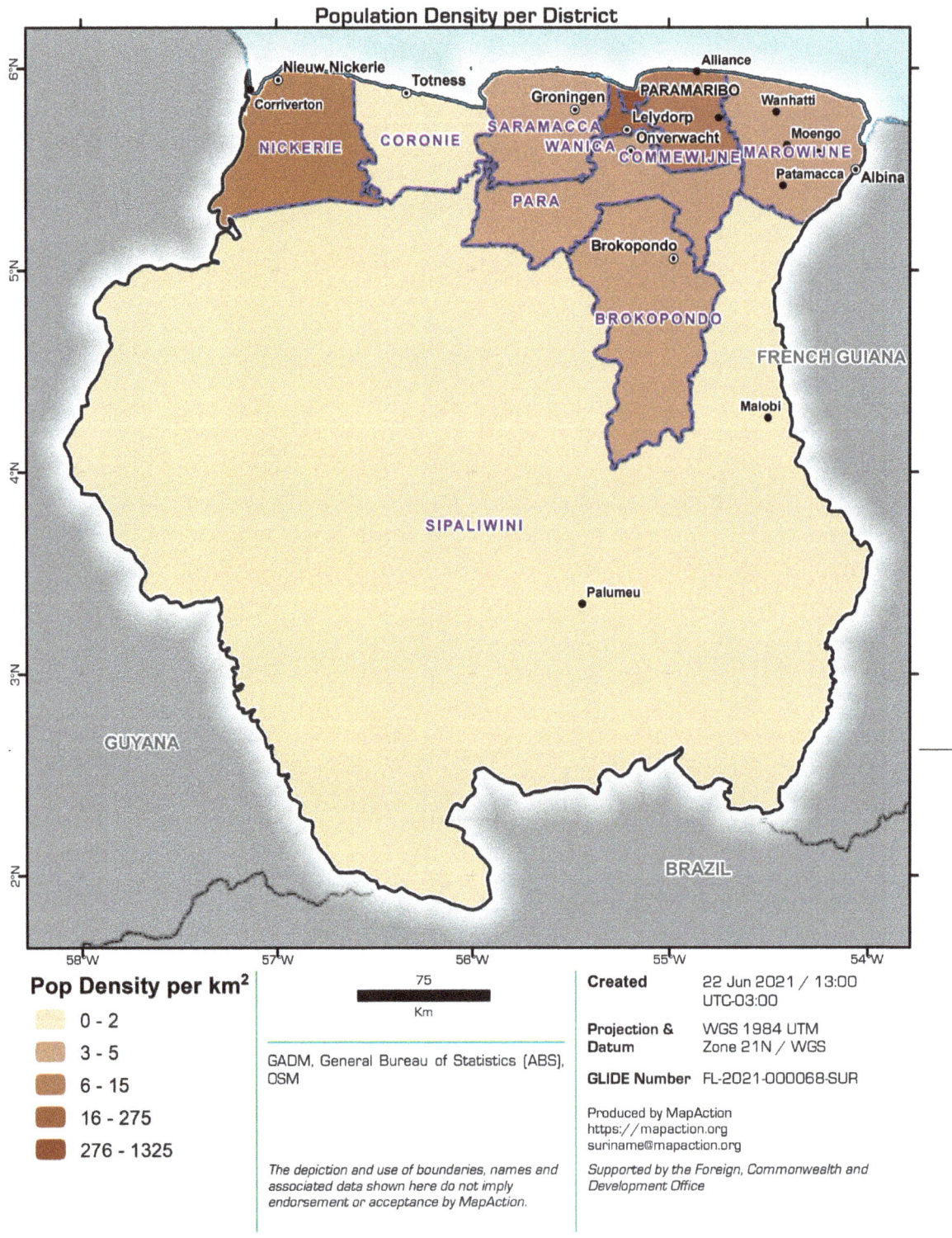

Figure 8.9 *Population distribution and density of Suriname - Continued*

Impact of under and over population on a country's development

Table 8.5 displays the relationship between development and population size.

Area of development	Under population	Overpopulation
Economic	– Too few workers to support an aging population and provide growth. – Fewer taxes collected.	Increases the price of food and demand for goods and other services such as health and education.
Social	Social services not being used and therefore forced to close.	Poor quality of life is visible as individuals may not access clean water and safe housing due to rising land and housing prices.
Environmental	Resources under used which prevents the area from realising its potential.	Overuse and overconsumption of resources can lead to higher greenhouse gas emissions worsening climate change.

Table 8.5

Interpreting maps showing population distribution and density

Representing data using a graphic representation or diagram can help users to understand it.

Population distribution is often depicted with the use of a **dot map**. Each dot represents a certain number of people and it is easy to read in terms of comparisons and concentrations. The map key explains the value of each dot, but if the area has a smaller number than the key can represent, no dot is used. This shows that a dot map is only useful when working with discrete data as opposed to continuous data.

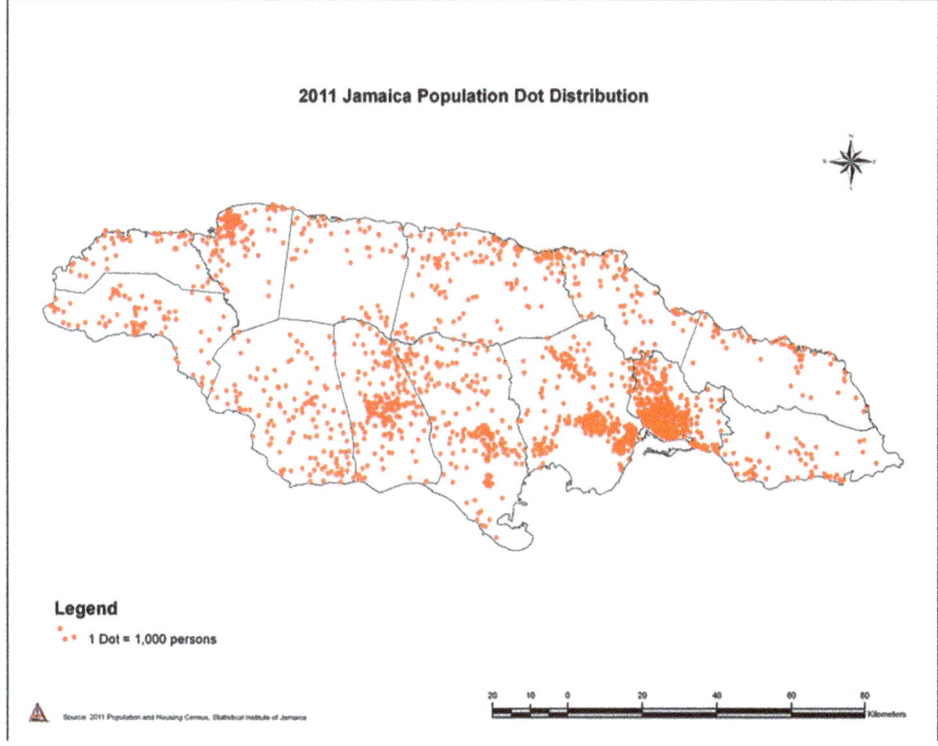

Figure 8.10 Dot map of Jamaica's population distribution in 2011

Population density is often represented with a **choropleth map**. This is a map which uses different shades of colour to show different levels of population density. Darker shaded areas indicate a higher concentration of people, while lighter shaded areas indicate a lower concentration of people. Once you calculate the density for each area, you can generate a key and apply that to the map. The choropleth map of Jamaica below shows the regions where the size of the population is most dense and the places which are least populated. Note that choropleth maps only show the average population density in an area, not variations within it.

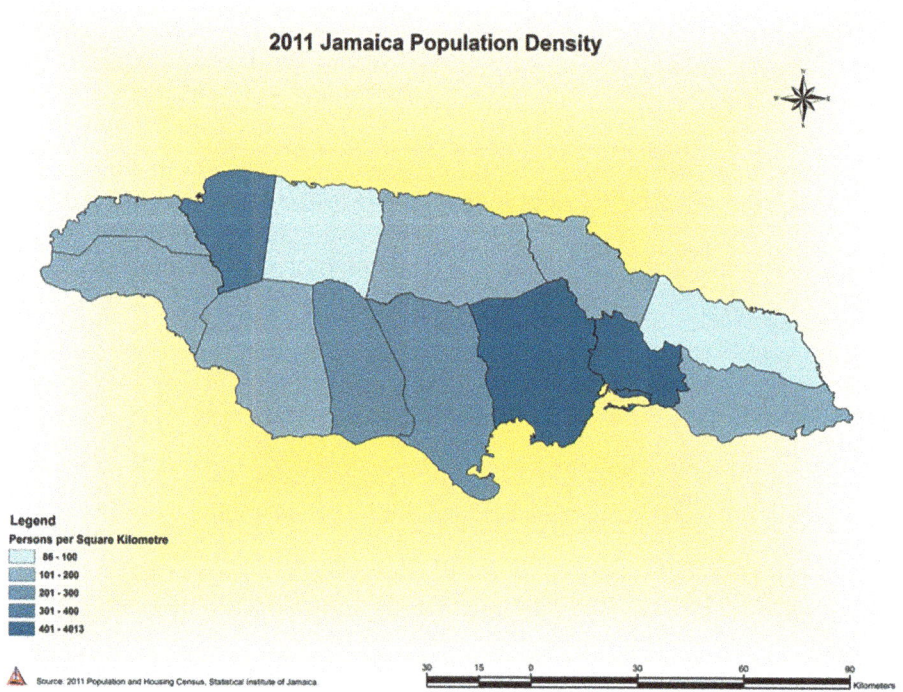

Figure 8.11 *Choropleth map of Jamaica's population density in 2011*

Map reading skills

Cartographers (mapmakers) are skilled at producing visual aids to navigate the best road routes, to prepare weather forecasts and even to plan the layout of a geographical area. These maps need to be accurate and clear, using an assortment of features.

Table 8.6 shows the key features of a map.

Title	Placed at the top of the map to state the purpose of the map
North arrow	Shows the direction of North
Key/Legend	Explains the meaning of each of the symbols used in the map
Scale	Shows the relationship between the distance on the map and the true distance on the ground. A bar scale is used to show a unit of distance
Border	A formatting 'frame' placed around the map
Source	The source of the map – who created it – should always be referenced

8 Population

Questions

Knowledge and comprehension

1 Define the following terms.
  a) Population density
  b) Infrastructure
  c) Key on a map

2 Outline ONE physical factor and ONE human factor to account for the population distribution of an area or country.

Use of knowledge

3 Explain the difference between population density and population distribution.

SBA skills

Look at the table below and answer the questions that follow.

Year	Population	Yearly % Change	Yearly Change	Migrants (net)	Median Age	Fertility Rate	Density (P/Km²)	Urban Pop %	Urban Population
2024	93,772	0.49 %	456	9	35.9	1.58	213	28.3 %	26,559
2023	93,316	0.51 %	476	0	35.5	1.58	212	28.2 %	26,313
2022	92,840	0.53 %	491	0	35.1	1.58	211	28.1 %	26,086
2020	91,846	0.53 %	482	0	34.3	1.57	209	28.0 %	25,682
2015	89,409	0.94 %	818	44	32.1	1.57	203	27.9 %	24,981
2010	85,320	1.39 %	1,142	291	30.2	1.79	194	29.1 %	24,837
2005	79,611	1.22 %	940	196	28.9	1.83	181	32.8 %	26,078
2000	74,912	1.90 %	1,345	263	27.4	2.20	170	35.8 %	26,853

Figure 8.12 *Population of Antigua and Barbuda 2000–2024*

The **median age** divides the population into two parts of equal size.

1. State the formula for population density.
2. Calculate the area of Antigua and Barbuda.
3. Describe any trends that you notice between 2010 and 2020.
4. There seems to be a gradual increase in the urban population from 2015 to 2020. Explain this gradual increase, keeping in mind that the fertility rate has remained the same during that time.

Section B(i)   Sustainable Development and Use of Resources

Population change

Populations are dynamic. Historically, populations grew due to agricultural and economic developments which improved nutrition and sanitation. Population decline happened because of disease and the effects of migration.

Learning objective

- Explain how different factors influence population change.

> **Important definitions**
>
> **Fertility rate** – the average number of children born to a woman during her childbearing years.
>
> **Infant mortality** – the number of child deaths below the age of 1 for every 1000 live births.
>
> **Migration** – the process where people move either within a country or to another country on a long-term basis.
>
> **Immigration** – the process where people move into a country.
>
> **Emigration** – the process where people move out of a country.
>
> **Net migration** – the difference between immigration and emigration.
>
> **Epidemic** – sudden increase in the number of cases of a disease in a particular geographical area.
>
> **Pandemic** – an epidemic that affects a whole country or the whole world.

Factors influencing population change

Positive population change means growth, which happens due to rising birth rates, declining death rates and an influx of people as a result of **immigration**.

Negative population change means a decline, which happens due to reduced births, an increase in deaths and **emigration**.

Births

Birth rates fluctuate every year within a country as well as across the world.

Table 8.7 highlights some reasons for the changes in birth rates.

Reasons for higher birth rates	Reasons for lower birth rates
Lack of appropriate family welfare services	Social and economic development of a country
Societies which depend on agriculture depend on a large workforce, so a high birthrate is encouraged	Social, economic and political empowerment of women
Some religions promote large families	Higher rates of infertility
Poverty, illiteracy and low standards of living where children are seen as future earners	Increased access to education

Table 8.7

The **fertility rate** indicates the number of children a woman of child bearing age can have.

Table 8.8 below highlights some reasons for the differential fertility rates.

Developed Country	Developing Country
Lower fertility rates due to marriage later in life	High fertility rates due to high levels of **infant mortality**
Smaller family sizes based on choice and occupation	Larger families help with agriculture
Education and use of family planning as outlined by governmental policies	Limited access and use of contraceptives and family planning
	Poor medical facilities

Table 8.8

The infant mortality rate is the number of child deaths below the age of one, per thousand of the population. This impacts the size and structure of a population and, if high, should signal to policy makers that improvement in post-natal care and proper medical facilities is needed.

Life expectancy gives an indication of the social and healthcare conditions in a country.

Table 8.9 highlights some reasons for the differential life expectancy rates between developed and developing countries.

Developed Country	Developing Country
Higher life expectancy	Lower life expectancy
Better public health services	Inadequate healthcare
High nutritional standards	Inadequate nutrition available to the average person

Table 8.9

In the Caribbean region, the average life expectancy among women is 75.53 years while among men the average is 69.22 years.

Deaths

Deaths are natural events which occur, but the death rate can increase due to poor healthcare and hygiene and infectious diseases spread under **epidemic** and **pandemic** conditions, as well as by an increase in violent crime and natural disasters.

Reduced death rates from one year to the next is a good indicator that the health of a population is improving and that measures put in place to reduce mortality are successful.

Table 8.10 gives some comparative statistics from various Caribbean countries.

	Population size (2022)	Death rate (2021)	Death rate (2022)	Life expectancy (2022)
Jamaica	2,818,596	8.8	7.6	74.77
Trinidad and Tobago	1,405,646	9.13	8.1	73.79
Antigua and Barbuda	93, 764	6.4	6.1	77.34
Guyana	808,726	9.9	9.8	70.15

Table 8.10

Migration

Migration changes the size and structure of a population. Positive **net migration** is when more people enter a country than leave it. Negative net migration shows that the rate of emigration is higher than the rate of immigration.

Migration flows fit into a number of categories based on distance or duration of time.

Internal migration

This is the movement of people within a country. Countries are made up of both **urban** and **rural** areas. Population shifts occur from rural to urban, urban to rural, rural to rural and also urban to urban areas.

Table 8.11 provides descriptions of internal migration.

Area	Rural to urban	Urban to rural	Rural to rural	Urban to urban
Scope	Large scale	Small scale	Small scale	Small scale
Reasons	Lack of employment opportunities and fewer facilities in rural areas.	Urban spaces with high population density suffer with pollution and congestion.	Looking for better, more fertile lands to continue farming.	City dwellers may move to another city area where there are similar amenities and comforts.

Table 8.11

Intraregional migration

This is the movement of people within a certain geographical area, like the Caribbean. This movement could be brought about by government policies or for human rights reasons. Both CARICOM's Caribbean Single Market and Economy and the OECS' Eastern Caribbean Economic Union have been instrumental in encouraging this type of migration in the region for employment reasons.

International migration

This is the movement of people across international borders for work, education and social services provisions. A number of Caribbean persons migrate to larger countries such as the USA and Canada for greater educational and employment opportunities. Laws such as International Human Rights Laws, Maritime Law and Humanitarian Law govern this type of movement.

Barriers to international migration

A barrier is something that prevents a person from migrating. Barriers can be personal, physical or legal.

Table 8.12 shows the types of barriers to international migration.

Personal barriers	Physical barriers	Legal barriers
Lack of finance	Countries are located far away	A visa is required to gain entry to the country
Family obligations	For refugees, the barrier could be the risk to life such as in navigating seas, mountains, etc.	Work permits are necessary for economic migrants
Emotionally tied to home country – place attachment		

Table 8.12

Forced/involuntary migration

Citizens of a country may feel threatened and fearful in their country due to political unrest, social and economic conflict situations as well as the aftermath of natural disasters. Leaving their home, life and family behind may seem the only choice for survival. These individuals often suffer from persecution and deprivation.

Seasonal migration

Opportunities are available for individuals to work in peak season activities where temporary labour might be required. In the agricultural sector, in several developed countries, seasonal migrants are encouraged to leave their home country to work on a legal, temporary basis. A variety of fruits and vegetables are harvested during the year. Migrants of this kind must apply for special work permits.

Questions

Knowledge and comprehension

1. Define the following terms.
   a) Fertility rate
   b) Migration
   c) Mortality rate

2. Describe TWO strategies to address rising birth rates in a country.

3. Describe TWO strategies to address rising death rates in a country.

4. a) Define 'internal migration'.
   b) State TWO reasons for the increase in internal migration from rural to urban areas.

5. List TWO countries that are attractive destinations to Caribbean migrants looking to move away from the region.

Use of knowledge

6. Discuss the importance of healthcare in maintaining sustainable development.

7. Rural to urban migration is on the rise in many Caribbean countries.
   Recommend TWO strategies that a 'rural planner' can take to reduce the number of young migrants away from the rural areas.

SBA skills

1. Look at Figure 8.12 which shows the numbers of immigrants and emigrants in Caribbean countries based on 2020 statistics.
   a) Calculate the net migration for each country.
   b) Identify the countries with the highest (positive, negative) net migration.

c) Identify the country with the lowest (positive, negative) net migration.
d) Suggest TWO reasons for the high emigration in a named Caribbean country based on the statistics provided.

Country Name	Population (total)	Immigration (stock)	Immigration (% of population)	Emigration (stock)	Emigration (% of population)
Antigua and Barbuda	97,928	29,386	30.0	66,561	68.0
Bahamas, The	393,248	63,583	16.2	53,793	13.7
Barbados	287,371	34,869	12.1	99,611	34.7
Belize	397,621	62,043	15.6	52,756	13.3
Dominica	71,991	8,284	11.5	78,191	108.6
Dominican Republic	10,847,904	603,794	5.6	1,608,567	14.8
Grenada	112,519	7,213	6.4	62,204	55.3
Guyana	786,559	31,169	4.0	438,413	55.7
Haiti	11,402,533	18,884	0.2	1,769,671	15.5
Jamaica	2,961,161	23,629	0.8	1,118,931	37.8
St. Kitts and Nevis	53,192	7,725	14.5	50,285	94.5
St. Lucia	183,629	8,338	4.5	71,227	38.8
St. Vincent Grenadines	110,947	4,738	4.3	55,525	50.0
Suriname	586,634	47,801	8.1	273,209	46.6
Trinidad and Tobago	1,399,491	78,849	5.6	330,519	23.6

Sources: UN DESA 2020; World Bank, World Development Indicators 2022.
Note: "Stock" is the term used by UN DESA. It refers to the number (or "stock") of international migrants.

Figure 8.13 *Immigration statistics for Caribbean countries in 2020*

Selection of appropriate statistical diagrams

It is important display your research data using charts and graphs, and to select the best and most appropriate illustrations to represent the data captured.

Line graphs

These graphs are usually used to display quantitative data over a period of time. It is a helpful choice to view drastic peaks and troughs over time.

The line graph below displays data collected from 1950–2020 and projects that the population size will drop to 1.8 million by 2099 based on predictions.

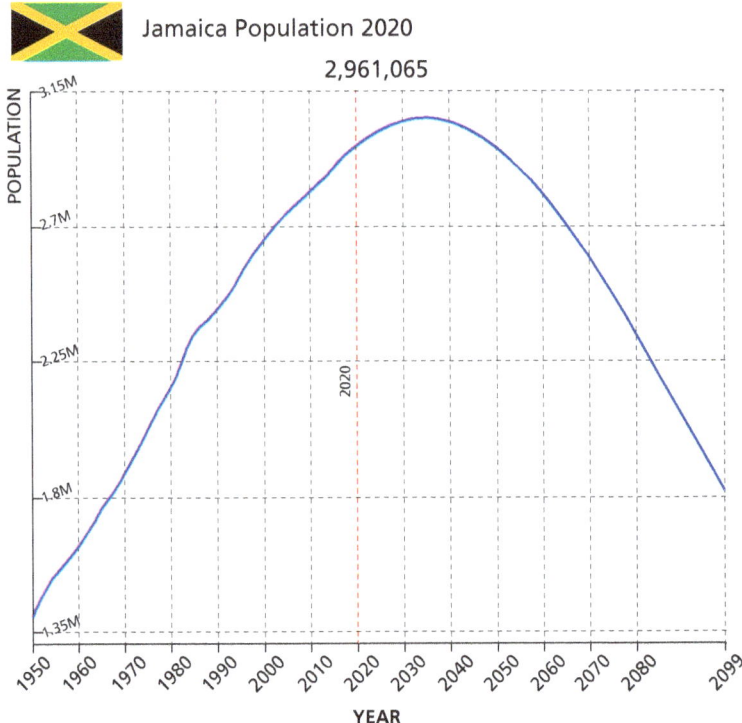

Figure 8.14 *Jamaica population line graph 1950–2099*

Bar graphs

These graphs are useful when showing population growth for a country as well as when comparing countries. The bars can be colour coded with an accompanying key to make for easy reading.

The bar chart here shows the age groups in Trinidad and Tobago taken from 2022 population statistics. The data presented here can also be used to construct an age-sex pyramid.

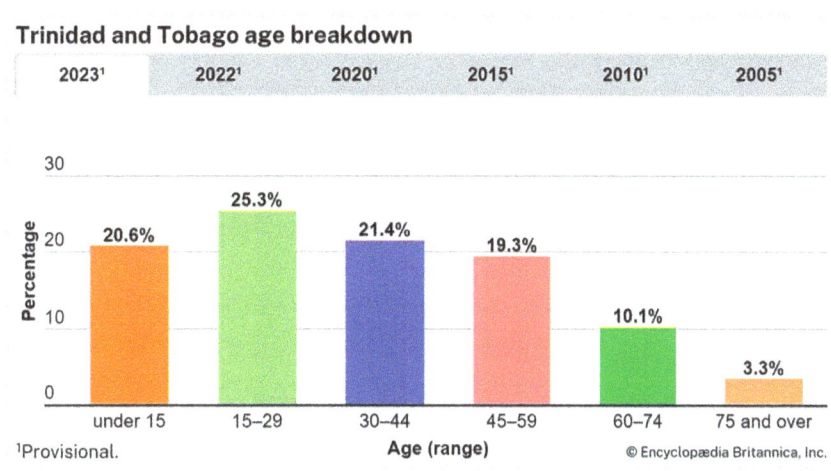

Figure 8.15 *Trinidad and Tobago age breakdown (2022)*

Pie charts

Pie charts resemble the segments of a circle where each variable is represented by a proportion of the whole. This type of chart is helpful since it can illustrate a large collection of data. For population statistics, it can be used to depict ages, occupations, ethnicities and religions. This chart can be colour coded and contain a key.

The pie chart below shows the ethnic composition of Grenada in 2011.

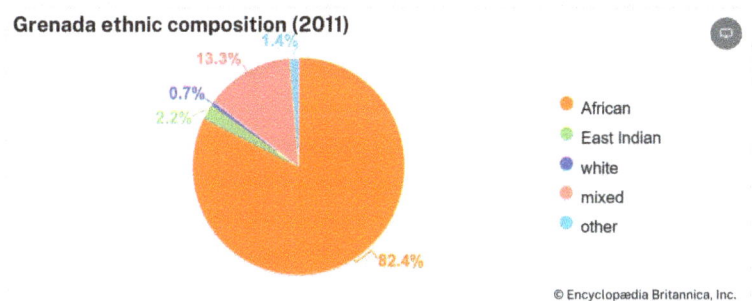

Figure 8.16 *Ethnic composition of Grenada in 2011*

End of chapter questions

1. a) Define the term 'dependency ratio'. (2 marks)
   b) Describe TWO uses of the dependency ratio in population planning. (4 marks)
   c) Life expectancy in the Caribbean ranges between 69.8 years in Guyana to 79.4 years in Antigua.
      (i) Suggest TWO actions governments may take to address the different life expectancies across the Caribbean. (4 marks)
      (ii) Explain why EACH action suggested in c) (i) is likely to be successful. (4 marks)

      TOTAL 14 marks

Section B(i)   Sustainable Development and Use of Resources

2. Population statistics are vital data used on the road to a nation's development. As a member of the Ministry of Planning and Development, prepare an address to be delivered to new data collection recruits.

Write an address in which you:
- define population
- outline TWO population indicators which reflect a nation's development
- explain TWO ways in which population statistics are used
- suggest THREE actions the Ministry will take by using the population statistics to drive development.
- explain how any TWO of the actions above are likely to be successful.

TOTAL 22 marks

Summary

The size, structure, composition and spread of a population is important in the understanding of any society. There are a number of social, economic, environmental and political impacts when a population is unmonitored and unprofiled. These include:

Social	Economic	Environmental	Political
Lack of social integration among ethnic or religious groups	Lack of jobs in particular fields	Strain on land and sea resources	Legislative decisions to control the population

Populations vary based on a number of indicators which can affect a country's level of development and sustainability. Experts analyse birth rates, death rates, life expectancy, dependency ratio, population density and distribution in a scientific manner to determine the effects of these on future life and levels of sustainability.

In order to obtain the raw data, several organisations are required to collect data and produce reports of their findings. One such data collection is a national census. The data collected is then used to inform decision-making in a current and long-term context. Population statistics are useful for development planning and decision-making. Some areas where planning is necessary include elections, housing, health care, education and employment.

Both population density and population distribution are affected by physical and human factors such as climate, soils, industry and agriculture. Maps are valuable when discussing these concepts as they help us visualise the data. Map reading is an essential skill to assist in the location of physical features, resources and patterns of settlement.

A population changes over time due to birth and death rates as well as migration. Birth rates are influenced by family planning methods, government policies, income and education levels and fertility rates. Death rates can be influenced by healthcare and nutrition, hygiene, epidemics, pandemics and natural disasters. Migration also accounts for movement into and out of a country which alters the structure and composition of the population.

Section B: Sustainable Development and Use of Resources
(i) Development and Use of Resources
9 Migration

The topics covered in this chapter are:
- the causes and consequences of migration
- the reasons for migration from Caribbean countries
- the global impact of migration from the Caribbean

The natural world has a migration season where some animals, such as the leatherback sea turtle, make their way to another destination to seek food or better weather conditions. Similarly, human migration involves a physical movement from one place to another, which can alter the size, density and distribution of a population. This impacts the economic, political, social and cultural dynamics of both the receiving and supply countries.

Causes and consequences of migration

Learning objectives
- Examine the causes and consequences of migration.
- Explore the reasons for migration from Caribbean countries.
- Analyse the global impact of migration from the Caribbean.

Important definitions

Migrant – an individual who has moved either within a country or to another country on a long-term basis.

Emigrant – an individual who has moved out of a country.

Immigrant – an individual who has moved into a country.

Refugee – an individual who arrives in another country having been forced to leave their country due to safety concerns.

Asylum seeker/asylee – an individual who is asking for international protection, as they cannot return to their home country due to safety issues.

Push factors – anything that prompts an individual to leave their place of origin.

Pull factors – anything that prompts an individual to move to a new area.

Brain drain – the movement of skilled individuals away from their home country.

Urban area – towns and cities with infrastructure and a high population density.

Rural area – agricultural lands with limited infrastructure and low population density.

Xenophobia – feeling of fear or dislike of people who originate from different cultural backgrounds.

Bigotry – prejudice or intolerance towards another social group.

Causes of migration

When we think about migration it is important to have an understanding of why people choose to move either within their region or further afield, and consider the challenges faced by those **migrants**. Statistics about current and historic migratory patterns are an important part of this understanding.

The Caribbean people in particular have always been on the move. The following shows some statistics from 2020.

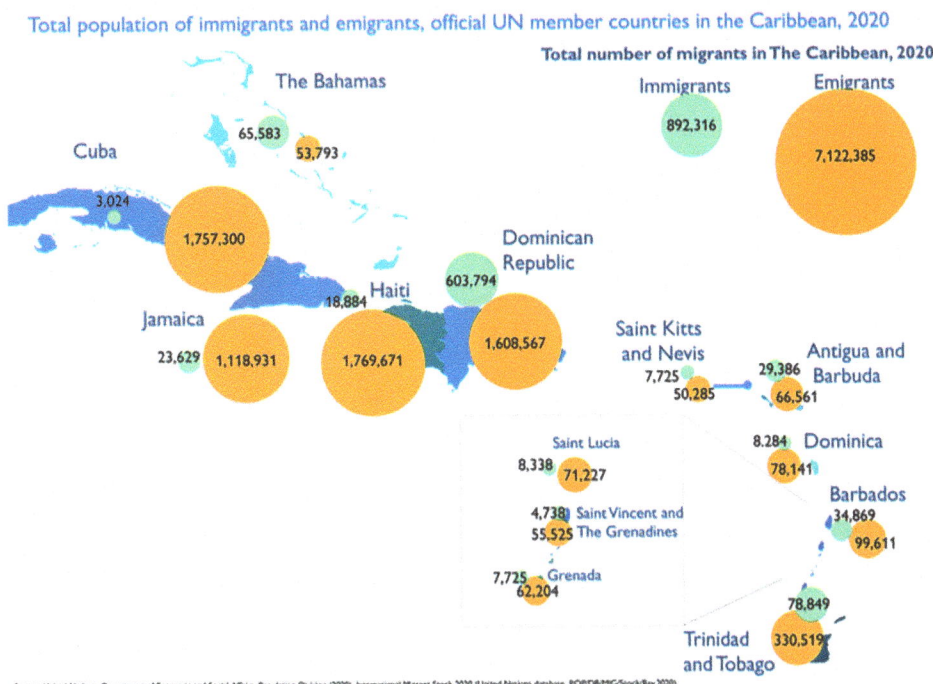

Figure 9.1 *Total number of immigrants and emigrants in the Caribbean, 2020*

Push and pull factors are what encourage individuals to move away from a place (emigration) or to move to a new destination (immigration).

Table 9.1 lists some push and pull factors.

Descriptors	Push factors	Pull factors
Economic	High unemployment rates can force people to move in search of work.	A stable economy will attract **migrants** for better job opportunities, better pay, better standard of living and quality of life.
Government policies	Strict government policies or unfair legal systems can encourage movement away from an area to find a fairer political environment.	Immigration policies such as Article 45 of the Revised Treaty (CSME) protects free movement of nationals of member states (CARICOM) to work.
Social factors	High crime rates and other social issues encourage people to move out of an area.	Improved communication networks and controlled social issues are attractive to migrants.
Educational opportunities	Poor educational infrastructure can prevent permanent settlement. People move to find better education prospects.	Access to recognised educational institutions can be attractive as it leads to employment in the future.
Variations in population growth	Too many people living in a geographical area (rural or urban) can encourage rural to urban or urban to rural movement.	People generally move to city areas with better facilities and amenities.

Section B(i) Sustainable Development and Use of Resources

Descriptors	Push factors	Pull factors
Conflict	Armed conflict and war force individuals to leave their home. Individuals are known as **refugees** and **asylum seekers**.	A generally safe area with greater security to live and work can convince a migrant to move.
Natural disasters	Floods, earthquakes, volcanic eruptions and hurricanes can force people to move.	Individuals are drawn to 'safe' zones, away from potential natural disasters such as in flood-controlled and inland areas.

Table 9.1

Case study

Montserrat has experienced a series of volcanic eruptions starting from 1995 which led to the displacement of people from the South of the island to the underdeveloped Northern region. Being a British Overseas Territory, the United Kingdom assisted with the relocation of about 75% of the population. In 1995 the population held at 10,324 but declined to 2,742 in 1998. The drastic decline has led to significant population changes and developmental concerns. The population now lies between 4000 and 5000 persons with an estimate of almost half being non-nationals from Jamaica, Guyana and the Dominican Republic. The local population have voiced their stereotypical beliefs about the newcomers which can impact the integration of the immigrants. The Jamaicans have been accused of violence and crime while the women from the Dominican Republican have been stigmatised as sex workers.

It is crucial for governments and international agencies to facilitate safe migration and collect quantitative data to better understand and manage migration flows. This can be challenging due to the consistent migration issues faced by Caribbean countries. Some useful steps to allow for effective migration controls would be:

- to monitor migratory patterns within the region among the documented and undocumented migrants
- to improve border management strategies while protecting vulnerable migrants
- promoting anti-trafficking legislation
- implementing policies to allow universal education for migrant school-aged children.

Consequences of migration

There are different consequences for each of the three 'actors' involved in migration. These three elements are the individual (migrant, refugee, **asylee**), the home country (country of origin) and the host country.

Refugees, IDPs, migrants... what's the difference?

CONCERN worldwide

Refugees
Flee their homes, cross an international border, and cannot return because they fear their lives are in danger.

IDPs
Flee their homes for the same reasons as refugees, but have not crossed an international border.

Asylum-Seekers
Flee their homes and claim they are refugees, but their status has not yet been definitively determined.

Migrants
Voluntarily leave their homes to settle permanently in another region of country for a variety of different reasons.

Figure 9.2 *Explanation of the different types of migrant*

IDPs are internally-displaced people.

Individual

An individual who voluntarily moves may have access to better educational opportunities in their new host country compared with their country of origin. This will improve the skills of the migrant and increase the possibility of employment. These individuals move with the prospect that their education and employment may be improved and they may return to their home country in the future.

Immigrants are usually seen as vulnerable groups facing a number of economic, social and cultural issues, which should be addressed with legal representation.

Economic	Social	Cultural
Largely underpaid, often receiving less than minimum wage	Exploited while working in unsanitary and unsafe conditions	Face racial discrimination

Migrant advocacy groups aim to provide support for these issues, help migrants fight exploitation in the workplace and lobby for fair treatment for these vulnerable groups.

The new concept of 'crimmigration', has contributed to a negative impression of immigrants in some countries, as encouraged by media coverage. Immigrants tend to be viewed with hostility and suspicion by the local population and labelled as 'illegal', leading to additional discrimination. This criminalisation of non-white migrants can lead to extreme situations of deportation or detention in the host country.

Individuals who become displaced due to armed conflict, unstable economies or natural disasters are often viewed as 'cheap' labour in the host country as they can be easily exploited. The local population may also be accused of **xenophobia** and **bigotry** as a result of their negative attitudes towards the refugees. These unfounded beliefs can make what is already a difficult situation for the refugees, even more challenging.

Country of origin

The movement of people away from the country of origin reduces the number of inhabitants in a particular geographical area which can lead to depopulation and **brain drain**. This can easily result in a high level of dependency as there is then pressure on the economically active to support the non-economically active population. Rural depopulation may be more pronounced as the amenities and facilities are less developed. Statistics presented by Our World in Data UN DESA (2020) revealed that many countries in the Caribbean experienced more emigration than immigration with only The Bahamas and Belize seeing higher immigration.

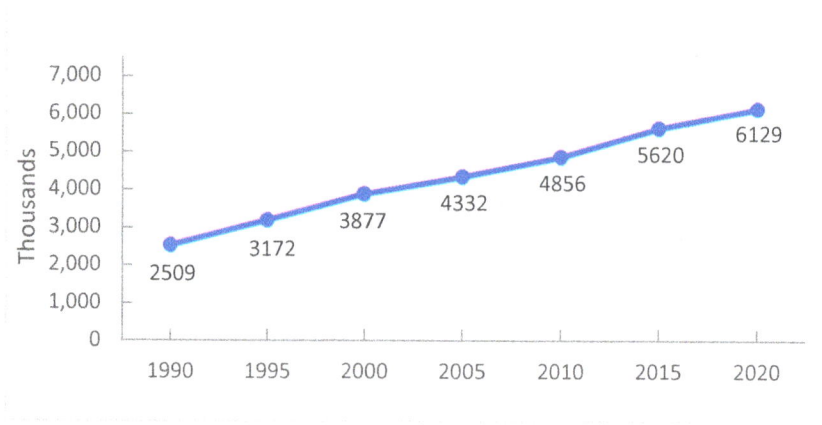

Figure 9.3a *Total number of emigrants in the Caribbean region 1990–2020*

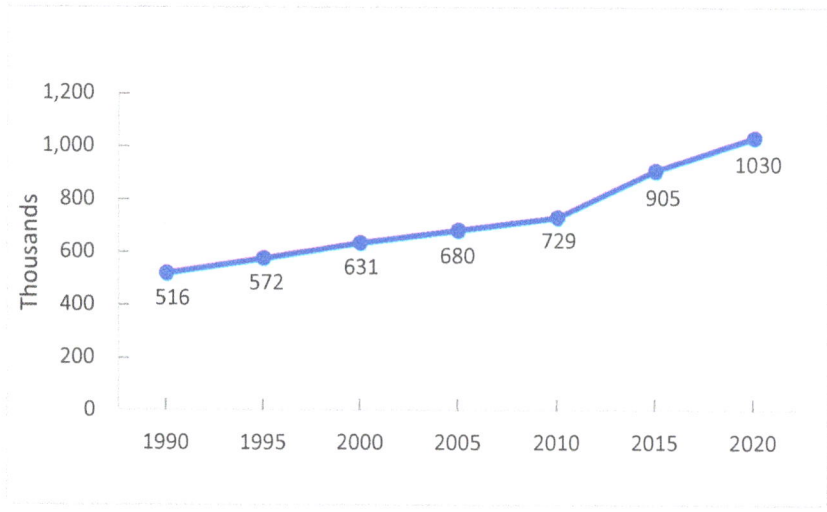

Source: UN DESA 2020.

Figure 9.3b *Total number of immigrants to the Caribbean region 1990–2020*

Another effect on the migrant's country of origin can be underpopulation, which is when there are not enough people in the country to use resources successfully.

Generally, emigration rates are caused by 'push' factors in the country of origin which encourages the movement. Evidence also suggests that the more educated an **emigrant** is, the more likely they are to want to move. Qualified, working age populations are more likely to explore better opportunities elsewhere leading to brain drain. The non-economically active population that remains can struggle with low productivity due to the lack of skilled individuals particularly in the health and education sectors.

Addressing the 'brain drain' issue

Country of origin	Host country
Create incentives to encourage people to stay	Enforce quotas. Immigration rates from supply countries should be fair otherwise the local population may be in competition with immigrants for jobs
Impose taxes on emigrants	Regulate the entry of migrants in high-skilled jobs

Return migration is also taking place in the Caribbean. The 2011 Jamaican census showed that more than 5% of the population were returnees with half of those being over 50 years old. Returnees can add value to the home country but if they only return at retirement age this can increase the dependency ratio.

Money sent back home from migrant workers to family members can be beneficial both to the welfare of the family as well as the economy. Family members have opportunities to improve nutrition, reduce poverty and offer their children more activities due to this extra money. In this way 'remittances', as they are known, generate finance for the home country. The United States is the preferred destination for Caribbean migrants and this is where most of the remittances come from.

The host country

The host country is the country that receives the immigrants. Migration brings challenges and opportunities for the host country. The influx of people can put a strain on infrastructure, resources and facilities. This can lead to overpopulation in some cases. Refugees and **asylum seekers** are often forced to live in low-quality housing which can result in 'squatting' or informal settlements in and around **urban areas**. This can have a negative impact on the sociocultural, economic and environmental landscape.

Sociocultural relates to social and cultural factors, including habits, traditions and beliefs.

Table 9.2 depicts the sociocultural, economic and environmental effects of migration in the host country.

Sociocultural	Economic	Environmental
Immigrants are able to live in a safe place.	Immigrants are able to use their skills to rebuild their lives and also contribute to the economy of the host country.	The host country creates new facilities and housing developments which both immigrants and nationals can occupy for better standards of living.
Immigrants bring their own cultures which add to diversity in the host country.	Individuals experience a high level of unemployment and underemployment. Any employment they can access is mainly informal.	A high density of people means more household refuse which could lead to rubbish on the streets if not collected.
The protection of migrant rights and the importance of migrant integration is included in government policies. **(SDG 10)**	Caribbean countries are small with comparatively small economies which can be negatively affected by the large arrival of undocumented migrants.	There is strain placed on land resources and use of fertile, agricultural areas for housing.

Table 9.2

Questions

Knowledge and comprehension

1. a) Define the terms 'push' and 'pull' factors.
   b) Describe TWO 'push' factors.

2. a) Define the term 'brain drain'.
   b) Describe how 'brain drain' can result from TWO 'push' factors which occur in the Caribbean.

3. a) Define the terms:
   (i) Immigration
   (ii) Emigration
   b) Outline TWO reasons why the rate of emigration can be greater than the rate of immigration.

Use of knowledge

4. 'Brain drain' and 'brain gain' are two sides of the same migration coin.'
   Examine this statement, giving suitable evidence from the Caribbean.

Reasons for migration

Employment

Starting in the 16th century, enslaved persons were brought to the Caribbean from West Africa to work on the sugar plantations. This was forced migration which ended in the 1800s in certain areas of the region. An alternative supply of labour came in the form of indentured labourers from India and China to continue the work on the sugar plantations.

Today, movement of people for work involves emigration to destination countries such as the United States, Canada and the UK, as well as within the Caribbean region, often due to high unemployment rates in the country of origin. Persons search for work outside of their immediate country to achieve better pay. A 2019 US American Community Survey showed that the healthcare and medical industry contained a lot of immigrant workers while the agricultural industry had far fewer Caribbean migrants working in it.

Some of key ideas should be noted:

- Between 2010 and 2020, emigration to Canada from Jamaica, Guyana and Trinidad increased. This was helped by the Canadian immigration system encouraging permanent residency to help their pandemic recovery. These new immigrants are helping to rebuild the economy by working, generating new jobs and supporting local enterprises.
- Within the Caribbean, in Guyana, Trinidad and Tobago, The Bahamas and Antigua and Barbuda, there was an increase in migration between 2010 and 2020. Guyana made significant oil and gas discoveries in 2015 which has encouraged regional movement of labour into this booming industry.

The COVID-19 pandemic saw the closure of many national borders. This government decision prevented nationals, migrants and refugees from entering countries in the hope of stopping the spread of the disease. Unemployment among migrants increased during this time, as businesses closed.

Natural disaster

The Caribbean region often suffers from natural disasters due to our location, dual seasons and the effects of climate change. Hurricanes such as Dorian in 2019 (The Bahamas), Maria in 2017 (Dominica) and the two earthquakes in Haiti (2010, 2021) left many people stranded, injured and displaced. In Haiti in 2010, people emigrated in large groups to South American countries as they did not require visas or admission arrangements. Later on, after the 2021 earthquake and continued political unrest in Haiti, people tried to reach the United States via difficult routes where migrants were largely undocumented. In 2021, La Soufriere volcano in St. Vincent erupted causing devastation to the island. More than 13,000 people were displaced with some wanting to leave to go to other countries. Neighbouring islands such as Barbados and Grenada were also affected by the ash and debris.

Figure 9.4 *Many Haitians have had to leave their country due to recent earthquakes*

Education

Education is a basic right for all individuals, including people on the move. Individuals who move for educational purposes can be:

- from middle-class backgrounds who want to train for white collar jobs and are able to pay for tuition and accommodation. A study visa for international purposes makes the travel process easier
- from areas with limited educational opportunities that may not be able to access secondary or tertiary education. Sometimes the assumption is that the 'right education' is considered to be a foreign one, and studying abroad brings prestige. This overseas education will then lead to better jobs, either in the home country or the host country
- from families who support and prioritise higher learning.

Some countries in the Caribbean offer students full scholarships upon success at the C.A.P.E level, giving them the opportunity to study in different parts of the world. In 2020, the Barbados Education Ministry announced that 11 students were successful at Exhibitions and received full tuition payment, health insurance and living allowance for further study in either the UK, United States or Canada.

Social services

Social services describes the public services offered to particular groups in society. Migrants and refugees often move to access quality health care in host countries. Caribbean migrants to the USA, UK and Canada are often looking for healthcare services which are more cost effective than local procedures. In some countries such as Jamaica and Trinidad and Tobago, nurses and other health professionals often move to seek better wages and more employment opportunities which reduces the number of these professionals available for the local population.

Asylum

Across the globe, people ask for international protection because of political, social and economic problems, conflict and food insecurity in their home country. Within the Caribbean, Venezuelans have moved both as migrants and as refugees to nearby countries such as Trinidad and Tobago, Guyana, Aruba and Curacao. The main 'push' factor has been the political turmoil brought on by the economic crisis, when world oil prices dropped suddenly in 2014 and 2016. Host countries such as the US and Canada have helped to accommodate the Venezuelans by creating refugee resettlement initiatives, which focus particularly on the needs of women, children, young people and those with disabilities.

Global impact of migration from the Caribbean

Economy

The economies of countries such as Canada, UK and the USA are boosted by migration, and their productivity levels are increased. Migrants spend money in their host countries, and pay taxes, boosting revenue. Temporary or seasonal work programmes such as SAWP (Seasonal Agricultural Worker Program) in Canada and H-2A in the US provides the agricultural sector with temporary labour from English-speaking Caribbean countries when there is a shortage of local labour. Canada in particular has low fertility rates and an aging labour force which makes economic immigrants essential. Young, skilled migrants are often employed in tertiary and quaternary sectors.

Jamaicans in particular have taken advantage of the Temporary Foreign Worker programme in Canada. Jamaicans with disabilities have also been able to take advantage of the programme.

Spread of Caribbean culture

Members of the Caribbean nations living abroad are known as the diaspora. They help preserve and spread our cultural practices in their host countries, supporting a relationship between the host country and the country of origin. There is evidence that immigrants in host countries feel a sense of reconnection, solidarity, pride and power being part of such a group.

Figure 9.5 *Notting Hill Carnival, London*

Canada has been considered the 'poster child' for multiculturalism since their open border policies embrace all cultures and religions. They have been celebrating Toronto Caribbean Carnival (formerly Caribana Toronto) since the 1960s promoting 'West Indian-ness' through dance, music and costumes. The United States and the United Kingdom have also recognised their Caribbean diaspora residents and their culture through the sale of local foods and grocery supplies, cultural education through the teaching of pan and carnival celebrations such as Notting Hill Carnival in London.

Increased presence and influence in the global sphere

Political influence

Host countries such as the USA can attribute a large chunk of their economic success to the Caribbean immigrants of Cuba, Jamaica, Dominican Republic and Haiti. In 2022, the US State Department renewed the 'Cuban Family Reunification Parole' program which allows green card holders the ability to apply

Figure 9.6 *Makeshift boat carrying Cuban migrants attempting to reach Florida, USA*

for Cuban relatives to be allowed to come to the USA to get a green card of their own. Previously, the 'wet foot, dry foot' policy (1995–2017), allowed Cubans the right to stay in America once they landed on American land. If they were intercepted at sea, they were returned to Cuba.

Cubans have a rich connection with the US ever since the 1959 Cuban revolution, which saw white, middle class, well-off political refugees move from Cuba to Miami, and develop it into a viable city. Although the dynamics have changed and Cubans are now viewed as economic migrants, their position among other immigrants remains recognised. There is hope that other Latinos such as Guatemalans, Mexicans and Colombians will benefit from new programmes and policies.

Cultural influence

Caribbean migrants practice their traditions which host governments recognise as a money-making opportunity. For example:

- Carnival celebrations in Toronto, Notting Hill and the US bring visitors from all parts of the world to participate, generating revenue. These celebrations are not only cultural but iconic and cohesive for the host country and the country of origin.
- Local, established businesses supplying Caribbean goods and foods, not only to migrant populations, but also to the locals.
- Caribbean musicians are recognised on an international scale. The steelpan, the national instrument of Trinidad and Tobago, is showcased in many international forums and included in the curriculum of some schools in the host countries.

Figure 9.7 *Toronto Caribbean Carnival*

Educational influence

Host countries promote Caribbean interests by including studies of the region in education programmes. At some foreign universities, cultural studies programmes now include Caribbean Studies to facilitate the understanding of culturally diverse migrant groups. Cuban history has also been included in Miami's school curriculum.

Social services

The high standards of social services provided by the host country is often one of the reasons why migrants choose to move there. However, heavy migration can put a strain on housing, health services and education systems.

Barriers to access of social services

Table 9.3 displays the barriers that migrants face to social services.

Housing	Health	Education
Limited availability of housing	High fees are incurred in host countries with no free healthcare	Language barrier
Housing often not affordable for migrants	Refugees and migrants are often excluded from national medical programmes	Lack of integration in formal settings

Table 9.3

Questions

Knowledge and comprehension

1 State the difference between a refugee and an asylum seeker.

2 a) List TWO types of natural disasters which have impacted the Caribbean and caused people to move from their country.

b) Outline TWO ways in which the receiving countries can reduce the negative effects on displaced individuals.

3 Read this quote from the Jamaica Observer newspaper.

'According to data provided by the Statistical Institute of Jamaica (Statin), Jamaica's "net migration" numbers amounted to 269,991 from 2002 to 2019.'

a) Define the term 'net migration'.

b) Outline TWO consequences of these statistics to Jamaican society.

Use of Knowledge

4 Explain the significance of Caribbean culture to a host country like Canada.

5 Suggest THREE ways that Caribbean countries can maintain a positive net migration.

6 Work in groups to discuss the reasons why some countries have placed barriers on migration.

SBA skills

1. Read the following case study and conduct research on ONE migrant support group located in your country. You can include items such as:
   - the group's history and (formal) structure
   - success stories
   - their programmes to meet migrant needs.

Case study

Little Amal

This 12-foot tall rod puppet was created by Handspring Puppet Company to bring the story to life, through theatre/public art, of a 10-year-old Syrian refugee girl in search of her mother due to war in her home country. Her name is Arabic, meaning hope, as she offers hope to all the displaced and marginalised people in the world. She uses non-verbal communication to send her message across the continents.

The message she communicates is simple: 'Don't forget about us.' Embrace and rethink the issue of refugees, especially children, encourage empathy and observe that these groups are vulnerable yet resilient.

Figure 9.8 Little Amal

Her journey started in Europe in 2021 during the COVID-19 restrictions and since then she has travelled 16 countries. As of 2024 she was in Australia, where she continues to spread awareness and stand in solidarity with asylum seekers.

2. Look at the bar graph below and make TWO comparative statements about the history of migration in Jamaica.

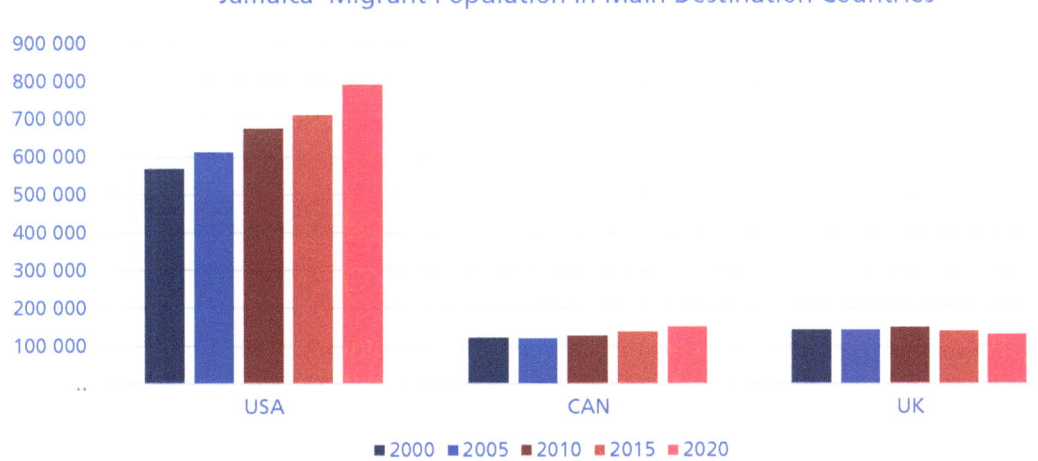

Figure 9.9 *Bar graph showing the history of migration in Jamaica*

Section B(i) Sustainable Development and Use of Resources

3. Conduct an interview with a migrant from your community about their experience of leaving their home country. Include details such as the language barrier, cultural differences and the treatment by the local population. You can use the following interview schedule as a reference point.

Migrant interview

Date:

Interviewee: (give some bio information)

Sex	Age range	Period of time in host country	Place of origin

Questions	Responses
Personal drives	
Why did you leave your home country?	
What did you hope to encounter when you decided to leave your country?	
Why did you select this destination?	
Was the decision yours to come here?	
Arriving here	
Do you feel safe here?	
Do you have a job?	
Do fellow nationals treat you differently?	
What are some challenges that you faced initially when you came?	
What do you appreciate here?	
What message would you send to other migrants like yourself?	

End of chapter questions

1. a) Define the term 'migration'. (2 marks)
   b) Outline TWO consequences of forced migration on young children. (4 marks)
   c) Caribbean emigration patterns have been increasing in recent years.
      (i) Suggest TWO actions Caribbean governments may take to address this. (4 marks)
      (ii) Explain why EACH action suggested in c) (i) is likely to be successful. (4 marks)
      TOTAL 14 marks

2. a) Define the term 'xenophobia'. (2 marks)
   b) Describe TWO consequences of migration on the individual. (4 marks)
   c) The movement of refugees and asylum seekers has been on the rise in the Caribbean.
      (i) Suggest TWO actions that Caribbean governments can implement to address this situation. (4 marks)
      (ii) Explain why EACH action suggested in (c) (i) is likely to be successful. (4 marks)
      TOTAL 14 marks

SUSTAINABLE DEVELOPMENT AND USE OF RESOURCES
The push and pull factors are the cornerstone of migration

3. A newly formed youth activist group for migrants in your community is having their first public meeting addressing the topic above.
   Prepare a formal speech in which you:

   - define the term 'migration'
   - identify a push and pull factor
   - outline TWO challenges which affect migrants in the host country
   - suggest THREE actions the government might take to meet the challenges of large migrant groups
   - explain why any TWO of these actions are likely to be successful.

   TOTAL 22 marks

Summary

The migration process has been very important in the development of the Caribbean. Historically, immigration played a big role in Caribbean economies while emigration, which came much later, is a more complex process.

People move for many reasons. We call these the 'push' and 'pull factors' of migration. Migrants, refugees and asylees are encouraged to leave their home countries due to:

- economic hardship
- social difficulties
- strict government policies
- severe effects of natural disasters
- conflict situations.

Migrants, refugees and asylees are attracted to:

- work opportunities
- open immigration policies
- educational prospects
- improved infrastructure
- safe environments.

In deciding whether to move, individuals take into account the distance to be covered (internal, intraregional or international), the cost, as well as their future prospects.

There are benefits and drawbacks to consider for both the country of origin and the host country when people migrate.

Table 9.4 shows some of the benefits and drawbacks of migration.

Descriptor	Country of origin		Host country	
	Benefits	Drawbacks	Benefits	Drawbacks
Economic	Remittances (money) are sent home to family members from migrants	Highly skilled population migrate reducing development 'Brain drain'	A 'cheap' supply of labour which boosts economic development 'Brain gain'	Money earned is often sent to home country
Political	Returning migrants add value to the society through skill transfer	Immigration policies can deny certain individuals	Immigration policies can be designed to 'invite' residents	Too many people seeking refugee and asylee status
Social	Better relations with other countries	Family members are apart for long periods	Integrated society	In some cases, human rights of migrants can be infringed
Cultural	Exposure to different ways of life through returnees	Loss of cultural practices as young, skilled people have migrated	The growth of a multicultural society	Spread of xenophobia and bigotry among nationals

Table 9.4

Section B: Sustainable Development and Use of Resources
(i) Development and Use of Resources
10 Human Resources

The topics covered in this chapter are:
- the need for developing human resources
- the factors that contribute to the development of human resources
- the factors that influence employment, unemployment and underemployment
- employment and career opportunities in different industries

The human population of a country can help it to reach its potential. The human resources of a country include the abilities, experiences, expertise, skills and talents of the population. If this **human capital** contains a skilled workforce with a strong work ethic, it can make a significant contribution to the development of a country.

Developing human resources

Learning objectives
- Explain the need for developing human resources.
- Explain the factors that contribute to the development of human resources.

Important definitions

Human capital – the skills, knowledge and innovation in a population, used to develop a nation.

Human resource – the people of a country who are able to perform tasks to develop the country.

Labour force – the number of people who are legally allowed to work, consisting of the employed and the unemployed of legal working age.

Nutrition – the food and water we take in to supply the body with nutrients for good health.

Health – the physical, social and emotional wellbeing of an individual.

Inclusive education – the involvement and acceptance of all types of learners in an educational space.

Food security – the 1996 World Food Summit describes food security as 'when all people, at all times, have physical and economic access to sufficient safe and nutritious food that meets their dietary needs and food preferences for an active and healthy life.'

Lifestyle diseases – any illness which happens due to the personal choices and habits that people adopt during their daily life.

Development of the human resource

The **human resource** consists of people who can work to improve the social, economic, political and cultural life of a country. It is therefore important and necessary that the human resource be trained to contribute in a way which suits the needs of the country.

Human resource development is necessary to give individuals the opportunity to improve their abilities in a wide range of areas. Persons can then complete tasks more efficiently and gain personal rewards and benefits as a result. 21st century skills are introduced in the classroom and help to prepare students for the workplace.

Organisations and businesses need productive workers who can show initiative and meet expectations. These workers also request regular feedback from their employers to work on their professional development.

Creativity, critical thinking and problem-solving skills are used by workers to solve challenges and issues. As the business world becomes more complex and competitive, workers need to adopt a universal approach to match the high levels of connection, integration and collaboration across the world.

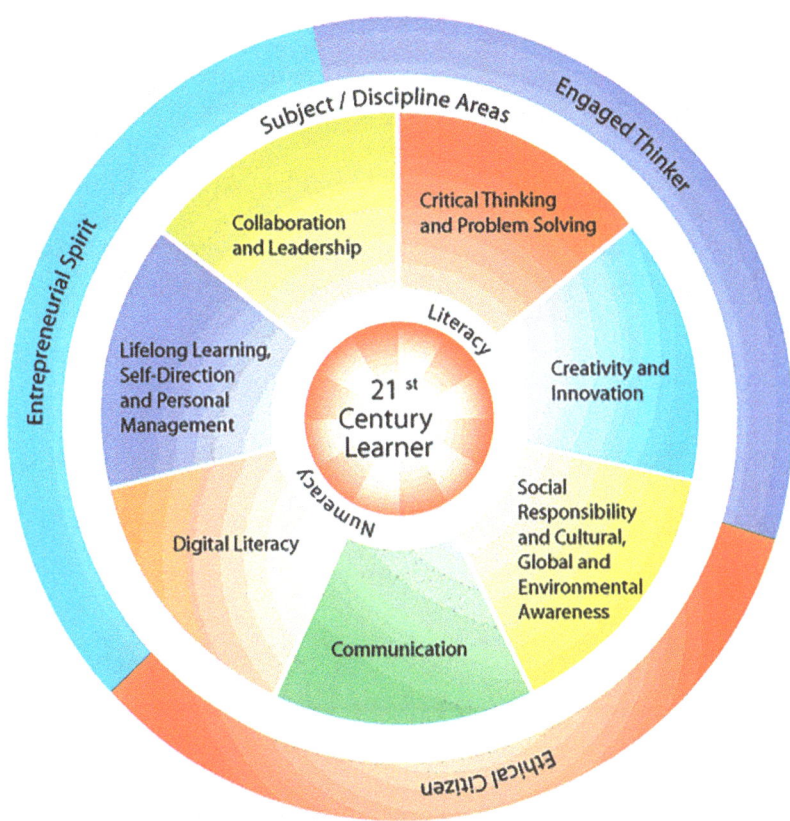

Figure 10.1 *21st century skills*

Factors that contribute to the development of the human resource

A high level of cooperation and integration is necessary among private and public agencies to deliver services across a country.

Nutrition and health

Figure 10.2 *Healthy food is very important*

Section B(i) Sustainable Development and Use of Resources

Nutrition and **health** go hand in hand in maintaining our wellbeing. Nutrition involves making sure we eat a variety of foods from different food groups in healthy portion sizes, to make sure we give our bodies all the nutrients they need. These nutrients are used for daily bodily functions. The UN SDG 2 aims to achieve **food security** and zero hunger, improving nutrition and promoting sustainable agriculture by 2030.

We can use nutrition as an indicator of a country's development. If the population of a country can access an adequate supply of healthy food, they can achieve proper nutrition. Conversely, poor nutrition indicates that people are not meeting daily nutritional requirements, are either underweight or overweight, or are not consuming specific micronutrients such as Iron, Zinc or Vitamin A.

Factors affecting nutrition include:

- Poverty: people not being able to afford much food, or quality food, due to their economic situation
- Income inequality: people not having access to formal education, meaning their earning power is limited, and thus continuing a cycle of poverty
- Lack of resources: people generally not having access to healthcare or education
- Inadequate food systems: poor agricultural practices rather than sustainable agriculture, lack of available farming land.

Malnutrition is when a person does not take in enough nutrients to allow their body to function properly. In the Caribbean there is concern about the 'double burden of malnutrition' which refers to the combination of 'overnutrition' (obesity and being overweight) in children and adults while undernutrition is also an issue within the same society.

Table 10.1 presents the effects of malnutrition.

Undernutrition	Overweight	Obesity	Non-communicable diseases
– Stunting – height measurements in relation to age – Wasting – weight measurements in relation to age	High weight measurements in relation to age	Excess body fat among the adult population	Chronic conditions which include diabetes, cardiovascular disease and some cancers

Table 10.1

This line graph shows the level of malnutrition in children under 5 in Jamaica between 2000 and 2020.

Prevalence of stunting, wasting and overweight in children under 5 years of age

Figure 10.3 *Infant and child nutrition statistics 2000–2020 in Jamaica*

When a country has high levels of malnutrition, there is a higher risk of early death and diseases which costs the country a lot to manage. Some Caribbean national nutrition policies include the promotion of healthy lifestyles through quality nutrition education (Trinidad and Tobago), educational campaigns within schools offering healthy food and drink options (Jamaica, Barbados, The Bahamas) and agricultural programmes geared towards food security (Guyana).

Health

You may have heard the phrase 'a healthy nation is a wealthy nation'. If the population has access to clean water, proper sanitation and suitable healthcare services, then they will be able to maintain a high level of productivity while reducing health costs.

The SDG 3 (good health and wellbeing), covers many areas including healthy diets, promoting breastfeeding in infants, nutritional care of pregnant women as well as the nutritional care of persons living with HIV and other conditions.

If a country can ensure its human resource is healthy it will benefit in terms of long term growth and development. However, many countries are currently not meeting their established nutrition targets. Climate change has severely impacted global temperatures leading to droughts, famines and altered ecosystems in different parts of the world. The secondary effects of the COVID-19 pandemic have continued to affect child nutrition.

Primary and curative healthcare

Healthcare services are geared towards the promotion, preservation and rehabilitation of the population's health. Both primary and secondary healthcare is needed to maintain universal health coverage and protect the fundamental right to health.

Primary or preventive healthcare

This type of healthcare is focused on personal choices and responsibilities, with the support of government healthcare policies and public information campaigns. However, some persons may still not appreciate the role they play in their own health, which may lead to poor lifestyle choices and ultimately poor health.

Lifestyle diseases including diabetes, cancer, cardiovascular disease and depression can be increased by both personal as well as secondary factors. There are several ways to prevent and potentially reduce these diseases by changing behaviours and habits. Exercise, reducing salt and alcohol intake, not smoking and reducing stress levels can prevent these lifestyle diseases.

In Caribbean countries, several initiatives have been undertaken to support primary healthcare. For example, in Antigua and Barbuda Health Aides and Assistant Nursing Personnel have been employed. In St. Lucia, the government has introduced policies to support the primary healthcare system and established universal healthcare regardless of a person's ability to pay. Dominica has also worked hard to provide equitable primary health care which is both affordable and accessible. There is a built-in level of resilience.

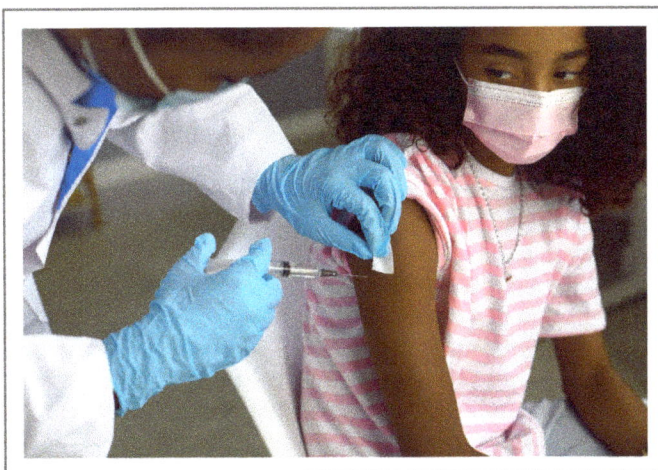

Figure 10.4 *Immunisation is a form of preventative healthcare*

Section B(i)　Sustainable Development and Use of Resources

There are however some countries that experience several challenges which affect the Universal Health Coverage standards. Trinidad and Tobago was rated as having one of the lowest proportion of primary health care physicians by PAHO (Pan American Health Organisation) in 2011. Specialised areas such as nutrition educators, psychologists, medical social workers and psychiatric social workers were also in short supply according to data collected in 2019. This personnel shortage has affected the distribution of healthcare workers between rural and urban areas as well as between the public and private sectors.

Secondary or curative healthcare

This type of healthcare involves the treatment of any health-related issues. Once an individual has contracted an illness or disease, they should seek medical attention or emergency care at doctor's surgeries, hospitals, rehabilitative centres and specialised institutions.

Table 10.2 outlines the practices and services received under the two types of healthcare.

Figure 10.5 *An ambulance in Grenada*

Primary healthcare	Secondary healthcare
Maintaining a healthy diet and proper hygiene	Specialist care for specific illnesses
Engaging in exercise	Referral from primary healthcare provider
Taking vitamins and ensuring immunisations are up to date	Vaccinations against certain infectious diseases
Environmental clean-up programmes	
National healthcare awareness drives through media adverts	
Public policies about food preparation in the service industry	

Table 10.2

There are instances where access to primary and secondary healthcare poses challenges. These instances prevent inclusive care and equal access to healthcare.

Table 10.3 highlights the barriers to healthcare access.

Economic	Shortage of medical personnel	Geographic distribution of healthcare services	Level of education
Socioeconomic status can contribute to reduced access to healthcare services	Doctors, nurses and specialists in short supply in relation to the size of the population	Majority of medical resources located in urban centres meaning the rural population is at a disadvantage	Access can be affected by the education level of potential patients

Table 10.3

Education

Apart from ensuring that the population has proper nutrition and is making healthy life decisions, governments must ensure that universal education is delivered in a structured manner. Education is the acquisition of skills needed for the future. It is delivered in many forms and at different levels to cater to the needs of society.

Basic education is classed as primary and lower secondary school education. Students are given basic instruction in literacy and numeracy and some wider concepts. These skills are very useful as they provide a sound foundation for the future.

Moral education teaches social values at a young age. Learning ethical, social and civic values can lead to well-rounded members of society, who can demonstrate resilience and empathy. Moral education starts at home, is extended in school and at places of worship and benefits the wider society.

The main goal of the Primary Health and Family Life Education Curriculum is to instil proper attitudes, morals and values. It has been adopted by many Caribbean countries.

Technical and vocational education and training (TVET) is a form of education where students receive training related to specific occupations. This type of formal and informal education teaches the specialised skills to contribute to the economy of the nation. Traditionally, face-to-face instruction and demonstrations were used in this kind of education. However, recently blended learning has been adopted to cater for different learning styles and to allow flexibility for the learner.

Professional training refers to quality training, skills training and team training. This involves keeping skills up to date and relevant to improve the working environment. This should be a regular exercise in every workplace as certain elements change and additional training is necessary.

Rehabilitation. Although education is universal, there is not always equal access to it. This can lead to individuals dropping out of school, juvenile delinquency, suspensions and expulsions. Student rehabilitation can help solve these situations through remediation, teacher training and the provision of alternative youth facilities.

Retraining is necessary to ensure that education providers can keep up with changes in curriculum, technology and students' experiences. In particular, teachers must retrain to learn how to incorporate new technology into their teaching through e-learning platforms, game-based learning and automated assessments, among others.

Lifelong learning is the process of absorbing new knowledge after traditional schooling has finished. It allows individuals the opportunity to gain new skills for employment but also for their own personal enjoyment. A lifelong learner should:

- develop a passion for reading
- keep the company of like-minded individuals
- teach others
- prioritise learning.

Types of educational institutions

In order to produce a workforce with various skills and abilities, education systems must be tailored to the different needs of the population. SDG 4 – **quality education** emphasises equal opportunities for all, where individuals are given fair access to lifelong learning. **Inclusive education** ensures all learners, no matter their financial, racial, learning or even health background can have equal access to an education. There are a number of levels of formal education in Caribbean countries.

Pre-primary educational institutions

The first level of learning starts between three and five years where children are brought together to learn social skills and simple concepts to prepare them for learning literacy and numeracy once they reach school. Early childhood development services work with children across the country to provide quality and equal access to these fundamental services across the country. These services are provided either by the government or private establishments, and are regulated by the government to ensure standards are maintained.

Figure 10.6 *A primary school classroom in Trinidad*

Primary educational institutions

The next level of formal education is primary school. Students aged five to 11 years old are taught a range of subjects as they progress to a national exam. This level is important to deliver core values across subjects and prepare students to be placed in secondary schools based on their merit and academic ability.

Figure 10.7 *Students at a primary school in St. Lucia*

The goal at all levels of education is to promote quality and equity but this is not always the case. In the primary school system, there is often a clear difference between the government schools and private institutions. There are high levels of illiteracy which can be linked to high levels of student absenteeism and low socio-economic status. This can place students at a disadvantage when entering the next educational stage.

Secondary educational institutions

At this level, students aged 11 to 18 are offered a broad range of subjects to equip them with a wide

Figure 10.8 *Secondary schools include Music in the curriculum*

variety of skills. Schools deliver education at various levels to help students access job opportunities in the future.

At the lower school level (Forms 1–3 / Grades 7–9) subjects can include Modern Languages (French and Spanish), Modern Studies (Geography, Social Studies and History), Visual and Performing Arts (Visual Arts, Theatre Arts and Music) and TVET (Home Economics, Food and Nutrition and Technology Education).

At the upper school level (Forms 4–5 / Grades 10–11) subjects can include Business (Principles of Business, Principles of Accounts and Economics), Science (Biology, Physics and Chemistry) and Mathematics (Mathematics, Additional Mathematics and Information Technology). At this stage, students sit the CSEC (Caribbean Secondary Education Certificate) examinations in a minimum of eight subjects, including Mathematics and English. If successful, they can either enter the world of work or continue in the secondary school system.

Form 6 / Grades 12–13 is an additional two years where students are able to select subjects to specialise in. Students build on their earlier education as some subjects have entry requirements. For example, in order to study Pure Mathematics, individuals should have successfully completed Additional Mathematics at the upper school level.

Subjects at this level range from Sociology, Law, Chemistry, Digital Media and Food and Nutrition. Students must also study Caribbean Studies and Communication Studies which involve developing cultural understanding, critical thinking and communication skills which will be useful in the workplace, or in further study. Students then sit the Caribbean Advanced Proficiency Examination (CAPE) which officially marks the end of secondary school.

Educational facilities come in various different forms, and produce students of varying academic abilities. Some people believe that single-sex schools, which are mainly religious schools, perform better academically. Co-educational schools, which are government funded, are often considered to perform less well academically. This reflects a number of differences: unequal opportunities, different levels of investment and competition to gain entry to top performing schools.

Tertiary educational institutions

Figure 10.9 *Woodworking students in Guyana*

This refers to organisations such as universities (public and private), colleges, technical training (teacher training) and vocational institutes which offer their students specialised courses. Individuals are able to gain varied skills which may be academic or vocational.

Continued higher education is beneficial as it increases the likelihood of finding employment, and earning more from that employment. Students are able to receive a certificate, associate's degree, bachelor's degree, master's degree or even a doctoral degree.

Tertiary studies can be expensive, but financial assistance is available to some students. This may be from the institution itself, through grants given by public and private donors as well as through student loans.

Table 10.4 shows numbers of students enrolled on undergraduate degree programmes at the University of the West Indies campuses.

Campus	2020/2021	2021/2022
Cave Hill, Barbados	5530	5231
Mona, Jamaica	5510	4824
St. Augustine, Trinidad	10,769	10,455

Table 10.4

From the numbers above, students were enrolled in Engineering, Food and Agriculture, Humanities and Education, Law, Medical Sciences, Science and Technology, Social Sciences and Sports.

Financial resources and scholarships

Governments around the region have invested funds in the education sector to help students get the most benefit from their time in the school system. School grants for textbooks, laptop and tablet distribution, school food programmes, teacher training and remedial education programmes are some of the ways in which financial support is given to raise educational standards.

Awarding scholarships is a continued investment in the human capital, as students are given opportunities to continue their education at home or abroad based on their academic excellence.

Sports

Earlier in the chapter we discussed that taking part in sports can be viewed as part of primary healthcare. It can also stand on its own merits in terms of development of the human resource. Encouraging and engaging young people in physical activities is a necessity for good living and developing a positive outlook on life.

Sports should be seen as:

- more than just leisure activities but as a way to forge an industry
- more than physical activity but as a way to build community through youth development
- more than competition but as a way to diversify tourism and bring about nation building.

Figure 10.10 *Under 11 badminton player from Barbados*

Physical Education was added to the school curriculum by CXC (Caribbean Examinations Council) in 2003. Teachers have been appropriately trained, but in some countries the physical infrastructure and equipment were not at the required standard and this continues to be a challenge in some areas.

Sports is directly linked to the employability of young people who continue with the subject at the tertiary level. A number of institutions offer degrees, masters and postgraduate diplomas in related fields such as sports management, sports coaching, sports studies and sports and physical literacy which have all become very attractive options in the job market.

Governments across the region have invested in recreational opportunities to ensure the people are physically and mentally well. For example, in Trinidad and Tobago the National Sports Policy 2017–2027 has as its themes: 'development of sport' and 'sport for development'. In Barbados, the National Sports Policy 2022–2032 aims at 're-imagining the future of Sports' by 'building a more active Barbados'.

Sportspersons are global professionals who:

- display high levels of discipline and focus which makes them effective role models and positive influencers in the community
- attract the attention of international media and corporate sponsorship. This can boost the economy and enhance sports professionalism in the region.

Figure 10.11 *Usain Bolt became the most well-known sprinter in the world*

Culture

The human resource of a country needs to be healthy, educated and given the opportunity to learn new skills and use them in the workplace. It is also important that the human resource feels connected to the society they live and work in.

Governments promote culture to recognise the talents that people possess, to promote traditional values, to protect cultural practices that may be losing significance and to generate local, regional and international interest. The population will feel invested in the nation when there is general appreciation and focus on the local cultural practices from all levels in society.

We live in a multicultural environment which means frequent cultural exchanges in the form of ideas, innovation and interactions. This can lead to a high level of tolerance which makes for a productive society.

Questions

Knowledge and comprehension

1. Define the following terms:
   a) Human resource
   b) Health
   c) Education

2. Describe TWO types of healthcare provided by your country.

3. Identify and describe the levels of education offered in your country.

4. Outline THREE ways that the government of your country can develop the human resources.

5. List TWO sporting activities offered in your country and describe the benefit of the activities to:
   a) the individual
   b) the country

Use of knowledge

6. Discuss the benefits of sports and physical education to the development of the human resource.

7. Examine TWO strategies that governments can use to attract more young people into the sporting field.

8. Suggest THREE ways that the government of the country can suitably prepare young people to become productive members in society.

9. Explain TWO drawbacks in the subject offerings at your school which might affect your preparedness and participation in the world of work. Suggest alternatives for a better outcome.

SBA skills

1. Read the following article and create a set of interview questions for secondary school students about their participation in the extra lesson classes.

> The Government will provide $1billion in the upcoming fiscal year, for the employment of temporary teachers to help students recover from learning loss experienced during the disruption of face-to-face classes.
>
> This will be primarily facilitated through the Ministry of Education and Youth's Extra Lessons Programme.
>
> The disclosure was made by Prime Minister, the Most Hon. Andrew Holness, while he made his contribution to the 2022/23 Budget Debate in the House of Representatives on Thursday (March 17).
>
> In his remarks, he noted that since the launch of the programme, 2,100 students have registered for the online teaching method, while 11,926 have registered and "are now engaged in the face-to-face extra-lesson classes".
>
> Further breakdown of the registration shows that 6,175 are secondary students, while 5,751 are from primary schools.
>
> "I want to encourage our students and parents to take advantage of this extra-lesson support, to begin to make up for the learning loss," he urged.
>
> *Jamaica Information Service*

Employment, unemployment and underemployment

Societal members, once they reach a certain age, engage in activities to provide for their overall existence. They are able to match their skills and qualifications with a particular type of job, so jobs are completed skillfully and efficiently. This is a necessary part of life so that they can satisfy their needs and wants.

Learning objectives

- Explain the factors that influence employment, unemployment and underemployment.
- Outline employment and career opportunities in different industries.

Important definitions

Employment – when an individual is in a job and receives payment for the work that they do.

Unemployment – when an individual does not have a job.

Underemployment – when an individual is overqualified for the job that they currently hold.

Unemployable – when an individual cannot find a job for a particular reason, for example due to a disability, lack of numeracy or literacy or where they possess a poor track record.

Self-employment – when an individual works for themselves rather than for someone else or a company.

Employable/Employability – when an individual has the right attributes to be able to find and keep a job. This means they have the correct skills and qualifications, a good work ethic and a good level of experience.

Entrepreneurship – when an individual or group of individuals use an innovative idea to start a business with the intent of making a profit.

Capital – the total of all the assets (money, land and equipment) held by a business or a country.

Technical skills – skills involving specific abilities and knowledge to carry out a task.

Transferrable skills – skills involving general abilities and knowledge which can be used in various different jobs.

Career – a profession in a particular area of work which requires specific education and skills and allows an individual to progress.

Factors that influence employment, unemployment and underemployment

Capital availability and use

When a country gains **capital** through investment, natural resources like oil and gas and tourism, it should channel this wealth into the human capital through job creation and productive **employment**. For example, new oil fields have recently been discovered in Guyana. This new wealth should be used to train new workers in this area in order to make best use of the discovery.

Not all countries experience the same economic growth and may suffer from high levels of **unemployment**. This puts a number of pressures on society.

Table 10.5 lists some of the social and economic issues concerning unemployment.

Social Issues	Economic Issues
Rise in poverty which has implications on health, education and housing	'Brain drain' as workers are not able to find jobs locally
Increase in criminal activity	Reduction in tax revenue as fewer workers generate less taxation
Increase in family conflict brought on by financial stress	Poor image as a viable tourist destination

Table 10.5

Even when a country does generate capital, a large amount must be used to repay any loans taken from agencies such as the Inter-American Development Bank (IDB), the International Monetary Fund (IMF) and the World Bank. These loans are generally used to help with growth and the economic development of the nation.

Availability of trained human resource

Governments must look after the social, economic and educational needs of the population.

Table 10.6 gives a summary of the extent to which human resources can be developed.

Social	Economic	Educational
Job training programmes offered by government agencies or private businesses	National minimum wage to ensure workers earn enough money to live on	Initiatives to encourage **entrepreneurship**
Safety net programmes to protect individuals from economic shocks and sudden crises		

Table 10.6

They also have to uphold the constitutional rights of individuals to work and recognise SDG 8 (decent work and economic growth). A highly trained workforce should occupy a variety of jobs to help the development of the country.

Some individuals are unable to find jobs matching their skill set which can lead to **underemployment** and in some instances, unemployment. Individuals may also choose not to work. Educational institutions need to offer the kinds of subjects that match the type of jobs available. In Guyana, training in technical skills will be necessary to support the recent boom in the oil and gas industry.

Level and range of skills demanded versus available skills

All potential employees should make sure they have a wide range of skills for the changing world of work, to ensure that they are as **employable** as possible. **Technical** skills, **transferrable** skills and information technology are vital in the 21st century.

Table 10.7 displays some of these skills.

Technical skills	Transferrable skills	Information technology
Data analysis	Communication	Data management
Health and safety compliance	Teamwork	Microsoft suite (Word, Excel, PowerPoint, etc.)
Finance and accounting	Problem solving	Use of hardware
Project management	Planning and organisation	
Use of Microsoft programmes	Leadership	

Table 10.7

Huge changes have happened to the workplace in recent years, from the way individuals communicate to the storage of data. Organisations must also train their workers to suit the needs of the changing market, through continuous professional development. This allows businesses to maximise their output and levels of productivity.

In the Caribbean, there are a number of situations which can make finding work more difficult. This can lead to the following various types of unemployment.

Seasonal unemployment

Individuals may be employed for a particular season. When that season finishes, their employment ends. The agricultural sector and the tourism industry are good examples. Harvest season relies heavily on a steady stream of workers, while international tourists often visit the Caribbean when it is winter in their own country, which means our region needs more staff at airports, hotels and resorts.

Frictional unemployment

This is a natural type of unemployment occurs in all societies. People who leave their current jobs may not find another one immediately afterwards. This temporary period of unemployment between jobs can result from family priorities, educational priorities or being fired from the previous job with limited notice.

Technological/technical unemployment

In some industries, technology has taken over the jobs that people used to do. Businesses are using artificial intelligence and robotics to reduce the number of people they need to employ.

Structural unemployment

This type of unemployment results from changes that occur in the economy. Closure of state-run businesses due to debt, competition from other industries and changing trade agreements can result in structural unemployment. This can affect a large number of people.

Cyclical unemployment

This happens when there are periods of depression or recession followed by economic expansion and recovery. During a recession, demand and production of goods are reduced which results in a reduction in spending and the need for labour. As the economy starts to recover, there is a gradual build up in the need for goods so production will increase.

Availability and creation of markets, trading patterns and preferences

Collecting recent, reliable and relevant data on the trends in the labour market can help persons know which employment area they should train in, and help workers to find jobs matching their skill set.

Sometimes the creation of new markets can lead to underemployment as workers' skills may have not been updated and they are unable to adapt quickly.

In the Caribbean region, patterns of trade have significantly changed over time. Multilateral agreements, in the form of the CARICOM Single Market and Economy (CSME), have removed many of the restrictions placed on goods and services and created freedom of movement and work.

Individual tastes will also always be a factor in the employment, unemployment and underemployment of a country or region. There is a direct link between consumer preference, the demand of a good or service and the supply of labour.

Availability of technology

Technology has had a huge impact on employment across the region and the wider world. While some countries are gradually embracing technology in the public and private sectors, others have developed very fast. For example, Barbados has committed to embracing technological advances while adopting the green economy principles.

Economic situation

Workers are the first to feel the brunt of a recession as there is a loss of jobs while productivity, consumption and levels of investment decline. A sharp oil price increase can trigger a recession since an increase in the energy supply will lead to increased prices overall.

Gender and employment

History

In the early part of the 20th century, women rarely worked as they were expected to get married and raise children. Paid work for women outside the home started to increase between the 1930s and 1970s as education became popular and public. As the education of women increased, so did the use of technology in the workplace. The number of clerical and secretarial jobs increased and were considered appropriate for women as these jobs were seen as clean and safe. General attitudes about women and work began to change after the Second World War when there was a better appreciation of the balance between family and paid employment, helped by the fact that many women had stepped up into traditionally male roles while the men were away fighting.

Women's rights

Women's liberation was an important development during the 19th and 20th centuries. It focused largely on voting rights, equal rights, gender equality and equal pay. Huge progress has been made as women now occupy key roles in society from presidents to prime ministers to chief justices and business owners.

Entrepreneurial opportunities

In the Caribbean, many people have used creativity and innovation and created small businesses to boost the economy. Small and medium-sized enterprises (SMEs) are growing and having a positive effect on employment rates in the region. Entrepreneurs use technology to reach new markets and expand regionally and internationally.

Grants are awarded to business owners who meet the criteria from a number of national and regional organisations such as NEDCO (Trinidad), Caribbean Export (Barbados) and Compete Caribbean.

Being WOW (world of work) ready

Once an individual has completed their education, they need to research available jobs. Sources of job opportunities and information may include:

Ministries of Labour
These ministries are responsible for managing the appropriate use of the country's labour force. They offer labour market information which is useful for both employers and potential employees, and support on-the-job training programmes.

Local and foreign universities
These institutions provide postgraduate programmes and job opportunities in research.

Specific tertiary-level educational institutions
As above, these offer additional training programmes and often research-based roles.

Companies
Private companies may offer internships which can teach relevant skills in a practical way.

Professionals already in the field
First-hand knowledge and advice from experienced individuals can be helpful to potential employees.

Workers can be categorised based on their hours of work and skills. Workers may fall into a number of categories which include:

Part-time workers
These are individuals who only work for part of a day or week, and their pay is calculated by how much time they have worked. If they are a permanent employee they receive benefits such as sick leave and paid holiday time, and may also receive extra benefits such as a car allowance and health insurance.

Full-time workers
These individuals work for a specific amount of time every week and receive a fixed amount of pay. Most countries have a standard working week of between 37 and 44 hours. Full-time workers also receive a number of benefits such as sick leave and paid holiday time, and may also receive extra benefits such as a car allowance and health insurance.

Temporary workers
These are individuals who work for a specified period of time, for which they are paid, and then their employment ends.

Contract workers
This is a form of temporary work where individuals perform a specific task for which a legal agreement is signed between them and the company, for an agreed amount of money. Once the job is completed the contract ends.

Interns
These are individuals who work for a particular company to help with project-based work while learning technical and transferrable skills that will help them in their search for permanent employment. Internships can be paid or unpaid, and can often lead to permanent employment at the same company.

Volunteers
Volunteers donate their time for free to help others and in so doing benefit the organisation they choose to work with. Volunteering can lead to a high level of employability as the volunteer can gain useful skills while demonstrating that they have a good work ethic.

Types of industries

There are four main industries which employees can work within. These industries are all interconnected.

Primary industry

The primary sector is the basis for the other sectors in the economy. It deals with the extraction of raw materials, like minerals and crude oil. It also involves farming, fishing and forestry. Certain primary industries can directly impact the environment and as such need to be monitored for environmental awareness and sustainability.

Agriculture

For many years the Caribbean region has largely been dependent on agriculture for food security, income generation and employment. It is important that countries are able to feed their own population, and also benefit economically from the crops and animals that are exported within and outside the region. Agriculture uses a lot of human labour, for example in Dominica where bananas, citrus, coconuts and cocoa are produced. In 2010, it was estimated that 31% of the male labour force in Dominica was employed in agricultural work. The industry has diversified to include hydroponic and aquaponic systems to grow plants in water without the use of soil. As innovative methods of planting, growing and harvesting crops become available, training needs to be offered to ensure the workforce has the right skills.

The agricultural sector in the Caribbean faces a number of challenges:

- impact of climate change
- frequency of natural disasters
- pests and diseases on the farms
- competition for arable land from other uses such as housing.

Agriculture is sometimes stigmatised in the region as an industry for less-educated, poorer individuals. Regional governments and the private sector should work to alter the negative impression of agriculture to attract younger workers into the sector.

Figure 10.12 *A banana plantation in Dominica*

Fishing

The fishing industry is very important to the Caribbean region. In Belize, fishing is done both for subsistence (for use by the fisher and their family) and for export which supports the economy. Fish is a main source of protein and the sector needs to be protected from overfishing and illegal fishing. Belize, Guyana, Barbados, Jamaica, Panama and St. Lucia all aimed to recognise sustainable fishing practices which can support the industry, aquaculture and tourism. According to the World Bank, the blue economy is the 'sustainable use of ocean resources for economic growth, improved livelihoods, and jobs while preserving the health of ocean ecosystem.'

Figure 10.13 *Fishermen sell their catch in Belize City*

Mining

Mining is the extraction of minerals from the ground, such as gold, bauxite and diamonds in Guyana. Mine exploration and development involves a number of disciplines which include geography, geology, chemistry and engineering. The mine will stop operating after some time when all the minerals have been mined or if it has become unprofitable to continue. Steps must then be taken to dismantle the mine and rehabilitate the land.

Figure 10.14 *Bauxite mine in Guyana*

Section B(i)   Sustainable Development and Use of Resources

Table 10.8 gives some examples of professions in the primary sector.

Agriculture	Fishing	Mining
Farmer	Fisher	Quarry worker
Farm hand	Aquaculture worker	Mine operator
Fruit picker	Fish sorter	Engineer

Table 10.8

Secondary industry

The secondary sector involves refining the raw materials which were extracted in the primary sector, and manufacturing them into other products. The industry also involves processing goods into a final product for consumption.

Manufacturing

Some of the manufacturing carried out in the Caribbean includes:

- oil refining
- food and beverage processing
- vehicle production
- clothing manufacturing.

These industries require a skilled labour force and management who can work to develop the product competitively. They must also find ways to reduce costs and enhance the quality of the final product.

Figure 10.15 *The Carib beer processing plant in Port of Spain, Trinidad*

Construction

Construction involves developing the physical landscape. Highways, housing, projects focused on education and health, and modernising existing urban spaces are necessary due to increased demand.

Figure 10.16 *A construction site in Ocho Rios, Jamaica*

Table 10.9 gives some examples of professions in the secondary sector.

Manufacturing	Construction
Tailor	Bricklayer
Machine operator	Tile setter
Assembly line worker	Concrete finisher
Mixologist	Ironworker

Table 10.9

Tertiary industry

This sector is sometimes known as the service industry as it provides direct services to businesses and consumers. Some services include banking, insurance and communications.

Tourism

Tourism is the movement of persons from one area to another for pleasure or business purposes. The tourism industry provides accommodation, facilities and amenities for visitors. It is considered one of the most important economic activities in the Caribbean, contributing between a third to a half of GDP (Gross Domestic Product) for many countries.

Figure 10.17 *A waiter at a restaurant in Barbados*

In the tourist industry, jobs may become full careers. Jobs and careers may be at the unskilled level such as a room cleaner, at the technical or skilled level such as a chef or watersports instructor, at the middle management level such as a restaurant manager or the management level such as a hotel manager.

The tourism industry is also referred to as the hospitality industry as workers must be able to interact with all types of people from many different areas and countries.

Technical staff must have primary or secondary education and have completed a training course conducted at a hotel or tourism agency. Such jobs include tour guides, bar staff and waiting staff, and reservation and accounting clerks.

Middle management jobs may be achieved after a number of years of service and on-going training programmes, through promotion or after completion of a two-year course at a technical institute or community college or a three to four-year programme at a college or university.

Management jobs require training beyond the first-degree level or are achieved as a result of promotion within the field.

Careers in tourism fall into the following categories:

- recreation
- airline and cruise ship
- hotel
- travel agencies
- maintenance and special services.

Banking

The banking industry is essential to any country. Banks offer a range of facilities and services which include providing various deposit accounts, loans and safeguarding assets.

Quaternary industry

Quaternary industry is the knowledge-based part of the economy. It really sits under the tertiary sector but has been considered as a separate industry due to its increasingly widespread nature.

Figure 10.18 *Banking is an example of a tertiary industry*

Information technology

The internet has completely revolutionised our way of life. The primary, secondary and tertiary sectors have all been significantly influenced by the use of various applications and technologies and nothing has been left untouched by it. An employee of any sector now requires a working knowledge of the internet and the technologies that use it.

Research and development

In all sectors, research is an important tool. In the primary sector it to helps to improve efficient and safe extraction of raw materials; in the secondary sector it leads to higher quality processed items and in the tertiary and quaternary sectors, it encourages innovative methods of working.

Table 10.10 gives some examples of professions in the quaternary sector.

Information technology	Research and development
Media	Graphic designer
Educator	Software developer
Robotics	Consulting

Table 10.10

Questions

Knowledge and comprehension

1 Define the following terms:
   a) Employment
   b) Unemployment
   c) Underemployment

2 Describe TWO types of unemployment found in the Caribbean.

3 Identify and describe THREE factors which influence the employment rate in your country.

4 Outline THREE ways that the government of your country can create more job opportunities for young people.

5 List TWO career opportunities offered in your country and describe the benefit of these to the:
   a) Tertiary sector
   b) Quaternary sector

Use of knowledge

6 Discuss the benefits of agriculture and fishing to nation building.

7 Examine TWO strategies that governments can use to attract more young people to the agricultural sector.

8 Suggest THREE ways that the government of your country can suitably prepare young people for the quaternary industry.

9 Explain the need to develop the tourism industry so that young people can participate in it.

SBA skills

Look at the unemployment rates for 2023 for four Caribbean countries below and answer the questions that follow.

Country	Unemployment rate (%)	Labour force	Population size	Unemployed people
Barbados	8.2	142,648	281,635	
Guyana	12.4	289,264	808,726	
Trinidad and Tobago	3.98	678,100	1,531,044	
Jamaica	6.6	1.572,790	2,827,377	

Section B(i) Sustainable Development and Use of Resources

1. Calculate the number of unemployed people for each country and complete the table provided.
2. What reasons can you give for the different unemployment rates in the different countries?

End of chapter questions

1. a) Define the term 'nutrition'. (2 marks)
   b) Outline TWO consequences of poor nutrition on young children. (4 marks)
   c) The Caribbean has seen an increase in the number of students choosing to study Sport at the secondary level and as an undergraduate degree at the tertiary level.
      (i) Suggest TWO ways that the Caribbean can promote sports in the region. (4 marks)
      (ii) Explain why EACH action suggested in (c) (i) is likely to be successful. (4 marks)
      TOTAL 14 MARKS

> **SUSTAINABLE DEVELOPMENT AND USE OF RESOURCES**
> **The COVID-19 pandemic has increased unemployment rates in the Caribbean.**

2. The Heads of Government of CARICOM are meeting to discuss the statement above to consider the economic impact of the pandemic in the region.

   Prepare a formal speech in which you:
   - define the term 'unemployment'
   - identify TWO types of unemployment which have been impacted
   - outline TWO effects of unemployment on the labour force
   - suggest THREE actions the government might use to reduce the unemployment rates in the Caribbean region
   - explain why any TWO of these actions are likely to be successful.

   TOTAL 22 MARKS

Summary

The human resource is the people of a country who all have various talents and abilities, creativity and innovation which are used to develop the country. If a country fails to use its human resource appropriately, it won't achieve economic success. Lack of investment in the human capital can slow economic growth in a country, even one which possesses natural resources.

Human resource development plays an important role in overall development and care should be taken with the workforce. Governments must provide for the proper nutrition and good health of the population so that individuals can work efficiently. The population should also be able to access healthcare services such as primary or preventive healthcare as well as secondary or curative healthcare. Both are essential to the general wellbeing of the individual.

Apart from health, the potential workforce should have access to education, from pre-primary up to tertiary levels and beyond. The skills attained through education should be relevant, based on values, technical and transferrable from one discipline to another. The human resource also benefits when given opportunities for sport and culture.

Levels of employment, unemployment and underemployment in a country should be monitored. High unemployment and underemployment rates can put a strain on the economy while too many workers in certain areas can indicate a need to diversify the economy.

Individuals can consider employment in a variety of careers in different industries. These industries can range from primary (extraction of raw materials) to secondary (manufacturing) to tertiary (service-based) and finally, quaternary (knowledge-based).

The development of the human resource brings a number of benefits to a country and should be placed high on any national agenda.

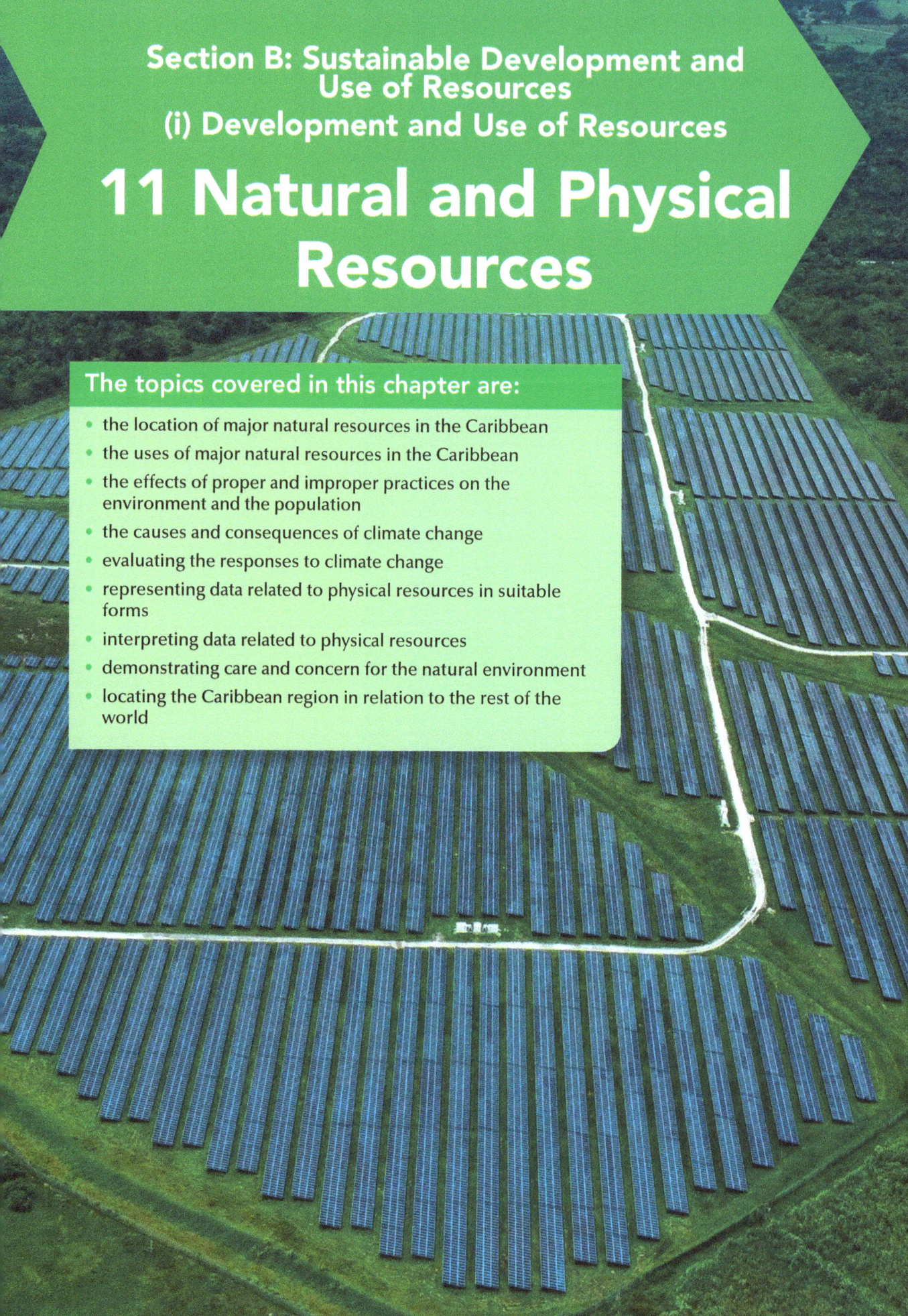

Section B: Sustainable Development and Use of Resources
(i) Development and Use of Resources
11 Natural and Physical Resources

The topics covered in this chapter are:

- the location of major natural resources in the Caribbean
- the uses of major natural resources in the Caribbean
- the effects of proper and improper practices on the environment and the population
- the causes and consequences of climate change
- evaluating the responses to climate change
- representing data related to physical resources in suitable forms
- interpreting data related to physical resources
- demonstrating care and concern for the natural environment
- locating the Caribbean region in relation to the rest of the world

As humans, we need food to live, shelter for protection and energy to satisfy our limitless wants. The natural light of the sun serves as a source of energy while the land gives us food. We, as the human resource, can use the knowledge and expertise to extract the raw materials nestled both on the land and in the sea for personal and commercial use. The Caribbean community possesses a multiplicity of **natural and physical resources** which can range from oil and natural gas to forestry and even climatic conditions ripe for tourism.

Major natural resources in the Caribbean

Learning objectives

- Locate the Caribbean region in relation to the rest of the world.
- Identify the location of the major natural resources in the Caribbean.
- Describe the economic and industrial uses of the major natural resources found in the Caribbean region.
- Examine the effects of proper and improper practices on the environment and the population.

Important definitions

Resource – anything that can be used to enhance one's quality of life.

Natural/Physical resource – anything that occurs in nature which can be used to generate profits for a country.

Renewable resource – any resource that occurs in nature which can be used repeatedly.

Non-renewable resource – any finite resource that occurs in nature; when it is finished, more cannot be made

Archipelago – a collection of islands.

Desalination – the process by which salt is removed from seawater to make it suitable for drinking and in agriculture.

Hydropower – generating electricity from the power of flowing water.

Habitats – places or environments where plants, animals and organisms live.

Conservation – the responsible use of resources to ensure the survival of the environment.

Slash and burn agriculture – the removal of trees and vegetation by cutting them down and burning them off, before growing new crops.

Mass wasting – the influence of gravity to move rocks and soils down a slope.

Ecology – the study of the relationships between organisms and their environment.

Flora and fauna – the indigenous plant and animal life in a particular geographical area.

Location of the Caribbean

The Caribbean is made up of an **archipelago** or chain of islands which are scattered across the Caribbean Sea to the southeast of the North American continent, and also includes the mainland countries of Guyana on the South American continent and Belize in Central America. The Caribbean is spread over 2,754 million km².

Figure 11.1 *Map of the Caribbean*

The equator divides the world equally between the northern hemisphere and the southern hemisphere. The Caribbean sits above the equator in the northern hemisphere. This gives us our latitude measure. The other reference is the Greenwich Meridian or prime meridian which gives us our longitude measure. This imaginary line which joins the North and South poles gives an east or west location. The exact location of the Caribbean using latitude and longitude coordinates is latitudes 9° and 22° N and longitudes 89° and 60° W.

Caribbean people are unique and have a number of cultural practices which define their 'Caribbean-ness'. Although in the same area of the globe, each country has a unique way of life. National identity is strong, but Caribbean people also embrace their wider Caribbean identity through their acceptance of differences, past and present and in the many common festivities.

Historically, colonisation, enslavement, emancipation, indentureship and independence produced reliance and connectivity among nations around the world. As a result of these processes Caribbean nations developed relationships with countries outside the region for trade and commerce.

Some countries in our region are seen as financial hubs due to their rapid technological transformation. Other countries have used their natural resources to attract foreign exchange through tourism.

Location of major natural resources

Natural resources can be divided into two main categories. A **renewable resource** is any resource that occurs in nature which can be replenished and replaced. It has an almost infinite supply.

Figure 11.2 *The rainforests of Guyana*

Figure 11.3 *Bauxite mine in Mandeville, Jamaica*

A **non-renewable resource** is any resource that occurs in nature which cannot be replaced when it runs out, which means we say it is finite.

Table 11.1 shows some examples of the two types of natural resource.

Renewable	Non-renewable
Agricultural land	Petroleum
Water	Bauxite
Forests	Gold
Marine and land life	Diamond
Energy in the form of solar, wind and geothermal	Other minerals

Table 11.1

Figure 11.4 *Bauxite*

Renewable resources

Agricultural land

The land as a resource is vital to the development of its people. Both commercial and subsistence agriculture can benefit the country as the soil conditions, together with the tropical climate, allow for food production.

Grenada, Jamaica and Guyana have thriving agricultural industries.

Figure 11.5 *A coffee plantation in the Blue Mountains, Jamaica*

Section B(i) Sustainable Development and Use of Resources

Table 11.2 gives an overview of the countries' agricultural industries

Country	Grenada	Jamaica	Guyana
Main soil type	Clay loam	Limestone	Diverse, ranging from sandy to sandy loam, clay and pegassy (peat)
Crops grown	Nutmeg and other spices	Coffee, cocoa, sugarcane	Sugar, rice, coconut
Size of agricultural land (hectares)	8000	417,000	200,000

Table 11.2

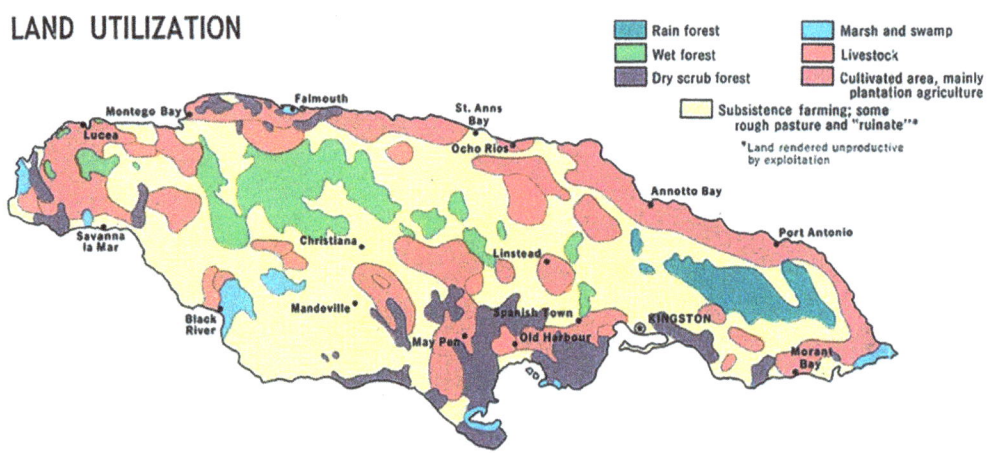

Figure 11.6 *Map showing the different land use across Jamaica*

Water

Water is obtained from a number of sources including ground water aquifers, freshwater sources and water which has undergone **desalination**. Aquifers are layers of rock that contain groundwater. In Jamaica, these rocks are either limestone or alluvium. Water also originates from springs, ponds, rivers and wells and has to be pumped, purified and stored before use. Water is necessary for all living things and should be potable (drinkable) for human consumption. In the agricultural sector, water is important for animals and plants as well as for cleaning.

Forests

Figure 11.7 *Desalination plant in Trinidad*

Tropical forests are indigenous to the Caribbean region as the climate provides the perfect temperatures and conditions for them to grow. Forests are valued for their wood used in the construction industry, but if managed well they can be important for tourism, and for wildlife management and soil fertility programmes. Belize has extensive forests and woodland areas in the form of broadleaf and pine forests as well as scrubby woodland areas. About 87% of Guyana is covered with forests and as such, a National Forest Policy and Plan has been put in place to manage and conserve the forest reserves.

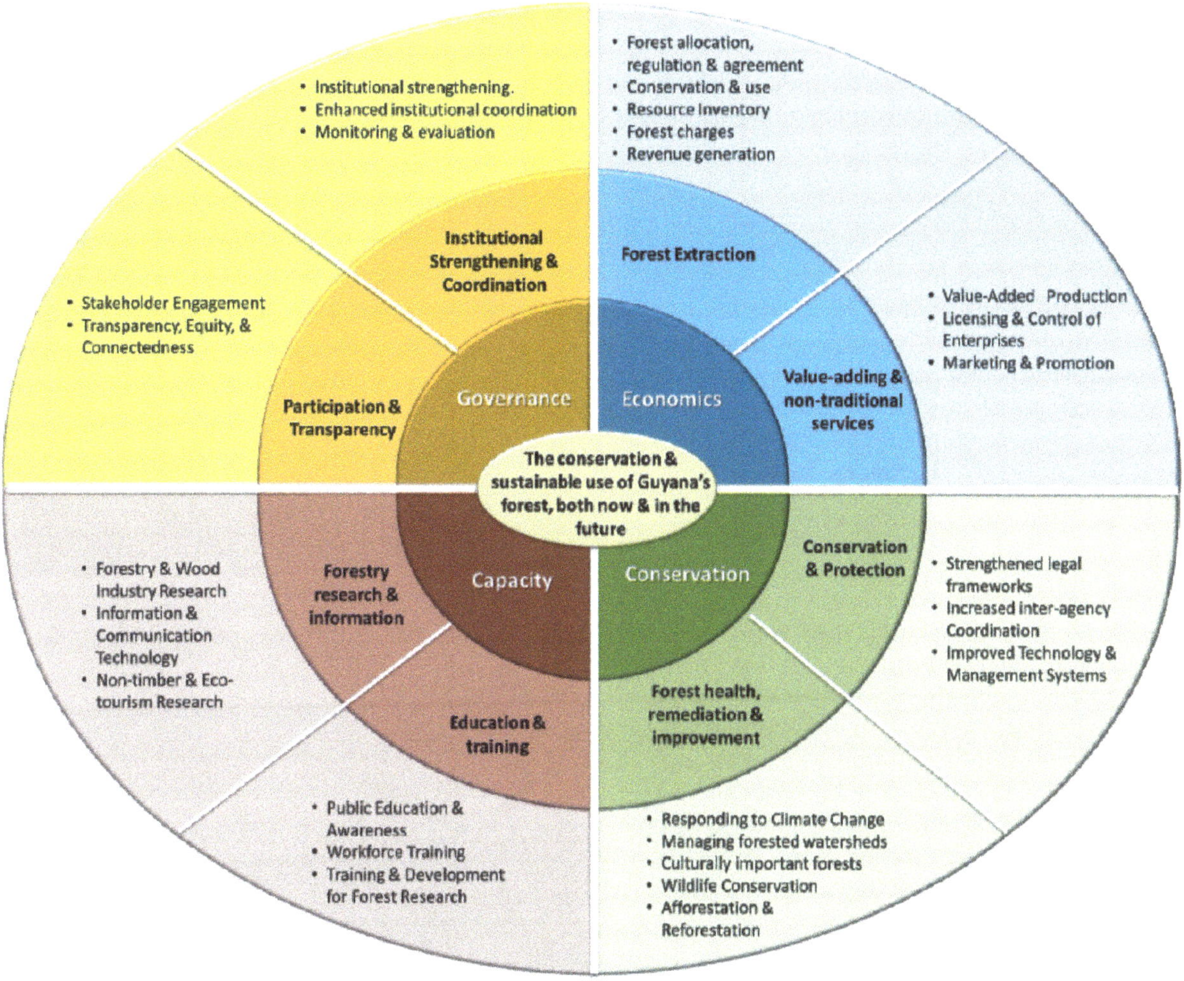

Figure 11.8 *Guyana National Forest Policy*

Land and marine life

Living organisms populate our oceans, coasts and mangroves. The waters around the Caribbean contain a variety of fish, crustaceans and other living things which live in a wide range of **habitats**. There are a number of food webs both on land and sea which can provide useful information on the **ecology** of the area.

Coral reefs can be found in Caribbean countries such as Tobago, Jamaica and Cuba and there are well-developed fisheries in Jamaica, St. Lucia and Antigua and Barbuda. In fact, most coastal areas within the Caribbean use fishing for food, family income and export.

Figure 11.9 *The waters around the Caribbean are full of life*

It is important that we take good care of our oceans as there are some endangered species that live there. Sea turtles migrate to our region during the nesting season. The leatherback turtle is an endangered species and we need to work hard to maintain and grow the population of

Section B(i) Sustainable Development and Use of Resources

these creatures. The turtles can be seen during their nesting season periods in Trinidad from March to September every year.

In the eastern Caribbean lies Ma Kôté, the largest mangrove forest in St. Lucia and home to juvenile fish. Mangroves survive in tropical regions and protect the coastline from harsh waves and tides.

Forms of energy

Solar energy

Solar water heating became more popular in Barbados during the 1970s as the government tried to provide renewable energy in light of the international oil crisis. Economic incentives and entrepreneurial thinking led to its success today. Solar now helps Barbados have greener infrastructure.

Figure 11.10 *Solar panels are popular in Barbados*

Wind energy

Energy from the wind is harnessed as the air moves through wind turbines. As the turbine blades move, the drive shaft turns the generator to produce the electricity. When there is more than one windmill in a location, it is referred to as a wind farm. This means more electricity can be generated. Jamaica has the largest wind-energy facility in the English-speaking Caribbean, consisting of three plants. It contributes 6% of Jamaica's renewable energy.

Figure 11.11 *Wind farm in Jamaica*

Geothermal energy

Geothermal energy comes from the Earth's core. The heat energy is still being generated from the Earth's formation, combined with decay of radioactive minerals. The Lesser Antilles are a good source of geothermal energy as countries such as St. Lucia, Dominica, St. Vincent and St. Kitts and Nevis are located around potentially active volcanoes. Dominica has made significant progress with geothermal energy as they signed a contract in 2022 to start drilling two new geothermal wells. The movement away from the use of fossil fuels provides environmentally friendly opportunities for energy generation.

Hydroelectric power

Hydroelectric power is the energy generated by moving water to produce electricity. Power plants regulate the amount of water which flows from the reservoir and captures the energy contained in the water as it flows downwards.

These forms of energy do have some drawbacks. Solar, wind and geothermal energy cost a lot to set up and need technical expertise throughout. Wind, solar and hydroelectric power can be unpredictable due to weather conditions. Using different forms of energy in a country can cause engineering difficulties as original power grids need to be upgraded.

Non-renewable resources

Petroleum

Black gold, as it is known, can be found both on land and in the sea. Sometimes known as crude oil, it is black in colour and is the main source of energy globally. High demand means there is a high price for this fossil fuel. Petroleum can be found in the southern part of Trinidad as well as offshore to the north of Tobago and in the seas around Trinidad. In recent years Guyana has discovered oil off their northern coast.

Bauxite

In the Caribbean, bauxite is mainly found in Suriname, Guyana and Jamaica. It is a rock found in tropical climates which contains minerals including aluminum. It varies in colour: white, grey or brown if iron is present. In Jamaica, bauxite mining is the third largest foreign exchange earner after remittances (money sent home from abroad) and tourism. Refining bauxite ore is not only expensive due to the amount of energy it uses, but it contributes significantly to water and air pollution as well as land degradation and deforestation.

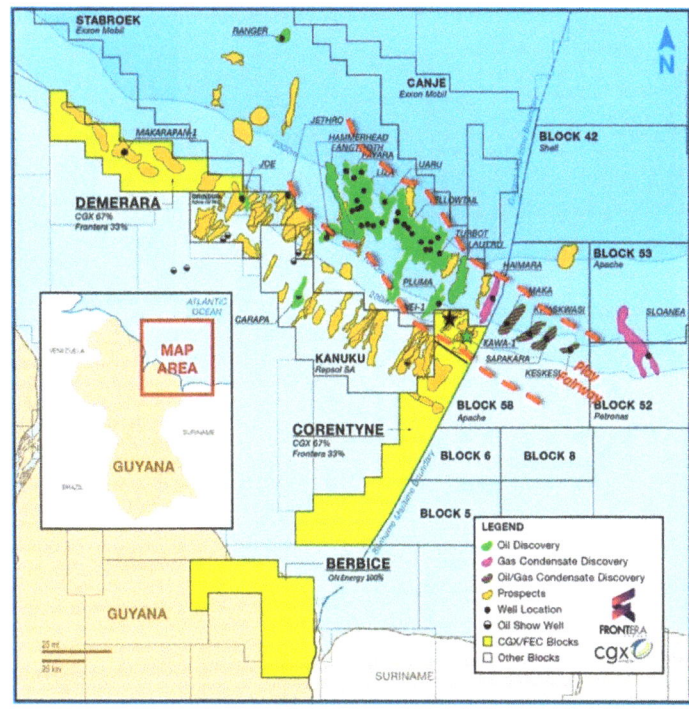

Figure 11.12 *Map of oilfields around Guyana*

Gold

This element is a precious, soft, yellow metal which can be easily shaped. Gold mining in Guyana accounted for 12% of the country's GDP between 2000 and 2019. Gold production in Guyana is big business as it forms one of its biggest exports. However, illegal gold mining together with medium scale gold mining have caused environmental damage, deforestation and mercury pollution in the air, water and soil.

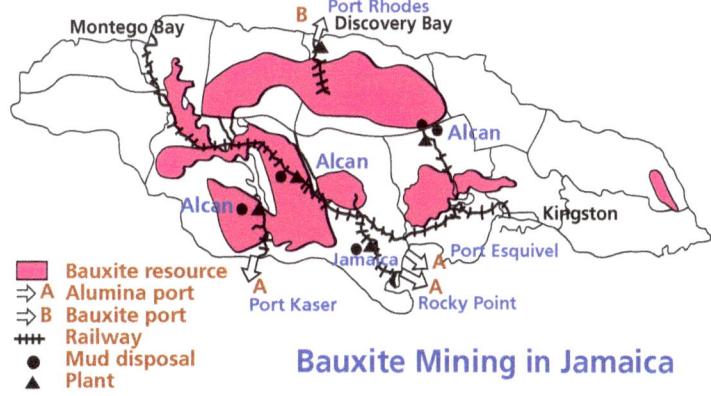

Figure 11.13 *Map of bauxite mining in Jamaica*

Diamonds and other minerals

Diamond and gold mining in Guyana are both located in similar areas. Diamonds only account for 2% of all exported minerals. Diamonds are an extremely hard gem which can be used for industrial purposes and, of course, in the jewellery business.

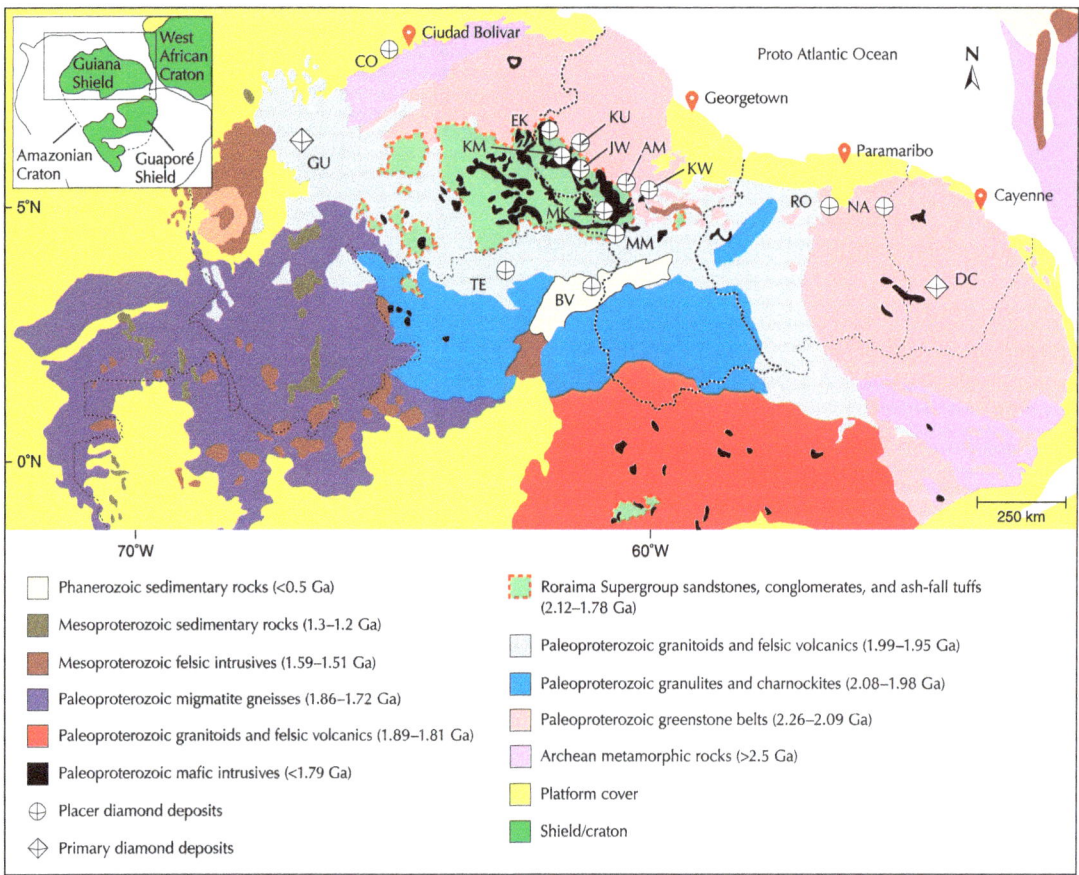

Figure 11.14 *Map showing location of diamond mines in Guyana*

Uses of resources

The countries of our region have various renewable and non-renewable resources which helps in terms of self-reliance, economic stability and development.

Agriculture

Agriculture has always been important to the region, as sugarcane was once the Caribbean's main export crop. A number of other crops became popular such as coffee, cocoa, coconuts, citrus and some spices, as the soil is ideal for food production.

Planting the land not only supports the economy through foreign exchange earnings but creates employment and develops rural areas.

However, food insecurity is becoming a problem in the region, as demonstrated by the huge food import bill. This means countries are unable to grow enough food to feed themselves. Efforts are being made to reduce food imports by 25% by 2025. A number of factors have caused this level of food insecurity including:

- natural disasters which have caused crop devastation
- climate change
- urbanisation which has impacted how the land is used.

Land and marine life

People need the ocean for food, oxygen, fresh water, trade and commerce as well as for employment and tourism. Table 11.3 describes the uses of the waters in our region.

Use	Examples
Food	Caribbean countries depend on the fishing industry for food in-country and export. Mangroves are a good source of fish.
Fresh water	Countries can construct desalination plants to remove salt from water for human consumption.
Trade	Water courses are used to transport goods within and between countries.
Commerce	Aquaculture is the name for the farming of marine life, such as fish and shrimp farms.
Employment	Employment opportunities in fisheries and tourism, as well as marine biology and ichthyology (study of fish).
Tourism	Coral reefs, water sports and opportunities to see endangered species all provide revenue for the economy.

Table 11.3

Figure 11.15 *Mangroves in Trinidad*

Figure 11.16 *The famous 'Blue Hole' is found in the Belize Barrier Reef*

Forests

Around 65% of Belize is forested, consisting of mainly broadleaf and pine forests. Almost 50% of the forests owned by the State are protected. Timber production, including harvest of mahogany and pine, are used to contribute to the economy. Other uses of the forests include:

- clean water in the form of ground water
- prevention of flooding in low lying, coastal areas
- prevention of soil sediment collecting at river mouths and infringing on coral reefs
- generation of rain through condensation
- storing excess carbon emissions by humans.

Forests play a crucial role in our daily lives and help to keep countries healthy.

Mineral resources

We have already discussed the mineral resources which are most important in the Caribbean region. They all have specific uses. Bauxite is mined for its use in the production of aluminium.

Once bauxite is extracted, it is refined into alumina and then exported. Alumina is the primary ingredient in making aluminium. The industry generates foreign exchange earnings as well as supporting a number of jobs in the primary and secondary sectors.

Petroleum or crude oil is used to manufacture gasoline. Other products it can be used for include synthetic material like fabrics, nail polish, rubbing alcohol, tyres, basketballs and even house paint.

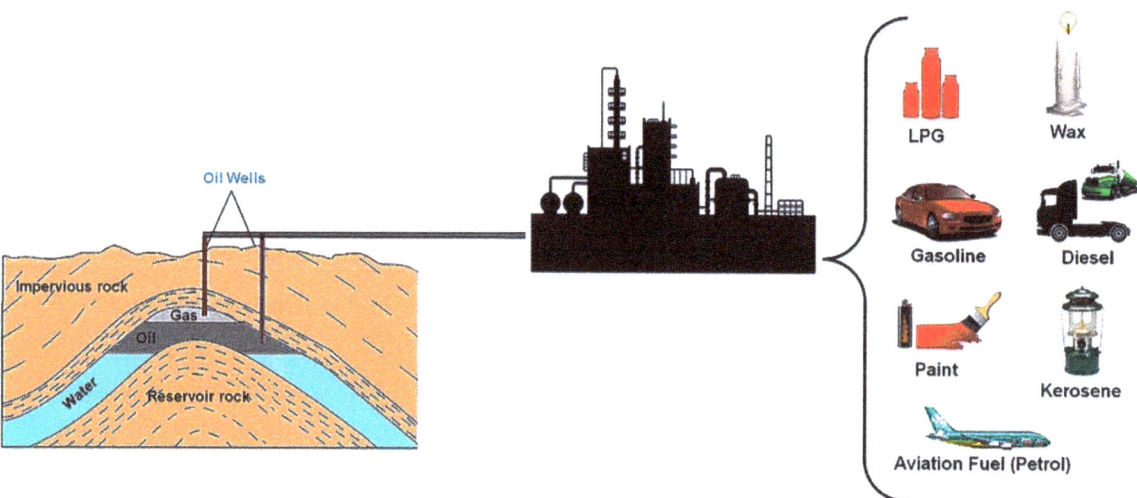

Figure 11.17 *Extraction and refining of petroleum to make various products*

Tourism products

Natural resources can attract local, regional and international travellers and visitors to the Caribbean. Tourism is when people move from one place to another for recreation or business. It is considered one of the most important economic activities in the Caribbean, contributing a third to a half of GDP in most countries.

Traditionally, Caribbean tourism has involved the usual attractions of reliable sunshine, beautiful beaches and seaside resorts, but with development in the sector, different types of tourism have emerged. These include:

- Nature and ecotourism: People are often interested in the environment and the **flora and fauna** of a country. The Caribbean offers attractions such as rainforests (Guyana), coral reefs (Belize), wetlands (Jamaica), bird sanctuaries (Trinidad) and nature reserves (Tobago).
- Health/medical tourism: As people research alternative medicine and different treatments for particular issues, they seek out specialist facilities. Mud volcanoes and even the water crevices in the Pitch Lake (Trinidad) have been used for skin rejuvenation. People also use facilities somewhere other than their own country due to cost, long waiting times for services and for specialist services such as cosmetic surgery.
- Sports tourism: This brings in both the individuals participating in the sport and also the spectators. Cricket in the region is a good example of sports tourism. In 2024, the Caribbean and the United States hosted the ICC Men's T20 World Cup which usually garners much attention and support locally, regionally and internationally. The host countries of organised sporting events such as the CARIFTA games benefit as many people from within the region and from elsewhere visit.
- Cultural and heritage tourism: Visitors are attracted by cultural elements in the form of food festivals, local cuisine, festivals, music, dancing, art and craft.

Alternative energy and sustainable development

We can harness the energy of the sun through Solar Photovoltaics as well as through Solar Thermal technologies. Solar Photovoltaics (PV) uses the direct rays of the sun to make electricity by using semiconductors, while Solar Thermal uses the sun's heat energy for heating and for electricity generation.

Wind energy, which is captured using turbines, is also used as a sustainable method of generating electricity in the region. In Jamaica, the north-east trade winds are providing renewable energy for both commercial and residential use which is cleaner and cost-effective. The goal is to use renewable energy for 33% of electricity generation by 2030 and by a further 50% by 2037.

Geothermal energy is used extensively in Dominica to provide cheaper electricity. This means fewer greenhouse gases will be emitted and other countries, such as Martinique, can benefit by purchasing this renewable energy.

In the Caribbean, water is also used as a source of energy. Starting in 2015, Dominica aimed to be carbon negative by 2020, meaning that they would be removing carbon dioxide from the atmosphere as opposed to releasing it. They have achieved this by diversifying their energy supplies. **Hydropower** is the main source of renewable energy used on the island which accounts for 28% of generated electricity. Guyana also uses hydroelectric power in their energy mix policies to generate clean energy.

Bioenergy is a type of renewable energy which is produced from organic material known as biomass. Traditionally, biomass was prepared from animal remains, wood and charcoal as well as from decayed plant material. Today, biomass comes from specific plant waste and other organic sources. Belize has been quite successful in creating a renewable energy mix as seen in the doughnut chart above.

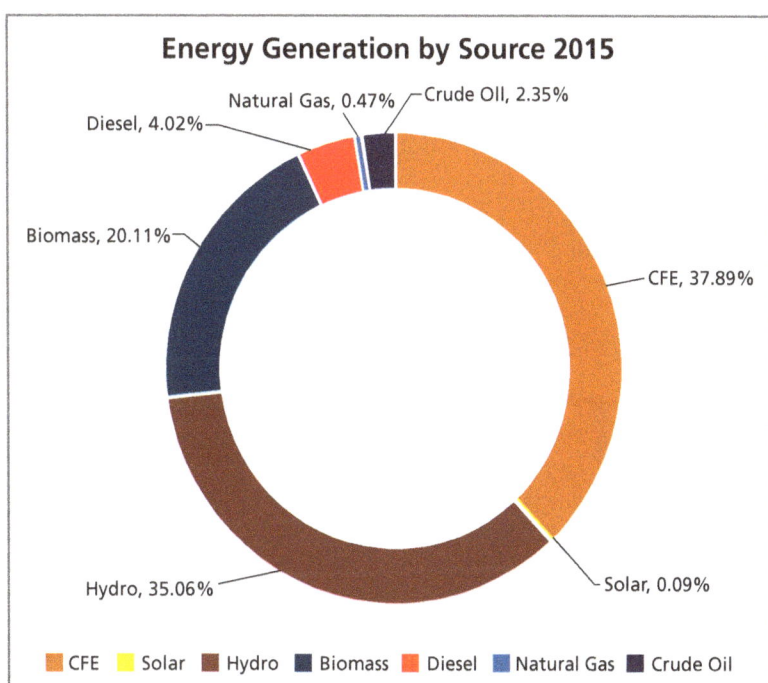

Figure 11.18 *Energy mix of Belize*

Proper practices on the environment and population

It is in our best interests to preserve and conserve the resources we have now, for future generations. Developing a conscious lifestyle of sustainable development can only work when best practices are adopted.

Sustainable development practices

Sustainable development involves greening, eco-friendliness and environmental stewardship. **Conservation** helps us to protect the environment and the people that live in it, by ensuring the continuity of a resource. Some actions are outlined on the following pages.

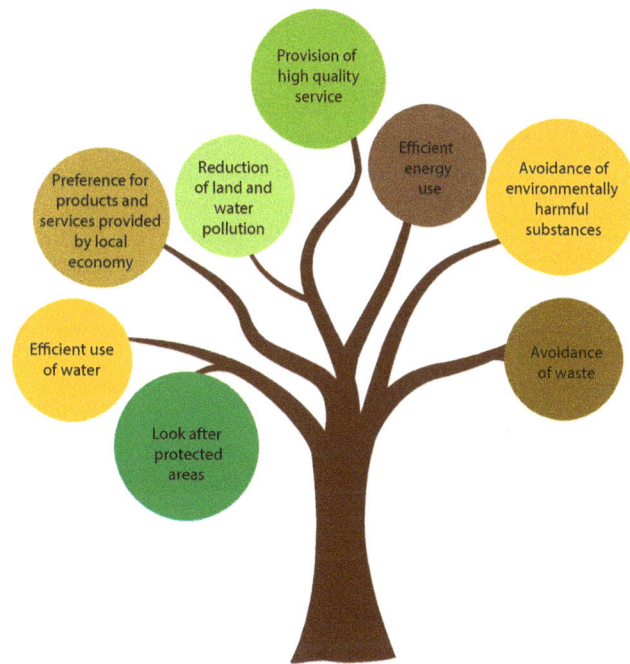

Figure 11.19 *Sustainable development best practice*

Section B(i)   Sustainable Development and Use of Resources

Reforestation

This is the replanting of trees to replace those which were cut down. An initiative by the Jamaican government aimed to plant three million trees over a three-year period with the hope of improving national development, increasing forest cover and creating green spaces on suitable land.

Farmers can also practice mulching to ensure that the soil has enough moisture and is not dried out by the intense heat. They should ensure that the soil is not left bare so that it isn't washed away during heavy rainfall.

Mangroves are trees bordering the land and sea. They are very important as they serve as store houses for carbon, and defend the coast from harsh conditions such as storms, tsunamis and coastal erosion.

Contour ploughing

Ploughing the land and planting crops on sloping land along the contours can prevent surface runoff and soil erosion. Conserving water and soil are the main goals of contour ploughing as when rain falls the water collects in small ridges and slowly infiltrates the soil.

Terracing

This soil conservation technique is usually used on slopes. It involves carving out ridges to form platforms. This helps water retention in the upper areas which will make its way down slowly to the lower levels. This method also reduces soil erosion making it a sustainable form of agriculture. However, it is labour-intensive and costly.

Figure 11.20 *Contour ploughing reduces runoff and soil erosion*

Crop rotation

Crop rotation involves planting a different crop each time in a particular area, so as not to deprive the soil of a particular nutrient. This practice may lead to fewer pests and crop diseases as well as better harvests. Farmers have to be careful when using this method to avoid nutrient overload.

Controlled logging

Most countries have placed controls on how much logging can be carried out and where, to avoid depleting our natural timber resources. Governments now specify areas where logging cannot take place, as illegal logging is on the rise. Only mature trees are earmarked for removal and there are severe penalties for illegal logging.

Figure 11.21 *Terracing helps water retention and soil erosion*

Zoning

In order to support sustainable development, governments must make sure land use is planned properly. Some countries have created 'green zones' or 'ecodistricts' to encourage sustainable practices, reduce environmental effects and rejuvenate the area. In Barbados, a groundwater protection zoning policy has been put in place to create areas where certain activities are not allowed.

Table 11. 4 looks at the water zones in Barbados.

Water zones	Requirements
Zone 1 (relaxed policy, existing buildings)	Septic tank with carbon activated filter bed and a well not more than 4 metres deep
Zone 2	Septic tank and a well not more than 6 metres deep
Zone 3	Two wells one each for sewage and domestic waste with each well a maximum of 12 metres deep
Zone 4 & 5	A single well of no specified depth

Table 11.4

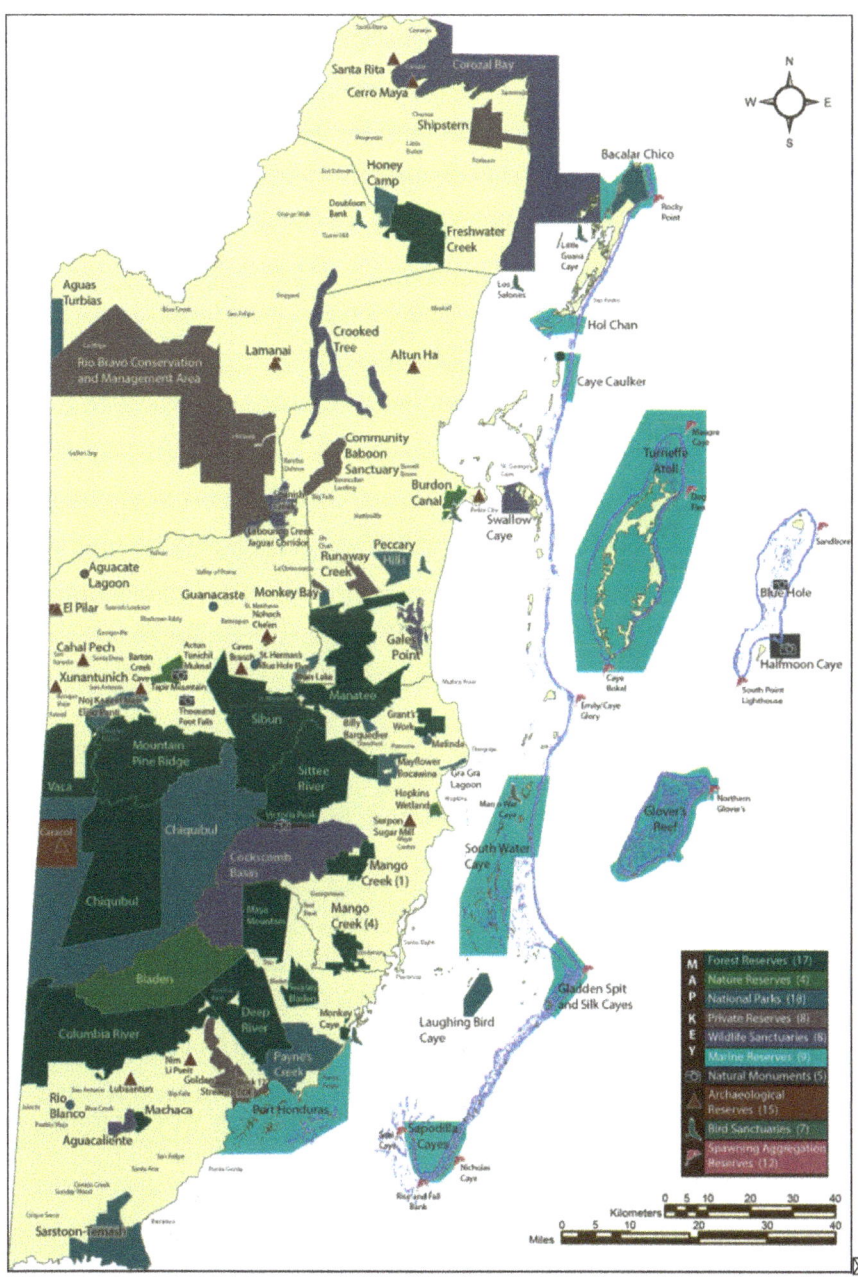

Figure 11.22 *Map of Barbados water zones*

Section B(i)   Sustainable Development and Use of Resources

Reserves

Forest reserves are now being identified in areas where forestry has to be protected. State lands can be monitored and improvements can be made to manage this resource more efficiently.

Improper practices on the environment and population

Status of land resources

The land can suffer from exposure, misuse and overuse from both human actions and natural events, leading to devastating effects. Some of these actions are as follows.

Improper use of soil leading to soil erosion

This can occur in nature when the top soil is removed by high winds and water during intense weather conditions, or by the poor use of soil during farming. This can also happen when vegetation is removed in forested areas which can expose the top layer of soil to the elements. **Slash and burn** agricultural practices can also degrade the quality of the soil especially during the dry season.

The overgrazing of animals and excessive weeding can have a negative effect on the land as vegetation does not have time to recover.

Overcropping

This practice is when a crop is grown on the same land repeatedly without a period of rest to replace lost nutrients. This can happen when the land resource is in short supply due to overpopulation or unequal distribution of land use. In some cases this can lead to food shortages, especially in subsistence farming.

Monocropping

Historically, the Caribbean had a monocrop economy, where sugar was the main crop grown. Every season this crop was harvested left the soil at a reduced pH level. Over time the yields reduced, limiting overall profits. These days, the agricultural industry in the region has developed to include a variety of crops which helps to return a variety of nutrients to the soil.

Improper tillage or ploughing

Tillage is turning over the soil ready for planting. Ploughing is one type of tillage. Although there are benefits to tillage, doing it too often can reduce the quality of the soil. Table 11.5 displays the benefits and drawbacks of tillage.

Benefits of tillage	Drawbacks of tillage
Used to prepare the seedbed	Disturbs the soil structure
Reduces weeds	Causes greater surface runoff
Buries previous crop remnants	Previous crop remnants can buffer heavy rains
Levels the soil	Leads to soil erosion in the form of **mass wasting**
Allows air to pass through soil	

Table 11.5

Ploughing slopes in a parallel pattern leads to less top soil as more sediment moves downhill, reaching water courses.

Destruction of biodiversity

The Caribbean has been described as one of the world's 'biodiversity hotspots' which means there are many important species which need protecting in our region. Some threats linked to biodiversity destruction include population pressures, pollution and the effects of climate change. Deforestation can cause species to become endangered as the removal of forests destroys plant and animal life and their habitats.

Table 11.6 demonstrates some causes and consequences of deforestation.

Causes	Consequences
Removal of trees for commercial and subsistence agriculture as well as for mining and quarrying.	Soil erosion as the surface protection is removed.
Cutting and processing trees for wood and pulp.	Tree roots are not there to keep the soil together, leading to landslides.
Wood used as a fuel source.	Tree cover is reduced so rain hits the surface of the soil directly, causing flooding.
Demands placed on housing as the population grows.	Less groundwater as more water runs off after rainfall as opposed to seeping into the ground.

Table 11.6

As temperatures increase due to climate change, the Freshwater Lake in Dominica seems to be 'dying' as the water level has declined sharply. The marine ecosystem will suffer as a result.

Poor housing development

Sustainable Development Goal 9: Industry, Innovation and Infrastructure encourages governments to consider how and where people live. Populations in urban areas are increasing and so additional housing must be planned in a sustainable way. In some countries, groups of people occupy informal settlements which are largely unplanned, which can impact on sustainable development goals.

Individual, industry and community practices

Some farmers use chemicals which can reach rivers and streams and damage marine life. Pesticides can alter the ecosystem so much that diversity is altered; some species may multiply while others decrease. A change in one part of an ecosystem will have a knock-on effect on another.

Solid waste disposal has always been a challenging issue. Some rivers and oceans are so polluted that when flooding occurs, the situation is made worse by the additional waste.

Bauxite mining uses an open-cast method which removes forest cover, pollutes water courses, damages agriculture and affects water and air quality due to large quantities of dust. Caustic soda is used to process bauxite which adds to dust particles in the air and the water.

Offshore drilling platforms, which are either anchored to the oceans' floor or constructed as a floating platform, can cause environmental issues due to malfunctioning equipment or human error. Oil spills present serious concerns for marine and land life. In 2010, an explosion on the Deepwater Horizon oil platform in the Gulf of Mexico claimed the lives of 11 workers, severely damaged marine life and polluted the ocean for months.

Resort development

Resort development can boost the economy, but at the same time weaken links with the local community. These negative effects include:

- lack of cooperation between stakeholders and the wider community
- tourists remain in the resort without exploring surrounding areas

- small enterprises rarely benefit from the resort which creates a sense of exclusion among local residents.

The environmental impact of resort development is also concerning. When developing a new resort, Environmental Impact Assessment Reports must be conducted together with a Certificate of Environmental Clearance to ensure that economic benefits do not outweigh the sustainability of the environment.

Table 11.7 gives details of resort development in Tobago and Jamaica.

Country	Location and size of resort	Project start date	Initial investment	Environmental concerns
Tobago	Kilgwyn, 500 room capacity, 46 acres	October 2023	US $100 million	- Potential destruction of mangroves - Impact on noise climate and air quality - Solid waste management issues
Jamaica	Negril, 6702 room capacity, 361 acres	2008	US $1 billion	- Potential destruction of delicate ecosystems such as forests and corals - Poor sewage and drainage solutions - Dredging to include a marina leading to poor waste management and air quality concerns

Table 11.7

Changes in ecology

Mismanagement of natural resources can have far-reaching consequences in various ecological systems. Table 11.8 outlines some practices and their ecological impacts.

Practice	Ecological impact
Waste disposal into bodies of water or soil	Land and water pollution which may lead to animal death or migration.
Accidental oil spills in oceans	Water pollution which may lead to animal death or migration.
Land reclamation and coastal development	Reduction in coral cover, coastal diversity and colony size (ecosystem degradation).
Overfishing	Destruction of species leading to instability in the marine environment.
Intensive agriculture	Sedimentation can affect the growth rates of corals.

Table 11.8

Tourism

The tourism industry has an important role to play to conserve biodiversity and minimise the effects on the environment, especially in Caribbean countries which are heavily dependent on the industry. The greening of the tourism industry and protection of flora and fauna is crucial to ensure sustainability.

In Jamaica, several land and marine parks and protected areas have passed regulations to stop the lighting of fires, fishing without a license and the collection of flora and fauna specimens.

Role of the Caribbean Conservation Association

The CCA, which is based in Barbados, was formed in 1967 in Grenada in response to the increasing impact of development on the Caribbean environment. Today, the organisation works with governments, NGOs (non-governmental organisations), overseas institutions and individuals as they:

- support environmental policies leading to sustainable development
- promote environmental awareness and education
- provide services to partnering countries.

Role of National Trusts

National Trusts aim to promote, protect and raise awareness of the built and natural heritage in a country.

Table 11.9 outlines some details of the National Trusts in the Caribbean.

Country	Year established	Main themes
Jamaica	1985	National pride
Trinidad	1991	Dedicated to the preservation of built and natural heritage
Barbados	1961	Awaken the public to a greater awareness of Barbados' historic riches
Guyana	1972	Conserve, preserve and promote the nation's heritage

Table 11.9

There are a number of areas which pose challenges to these organisations:

- difficulty accessing funding from governments for specific projects
- lack of appreciation and understanding of national heritage sites by the general public
- erosion of national culture by globalisation
- environmental challenges.

The Environmental Law Institute, established in 1969, is largely responsible for creating policy concerning environmental law in a number of territories within and outside the region. They are instrumental in reviewing laws relating to coastal and marine management, fisheries, conservation of the biodiversity, general environmental protection and land-use planning. Their assessment of the applied laws can draw attention to the environmental policy makers and other stake holders to issues concerning enforcement powers and penalties.

Questions

Knowledge and comprehension

1. Define the following terms:
    a) Natural resource
    b) Renewable resource
    c) Non-renewable resource

2. Describe TWO natural resources found in the Caribbean.

3. Identify TWO countries where bauxite is mined and describe its uses.

4. List FOUR uses of petroleum.

5. Outline TWO benefits of geothermal energy used in the Caribbean.

6. Describe TWO unsustainable practices which can harm coral reef biodiversity in a named Caribbean country.

Use of knowledge

7. Discuss TWO strategies to address the improper use of soil in a named Caribbean country.

8. Suggest TWO actions that can be taken to reduce deforestation.

9. Explain TWO uses of forests in the Caribbean.

10. Evaluate TWO sustainable agricultural practices in the Caribbean region.

11. Suggest THREE actions that a government can take to promote sustainable agricultural practices in communities.

SBA skills

Overview of countries in the Caribbean

Country	Total population (million)	Rural population (%)	Electricity access (%)	Electrical capacity (MW)	Electricity generation (GWh/year)	Hydropower capacity (MW)	Hydropower generation (GWh/year)
Cuba	11.5	23	100	6,407	20,459	66	64
Dominica	0.07	30	100	27	112	7	36
Dominican Republic	10.6	20	99	3,460	15,892	616	1,510
Grenada	0.1	64	92	51	223	0	0
Guadeloupe	0.4	2	N/A	573	1,791	11	34
Haiti	11.0	46	39	349	1,089	61	131
Jamaica	2.7	45	98	941	4,363	30	157
Puerto Rico	3.7	6	85	6,161	16,372	100	51
Saint Lucia	0.2	81	98	91	400	0	0
Saint Vincent and the Grenadines	0.1	48	97	58	166	7	37
Total	40.4	-	-	18,118	60,867	898	2,020

Source: WSHPDR 2016,[1] WSHPDR 2019,[1] WB,[4] WB[5]

Figure 11.23 Overview of energy generation in the Caribbean

Look at the table above and answer these questions.

1. a) Define 'hydropower'.
   b) Which country generated the largest amount of hydropower?
   c) List TWO countries where land is used extensively for agriculture.
   d) Examine the countries with the highest and lowest rates of electricity generation and explain the variations.

2. Look at the table below showing land use in Grenada in 2000 and answer the questions which follow.

Vegetation category	Area (ha)[1]	(%)
Foodcrops and vegetables	441	1.4
Foodcrops, vegetables, and fruit trees	790	2.5
Mixed cultivation	10305	33.1
Sugarcane	224	0.7
Abandoned cultivation	337	1.1
Bananas	22	0.1
Bananas with cacao and/or nutmeg	1095	3.5
Cacao	575	1.8
Coconut	498	1.6
Nutmeg	3382	10.9
Nutmeg and cacao	245	0.8
Moist deciduous and semi-deciduous rainforest	4007	12.9
Mixed primary and secondary evergreen rainforest	5247	16.9
Scrub/cactus	1718	5.5
Mangrove	172	0.6
Inland swamp	17	0.1
Pastures	182	0.6
Urban/suburban	1650	5.3
Industrial	44	0.1

[1] Based on data provided December 2005 by the Land Use Division, Ministry of Agriculture.

Figure 11.24 Land use in Grenada, 2000

a) What accounted for the greatest land use area?

b) What accounted for the smallest land use area?

c) Calculate the total percentage of the forested areas.

Climate change

Climate change is caused by humans, as a result of the burning of **fossil fuels** to generate energy for electricity, transportation and industry. Today, it is high on the international agenda due to its severe and intense effects. Halting climate change is essential if we want to ensure quality of life for future generations.

Learning objectives

- Explain the causes and consequences of climate change.
- Evaluate the responses to climate change.

> **Important definitions**
>
> *Anthropogenic* – environmental change caused by humans.
>
> *Climate change* – drastic changes experienced on a long-term basis affecting global temperatures and weather patterns.
>
> *Global warming* – the increase in temperatures around the world caused by the increase in carbon dioxide and other gases in the atmosphere.
>
> *Greenhouse effect* – heat is trapped in the Earth's atmosphere by greenhouse gases such as carbon dioxide, methane, nitrogen oxide and CFCs.
>
> *Fossil fuels* – deposits such as coal, oil and natural gas which contain carbon and hydrogen and are used for energy.
>
> *Deforestation* – cutting down large areas of forest without replanting.
>
> *Oxygen cycle* – the process by which plants use carbon dioxide, water and sunlight to make food through photosynthesis and then release oxygen.
>
> *Glaciers* – huge pieces of slowly moving ice which contain rock, snow and sediment.
>
> *Bleaching* – whitening of coral caused by warmer sea temperatures which destroy the microalgae, a supply of food for the corals.
>
> *Carbon footprint* – the measure of carbon dioxide and other greenhouse gases which an individual or company uses.
>
> *Biochar* – the product made after heating biomass without oxygen.
>
> *Carbon neutral* – when carbon emissions are balanced with emission reducing projects.

Causes and consequences of climate change

Causes of global warming

Global warming is considered to be the biggest environmental issue facing the world. Average global temperatures are rising quickly which is affecting life on land and in the sea. SDG's 14 and 15 are relevant here to ensure conservation and sustainability of land and sea use. The main cause of global warming is human activity. Human activities have caused large quantities of greenhouse gases to be released into the atmosphere, creating the **greenhouse effect**. This means the earth is like a greenhouse; heat cannot escape and so the planet warms up. Burning fossil fuels for energy results in the rising temperatures, as fossil fuels contain large amounts of carbon dioxide.

Figure 11.25 *A Trinidad oil refinery*

Another practice which causes high carbon emissions is **deforestation**. The removal of trees interrupts the **oxygen cycle** as fewer plants means more carbon dioxide in the atmosphere. Dead or decaying plant material also adds to the carbon release.

Methane is another greenhouse gas which is released from oil and gas wells, landfill, coal mines, agricultural activities and in livestock rearing. Methane traps even more heat than carbon dioxide and so we must work to control its emission levels. Coal mines are considered to be the biggest human cause of methane release.

Chlorofluorocarbons are also greenhouse gases and can be found in aerosol cans and refrigeration.

Consequences of global warming

Global warming is an indication that our overuse of natural resources is harming the atmosphere and environment. The most obvious signal is the melting of the ice caps and **glaciers** which is occurring in places like Greenland and the Antarctic Peninsula. This in turn raises sea levels which can be catastrophic in low-lying areas such as the Caribbean. The temperature rises are affecting both land and sea environments and can have devastating effects globally.

Table 11.10 highlights some of the land and sea changes brought on by global warming.

Land changes	Sea changes
Air temperature rises	Sea temperature rises
Changes to precipitation such as acid rain	Affects fish population and damages coral reefs
Regular, extreme weather conditions such as heavy rains, heatwaves and extreme cold	Rising ocean temperatures develop into extreme storms
	Algal bloom which can harm ecosystems
	Sea level rises

Table 11.10

Causes of climate change

The earth's atmosphere is designed to trap some of the heat from the sun, acting like a greenhouse. This process is important as the earth's temperature needs to be ideal for life to exist. However, global warming happens when excessive carbon dioxide in the atmosphere traps too much heat, resulting in rising global temperatures. In the last 60 years, evidence has proven that human actions have increased climate change. The burning of fossil fuels has been the main reason for increased carbon dioxide emissions.

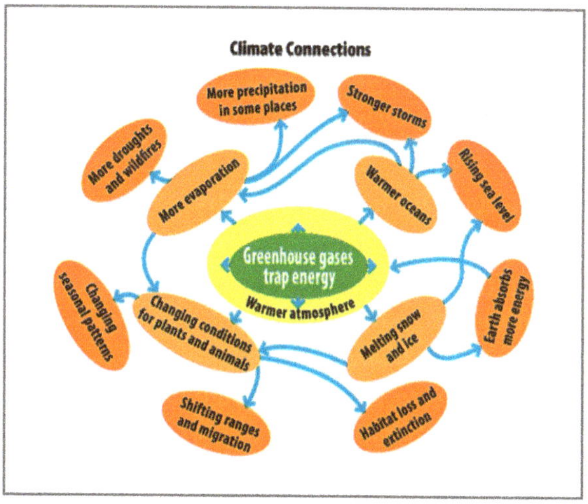

Figure 11.26 *Fossil fuel processing*

Consequences of climate change

Sea levels rise

Evidence suggests that sea levels are rising. In the last 100 years there has been a rise by as much as 20 centimetres which can have catastrophic effects on coastal areas. If this continues, low-lying areas will need to construct sea defences to protect themselves from the severe weather patterns.

Extreme climate variability

Extreme weather events become more common. Heavy rains and hurricanes are more regular and extreme as there is more water in the atmosphere. This can lead to flooding. Droughts and intense heat are also more frequent, causing forest fires and serious issues for agriculture.

Destruction of coral reefs

The National Oceanic and Atmospheric Administration has reported that higher sea temperatures in Trinidad and Tobago are causing damage to coral by a process of **bleaching**. As the coral dies, other marine life will be affected, altering the carefully balanced ecosystem.

Health related concerns

The Caribbean has a tropical climate which is very pleasant to live in. However, as temperatures rise due to climate change, people are being affected by heat-related illnesses and the spread of disease. Insects such as mosquitoes thrive in warm temperatures and are the carriers of a number of diseases such as malaria, dengue and the Zika virus. The graphic shown here presents a number of other health issues related to climate change.

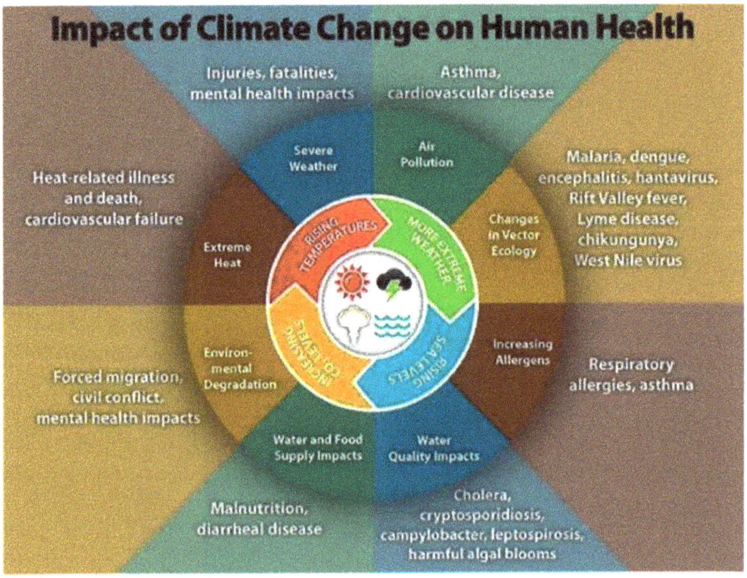

Figure 11.27 *Impact of climate change on human health*

Impact of climate change

Tourism

The Caribbean is a popular destination for tourism as the climate has the right characteristics for the industry to flourish. However, the industry is at risk as that same climate is undergoing changes. Small island developing states (SIDS) such as Barbados may experience beach erosion as a result of rising sea levels, leading to coastal degradation. The extreme and intense weather events such as heavy rainfall and gusty winds may damage infrastructure.

Agriculture, fishing and forestry

The development of the agricultural sector is also impacted by climate change. Agricultural production is hampered by natural disasters and extreme weather patterns which can interfere with economic growth.

The fishing industry is particularly vulnerable to sea temperatures rising as fish migrate to colder areas to survive. Climate change can affect the social and economic life of people who depend on fishing for a livelihood.

Tropical forests generally thrive in warm, wet conditions. As weather patterns change, temperatures in the Caribbean are predicted to rise which can lead to droughts in the dry season and significant rainfall leading to flooding and landslides in the wet season.

Table 11.11 gives some examples of climate change on agriculture, fishing and forestry.

Agriculture	Fishing	Forestry
Irrigation issues due to lack of water	Food insecurity when fish is a main part of the diet	Intense hurricanes can damage forests
Soil depletion	Ecosystem disruption	Trees prone to diseases
Coastal erosion	Fish extinction	Landslides

Table 11.11

Water supply

Water is an essential commodity that becomes even more essential during long periods of intense heat brought about by climate change. During droughts, water is scarce and there can be issues with water quality and safety. Regular natural disasters can affect the water supply so that water-borne diseases can be spread easily.

Water salinity can occur when water particles evaporate from seas, oceans and the land due to intense heat, raising the salt content in water and in the soil. In Barbados, ground water aquifers are the main water source and so the country is vulnerable during the climate crisis.

Responses to climate change

As a global phenomenon, climate change needs to be addressed at all levels.

Individuals

If everyone in the world makes an effort, a difference can be made to climate change. The personal goal should be to reduce your **carbon footprint**. In all aspects of our life, we are able to make subtle changes like reduce (waste), reuse (rather than throwing away) and recycle (re-invent). This principle became popular in the 1970s in the USA and contributes to sustainability.

In travel, we should aim to use shared modes of transport if we cannot walk or cycle. This can be carpools or public transport. Investing in an electric car is a good step to take. Both Barbados and Jamaica have encouraged the use of electric vehicles on the road by providing charging facilities.

Home owners can improve their energy efficiency by using the 'IoT' (Internet of Things) to turn their home into a smart home. This means devices can operate and switch off and on when owners are away. This can save energy and reduce emissions.

Figure 11.28 *Reduce, reuse, recycle*

Communities

Agricultural communities can improve their sustainability by using **biochar** instead of nitrogen-based fertilisers to help with plant growth. Farmers can also use waste materials in different areas of the farming process, and use renewable energy sources such as wind turbines and solar panels to power machinery.

Planting trees not only adds beauty to an urban area but absorbs more carbon dioxide from the atmosphere, as plants use it as part of photosynthesis.

Organisations

A number of organisations are working hard to tackle climate change. The movement known as '350' are promoting international use of renewable energy as opposed to oil and gas. Environmental NGOs (non-governmental organisations) such as Climate Action Network (CAN) also do their part to educate people and put pressure on governments about the climate crisis.

The Carbon Zero Initiative (CZITT), an NGO in Trinidad and Tobago, organised a 1000 tree planting challenge in 2019 to celebrate World Environment Day on 5th June. At this event, it was pledged that the country should aim to become **carbon neutral** by 2050.

Government

Adapting to climate change is essential in order to mitigate the impact on urban planning. This means conducting risk assessments and zoning land for different categories: industrial, historical, residential and commercial.

Government building regulations must consider flood risk due to the increase in sea levels as well as climate proofing of buildings against extreme heat. Rebuilding after natural disasters is costly so it is wise to rebuild with future issues in mind.

Figure 11.29 *An electric vehicle charging point in Jamaica*

Many governments have taken action to deal with climate change head on. Barbados introduced a National Resilience Programme called 'Roofs to Reefs', which aimed to make homes more resilient to extreme weather, increase water storage capacity and make its use more efficient, reduce emissions and pollution, make infrastructure climate resilient and restore reef ecosystems.

The Barbados National Energy Policy 2019–2030 outlined a number of ways to mitigate climate change. One way is to prepare the workforce with the new skills needed to transition from an energy-based industry to a renewable energy-based industry. Climate change is happening and governments need to take a proactive approach to the issues it presents.

SDG 13 is climate action. Work needs to be done to not only deal with the environmental impact of climate change but the pressures placed on socioeconomic development and sustainability. Trinidad, being a small island developing state, was the biggest producer of carbon dioxide emissions in the Caribbean. In order to address climate change there needs to be partnership between governments, the private sector, individuals and even with CARICOM.

In order for governments to move towards being carbon neutral or negative they can take steps such as partnering with utilities and the private sector and offering incentives to reduce carbon emissions through electrifying transportation. This has been done in Jamaica.

Regional and international bodies

The United Nations Framework Convention on Climate Change (UNFCCC), established in 1994, aimed to steady the levels of greenhouse gases released by humans. Most countries have agreed to this Convention. Developed countries were required to cut emissions to 1990 levels by the year 2000. It is also a requirement that developed countries assist developing countries in their efforts and report on the actions taken.

The Kyoto Protocol, which formally came into effect in 2005, was administered by the UNFCCC. The Protocol has systems to monitor, review and verify the work countries do, as well as providing assistance to cope with the effects of the climate change.

The Paris Agreement was made at the UN Climate Change Conference known as COP21 (21st Conference of the Parties), and officially came into effect in 2016. This treaty aimed to limit global warming levels to an increase of 1.5°C and participating countries had to outline the actions taken to reduce their greenhouse gas emissions.

The Caribbean Community has established the CCCCC (Caribbean Community Climate Change Centre) which is able to provide forecasts, give feedback about climate change impacts and help create sustainable development programmes.

Questions

Knowledge and comprehension

1. Define the following terms:
    a) Climate change
    b) Global warming
    c) Conservation of resources

2. Describe TWO effects of climate change in the Caribbean.

3. Identify and describe THREE anthropogenic practices which can lead to high emissions of greenhouse gases.

4. Outline THREE ways that climate change can be addressed on an individual basis.

5. List TWO actions that organisations can take to tackle climate change.

Use of knowledge

6. Discuss the impacts of climate change on the tourism industry.

7. Examine TWO strategies that governments can take to respond to climate change.

8. Suggest THREE areas, other than the tourism industry, which are affected by climate change and describe the impact on each.

End of chapter questions

1. a) Define the term 'soil erosion'. (2 marks)
   b) Outline TWO practices which lead to soil erosion. (4 marks)
   c) Industrial negligence is to blame for the damage to the environment.
      (i) Suggest TWO actions that Caribbean governments can take to mitigate this negligence. (4 marks)
      (ii) Explain why EACH action suggested in c) (i) is likely to be successful. (4 marks)

      TOTAL 14 MARKS

2. a) Define the term 'greenhouse effect'. (2 marks)
   b) Outline TWO consequences of climate change on SIDS (Small Island Developing States). (4 marks)
   c) Anthropogenic factors play a huge role in the climate crisis in the Caribbean.

(i) Suggest TWO ways that Caribbean governments can reduce these factors in the region. (4 marks)

(ii) Explain why EACH action suggested in c) (i) is likely to be successful. (4 marks)

TOTAL 14 MARKS

SUSTAINABLE DEVELOPMENT AND USE OF RESOURCES

The natural environment is being destroyed at an alarming rate due to anthropogenic influences.

3. The Environmental club at your school is hosting an educational symposium in celebration of Earth Day 2025 to discuss the statement above.

Prepare a formal speech in which you:

- define the term 'anthropogenic'
- identify two practices which are anthropogenic
- outline TWO effects of these anthropogenic practices on EITHER the marine life OR land
- suggest THREE actions the government might use to reduce the impact of these practices in your country
- explain why any TWO of these actions are likely to be successful.

TOTAL 22 MARKS

Summary

Natural resources enable a population to support themselves economically, socially and culturally. The Caribbean region has a healthy blend of renewable and non-renewable resources which, if used sustainably, can meet national development targets.

The natural resources can be used to feed, house and protect the citizens of a country. Economies can develop through agriculture, forestry and tourism. However, some practices are unsustainable and have a negative impact on the environment.

Climate change is the biggest issue facing the world at the moment. As a region, we can play our part to reduce negative anthropogenic influences while monitoring the changes in our climate.

The Caribbean region has witnessed the impact of climate change first hand as the islands are small and low-lying and have felt the impact of harsh weather conditions. The tourism, agriculture and forestry industries have also been severely affected by climate change.

Several agencies and institutions are working hard to address climate change urgently, but we must all play our part.

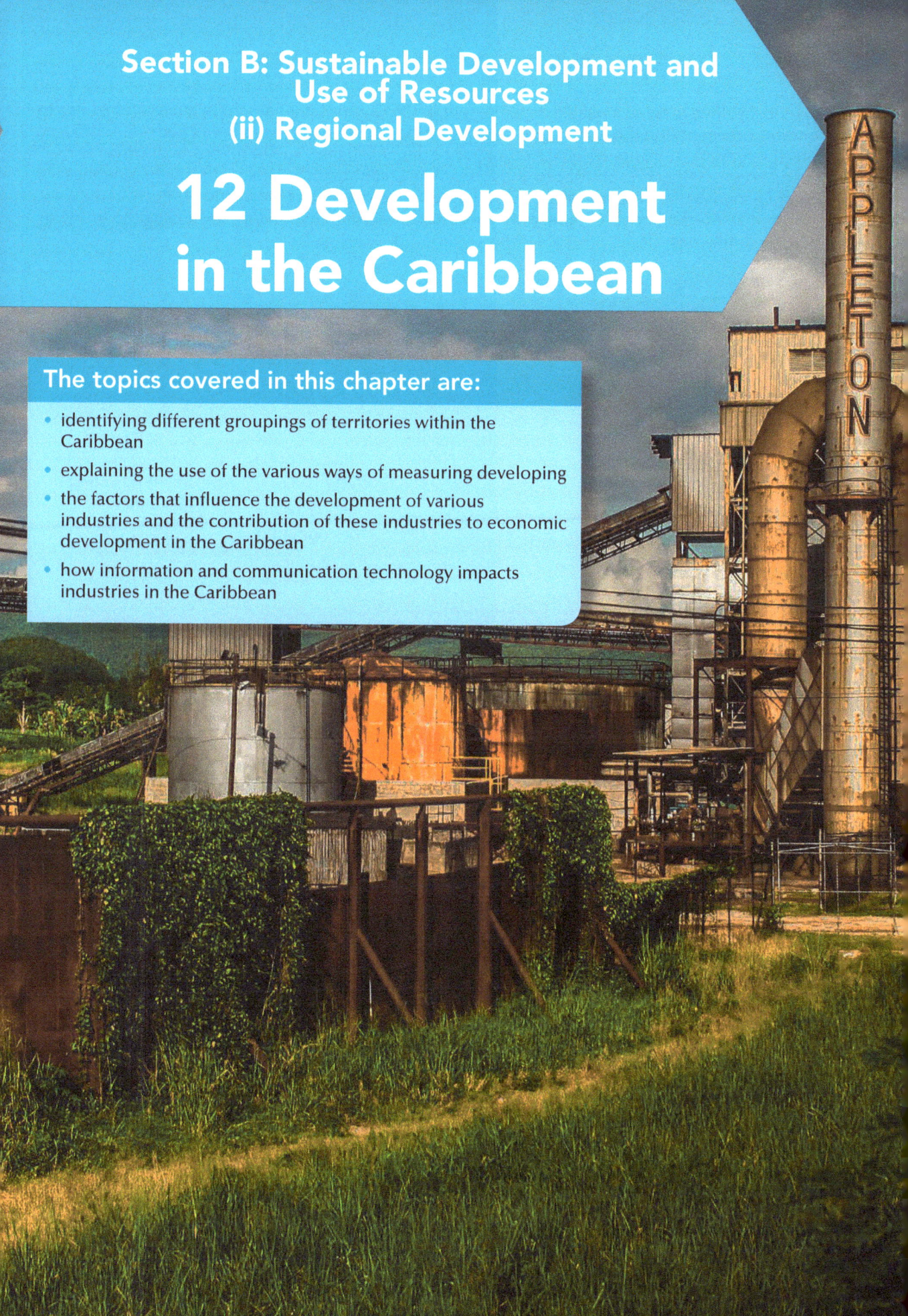

Section B: Sustainable Development and Use of Resources
(ii) Regional Development
12 Development in the Caribbean

The topics covered in this chapter are:
- identifying different groupings of territories within the Caribbean
- explaining the use of the various ways of measuring developing
- the factors that influence the development of various industries and the contribution of these industries to economic development in the Caribbean
- how information and communication technology impacts industries in the Caribbean

Development in the Caribbean

Can tourism alone drive sustainable development in the Caribbean, or are there alternative routes to economic prosperity? In this chapter we will look at the contrasting development paths of Caribbean countries, from the tourism-dependent economies of the Bahamas and Barbados to the diverse industrial base of Trinidad and Tobago and the growing tech sector in Jamaica. By comparing these different economic models, we will learn about the varied nature of growth and progress in the region and assess the impact of information and communication technology in shaping the future of Caribbean industries.

Case study

Country	Development Model	Economic Strengths	Challenges	What Can We Learn?
The Bahamas	Mostly relies on tourism	– Tourism brings in a lot of money – Creates many jobs – Helps build hotels, airports, etc.	– Economy suffers if fewer tourists come – Damage to the environment – Too dependent on one industry	– Tourism helps, but relying on just one thing is risky. The Bahamas needs to add other industries to be stronger.
Barbados	Tourism and financial services (like banks)	– Has both tourism and international business – More stable economy	– Can be affected by global financial issues – Has to stay competitive with other tourist destinations	– Mixing tourism with other industries makes Barbados stronger. It should continue to explore new business opportunities.
Trinidad and Tobago	Industrial economy focused on oil and gas	– High income for the country – Strong industrial growth – Big energy exporter	– Depends too much on oil and gas – Environmental damage from oil extraction	– Oil and gas have made the country rich, but it needs to diversify since fossil fuels aren't sustainable long-term.
Jamaica	Growing technology (ICT) and creative industries	– New tech jobs being created – Innovation attracts international interest	– Needs better internet and infrastructure – Skills gap in tech – Rural areas left behind in tech growth	– Jamaica's tech sector has great potential. More investment in technology and education will help the economy grow sustainably.

Country	Development Model	Economic Strengths	Challenges	What Can We Learn?
Dominica	Eco-tourism and agriculture	– Focus on eco-friendly tourism – Agriculture, especially bananas, supports the economy	– Vulnerable to hurricanes and climate change – Small size limits industry growth	– Dominica's eco-tourism model is promising, but it needs to protect its environment and develop other sectors like green energy and tech.
Guyana	Emerging oil industry and agriculture	– Huge potential with new oil discoveries – Strong agricultural base (rice, sugar)	– Environmental risks from oil production – Risk of over-dependence on oil	– Guyana can become wealthy from oil, but it must manage its natural resources carefully and use the money to develop other industries.

Different groupings of territories in the Caribbean

Learning objectives

- Learn about the Caribbean's main areas: Greater Antilles, Lesser Antilles, Leewards and Windwards.
- Explore the Eastern Caribbean and its islands.
- Study the Caribbean's mainland countries: Guyana, Suriname and Belize.

Important definitions

Greater Antilles – a group of larger islands in the Caribbean region, including Cuba, Hispaniola (the island containing Haiti and the Dominican Republic), Puerto Rico and Jamaica.

Lesser Antilles – a chain of smaller islands in the Caribbean, extending from the Virgin Islands in the north to Trinidad and Tobago in the south.

Mainland territories – countries situated along the Caribbean coast of Central and South America, including Belize, Guyana and Suriname.

Leewards – a group of islands in the northern Lesser Antilles, sheltered from the prevailing trade winds. Key islands include Anguilla, Antigua and Barbuda, Saint Kitts and Nevis, Montserrat and the Virgin Islands.

Windwards – the southern islands of the Lesser Antilles, exposed to the trade winds. Key islands include Dominica, Saint Lucia, Saint Vincent and the Grenadines, Grenada and Martinique.

Eastern Caribbean – the easternmost part of the Caribbean Sea, including islands from the Virgin Islands to Grenada. It features diverse landscapes, rich cultures and economies driven by tourism, agriculture and financial services. Key countries include Antigua and Barbuda, Dominica, Saint Lucia and Barbados.

Territorial dynamics in the Caribbean

The Caribbean is a group of islands with coastal areas, each with its own story shaped by Indigenous, African and European colonisers, trade and cultural mixing. Think of the **Greater Antilles** as the big historical stage where Europeans first arrived and started using the land and resources. The **Lesser Antilles**, **Leeward** and **Windward** islands were important for ships travelling with the trade winds, which helped them move goods and influence cultures. The **Eastern Caribbean** countries, often connected by their British colonial past, work together economically and politically. Then there are places like Guyana, Suriname and Belize on the mainland of South and Central America; they are part of the Caribbean family too because of their history and culture. All these parts make up the Caribbean, showing us how history, trade and shared experiences have shaped this diverse region, affecting issues like climate change, migration and how these countries work together.

Figure 12.1 *Independent states*

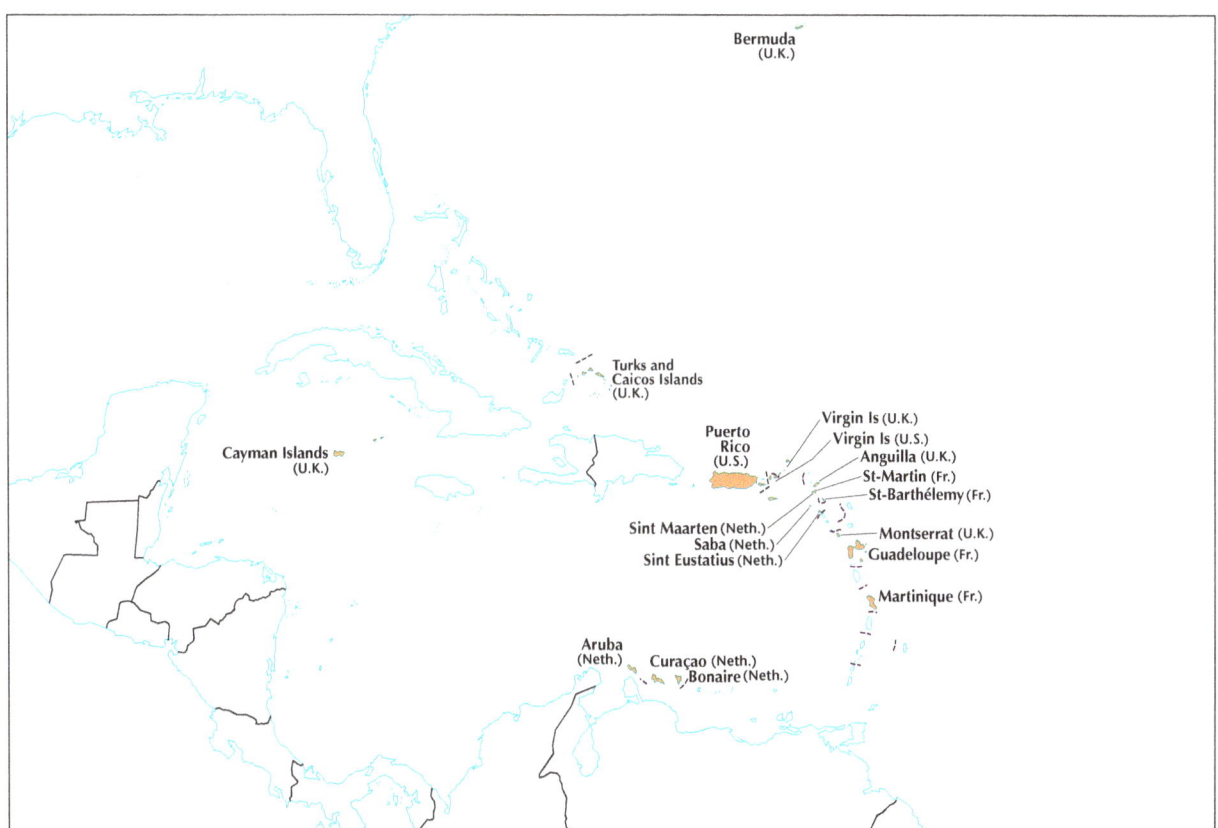

Figure 12.2 *Dependent states*

Table 12.1 shows the economic integration of the Caribbean region.

Economic integration		
Caribbean Community (CARICOM)	Antigua and Barbuda, Bahamas, Barbados, Belize, Dominica, Grenada, Guyana (associate member), Haiti, Jamaica, Montserrat, Saint Kitts and Nevis, Saint Lucia, Saint Vincent and the Grenadines, Suriname, Trinidad and Tobago	This is a regional trade bloc that promotes economic cooperation and development.
Organisation of Eastern Caribbean States (OECS)	Antigua and Barbuda, Dominica, Grenada, Montserrat, Saint Kitts and Nevis, Saint Lucia, Saint Vincent and the Grenadines	This is a regional grouping of smaller Eastern Caribbean islands that promotes economic and political cooperation.
Other:	Anguilla, Aruba, Bermuda, Bonaire, British Virgin Islands, Cayman Islands, Curaçao, Guadeloupe, Martinique, Saba, Saint Barthélemy, Sint Eustatius, Sint Maarten, Turks and Caicos Islands, United States Virgin Islands	These territories are not members of any major regional economic integration group.

Table 12.1

Historical creation

These groupings came about due to the region's colonial past, economic development and cultural diversity. Understanding these groupings provides insights into the historical forces that have shaped the Caribbean over the centuries.

Greater Antilles and Lesser Antilles

In the Caribbean, the Greater and Lesser Antilles share a rich historical colonial past. The Greater Antilles, home to larger islands like Cuba, Hispaniola (Haiti and the Dominican Republic), Puerto Rico and Jamaica, were among the first to encounter Spanish, French, and English colonisers. These islands became colonial powerhouses, strategically important for their locations and wealth of resources.

The Lesser Antilles, a chain of smaller islands stretching from the Virgin Islands to Trinidad and Tobago, specialised in certain crops like sugar and tobacco.

The influence of Spanish, English and Dutch is evident across these islands, each leaving a distinct mark on cultural expressions, traditions and interactions, such as Barbados with its English heritage and Dominica, Grenada and Saint Lucia's blend of French and English influences.

Leewards and Windwards

Figure 12.3 *The Leeward and Windward Islands within the Caribbean*

The Leeward and Windward Islands in the Lesser Antilles played a significant role in the region's maritime history, due to the prevailing trade winds used by European navigators. The Leeward Islands, including Antigua and Barbuda, Saint Kitts and Nevis and Anguilla, are positioned to the west and north, making them the first port of call for ships sailing from Europe. This strategic location made them useful in establishing trade routes, colonial outposts and economic hubs.

The Windward Islands, such as Dominica, Saint Lucia and Saint Vincent and the Grenadines, located to the south and east, were encountered later by European explorers. Their position influenced their development, with these islands often becoming centres for agriculture and later, tourism, due to their lush landscapes and strategic ports.

Dominica's mountainous terrain and dense forests made large-scale plantation agriculture challenging, leading to a smaller plantation economy compared to other Caribbean islands. The island's location in the Eastern Caribbean made it a valuable asset for monitoring and controlling the surrounding ocean, especially given its proximity to the French territories of Martinique and Guadeloupe.

Trade and cultural exchange flourished between the Leeward and Windward Islands, with the movement of goods, people and cultural practices.

Competition and conflict have existed between these groups of countries as a result of political tension due to differing alliances, economic competition with regards to tourism and investment and environmental concerns such as climate change and natural disasters which have placed strains on resources and access to international aid.

Eastern Caribbean

The Eastern Caribbean reflects historical ties dating back to colonial times. Many Eastern Caribbean countries were British colonies and share a history of British colonial administration. These states have a shared history of economic cooperation and integration, such as the Eastern Caribbean Currency Union, supported by regional organisations like the Eastern Caribbean Central Bank.

Mainland territories: Guyana, Suriname and Belize

The historical connections between Guyana, Suriname and Belize and the wider Caribbean are rooted in their colonial pasts, which have influenced their languages, legal systems and cultural landscapes. In Guyana and Suriname, Dutch colonial rule has left a lasting mark. For instance, in Suriname, Dutch is still the official language, and the country's legal system and administrative structures are based on Dutch models. Even though Guyana is primarily English-speaking today, it retains Dutch-influenced place names and legal principles from its period under Dutch rule.

In Belize, British colonisation is evident in its official language, English, making it unique in Central America. British influence extends to the legal system, which is based on English common law, and cultural practices that mirror those of the English-speaking Caribbean, such as cricket and other British sports.

The Creole cultures in these countries mirror the blend of African, Indigenous, European and Asian influences found throughout the Caribbean islands. Indigenous populations have also left their mark on the cultural identity of these territories, further connecting them to the heritage of the wider Caribbean. The **mainland territories**' active participation in Caribbean regional organisations like CARICOM reflects their shared historical and cultural ties and their collaborative approach to regional development and integration.

Historical significance of groupings by language

- Spanish-speaking Caribbean (Greater Antilles)

The impact of Spanish rule is evident in the language, culture, and architectural heritage of countries like Cuba, the Dominican Republic and Puerto Rico. This shared linguistic heritage reflects a common colonial past and historical ties.

- English-speaking Caribbean

English-speaking Caribbean territories, including islands in the Lesser Antilles and mainland territories like Belize, have a historical connection

Figure 12.4 *Spanish architecture in Havana, Cuba*

to British colonial rule. The English language remains a lasting legacy of this period. These countries share their historical struggle against enslavement the impact of the British Empire on governance structures and the development of trade networks, contributing to a collective identity.

- Dutch-speaking Caribbean (Suriname)

Suriname, situated on the northeastern coast of South America, shares historical ties with the Dutch Caribbean. The significance of the Dutch language in Suriname is rooted in its colonial past under Dutch rule. This linguistic connection underscores the shared history and cultural exchanges between Suriname and Dutch-speaking Caribbean territories.

Figure 12.5 Rose Hall Great House in Jamaica is an example of British architecture

Historical significance of groupings by economic integration

- Eastern Caribbean Currency Union (ECCU)

The Eastern Caribbean Currency Union, comprising countries like Saint Kitts and Nevis, Antigua and Barbuda, Dominica, Saint Lucia, Grenada and St. Vincent and the Grenadines reflects a historical commitment to economic collaboration post-colonisation. The establishment of a common currency, the Eastern Caribbean Dollar, and monetary policies illustrates efforts to integrate economies and strengthen regional resilience, acknowledging historical ties under British colonial rule.

Figure 12.6 Dutch architecture in Paramaribo, Suriname

- CARICOM (Caribbean Community)

CARICOM is historically significant for fostering economic cooperation among Caribbean nations, both English-speaking and non-English-speaking. It was founded in the post-independence era to promote economic development, trade and political collaboration. The historical context includes a shared desire for economic self-determination and resilience in the face of global challenges.

- ALBA-TCP (Bolivarian Alliance for the Peoples of Our America – Peoples' Trade Treaty)

Some Caribbean nations, including Cuba and several in the Lesser Antilles, have engaged in alliances such as ALBA-TCP, reflecting historical ties and shared political ideologies. The significance lies in the pursuit of economic integration based on principles of solidarity and cooperation, challenging historical patterns of dependence on former colonial powers.

Questions

Knowledge and comprehension

1. What are the Greater Antilles and which major islands are included in this group?
2. Define 'Leeward Islands' and list two islands that belong to this group.

3 Explain the significance of the Eastern Caribbean in the context of regional cooperation and economic integration.

4 What role did the trade winds play in the historical development of the Windward and Leeward islands?

5 Describe how information and communication technology impacts industries in the Caribbean.

Use of knowledge

6 How do the historical groupings of Caribbean territories (such as the Greater Antilles, Lesser Antilles, and mainland territories) impact their current economic activities and regional cooperation?

7 What role does economic integration (such as CARICOM and the OECS) play in promoting sustainable development across the Caribbean? Provide examples of how these organisations support economic cooperation.

Measuring development

Development is a concept that includes economic measures such as GDP growth, but also improvements in key areas that contribute to the wellbeing and quality of life of the population. For example, development includes access to quality education, comprehensive healthcare services for physical and mental wellbeing, and environmental sustainability practices that protect natural resources for future generations. Development also involves promoting cultural autonomy, allowing communities to preserve and celebrate their heritage and traditions. Citizens must also have the right and means to engage in the political process and decision-making processes.

In essence, development is about expanding the range of choices, freedoms and opportunities available to people, enabling them to lead lives of value.

In the global context, development for Caribbean nations involves achieving internal progress but also positioning themselves favourably on the world stage.

Learning objectives

- Learn the difference between economic growth and overall development.
- Look at how GDP, income per person and living costs show economic health.
- Study how education, health and social services indicate social progress.
- Learn about the Human Development Index as a way to measure a country's development.
- Use these measures to understand a country's economic and social health.

> **Important definitions**
>
> *Development* – the process through which a society improves the economic, political and social wellbeing of its people. It involves increasing the standard of living and quality of life, reducing poverty and ensuring sustainable access to resources and essential services such as education, healthcare and clean water.
>
> *Human Development Index (HDI)* – a statistical measure of a country's average achievements in three categories; health (life expectancy at birth), education (mean and expected years of schooling) and standard of living (Gross National Income per capita).
>
> *Gross Domestic Product (GDP)* – the total value of all goods and services produced within a country over a specific time period. It is a key indicator of a nation's economic performance.
>
> *Gross National Product (GNP)* – the total market value of all goods and services produced by the nationals of a country, whether within the country or abroad.
>
> *Multidimensional Poverty Index (MPI)* – a measure that assesses poverty from a multidimensional perspective, considering various factors such as health, education and standard of living, providing a more comprehensive understanding of deprivation beyond income alone.
>
> *Natural resources* – raw materials found in the environment that are used by humans for economic production and consumption. These can include minerals, water, forests and agricultural products.
>
> *Infrastructure* – the basic physical and organisational structures and facilities needed for the operation of a society, industry or enterprise. This can include transportation systems, communication networks and utilities.
>
> *Government policies* – intentional plans, decisions and actions adopted by a government to address specific issues or guide the overall direction of the country. These policies can encompass economic, social, environmental and foreign affairs.
>
> *Tourism* – the activities of individuals travelling to places outside their usual environment for leisure, business or other purposes. It is a significant industry in many regions, contributing to economic development.
>
> *Agriculture* – the cultivation of the soil for the purpose of producing food and other goods. It includes activities such as farming, livestock rearing and the cultivation of crops.
>
> *Offshore finance* – financial services conducted in a jurisdiction other than a person or company's home country. It often involves activities such as banking, investment and asset management in low-tax or tax haven locations.

Ways of measuring development

- Economic
- Social
- **Human Development Index (HDI)**

Economic measures

Gross Domestic Product (GDP) and **Gross National Product (GNP)** are measures used to assess the economic **development** of Caribbean countries. These indicators look beyond economic output, offering a greater understanding of a nation's economic health.

Gross Domestic Product (GDP): This represents the total market value of all goods and services produced within a country during a specific period. GDP measures the overall economic activity within a territory. It encompasses looking at the combined economic activity of the different sectors such as **agriculture**, manufacturing, services and more. Comparing the GDP of Caribbean countries to that of other nations gives a relative assessment of economic size and productivity.

Gross National Product (GNP): Unlike GDP, GNP accounts for the total market value of all goods and services produced by the nationals of a country, whether within the country or abroad. GNP includes the income earned by a nation's residents from foreign investments. This indicator is especially useful for nations that are heavily involved in international trade and investments.

Examining the contribution of different economic sectors to GDP and GNP provides information about the diversification of the economy. For instance, a heavy reliance on a single sector, such as **tourism** or agriculture, may indicate vulnerability to external shocks.

While GDP and GNP give an overall view of economic performance, evaluating these figures on a per capita (per person) basis provides more understanding. This measure divides the total economic output by the population, giving us figures for the average income and standard of living for individuals.

Tracking the trajectory of GDP and GNP over time can indicate economic trends. Whether experiencing growth, stagnation or contraction, these trends inform policymakers and stakeholders about the effectiveness of economic policies and potential areas for improvement.

By comparing the GDP and GNP of Caribbean countries to global benchmarks, we can assess their competitiveness on the international stage. Understanding the relative position of these nations in the global economy helps to identify opportunities for trade, investment and economic partnerships.

Development enhances people's lives by improving education, healthcare and job opportunities. For example, better schools increase career choices, while improved healthcare ensures longer, healthier lives. In the Caribbean, while GDP and GNP measure economic growth, true development also involves sustainable jobs, environmental protection and social inclusion, offering a holistic view of progress that expands individual freedoms and opportunities.

Table 12.2 shows the GDP and GNP of Caribbean countries.

GDP and GNP of Caribbean Countries (2024)				
Country	GDP (USD, billions)	GNP (USD, billions)	Key economic sectors	Comparison with other Caribbean countries
Bahamas	13.7	11.4	Tourism, financial services	The Bahamas has a relatively high GDP per capita compared to many Caribbean countries, largely driven by tourism and banking, but it is highly vulnerable to global tourism fluctuations.
Barbados	5.3	4.8	Tourism, financial services, agriculture	Barbados has a diversified economy, with a stable financial services sector, making it more resilient than economies solely dependent on tourism.
Trinidad and Tobago	24.1	22.3	Oil, natural gas, petrochemicals	Trinidad and Tobago has one of the highest GDPs in the Caribbean due to its energy sector, making it less dependent on tourism and more industrialised than many of its neighbours.
Jamaica	16.3	15.5	Tourism, agriculture, ICT, manufacturing	Jamaica's economy is heavily reliant on tourism, but its growing tech sector and agriculture provide additional sources of income, making it more diversified than some smaller islands.

GDP and GNP of Caribbean Countries (2024)				
Country	GDP (USD, billions)	GNP (USD, billions)	Key economic sectors	Comparison with other Caribbean countries
Dominica	0.6	0.5	Ecotourism, agriculture (bananas), geothermal	Dominica's GDP is much lower compared to larger islands due to its smaller size, but it is increasingly focusing on ecotourism and geothermal energy as sustainable development pathways.
Guyana	17.3	15.2	Oil, agriculture, gold mining	With recent oil discoveries, Guyana has seen significant growth in its GDP, making it one of the fastest-growing economies in the region. It surpasses many Caribbean islands in growth.
St. Lucia	2.1	1.9	Tourism, agriculture, financial services	St. Lucia's economy is primarily tourism-based, with financial services also playing a role. Its GDP is higher than smaller Eastern Caribbean islands but still tourism-dependent.
Haiti	21.6	19.8	Agriculture, textiles, remittances	Despite having a relatively high population, Haiti's GDP per capita is among the lowest in the Caribbean, reflecting deep economic struggles and reliance on foreign aid.
Cuba	100	95.5	Tourism, healthcare, biotechnology, agriculture	Cuba's economy is state-controlled and more diversified, with strong sectors in healthcare and biotechnology. It has the highest GDP among Caribbean nations, due to its large population.

Table 12.2
Source: World Bank Open Data

> We can use Antigua, an island nation in the Caribbean, as an example. It has a vibrant economy with different sectors contributing to its overall wealth.
>
> **Gross Domestic Product (GDP) = The total earnings of everyone living and working on Antigua.**
>
> – Antigua has three main sectors: Fishing, Tourism and Agriculture.
> – The fishers catch fish, the farmers grow crops and the tourism sector involves hotels, restaurants and attractions.
> – The total value of all fish caught, crops grown, and money spent by tourists in Antigua in a year is the GDP.
>
> **Gross National Product (GNP) = The total earnings of everyone from Antigua, including those who work abroad.**
>
> – Antiguans working in other countries such as the United States or Canada, who send part of their earnings to their families in Antigua.
> – The GNP includes the money earned by Antiguans both at home and abroad.

Per capita income

Per capita income is the average income of individuals in Caribbean countries. Comparing this measure on a global scale gives us an understanding of the standard of living relative to other nations.

Per capita income is like looking at the average money each person in a country has earned in a year. It helps us understand how well-off, on average, the people in a country are.

We can use Antigua again to illustrate this.

- Antigua has a total income, which is the combined money earned by everyone on the island.
- It also has a population, which is the total number of people living in Antigua.
- To find per capita income, you divide the total income by the population. It is like sharing all the money earned equally among every person.

Example calculation:

- If Antigua has a total income of $100 million and a population of 1 million people, the per capita income would be $100 million / 1 million people = $100 per person.

Cost of living

The cost of living index is a tool that helps us understand how much money people need in a particular place to afford a standard set of goods and services. It's a way to measure how expensive or affordable it is to live in a specific location.

The cost of living index considers a standard set of goods and services that people typically need, such as food, housing, transportation, healthcare and education. Researchers gather data on the prices of these items in a country. They then compare this data to a global standard or average.

Example:

- Imagine the global average cost for the standard set of goods and services is $1,000. If the cost of the same items in the Caribbean country is $1,200, the cost of living index for this country would be 1.2 (because $1,200 / $1,000 = 1.2).

If the cost of living index is higher than 1, it means that, on average, living in that country is more expensive than the global standard. If it is lower than 1, it indicates that the cost of living is relatively more affordable.

Social measures

Education: Measuring the number of educational institutions, enrolment rates and educational attainment in Caribbean nations provides a basis for understanding the development of human capital and how it compares globally.

Literacy rate: Literacy rates in the Caribbean reflect the educational achievements of the population, showing how well these countries fare in terms of basic literacy compared to other regions.

Life expectancy: Life expectancy at birth in Caribbean countries is a critical health indicator, offering insights into the overall wellbeing of the population in comparison to global standards.

Infant mortality rate: Comparing the infant mortality rate in the Caribbean to global averages provides valuable information about the effectiveness of healthcare and sanitation practices in these nations.

Availability of social services: Assessing the availability and accessibility of social services, including healthcare and housing, helps gauge the overall quality of life in the Caribbean relative to other parts of the world.

Human Development Index (HDI)

The **Human Development Index (HDI)** is a composite statistic used to measure a country's overall achievement in its social and economic dimensions. The HDI focuses on three main factors:

1. **Life expectancy at birth:** Measures the ability to live a long and healthy life.
2. **Education:** Combines the average number of years of schooling for adults aged 25 years or older and the expected years of schooling for children entering the educational system.
3. **Gross National Income (GNI) per capita:** Reflects the standard of living in terms of income, adjusted for purchasing power parity (PPP).

How HDI scores are interpreted

- **HDI Scores** range from 0 to 1, where:
    - **0.800 or above:** Very high human development
    - **0.700 – 0.799:** High human development
    - **0.550 – 0.699:** Medium human development
    - **Below 0.550:** Low human development

Table 12.3 shows the HDI of several Caribbean countries compared to global countries.

Country	HDI (Most Recent)	Global ranking (approximate)	Development category
Bahamas	0.814	58th	Very high human development
Barbados	0.788	70th	High human development
Trinidad and Tobago	0.796	67th	High human development
Jamaica	0.726	101st	High human development
Guyana	0.682	122nd	Medium human development
Haiti	0.510	170th	Low human development
Cuba	0.783	72nd	High human development

Table 12.3

Analysis of Caribbean countries' HDI

- The Bahamas and Trinidad and Tobago are among the highest-ranked Caribbean countries, scoring in the very high to high human development categories, largely due to their strong income levels and improved life expectancy.
- Barbados, Jamaica and Cuba also fall into the high human development category, with steady progress in health and education.
- Guyana has a medium HDI score, reflective of the country's developmental challenges despite recent economic growth due to oil discoveries.
- Haiti ranks very low, struggling in almost all indicators, particularly life expectancy and income, which severely impacts its HDI score.

Global comparisons

The highest-ranking HDI countries globally are Norway, Switzerland and Ireland, with scores above 0.950, showcasing advanced living standards, healthcare and education systems compared to Caribbean nations.

Uses of development indicators

Policy planning

Development indicators help Caribbean policymakers to craft strategies and policies to address specific challenges and encourage overall development. These indicators range from economic measures like GDP to social indicators such as literacy rates and life expectancy. They provide essential data that policymakers analyse to create strategies and policies tailored to the unique challenges and opportunities of the region.

Economic development indicators such as Gross Domestic Product (GDP) and Gross National Product (GNP) are benchmarks for assessing the overall economic health of Caribbean nations. By examining economic indicators like GDP and GNP, policymakers can determine economic strengths, weaknesses and trends, guiding them to encourage growth or mitigate inequalities. These interventions can involve measures for health **infrastructure**, such as building hospitals or improving public health services, reforming educational policies to increase access and quality of education, allocating economic resources for certain sectors, and strategies to reduce income inequality, ensuring a more equal distribution of wealth and opportunities.

Social development indicators, including in education and healthcare, offer insights into the human capital of the Caribbean population. Policymakers use literacy rates, educational attainment levels, and health-related indicators to find out if existing education and healthcare systems are effective. This information guides the design of policies aimed at improving access to quality education and healthcare services, ultimately contributing to the overall wellbeing and productivity of the population.

The Human Development Index (HDI), which combines economic and social indicators, provides a comprehensive snapshot of a nation's development. Policymakers can use the HDI to prioritise areas that require attention, ensuring a balanced and inclusive approach to development.

Development indicators not only assist in identifying challenges but also serve as tools for monitoring the impact of implemented policies. By regularly assessing these indicators, policymakers can track the progress of initiatives and make adjustments to ensure that policies are producing the right outcomes.

International comparisons

International comparisons of these development indicators allow Caribbean policymakers to determine where their nations sit in relation to others. Understanding how their countries fare in relation to other nations provides information for best practice and improvement. Policymakers can learn from successful strategies implemented elsewhere and tailor them to suit the specific context of the Caribbean.

International comparisons provide Caribbean nations with useful information about their progress and standing on the global stage. These comparisons enable countries in the Caribbean to assess their development path, identify areas of strength, and pinpoint aspects that may need improvement. Here are the benefits of international comparisons using development indicators:

– Benchmarking progress:

Development indicators serve as benchmarks against which Caribbean nations can measure their progress in various dimensions, including economic growth, education, healthcare and overall wellbeing.

– Identifying best practice:

International comparisons allow Caribbean nations to identify best practice and success stories from other regions to enhance the efficiency of policy implementation and encourage innovation in development approaches.

– Targeted policy formulation:

Analysing development indicators on a global scale helps Caribbean policymakers to formulate targeted and evidence-based policies.

– Global collaboration opportunities:

Comparisons with global benchmarks helps international collaboration. Caribbean nations can engage with other countries, regional organisations and international agencies to share experiences, expertise and resources.

– Advocacy and diplomacy:

Armed with data from international comparisons, Caribbean nations can engage in diplomatic efforts and advocate for their unique needs on the global stage.

Resource allocation

Policymakers can prioritise sectors needing attention, allocate resources strategically and increase the impact of their investments. This ensures that resources are directed towards areas with the greatest potential for positive change.

Development indicators highlight areas that may be lagging or facing challenges within a country. By analysing indicators such as GDP, education, healthcare and infrastructure, policymakers can identify sectors that need improvement. Subsequently, they can allocate resources strategically to address deficiencies and enhance overall development.

We know that social indicators like education, literacy rates, and healthcare are helpful to determine the overall wellbeing of the population. Governments in the Caribbean use these indicators to prioritise investments in human development. For example, if literacy rates are lower than desired, allocating resources to education programs and initiatives becomes a priority to enhance the skills and capabilities of the workforce.

Economic indicators such as GDP growth, per capita income, and unemployment rates inform policymakers about the state of the economy. During periods of economic downturn, such as after the COVID-19 pandemic, governments may allocate resources to stimulate economic growth through infrastructure projects, job creation programs and targeted investments in key industries.

Development indicators related to environmental sustainability, such as carbon emissions or biodiversity, help governments to allocate resources to protect **natural resources** and promote sustainable practices. Investing in renewable energy, conservation efforts and eco-friendly infrastructure can be influenced by these indicators.

The V.C. Bird International Airport has a 23,000 square foot modern facility, equipped with a solar power plant that supports its energy self-sufficiency. As a result, the airport has successfully cut Antigua's carbon emissions by 3 019.5 tons each year.

Figure 12.7 *V.C. Bird International Airport in Antigua*

Infrastructure indicators, including access to clean water, sanitation and transportation, help governments identify areas that require infrastructure development. Resources can then be allocated towards building and improving essential infrastructure, contributing to the overall quality of life for citizens.

For the Government, development indicators are not only used for initial resource allocation but also for ongoing monitoring and evaluation of projects and programmes. Governments can assess the impact of investments over time, ensuring that resources are used efficiently and effectively to achieve the desired outcomes.

Indicators related to social services, such as healthcare accessibility and educational attainment, help governments to address the needs of the population. Resource allocation can be adjusted to meet the demand for healthcare facilities, educational institutions and other essential services.

In essence, development indicators serve as a compass for governments in the Caribbean, helping them with resource allocation. By aligning investments with areas of need identified through these indicators, policymakers can maximise the impact of limited resources, promote sustainable development and enhance the overall wellbeing of their citizens. This strategic approach ensures that funds are directed towards initiatives that contribute most effectively to the long-term progress and prosperity of the Caribbean nations.

Global partnerships

Global partnerships help to drive progress and sustainable development in Caribbean countries. These partnerships are formed on the basis of shared goals and mutual interests in various sectors, using strengths and resources for collective benefit.

Development indicators such as GDP growth, education levels, health outcomes and technological advancements provide a basis for collaboration. They help identify areas where Caribbean countries excel and where they need assistance, allowing for targeted and effective partnerships.

Partnerships often focus on advancing technology and innovation. For instance, collaborations with technology companies or foreign governments can help Caribbean nations access new technologies, build ICT infrastructure and create innovation ecosystems. These partnerships can lead to the development of smart cities, improvement in digital services and enhancement in sectors like agriculture and tourism through technology.

Collaborative efforts often focus on education and skill development. Partnerships with educational institutions and international organisations can provide Caribbean populations with access to higher education, vocational training and skill development programs, vital for sustaining economic growth and technological advancement.

The Global Partnership for Education (GPE) is a multi-stakeholder partnership and funding platform that aims to strengthen education systems in developing countries to increase the number of children who are in school and learning. In the Caribbean, GPE's involvement typically involves providing funds to support education programs, capacity building, policy planning and implementation, with a focus on marginalised groups and also crisis response.

Each Caribbean country's engagement with GPE depends on its specific needs and the status of its education system. The partnership's approach is designed to address unique local challenges to improve education outcomes.

– Sustainable Development Goals (SDGs):

Global partnerships in the Caribbean are frequently aligned with the United Nations' Sustainable Development Goals. These goals provide a framework for addressing key challenges such as poverty, education, health and climate change. International partners often collaborate on projects that advance these goals, bringing in investment, expertise and technology.

Other global partnerships include healthcare improvement, especially in the wake of challenges like the COVID-19 pandemic, environmental protection and climate change and finally economic development, where trade agreements, investment partnerships and economic development initiatives help Caribbean countries diversify their economies, access new markets and attract foreign investment.

Industry development and economic contributions in the Caribbean

Agriculture

- Investment: In agriculture, investment in modern farming equipment and sustainable practices boosts productivity.
- Markets: Agriculture and fishing benefit from access to both local and international markets.

- Infrastructure development: Reliable transportation networks are critical for sectors like agriculture, mining and tourism.
- Policy and regulations: This includes agriculture subsidies, tourism incentives, trade policies for manufacturing and intellectual property rights for the creative industries. Environmental regulations also impact industries like mining and forestry.
- Technology: In agriculture, technology enhances crop yields.
- Education: Improving worker's skills.

Figure 12.8 *Farming in Jamaica*

Tourism

- Investment: For tourism, investment in infrastructure and service quality enhances the appeal of destinations.
- Markets: Tourism relies on international visitors.
- Infrastructure development: Reliable transport networks are critical for sectors like agriculture, mining and tourism.
- Technology: In tourism, digital platforms improve customer experience.
- Trained professionals in tourism enhance service quality.

Figure 12.9 *Cruise ships docked in Grenada*

Case study

The Jamaican Government plans to start generating real-time data on the millions of persons entering the country by air and sea, using face scans and other biometric information that will be accessible by local and overseas law enforcement.

It will be the largest upgrade of the nation's border system in two decades, according to the Passport, Immigration and Citizenship Agency, PICA, the agency leading the project.

PICA says its aim is to create a "seamlessly integrated and smooth border control operation from 2024 onwards". It has put out a tender for a large 'high-level' contractor to implement the new system. The cost of the project is unknown.

"Various automated solutions are expected to form a complex loop with the introduction of an integrated border management ecosystem," PICA stated in the tender.

The document explicitly highlights biometrics as a key aspect of the upgrade.

Manufacture and mining

- Investment: In manufacturing and mining, investment in technology and safety measures is vital.
- Markets: Manufacturing industries need markets for their products.
- Technology: Manufacturing and mining benefit from technological advancements in processes and safety.
- Engineers and technicians advance manufacturing and mining.

Figure 12.10 *Coffee processing plant, Jamaica*

Case study

Over the years, Jamaica Promotions Corporation (JAMPRO) has been assisting various companies from different sectors to gain access to overseas markets for their products.

Due to the impact of the COVID-19 pandemic, the agency has had to pivot and change the way it assists these businesses.

Marlene Porter, Manager, Sales and Promotions Division, with a focus on agribusiness at JAMPRO, said that the agency's role is not only about attracting investments into the country and supporting the investments here in Jamaica.

"We also have to help our producers to get their products into markets, to understand the markets, and to link them with buyers and bring back market intelligence to them," Porter said.

"Even outside of that, they sometimes come upon problems as they seek to export, and so we have to advocate for them on a number of different areas. So, market research, market intelligence, business matchmaking, all of these are things that we do from JAMPRO standpoint to help our exporters," she added.

TRADE SHOWS

Porter explained that in the past, JAMPRO would take companies to trade shows in countries such as the United States or Canada.

"We would facilitate them by helping to set up a booth… bring the companies there, find buyers and put [the companies] in touch with them, take them into the market so that they can see for themselves what is happening on the ground, collect information on their competition, that kind of thing," she explained.

"We used to bring buyers as well into Jamaica, and then take them into the different companies so that they can meet with them. The buyers get a chance to see for themselves that these companies have the capability and the capacity to supply them. But with COVID, that doesn't quite happen," Porter added.

She further noted that even when there is not a show happening, JAMPRO creates its own show in the market called a trade mission.

"We take the company in the mission, into the market, and set up meetings for them with players on the ground, the buyers; and so we have to engage with influencers in the market. We have to know who they are, everything, and be able to set these meetings with these potential buyers for the products that the companies are going with. With COVID, those traditional channels were not quite there; we didn't have any real fancy shows, none of these were happening," Porter pointed out.

"So, we had to create our own… we had to pivot. We searched thoroughly online [for] virtual platforms that we could use, where we could bring in a show like a trade show, except that it's all virtual," she explained.

She added that a particular platform called ECRM has been successful.

"All the companies that have gone on it have been so pleased with the quality of the buyers that they have had and orders we have seen already. Even though it's such a short period, we have seen the development to the point where a company is now sending out a first shipment," Porter said.

"Sometimes the companies are the ones who initiated the contact. They probably have some new products, and they want to understand how they could get out there with this product. And so, we would help them to get a better understanding of that. Even though it's not a core [service] to what we do, companies ask us for feedback on their packaging and on their labelling. We help them to understand how to negotiate, how to position their product. So as best as possible, we do that," she added.

Export Max III

Porter also mentioned the Export Max III Programme, which is being undertaken in partnership with the Jamaica Business Development Corporation and the Jamaica Manufacturers and Exporters Association.

"We have 50 exporters that we're working with, to help them to get their products into market," Porter noted.

In terms of sector breakdown, 40 per cent are in the food processing industry, 29 per cent in non-food manufacturing, 10 per cent in the service sector, and, for the first time, there are creative industry companies in the programme, which account for 13 per cent of the number of enrolled companies.

"So, we have to build the capacity of these companies and we have to get into the market as well. A lot is happening behind the scenes in terms of some of the work that we do with these exporters," the agribusiness manager said.

Meanwhile, Porter noted that JAMPRO has representatives in markets such as the United States, Canada and the United Kingdom.

Source: Jamaica Gleaner

Cultural and creative industries

- Investment: The cultural and creative industries require investment in talent, innovation and infrastructure.
- Markets: The cultural and creative sector thrives with both local support and global outreach.

- Infrastructure development: Efficient ports and logistics are essential for export-oriented industries. Digital infrastructure supports the tech and services sector.
- Technology: The creative industry is increasingly tech-driven.
- Skills: In the cultural and creative sector, skilled artists and creators are essential.

Figure 12.11 *Carifesta*

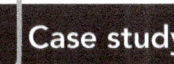

Case study

Kingston Creative is a registered non-profit organisation founded in February 2017. Its mission is to enable creatives to succeed so that they can create economic and social value, gain access to global markets and have a positive impact on their community.

Contributions of various industries to economic development

The development of industries in the Caribbean, such as agriculture, tourism, manufacturing and the creative sector, is driven by multiple factors like investment, market access, infrastructure, policy support, technology and skilled labour. These sectors are important for the region's economy, providing foreign exchange, creating jobs and generating government revenue.

For example, investment in modern farming techniques and sustainable practices in Jamaica's coffee industry has enhanced productivity, while global market access has increased demand for premium Jamaican Blue Mountain coffee.

Figure 12.12 *Jamaican Blue Mountain coffee*

Infrastructure improvements, such as roads and processing facilities, support the industry's logistics. **Government policies**, including quality standards and export incentives, have helped the sector's international competitiveness. Technology adoption in farming and processing has increased efficiency, and training programmes have equipped workers with necessary skills. This comprehensive development approach has made Jamaican coffee a renowned global brand, contributing significantly to the country's economy.

Tourism is a major foreign exchange earner. Agriculture, especially export crops, also contributes significantly. Mining extracts valuable resources for export. The cultural and creative industries, through global reach, can also generate foreign income.

Figure 12.13 *Tourists shopping in St. Lucia*

These industries provide varied employment opportunities – hotel workers in tourism, farm managers in agriculture, engineers in manufacturing and mining, and artists in the cultural sector. They also create indirect employment through links to other sectors. Industries like tourism and agriculture create additional jobs in transportation, arts and crafts, and services. Manufacturing stimulates demand in sectors like logistics and raw materials.

Industries contribute to government revenue through taxes; tourism through hotel taxes and fees, agriculture through land taxes, mining through royalties, and manufacturing with corporate taxes. The cultural and creative industries also contribute through business and sales taxes.

Figure 12.14 *A gold mine in Guyana*

Questions

Multiple choice

1. The Human Development Index (HDI) measures a country's development based on:
   a) Population size and density
   b) Economic growth and export rates
   c) Health, education, and standard of living
   d) Natural resources and industrial output

2. The impact of ICT in Caribbean industries can be seen through:
   a) The decline of traditional sectors like agriculture
   b) The increase in remote tourism services
   c) The transformation and growth of sectors like finance and education
   d) The decrease in international trade

3. The colonial history of Caribbean territories affects their current economic landscape by:
   a) Limiting their economic activities to agriculture
   b) Influencing the languages spoken and types of governance
   c) Preventing technological advancements
   d) Ensuring economic equality among the islands

Knowledge and comprehension

4. Define the Human Development Index (HDI) and explain how it can be used to assess a country's level of development.

5. Describe the economic significance of tourism in the Caribbean, particularly in the Bahamas and Barbados.

6. What are the main industries in Trinidad and Tobago, and how do they contribute to its economy?

Use of knowledge

7. Analyse how the diverse industrial base of Trinidad and Tobago differs from the tourism-dependent economies of the Bahamas and Barbados.

8. Discuss the role of information and communication technology (ICT) in shaping the future of industries in the Caribbean.

9. Evaluate the impact of colonial history on the current economic and cultural landscape of the Caribbean countries.

The transformational impact of information and communication technology on Caribbean industries

Information and Communication Technology (ICT) has a transformative role in reshaping industries across the Caribbean. ICT has been incorporated in sectors such as agriculture, tourism, manufacturing, financial services, education, cultural/creative industries, and healthcare. The adoption of ICT has enhanced efficiency, competitiveness and innovation, contributing significantly to economic development in the region.

Learning objective

- Describe how information and communication technology impacts industries in the Caribbean.

> **Important definitions**
>
> ***Information and communication technology (ICT)*** – the technologies and infrastructure used to process, transmit and store information. It includes computers, networks, software and telecommunications.

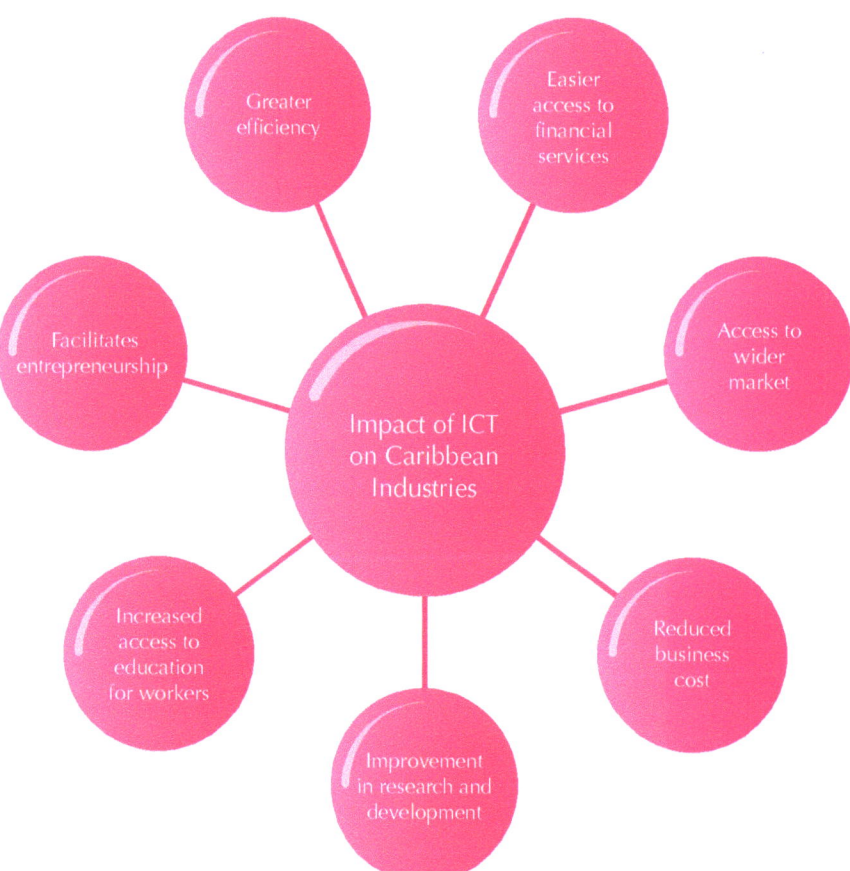

Figure 12.15 *Impact of ICT on Caribbean industries*

ICT has had a number of impacts on industries in the Caribbean.

Greater efficiency

ICT has automated many processes across industries, which has increased efficiency. In sectors like manufacturing, automated systems have streamlined operations, reducing human error and increasing productivity.

The ability to analyse data in real time has improved decision-making in industries such as agriculture and tourism, where quick responses to changing conditions are crucial.

Access to wider market

The rise of e-commerce has allowed Caribbean businesses to reach a global audience. This is especially beneficial for smaller businesses that can now access markets previously beyond their reach.

Social media and digital advertising have opened new avenues for market expansion, allowing Caribbean industries to target and engage with a broader customer base.

Figure 12.16 *Social media gives businesses another way of advertising*

Greater accessibility

Industries such as healthcare and education have used ICT to provide services remotely, reaching populations in more isolated areas.

The widespread use of mobile technology has made services more accessible, with applications across banking, retail and government services. Mobile banking apps have allowed users to perform a variety of financial transactions directly from their smartphones. This accessibility is particularly crucial in rural areas where traditional banking infrastructure may be limited. Customers can now check balances, transfer funds, pay bills and even access loans without needing to visit a physical bank branch.

Reduced business cost

Cloud computing has reduced the need for physical infrastructure, lowering operational costs.

Remote work models have decreased overhead costs like office space and utilities, a trend rapidly adopted across various sectors.

Improvement in research and development

ICT provides platforms for collaboration among researchers, enabling sharing of knowledge and resources across borders.

Digital libraries and online databases have made global research accessible, supporting innovation and development in industries like pharmaceuticals and engineering. For example, the University of the West Indies (UWI) has made extensive use of digital libraries and online databases to provide access to a wealth of global research materials.

Facilitates entrepreneurship

ICT has encouraged a vibrant startup ecosystem in the Caribbean. Easy access to online resources and digital tools has lowered the barriers to entry for entrepreneurs.

The establishment of tech hubs has encouraged innovation and supported budding entrepreneurs in translating ideas into businesses.

Increased access to education for workers

The post pandemic era has created a rise in online training and development. The availability of online courses and training programmes has made continuous education and skill development accessible for workers, enhancing their employability and productivity.

Initiatives to improve digital literacy are equipping the Caribbean workforce with the skills needed in a technology-driven world, benefiting industries across the board.

Questions

Multiple choice

1. What does Gross Domestic Product (GDP) measure?
    a) The total income of a country's citizens living abroad
    b) The total market value of all goods and services produced within a country
    c) The total market value of all goods and services produced by the nationals of a country, regardless of location
    d) The total export earnings of a country

2. How might a decline in global tourism due to a pandemic affect the GDP of a Caribbean island primarily dependent on tourism?
    a) Increase in GDP due to diversified economic activities
    b) No change in GDP as tourism is not a significant sector
    c) Decrease in GDP due to reduced income from tourism
    d) Increase in GDP due to increased local tourism

3. Life expectancy in the Caribbean is used to measure:
    a) The average number of years a newborn is expected to live
    b) The total population of the Caribbean
    c) The number of people living above the poverty line
    d) The literacy rate of the population

4. Which of the following would likely result from an improvement in the literacy rate of a Caribbean country?
    a) Decreased economic development
    b) Reduced life expectancy
    c) Enhanced social and economic opportunities
    d) Increased unemployment rates

5. The Human Development Index (HDI) includes which of the following indicators?
    a) Gross Domestic Product (GDP) and Gross National Product (GNP)
    b) Life expectancy, education and per capita income
    c) Tourism revenue and agricultural output
    d) Unemployment rate and inflation rate

6. If a Caribbean country significantly improves its educational system, what is the most likely effect on its HDI?
    a) The HDI will decrease
    b) The HDI will remain unchanged
    c) The HDI will increase
    d) The HDI is not affected by education

End of chapter questions

1. Define Gross Domestic Product (GDP) and Gross National Product (GNP). (2 marks)
2. How do GDP and GNP differ in terms of what they measure for a Caribbean country? (4 marks)
3. What is the significance of the literacy rate in measuring a country's development? (4 marks)
4. Describe how life expectancy can reflect the health and wellbeing of a population in the Caribbean. (4 marks)
5. Analyse how the economic reliance on tourism might affect the GDP of a Caribbean island during a global pandemic. (4 marks)
6. Discuss how a country's GNP could be impacted if a significant number of its citizens work abroad. (4 marks)
7. Evaluate the potential impact of improving education quality on the social development of a Caribbean nation. (4 marks)
8. Propose strategies that Caribbean countries could adopt to improve their life expectancy and literacy rates. (6 marks)

Summary

This chapter looks at the development trajectories of Caribbean territories, examining the role of tourism, industry diversification and the impact of Information and Communication Technology (ICT) on economic growth.

Key concepts and definitions:

Territorial groupings in the Caribbean
- Greater Antilles: Consists of larger islands like Cuba, Hispaniola (Haiti and the Dominican Republic), Puerto Rico and Jamaica. These islands have played significant historical and economic roles due to their size and resources.
- Lesser Antilles: A chain of smaller islands extending from the Virgin Islands to Trinidad and Tobago, known for their diverse economies and reliance on tourism and agriculture.
- Leeward Islands: Located to the north and sheltered from prevailing trade winds, including islands like Anguilla and Antigua.
- Windward Islands: Situated facing the trade winds, including Dominica and Saint Lucia, known for their lush landscapes and agricultural focus.

Section B(ii) Sustainable Development and Use of Resources

- Economic development metrics
    - Gross Domestic Product (GDP): The total market value of all goods and services produced within a country. It's a primary indicator used to gauge the economic health of a country.
    - Human Development Index (HDI): A composite index measuring average achievements in three basic aspects of human development – life expectancy, education and per capita income.
- Industries contributing to economic development
    - Tourism: Vital for islands like the Bahamas and Barbados, where it is a major economic driver.
    - Agriculture and manufacturing: Important in islands with more diversified economies like Trinidad and Tobago.
- Impact of ICT on Caribbean industries
    - The role of ICT in transforming industries by improving efficiency, connectivity and competitiveness is emphasised. The sector helps modernise other industries, expand market access and improve service delivery, crucial for regional development.

Regional development differences: Understanding how geographical and historical factors influence the economic paths of Caribbean territories helps in appreciating the diverse developmental strategies employed across the region.

Economic measures: Knowing how GDP and HDI are calculated and what they indicate about a country's economy and quality of life is crucial for grasping the broader economic health of the region.

Section B: Sustainable Development and Use of Resources
(ii) Regional Development

13 Challenges to Caribbean Development

The topics covered in this chapter are:

- the major challenges facing development in the Caribbean region
- proposing strategies to mitigate challenges faced by the Caribbean region
- justifying strategies proposed to mitigate challenges faced by the Caribbean region

Challenges to Caribbean development

In this chapter, we take a look at the challenges to Caribbean development, highlighting key obstacles such as **trade barriers**, political discord, and a workforce with limited skills, while not overlooking the ever-present threat of natural disasters. Together with economic constraints and social issues, these challenges can block to the path to progress.

Trade barriers and political strife, often rooted in historical rivalries and conflicting interests, can present hurdles. These issues create mistrust between governments, limit economic collaboration and prevent unified regional policies.

Integration is also complicated by transportation and communication barriers. The Caribbean's struggle with infrastructure issues, high travel costs and fragmented communication networks poses serious challenges to regional cooperation and unity.

A workforce with limited skills together with **brain drain** threaten to undercut the development of the region. This scenario of skill shortages and the exodus of talent hampers economic growth and innovation, presenting a critical challenge to **Caribbean integration**.

However, within these challenges there are also opportunities for growth, innovation and unity. This chapter maps out these hurdles and presents strategic solutions, aiming to transform these barriers into stepping stones towards a more integrated and prosperous Caribbean.

A look at the challenges to Caribbean development

Learning objectives

- Understand the major challenges facing development in the Caribbean region.
- Learn about the physical, economic and social challenges in the Caribbean.

> **Important definitions**
>
> *Trade barriers* – rules or taxes that make it harder or more expensive to buy and sell goods between countries.
>
> *Brain drain* – when skilled or educated people leave their country to work in another country, often for better opportunities.
>
> *Caribbean integration* – the process of creating closer economic, political and social ties among the countries in the Caribbean region.
>
> *Natural hazards* – potential threats to life or property that occur naturally, such as hurricanes, floods, drought, earthquakes, volcanoes and tsunamis.
>
> *Disasters* – the results of natural hazards, causing significant damage to life or property.

Understand the major challenges facing development in the Caribbean region

In international affairs, Caribbean countries often do not vote as a single block but as separate states. Each country in the Caribbean makes independent decisions based on its national interests. However, there are instances where Caribbean nations coordinate their positions on certain issues, especially when their collective interests are at stake.

Regional organisations like the Caribbean Community (CARICOM) facilitate coordination and cooperation among member states on various matters, including foreign policy, economic relations and development initiatives. While CARICOM aims to promote unified positions on certain international issues, the degree to which its member states act as a cohesive block can vary depending on the issue at hand.

In multilateral forums like the United Nations, Caribbean states often align with broader groups such as the Group of 77 (G77) and China or the Alliance of Small Island States (AOSIS) to advocate on issues of common interest, such as climate change, economic development and challenges facing small island developing states. However, when it comes to voting on resolutions or in international elections, Caribbean countries may vote independently, reflecting their national policies and interests.

The Caribbean region faces many challenges that hinder its development. These can be categorised into physical, economic and social challenges.

Physical challenges

The Caribbean faces **natural hazards** like hurricanes and earthquakes, worsened by human actions such as deforestation and poor urban planning. For example, in Haiti, deforestation has led to deadly floods and landslides. To tackle these issues, the region can improve disaster preparedness and sustainable development.

Figure 13.1 *Eroded and deforested farmland in Haiti*

Specific measures include reforestation, enforcing building codes and enhancing early warning systems. A collective approach involving local and international efforts is important to ensure these measures are successful and sustainable.

- **Climate change**: The Caribbean region is particularly susceptible to the impacts of climate change. Rising sea levels and increased temperatures can increase the frequency and intensity of natural disasters. Additionally, climate change can lead to coral bleaching and loss of biodiversity, which are crucial to the region's tourism industry.
- **Environmental degradation**: Activities such as deforestation, overfishing and pollution can lead to environmental degradation, increasing the region's vulnerability to natural hazards.
- **Infrastructure**: Many Caribbean countries lack the infrastructure necessary to withstand natural disasters. Buildings, roads and other structures may not be built to withstand the forces of hurricanes or earthquakes, leading to significant damage and loss of life during these events.
- **Limited resources for disaster response**: Caribbean countries often have limited resources for disaster response. This includes a lack of funding for emergency services and a lack of equipment and supplies necessary for rescue and recovery efforts.
- **Geographic dispersion**: The Caribbean region is made up of numerous islands and mainland countries spread out over a large area. This geographic dispersion can make it difficult to coordinate disaster response efforts and can slow down the delivery of aid and resources.

Economic challenges

Many Caribbean economies are small, with small national markets, which leads to low levels of production and productivity, higher costs and lower competitiveness. Other economic challenges include lack of diversification, high unemployment and underemployment rates, differences in resource distribution, high debt burdens, high level and cost of imports, shortage of skilled workers, inadequate technology, low value of exports, difficulties in accessing the markets of developed countries and shortage of capital.

- **Size constraints**: The small size of Caribbean nations and their corresponding markets restricts the scale of production and productivity, potentially undermining their competitiveness on a global scale.
- **Economic monoculture**: A significant proportion of Caribbean economies are heavily reliant on single sectors, such as tourism or specific exports. This lack of economic diversification makes them vulnerable to fluctuations in the global market.
- **Employment discrepancies**: The region has substantial unemployment and underemployment rates, leading to underuse of human capital and potential socioeconomic instability.
- **Resource disparity**: The distribution of resources across the region is uneven, leading to socio-economic disparities that can restrict overall regional development.
- **Debt**: A considerable number of Caribbean countries have high levels of public debt, which can limit their ability to generate revenue and slow economic growth.
- **Import dependence**: The economies of the Caribbean are often import-heavy, which can be financially difficult and lead to trade imbalances.
- **Skills deficit**: There is a shortage of skilled labour within the region. This deficit can limit economic development and cause a 'brain drain' phenomenon, where skilled individuals emigrate in search of better opportunities.
- **Technological insufficiency**: Limited access to advanced technology can slow productivity and competitiveness within the region.
- **Export undervaluation**: The goods and services exported by Caribbean countries often command low value in the global market, which can limit their foreign exchange earnings.
- **Market access barriers**: Caribbean countries often encounter difficulties in reaching markets in developed countries due to trade barriers or geographical distance.

Social challenges

The region faces several social challenges such as high levels of crime and violence, health crises and the **influx of migrants**. These issues cause further challenges to development in the Caribbean region.

- **Criminality and violence:** The Caribbean region as a whole has high levels of crime and violence. This poses a significant hurdle to social development and economic growth.
- **Health emergencies:** The region has been severely impacted by health crises, most notably the COVID-19 pandemic, which disrupted essential health services, interrupted regular immunisation programmes, care for expectant mothers and individuals with chronic conditions. The pandemic also led to a significant reduction in life expectancy and population growth.
- **Migration influx:** The Caribbean has experienced significant shifts in migration patterns due to factors such as climate change, natural disasters and global mobility trends. The influx of migrants can strain local resources and services, worsening existing social and economic challenges. The International Organization for Migration's Missing Migrants Project documented at least 321 deaths and disappearances of migrants in the Caribbean in 2022. In 2020, there were an estimated 859,400 intraregional and 745,700 extra regional immigrants living in Caribbean countries.

Political challenges

The path to Caribbean integration is not only shaped by economic, social and physical factors but also by significant political challenges. These include governance issues, diplomatic relations, policy alignment and the effectiveness of regional organisations.

Political challenges are key in Caribbean integration, involving governance variations, diplomatic relations, policy harmonisation and the role of regional bodies like CARICOM. Governance issues like corruption get in the way of cooperation, while differing political relations and unresolved conflicts between states affect regional unity. Aligning national policies with regional goals is essential for seamless integration. Strengthening regional organisations and ensuring that member states commit to shared objectives is crucial for successful integration and a cohesive Caribbean community.

Questions

Multiple choice

1. Which of the following is a major physical challenge in the Caribbean?
   a) Frequent snowstorms
   b) Volcanic eruptions
   c) Desertification
   d) Tornadoes

2. What contributes to economic challenges in the Caribbean?
   a) Large market sizes
   b) High diversification in economic sectors
   c) Dependency on a few key industries
   d) Low levels of public debt

3 Which of the following is a significant social challenge in the Caribbean?
   a) Low crime rates
   b) Health crises like the COVID-19 pandemic
   c) Decreasing migration patterns
   d) Stable employment opportunities

4 Which strategy is vital for mitigating the impact of natural disasters in the Caribbean?
   a) Reducing investment in early warning systems
   b) Promoting deforestation
   c) Enhancing infrastructure resilience
   d) Isolating national disaster response efforts

Knowledge and comprehension

5 a) Describe the main physical challenges faced by the Caribbean region and how they impact development.
   b) How do human activities worsen these challenges?

6 Analyse the economic constraints in the Caribbean, focusing on the impact of small market sizes and lack of diversification on productivity and growth.

7 Discuss the social challenges in the Caribbean, including crime and violence, health crises and migration. How do these issues affect regional stability and development?

Use of knowledge

8 Propose solutions to mitigate the impact of natural disasters in the Caribbean, considering both local actions and international cooperation.

Addressing the major challenges faced by the Caribbean

Learning objectives
- Explore strategies to mitigate these challenges.
- Justify the proposed strategies for their effectiveness.

> **Important definitions**
>
> **Disaster management and resilience** – *the strategies and measures taken to predict, prevent, mitigate and respond to disasters.*
>
> **Economic diversification** – *the process of expanding the range of economic activities in a country to reduce dependence on a single economic sector.*

We will now look at how the region can overcome its challenges through unity and innovation and what strategies can be used for development and change. We will learn how interconnectedness and cooperation are not just ideals but essential strategies for the Caribbean, as nations come together to craft sustainable solutions.

Physical challenges

Enhancing disaster preparedness and management

To improve disaster preparedness and management in the Caribbean, countries must use strategies that address both immediate and long-term needs. The approach should combine infrastructure improvements and regional collaboration, and focus on enforcing disaster-resistant building codes for new buildings and improving existing structures to withstand natural disasters. Nature-based solutions, such as mangrove restoration, should be used to protect against coastal hazards.

Regional collaboration is essential. Caribbean nations should unite to develop a centralised early warning system, and exchange best practices for evacuation and emergency response. This could include community-based early warning mechanisms, accessible evacuation routes for vulnerable communities and regular disaster drills for everyone. By pooling resources and expertise, the region can develop a more robust and coordinated approach to disaster management, ensuring countries are prepared for future threats.

Promoting environmental sustainability

To mitigate environmental degradation and improve disaster resilience in the Caribbean, policies must promote sustainable resource management. Key initiatives include phasing out harmful agricultural methods, enhancing sustainable waste management and restoring vital ecosystems like coral reefs and mangroves. These actions will preserve natural barriers against disasters, support biodiversity and ensure sustainable community livelihoods for the region.

Investing in research and technology

Investing in research and technology will help Caribbean nations to predict and manage natural disasters. Due to limited resources, countries should seek international support and finance to acquire advanced tools like improved weather forecasting systems. Public–private partnerships and prioritising technology budgets can also help. This approach will enhance disaster preparedness and response capabilities in the region efficiently.

Case study

Consider the current situation in three Caribbean countries and proposed actions.

Country 1

Background:

A Caribbean island is known for its vibrant culture and breathtaking landscapes. However, it is also prone to natural disasters like hurricanes, floods, and occasional earthquakes. The island's economy heavily relies on tourism and agriculture, both of which are vulnerable to environmental impacts. Limited weather forecasting technology exacerbates the challenges.

Current situation:

Lack of preparedness for disasters: The island recently faced a devastating hurricane, revealing significant gaps in disaster preparedness and response. The early warning systems were outdated, evacuation plans were inefficient, and there was a lack of emergency shelters resistant to such disasters.

Section B(ii)   Sustainable Development and Use of Resources

Environmental degradation: Unregulated tourism and agriculture practices have led to deforestation and coastal erosion, exacerbating the island's vulnerability to natural disasters. The loss of natural barriers like mangroves has made coastal areas more prone to storm surges.

Limited technological resources: The island's meteorological department lacks advanced tools for accurate weather prediction and tracking of hurricanes, leading to delayed and sometimes inaccurate forecasts.

Proposed actions:

Addressing disaster preparedness and environmental degradation:

1. Upgrade disaster management infrastructure: implement modern early-warning systems, establish well-defined evacuation routes and construct resilient shelters strategically located across the island.
2. Invest in ecosystem restoration: initiate reforestation projects, particularly mangroves, to buffer coastal areas and promote sustainable land management practices in agriculture.
3. Promote environmental awareness and education: educate residents and tourists about the island's delicate ecosystem and encourage responsible practices to minimise the environmental impact.

Addressing limited technological resources:

Seek international support and finance to acquire advanced tools, like improved weather forecasting systems.

Economic challenges:

1. Diversifying the economy: encourage development in various sectors like tourism, agriculture and technology to reduce dependency on a few industries.
2. Boosting productivity and innovation: invest in education and training programs to enhance skills and productivity. Foster a culture of innovation and entrepreneurship.
3. Improving trade and market access: source better trade agreements to access international markets, and improve port and transportation infrastructure to facilitate trade.
4. Debt management and financial stability: work with international financial institutions for debt restructuring and seek ways to improve fiscal management.
    - Seeking debt restructuring: Collaborate with international financial institutions to restructure existing debt and secure favorable terms for future borrowing.
    - Improving fiscal management: Implement transparent and accountable financial practices to optimise resource allocation and minimise wastage.
    - Exploring innovative financing mechanisms: Investigate public–private partnerships, green bonds, and other sustainable financing options for infrastructure development and environmental projects.
5. Promoting sustainable tourism: develop eco-friendly and sustainable tourism models that leverage natural and cultural assets without harming the environment.

Country 2

Background:

This small Caribbean nation has a breathtaking landscape and vibrant cultural heritage. However, the economy is traditionally reliant on a single agricultural export and faces instability due to global market fluctuations and natural disasters. Limited diversification, skill gaps and outdated infrastructure are getting in the way of sustainable growth.

Current situation:

Over-reliance on traditional agriculture: the nation's economy is largely dependent on exporting one primary crop, which is vulnerable to market changes and environmental factors. This has resulted in economic instability and limited growth opportunities.

Low productivity and lack of innovation: the workforce lacks access to advanced training and education, leading to low productivity levels. There's a lack of innovation-driven enterprises and entrepreneurial activities.

Limited market access and poor infrastructure: trade barriers and limited market access have restricted economic growth. Additionally, outdated port and transport infrastructure have limited efficient trade operations.

High national debt and financial instability: the country faces a high level of national debt, limiting the funds available for development initiatives. The government struggles with balancing debt repayment and investing in critical sectors.

Unsustainable tourism practices: while tourism is a growing sector, current practices are not sustainable and threaten the environmental and cultural assets of the country

Proposed actions:

Diversifying the economy and building resilience:

1. Embrace agricultural diversification: encourage and support the production and export of high-value crops, resilient varieties and value-added products.
2. Promote innovation and entrepreneurship: Encourage partnerships between academia, industry and government to stimulate innovation in sectors like renewable energy, eco-tourism and the creative industries.
3. Develop a blue economy: leverage the ocean's potential for sustainable fisheries, aquaculture and marine tourism.
4. Invest in climate-smart agriculture: adopt practices that enhance resilience to droughts, floods and other climate risks.

Enhancing human capital and access:

1. Improve education and training: provide accessible and relevant education focused on critical thinking, digital skills and entrepreneurship.
2. Upskill the workforce: offer targeted training programs to bridge skill gaps and meet evolving industry needs.
3. Promote gender equality and empower women: increase access to education, financial resources and leadership opportunities for women.
4. Improve healthcare: expand access to preventive and quality healthcare services for all citizens.

Strengthening trade and infrastructure:

1. Negotiate favourable trade agreements: secure better market access for diversified exports and attract foreign investment.
2. Modernise infrastructure: upgrade ports, transportation networks and digital infrastructure to facilitate trade and connectivity.
3. Embrace sustainable tourism: develop ecotourism models that protect the environment, preserve cultural heritage and benefit local communities.

Managing public finances and debt:

1. Seek debt restructuring: collaborate with international institutions to restructure existing debt and secure favourable terms for future borrowing.
2. Improve fiscal management: implement transparent and accountable financial practices to optimise resource allocation and minimise wastage.
3. Explore innovative financing mechanisms: investigate public-private partnerships, green bonds and other options for infrastructure development and social programmes.

Addressing social challenges:

1. Build community resilience: invest in community-based programmes that address crime prevention, rehabilitation and social integration.
2. Empower youth: partner with organisations like JCI, Cadet Corps and Scouts to provide leadership training and positive engagement opportunities.
3. Implement humane migration policies: develop frameworks for managing migration humanely while addressing root causes.
4. Promote social inclusion and equity: create a society where everyone has equal opportunities to contribute and benefit from economic and social progress.

Social challenges:

1. Addressing crime and violence: implement community-based programmes focusing on crime prevention, rehabilitation and social integration. Partnerships with organisations like Junior Chamber International, Cadet Corps and Scouts to provide leadership training and positive engagement for young people.
2. Improving healthcare systems: strengthen healthcare infrastructure, focus on preventive care and improve access to healthcare services.
3. Managing migration effectively: develop policies for the humane treatment of migrants and integrate them into society, while also addressing the root causes of migration.

Country 3

Despite its natural appearance, this Caribbean nation struggles with social issues including rising crime rates, an overburdened healthcare system and challenges posed by increasing migration.

Current situation:

High crime and violence: the country has seen an increase in crime and violence, particularly among the youth. This is due to unemployment, lack of educational opportunities and inadequate social programmes.

Inadequate healthcare facilities: the healthcare system is strained, with limited resources, outdated equipment, and insufficient healthcare professionals. There's also a lack of focus on preventive care and health education.

Challenges with migration: A recent influx of migrants has placed additional strain on the country's social services. There are tensions between locals and migrants, and the government lacks effective policies for migrant integration.

Proposed actions:

Tackling high crime and violence:

1. Improve employment opportunities
   Develop job creation programmes targeting youth, including vocational training and apprenticeships.
   Encourage private sector investment in local businesses through incentives and support.
2. Enhance educational opportunities
   Invest in education by building more schools, improving facilities and providing scholarships for higher education.
   Implement after-school programmes and extracurricular activities to engage youth positively.
3. Strengthen social programmes
   Expand and improve social services focused on at-risk youth, including counselling, mentorship and community centres.

Addressing inadequate healthcare facilities:

1. Increase healthcare funding
   Allocate more government budget to healthcare to improve facilities, purchase updated equipment, and increase salaries for healthcare professionals.
   Seek international aid and partnerships for funding and technical support.
2. Focus on preventive care and health education
   Launch nationwide campaigns promoting healthy lifestyles, regular check-ups and disease prevention.
   Integrate preventive care programmes into the healthcare system, such as vaccination drives and health screenings.
3. Train and recruit healthcare professionals
   Offer incentives such as scholarships, loan forgiveness and competitive salaries to attract and retain healthcare workers.
   Establish partnerships with international medical institutions for training and exchange programmes.

Managing migration challenges:

1. Develop effective migration policies
   Create comprehensive policies for migrant integration, including legal pathways for residency and employment.
   Ensure fair treatment and protection of migrant rights while addressing community concerns.
2. Promote social cohesion
   Organise community-building activities that foster positive interactions between locals and migrants.
   Launch public awareness campaigns to reduce xenophobia and promote the benefits of cultural diversity.
3. Strengthen social services
   Enhance social services to support both locals and migrants, such as housing, education and healthcare access.
   Partner with NGOs and international organisations to provide additional support and resources for integration programmes.

Justification of strategies

Learning objectives
- Develop skills such as research, discussion, creativity and communication.
- Apply these skills in the context of Caribbean development and integration.

> **Important definitions**
>
> **Debt burden** – *the total amount of money that a country owes to its creditors, which can hinder economic development.*
>
> **Underemployment** – *where individuals are working less than they could be, either in terms of hours (part-time when they prefer full-time) or in jobs that don't fully utilise their skills and abilities.*
>
> **Influx of migrants** – *a large number of people moving into a country or region, often in search of better economic opportunities or safety. This can put pressure on local resources and services.*

Justification of strategies

To solve the problems of integration in the Caribbean, we need to consider all the economic, social, and political details. The Caribbean has been working towards becoming more united, which is important because it helps the countries work together, improve trade and support each other.

To make integration work well, it is important to focus on a few key things: reducing debt, creating more job opportunities and managing migration. High debt makes it hard for countries to function well and join in regional activities. More employment opportunities can boost the economy and make society more stable. Managing how people move between countries in the Caribbean can help make sure that this movement is good for everyone and does not overload any particular country.

By addressing these issues, Caribbean countries can build a strong base for working together more effectively. This is not just about fixing problems; it is about opening doors to new opportunities for growth and cooperation across the Caribbean.

Debt burden

High national debt can significantly limit a country's economic development and its ability to cooperate regionally. When a country has a lot of debt, a large portion of its revenue goes towards paying off this debt rather than investing in important sectors like education, healthcare and infrastructure. This situation can limit economic growth and reduce the country's capacity to engage in regional projects and initiatives, as it has fewer resources to contribute and may be more focused on its own financial issues.

Underemployment

Underemployment, where individuals are employed at less than full capacity, either by working fewer hours than they wish or by working in jobs that do not use their full set of skills, has significant effects on economic growth and regional stability.

Effects on economic growth:

- Reduced productivity: Underemployment leads to a waste of human capital, as people are not working to their full potential, which lowers overall productivity.
- Decreased income and consumption: Individuals who are underemployed earn less than they would in full employment, which means they have less money to spend. This reduced consumption can lead to slower economic growth.

- Inefficient labour market: Underemployment indicates that the labour market is not functioning efficiently. Skills mismatches and lack of job creation limits economic progress and competitiveness.

Effects on regional stability:

- Social unrest: Persistent underemployment can lead to frustration and dissatisfaction among the workforce, potentially causing social unrest and affecting political stability.
- Migration pressures: In search of better employment opportunities, underemployed individuals may migrate to other regions, which can strain relationships between countries and lead to imbalances in labour markets across the region.
- Resource allocation challenges: Underemployment can complicate efforts to achieve regional integration, as countries may prioritise national employment concerns over collective regional strategies.

Research activity

A tale of debt and **employment**.

In the country of Hope, life was both beautiful and challenging. The island's people were resourceful and hardworking, but they faced significant economic hurdles. Hope's government had accumulated a high national debt over the years, trying to modernise its infrastructure and improve public services. However, this debt burden strained the country's finances, limiting further investments in crucial sectors like education, healthcare and infrastructure.

Many young people in Hope were underemployed. They had skills and degrees but couldn't find jobs that matched their qualifications. Instead, they took on part-time or low-paying jobs, leading to frustration and a sense of wasted potential. This underemployment resulted in reduced productivity and decreased income, which in turn affected consumption and economic growth.

The community began to see the social implications of these issues. Social discontent grew as more people struggled to make ends meet. The lack of opportunities drove some to migrate to other countries in search of better prospects, while those who stayed faced an uncertain future.

Recognising the urgent need for change, the island's leaders started to focus on financial management and sustainable employment practices. Inspired by a story similar to *One Hen*, where a small loan helped a young boy transform his life and community, they launched microfinance programmes to empower local entrepreneurs. They also invested in vocational training to help citizens gain practical skills that matched the job market's needs.

These initiatives began to show promising results. Small businesses flourished, creating jobs and boosting the local economy. Improved financial management reduced the debt burden, allowing the government to reinvest in education, healthcare, and infrastructure. This holistic approach not only improved individual livelihoods but also enhanced the island's overall economic stability and regional cooperation.

Guided questions:

1. How do the themes of financial management and employment in the island of Hope relate to the broader economic issues faced by Caribbean countries?
2. In what ways can underemployment and high national debt hinder regional integration and stability in the Caribbean?

Influx of migrants

Migration can impact local resources and influence regional policy and integration efforts in the Caribbean. When large numbers of people move from one country to another, it often puts pressure on the receiving country's resources, such as housing, healthcare, education and employment opportunities. This influx can strain public services and infrastructure, leading to challenges in maintaining quality and accessibility for both migrants and the local population.

Caribbean nations must work together to develop migration policies that address the root causes of migration, such as economic instability, political unrest, or environmental disasters, while also ensuring the fair distribution of resources and responsibilities among countries. Effective regional integration requires management of migration in a way that supports both the migrants and the host communities, encouraging social cohesion and economic stability.

Case study

The impact of Venezuelan migration on neighbouring Caribbean countries

Recently there has been a significant migration flow from Venezuela into neighbouring Caribbean countries, demonstrating the challenges and implications for regional relations. Countries like Trinidad and Tobago, Guyana and others faced an influx of Venezuelan migrants seeking refuge from economic hardship and political instability.

Effects on local resources: These countries experienced increased demand for social services, including healthcare, education and housing, which strained local budgets and infrastructure.

Regional policy implications: The situation required a coordinated regional response to manage the humanitarian aspects of the migration, share resources effectively, and address the political and economic impacts. It highlighted the need for a unified strategy to handle such crises in the Caribbean, balancing national interests with regional solidarity and cooperation.

Impact on regional relations: The diplomatic relationships and humanitarian policies of Caribbean nations were challenged, prompting debates on immigration policies, border control and the role of regional bodies like CARICOM in managing cross-border issues.

Research activity

Regional cooperation on migration issues

Research how Caribbean regional organisations like CARICOM address migration challenges. Students should work in groups to research and find out about the strategies and programmes that exist to address migration issues in the region. It could be by CARICOM or by individual countries; each group should critique these strategies and present their findings and conclusions to a panel; and they should propose an alternative strategy or ways of improving the existing ones.

What initiatives or programmes have been developed to manage migration flows, and how effective have they been? Promoting creativity and communication is essential for overcoming challenges in Caribbean regional integration. Encouraging innovative thinking can lead to new solutions for common problems, such as economic instability and social disparities. By fostering a culture of creativity, the region can develop unique products and services that boost trade and tourism. Effective communication is equally vital, as it ensures that ideas and strategies are shared across borders, enhancing cooperation and mutual support. Strengthening communication channels between governments, businesses, and communities can build trust and facilitate the coordination needed for successful regional integration. By prioritising creativity and communication, Caribbean countries can work together more effectively, paving the way for a more united and prosperous future.

Targeted strategies to address these barriers

Economic challenges and solutions

Debt burden: High national debts limit economic growth and regional collaboration. Strategies like debt restructuring, financial management reforms and seeking favourable trade agreements can help.

Underemployment: Underutilised human capital weakens economies. Solutions include vocational training, education reform and investment in sectors that can absorb underutilised workers.

Social and political factors

Cultural and historical influences: Promoting cultural exchange and understanding historical integration attempts can build unity. Initiatives might include regional cultural festivals and educational programmes about Caribbean history.

Figure 13.2 *A fashion show at Carifesta*

Political will and governance: Strengthening democratic institutions and political commitment to integration is crucial. Regional forums and summits can add to political dialogue and cooperation.

Environmental sustainability and climate change

Climate change impacts: Joint efforts in environmental protection and disaster management are vital. Regional climate change adaptation and mitigation strategies, such as shared renewable energy projects, can be implemented.

Sustainable development goals (SDGs): Aligning integration efforts with the SDGs will promote environmental, economic and social sustainability in the region.

Technology

Bridging the digital divide: Enhancing access to technology and improving ICT infrastructure can boost economic and social integration. Regional initiatives should focus on expanding internet access and digital literacy programmes.

Technology for development: Collaborative tech projects can solve common issues like healthcare, education and disaster management, driving integration forward.

Trade, economic policies, and market access

Harmonising economic policies: Synchronised economic policies can help trade and investment, strengthening the regional market. Key areas include government spending, investment regulation, and labour standards.

Trade agreements and economic partnerships: Negotiating collective trade agreements can enhance market access and economic opportunities for Caribbean countries.

Educational exchange and skill development

Regional education and training programmes: Initiatives like student exchange programmes, regional training centres and online educational platforms can build skills relevant to regional integration.

Focus on innovation and entrepreneurship: Supporting innovation through regional research grants, startup incubators and entrepreneurship education can drive economic growth and integration.

Research, innovation, and collaboration

Joint research initiatives: Encouraging collaborative research on regional issues like sustainable agriculture, health and energy can support integration.

Innovation in governance and policy making: Innovative approaches to governance, such as e-governance and regional policy think tanks, can streamline integration processes and decision-making.

End of chapter questions

1. Name three major trade barriers that affect Caribbean integration. (3 marks)
2. What does 'Caribbean integration' mean, and why is it significant? (5 marks)
3. How does brain drain affect the skilled workforce in the Caribbean? (5 marks)
4. What role does deforestation play in exacerbating natural disasters in the Caribbean? (5 marks)
5. What are common investigative methods used to study the economic impacts of political discord in the Caribbean? (3 marks)
6. How do political challenges like governance issues and policy alignment affect Caribbean development? (5 marks)
7. Suggest strategies that Caribbean nations can use to overcome the limited skilled workforce problem. (5 marks)
8. Assess the role of technological advancement in enhancing Caribbean integration and development. (5 marks)
9. Analyse the impact of geographical dispersion on disaster response and economic development in the Caribbean. (5 marks)
10. How does environmental degradation contribute to the economic and social challenges in the Caribbean? (5 marks)

SBA skills

1. Plan a simple survey to understand how import taxes (a form of trade barrier) affect the prices of goods in your country. What questions would you ask in your survey? (10 marks)
2. Create a basic plan for a school-based disaster preparedness programme in your community, including drills and educational workshops. What local resources would you use? (5 marks)
3. Write a short analysis on the effect of a new regional trade agreement on job opportunities in your community. What factors would you consider in your analysis? (5 marks)
4. Design a project to study the impact of beach erosion (a consequence of climate change) on local tourism. What steps would you take to gather information? (5 marks)
5. Develop a proposal for a youth-led initiative to reduce littering and improve waste management in your community. What activities would be included, and how would you measure the project's success? (10 marks)

Summary

This chapter examines the significant obstacles to Caribbean integration, focusing on trade barriers, political discord, a limited skilled workforce and natural disasters. These challenges, compounded by economic constraints and social issues, slow the progress towards regional unity and development.

Trade barriers such as high import tariffs and non-tariff restrictions limit economic collaboration, while political discord stemming from historical rivalries creates mistrust between governments, stifling the creation of unified regional policies.

Transportation and communication barriers, including inadequate infrastructure and high travel costs, further hinder regional cooperation and unity.

The limited skilled workforce and the emigration of talented individuals, or brain drain, hamper economic growth and innovation, exacerbating these challenges.

Despite these significant hurdles, opportunities for growth, innovation, and unity exist.

There are strategic solutions to transform these barriers into stepping stones for a more integrated and prosperous Caribbean. By addressing these issues, Caribbean countries can work towards creating a stronger foundation for regional cooperation, improving trade and supporting each other more effectively. Key points to remember:

- Trade barriers:

High import tariffs
Non-tariff barriers (quotas and import licenses)
Trade regulations and restrictions

- Political discord:

Historical rivalries
Conflicting interests
Mistrust between governments

- Transportation and communication barriers:

Inadequate infrastructure
High travel costs
Fragmented communication networks

- Workforce and brain drain:

Shortage of skilled labour
Emigration of talented individuals

- Natural disasters:

    Hurricanes, floods, earthquakes

    Impact of climate change

    Need for disaster preparedness and resilient infrastructure

- Economic constraints:

    Small market sizes

    Lack of diversification

    High levels of debt

- Social issues:

    Crime and violence

    Health crises

    Migration pressures

- Opportunities for growth:

    Promoting innovation and entrepreneurship

    Improving regional communication and collaboration

    Investing in education and skill development

- Strategic solutions:

    Debt restructuring and financial management reforms

    Vocational training and education reform

    Sustainable tourism and environmental protection initiatives

    Technological advancement and digital infrastructure improvement

Section B: Sustainable Development and Use of Resources
(ii) Regional Development
14 Regional Integration

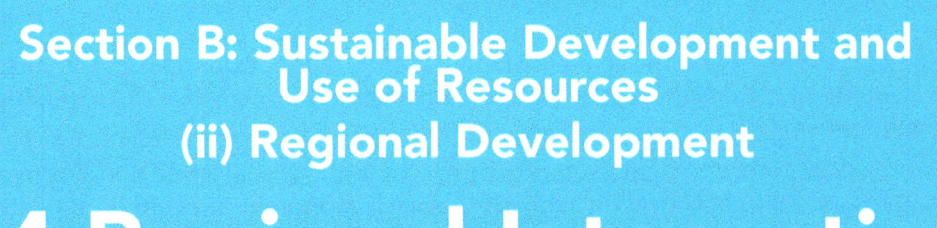

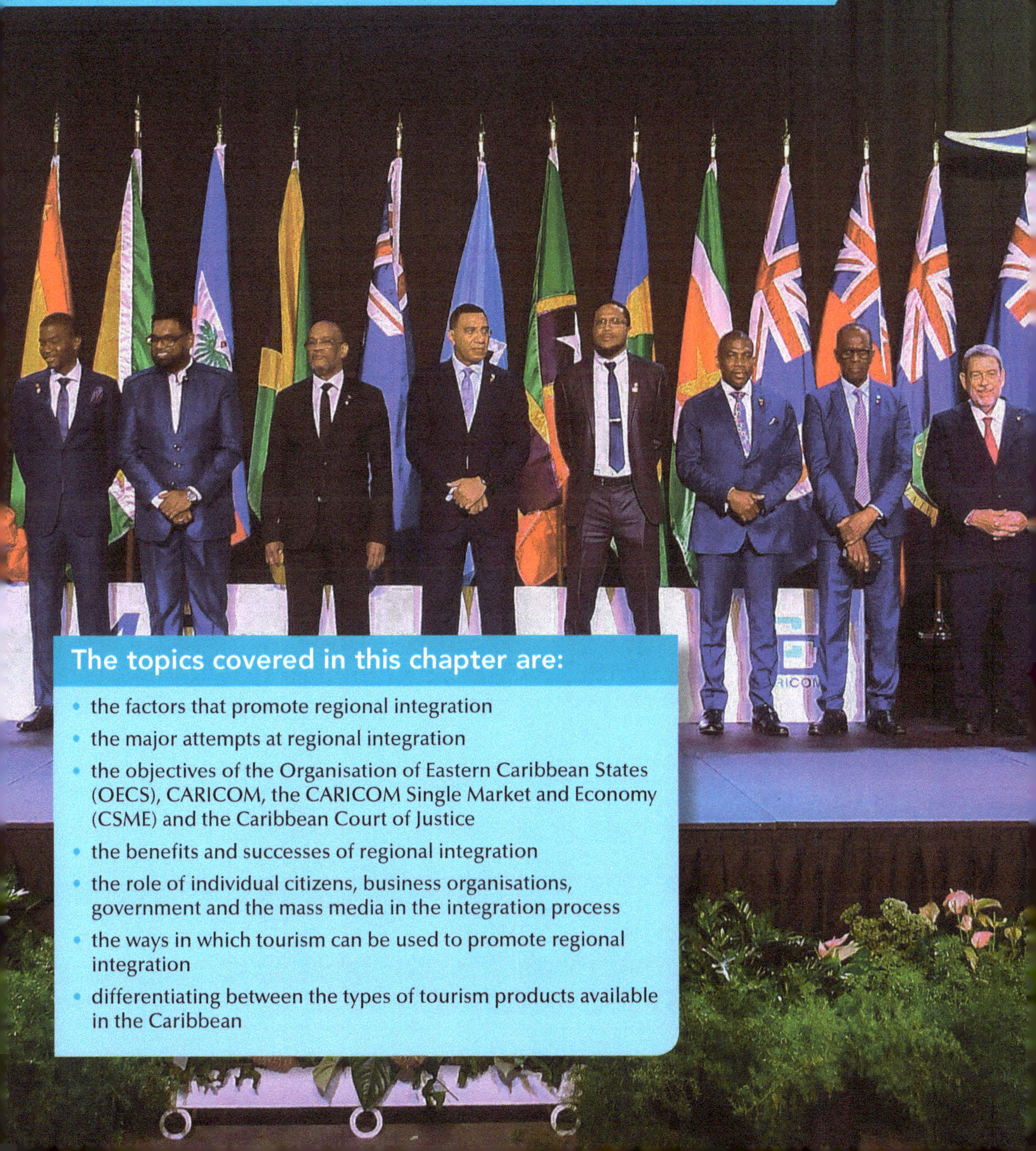

The topics covered in this chapter are:

- the factors that promote regional integration
- the major attempts at regional integration
- the objectives of the Organisation of Eastern Caribbean States (OECS), CARICOM, the CARICOM Single Market and Economy (CSME) and the Caribbean Court of Justice
- the benefits and successes of regional integration
- the role of individual citizens, business organisations, government and the mass media in the integration process
- the ways in which tourism can be used to promote regional integration
- differentiating between the types of tourism products available in the Caribbean

Factors that promote regional integration

The Caribbean region, with its interconnected physical features, human experiences and historical connections, is made up of nations that often rely on similar economic activities like agriculture, mining, fishing and tourism.

In order for these small countries to operate successfully within the global landscape, strong regional cooperation is important. This collaboration can lead to social, economic and cultural stability across the region.

The World Bank highlights regional integration as a key strategy to tackle the economic challenges facing the Caribbean. By joining forces, these nations can create a unified market that allows for easier movement of goods, services, capital and people.

This chapter will look at the benefits of regional integration, illustrating how it can make everyday items more affordable, simplify travel between nations and increase employment opportunities. We will explore the driving forces behind regional integration, the roles of different stakeholders and the successes and obstacles encountered in the journey towards regional unity and **sustainable development**.

Learning objectives

- Identify key factors promoting regional integration.
- Outline historical milestones in regional integration efforts.

Important definitions

Economic interdependence – when countries rely on each other for economic stability and growth. This often involves shared resources, markets and financial cooperation for mutual benefit.

Sovereignty – the independent authority and autonomy of a country, allowing it to govern itself without external interference. In the context of regional integration, countries may need to balance sovereignty with collaborative efforts for shared goals.

Harmonisation – aligning policies, regulations and practices among participating nations. This process is crucial for effective regional integration, ensuring consistency in approach and implementation.

Sustainable development – ensures long-term viability of the region's economic, environmental and social aspects, a key benefit of regional integration.

Trade liberalisation – the removal or reduction of barriers among countries to encourage trade of goods and services.

Figure 14.1 *Raising the flags of some of the CARICOM countries*

There are many factors that contribute to regional integration:

- Geographical location
- Common cultural heritage
- Common economic and social issues
- Effects of globalisation, **trade liberalisation** and trading blocs
- Vulnerability to economic shocks, climate change and natural disasters, shared security concerns
- Advancements in communication technologies that assist with the transfer of cultural heritage
- Tourism and maritime cooperation
- Common legal framework
- Youth engagement

Geographical location

The Caribbean, a region of islands and coastal nations, is heavily influenced by its geographical location. As the nations are located close together, shared space and interconnected coastlines contribute to economic, cultural and social collaboration.

Geographical location is important to the Caribbean in terms of regional integration, influencing economic collaboration, cultural identity and shared environmental responsibility. By taking advantage of their unique geographic setting, Caribbean nations can continue to build on their interconnected history, creating a more integrated and resilient Caribbean community for the future.

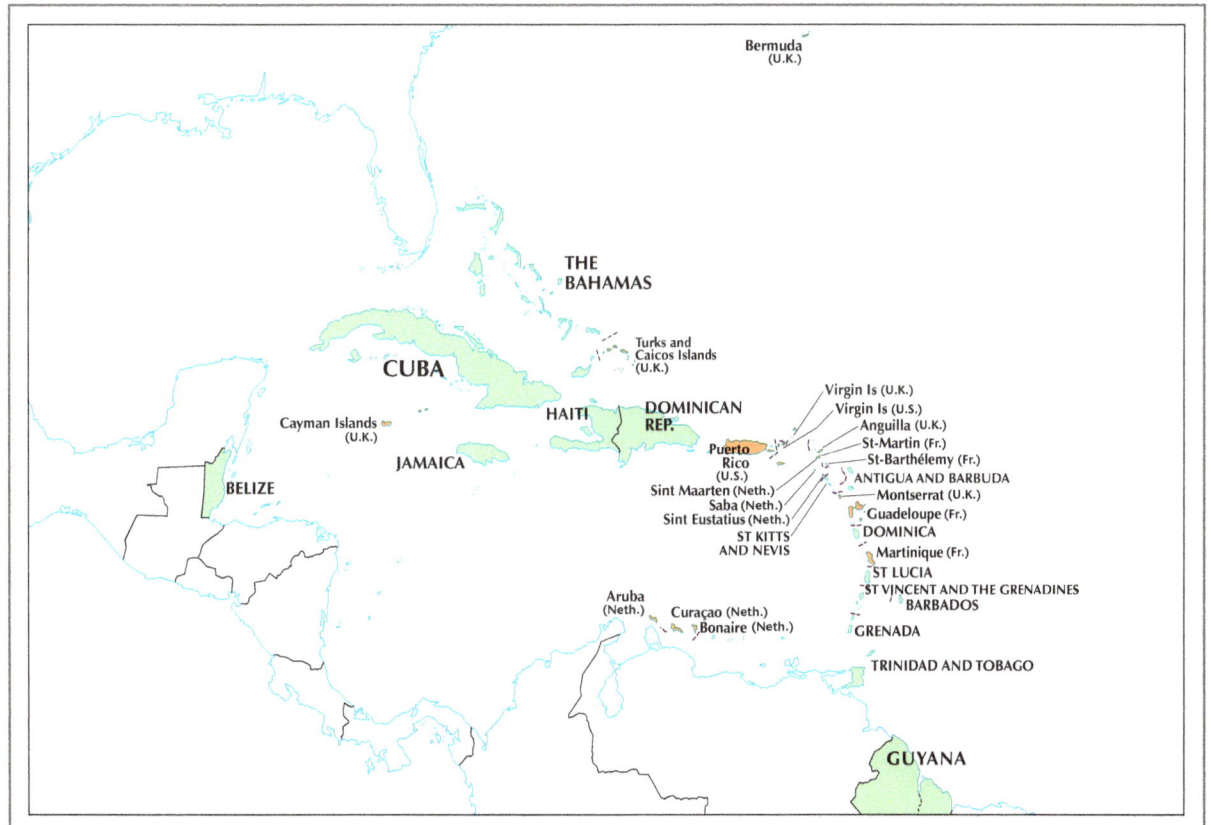

Figure 14.2 *The Caribbean*

1. Locations and economics

   The clustering of islands in the Caribbean fosters economic synergy. The close proximity of nations within island clusters promotes collaborative economic initiatives, trade agreements and shared markets, laying the foundation for economic integration. This geographical arrangement encourages countries to work together, enhancing their economic strength and resilience.

2. Maritime trade routes and connectivity

   The Caribbean's strategic location along major maritime trade routes has historically facilitated commerce and cultural exchange. This prime positioning has contributed to the development of interconnected trade networks, enhancing economic ties and providing avenues for regional integration. The flow of goods and services through these routes supports the region's economic vitality.

3. Environmental interdependence

   Caribbean nations share common environmental challenges, including susceptibility to hurricanes and rising sea levels. This shared vulnerability creates a mutual interest in environmental sustainability, prompting joint efforts to address climate change and natural disasters. Collaborative initiatives in environmental protection are crucial for the region's long-term survival and prosperity.

4. Cultural proximity and identity

   Geographical closeness fosters a shared cultural identity among Caribbean nations. The physical proximity contributes to the blending of cultural practices, languages, and traditions, creating a unique Caribbean identity. This cultural integration strengthens the bonds between nations, promoting unity and mutual understanding.

5. Interconnected tourism hubs

   The Caribbean's geographical layout often positions nations as interconnected tourism hubs. Collaborative tourism initiatives capitalise on shared attractions, promoting regional tourism and contributing to economic integration through the hospitality industry. By working together, Caribbean nations can enhance their appeal as a prime tourist destination.

6. Cross-border environmental conservation

   Proximity facilitates collaborative efforts in environmental conservation. Neighbouring Caribbean nations work together to protect marine ecosystems, biodiversity and natural resources, contributing to **sustainable development** and regional cooperation. Joint conservation efforts are vital for preserving the region's natural beauty and ecological health.

7. Shared maritime security

   The region's geography, with numerous coastlines, underscores the importance of shared maritime security. Collaborative efforts among Caribbean nations address common security challenges, such as piracy and illicit activities, promoting regional stability. By working together, these countries can ensure the safety and security of their maritime borders.

Common cultural heritage

The Caribbean region has a rich and diverse history that extends far beyond the colonial period. The Indigenous people were an integral part of this history, and their contributions have helped shape the region into what it is today. However, with the arrival of European colonists, the course of Caribbean history was forever altered. The legacy of this history remains a fundamental part of our cultural heritage. As Caribbean people, we are proud of our past and the unique identity that it has given us.

The cultural heritage links

Food: Caribbean cuisine is a blend of culinary influences from all over the world, including Africa, France, Spain, India, Netherlands, America, Britain and Asia. This combination creates a unique flavour and technique exclusive to Caribbean cuisine.

Family life: This is heavily impacted by the heritage of enslavement in the Caribbean. During this time, enslaved people were legally forbidden to marry; sexual exploitation of women by their masters was common and family groups were broken up and separated. These shaped the patterns of family life and have impacted the Caribbean community in relation to family types, maternal bonds and poverty.

Language: Languages spoken in Caribbean countries are a symbol of our historical bonds. Most of the languages in the Caribbean result from our colonial heritage and include five official languages in the region, including Spanish, English, French, Dutch and indigenous languages.

These languages are not just a means of communication, but they connect us to our ancestral relations. Our Creole language came about when the European languages mixed with the West African languages spoken by the enslaved people in the Caribbean to create unique Caribbean Creole. Terms such as 'Mama', 'Belly' and 'pickney' are recognised and used throughout the region, demonstrating the power of language to bring people together.

Music: In Caribbean music, many different influences come together to create truly amazing sounds. From the instruments used to the lyrics being sung, everything plays a role in shaping the unique rhythms and beats that define the Caribbean region. Many musical genres are identified with the Caribbean, such as Calypso, Reggae, Soca, Dancehall, Bouyon, Zouk, Fra Fra and Chutney.

Religion: The Caribbean is a melting pot of different religious practices that have evolved over time. Christianity is the most widely followed faith in the region, followed by Hinduism and Islam. The religious landscape in the Caribbean reflects the history of European colonialism, with Roman Catholicism being the dominant faith in countries that were colonised by the French and Spanish, and Anglicans and Methodists being prominent in countries with British colonial links. Alongside these, several Afro-Caribbean religions such as Rastafarianism, Vodou, Pocomania, and Orisha, have strong roots in African religious traditions. These diverse religious practices have contributed to the rich cultural heritage of the Caribbean and continue to play an important role in the lives of its people.

Figure 14.3 *Orisha ritual in Trinidad*

Festivals: Many of our Caribbean festivals have deep roots in African traditions and have religious significance. Countries in the region celebrate events like Carnival, Crop Over, Junkanoo, Mashramani and Owruyari. There are also religious celebrations such as Christmas, Easter, Diwali, Phagwah and Eidul-Fitr. These celebrations are unique because they often blend religious and historical heritage, such as the harvest and village feast. These community observances are an essential part of Caribbean culture and are celebrated enthusiastically by locals and visitors alike.

Figure 14.4 *Mashramani celebrations in Guyana*

Sports: Sport in the Caribbean is infused with the vibrant heritage and cultural display of the region. It is commonly referred to as the 'Calypso Experience' or 'Island Experience'. While there are many different sports played in the Caribbean, the main ones are cricket, football, track and field and netball. Cricket is the dominant unifying sport in the region, with the West Indies Cricket team bringing together players from different Caribbean territories and creating a powerful symbol of unity among Caribbean people.

Figure 14.5 *Shai Hope of Barbados batting for the West Indies*

Common economic and social issues

The Caribbean region is bound by common socioeconomic challenges. In the face of unique historical legacies and national issues, there are shared challenges for the economic resilience and social fabric of the region. These include fragile economies, vulnerability to natural disasters and a collective struggle for sustainable development. The following are a few mutual economic and social issues.

Limited national resources and small markets

The relatively small size of Caribbean nations means they have limited physical and human resources. This not only limits the scale of individual economic policies but also highlights the fragility of their economies. Due to the small size of domestic markets, the potential for robust economic growth is limited. To address these challenges, the Caribbean region should pool resources, knowledge and expertise. Through this kind of collaboration, the region can increase its collective impact, turning limitations into opportunities for sustained economic development.

Fragile economies and underdeveloped infrastructure

The fragility of some Caribbean economies, together with underdeveloped institutional infrastructures, creates a barrier to sustained economic growth. Some Caribbean countries face challenges that make it hard for their economies to grow and become stronger. These challenges include not having enough money, rules for businesses that are not good enough, and not having strong organisations to support economic growth. The lack of good infrastructure, like roads and communication systems, makes it even more difficult for businesses to run smoothly. To overcome these issues, it is important for these countries to work together on solutions. By joining forces, they can make their rules better, strengthen organisations, and improve essential infrastructure. This teamwork can help the Caribbean nations become stronger and more resilient.

Case study

Background: St. Lucia, a small island nation in the Caribbean, has a fragile economy due to its limited financial resources and underdeveloped infrastructure. The country's economy relies heavily on tourism and banana exports, making it vulnerable to external shocks such as natural disasters and global market fluctuations. The inadequate infrastructure, particularly in transportation and digital communications, creates further problems for economic development and discourages foreign investment.

Imagine St. Lucia as a small boat in a vast ocean, heavily relying on tourists and bananas for survival. But the boat faced big waves: weak roads, slow internet and not enough variety in its businesses.

Challenge: St. Lucia was like a boat relying on one sail. When storms (like global economic downturns) hit, it struggled to stay afloat.

Action plan: St. Lucia teamed up with its island neighbours to build more sails (diversify the economy), fix the boat (improve infrastructure) and strengthen the crew (enhance business rules).

Happy ending: With these changes, St. Lucia became a stronger ship, ready to sail smoothly through stormy seas.

Question:

Imagine you're the captain of St. Lucia's ship. How would you use your new sails (diverse economy) and sturdy boat (better infrastructure) to keep sailing smoothly during a storm (economic shock)? Why is having friends (neighbouring islands) helpful on this journey?

Non-independence and impact of global corporations

If small Caribbean countries are not fully independent, it means they cannot make all their own decisions, often because outside groups or bigger countries have a lot of influence. This can cause problems for local businesses and people. Sometimes, big companies might bring in ways of doing things that don't really help the local area or its residents. This situation makes it hard for these countries to grow economically while also taking care of the needs of their own community.

To tackle these economic challenges, Caribbean countries need to work together. By joining forces, they can create joint policies to protect their economies from outside influences. These efforts help maintain economic growth and support local businesses and people. The goal is to balance being part of the global economy while keeping the unique character and needs of small Caribbean nations in mind.

Economic development and import dependency

Some Caribbean countries have trouble growing their economies, which means they are not as rich or prosperous as they would like. One big problem they face is spending a lot of money buying things from other countries, which is called a high import bill.

For example, imagine a Caribbean island that buys lots of toys, food and cars from other places because it does not make enough of these things itself. Every time it buys these items, it is like the island is using its pocket money. If it spends too much on these, it will not have enough left for other important things, like building schools or fixing roads.

This high dependency on imports can create vulnerabilities in economies. Such a reliance on imports may expose these nations to economic risks, especially in times of global uncertainty or disruptions in the supply chain.

Here are some of the issues they might face:

- Changing prices: If the cost to buy goods from abroad increases, these countries will have to pay more, which could make it hard for them to manage their money.
- Money value risks: If the value of their money drops compared to other countries' money, they will need more of their own currency to buy the same amount of imported goods, which can cause financial trouble.
- Not getting enough supplies: If global problems like bad weather or political issues stop the flow of goods, these countries might not get important items they need, like food and medicine.
- Depending too much on others: If they rely heavily on goods from other countries, any economic problems in those countries can hurt the Caribbean economies too.
- Less growth at home: Spending a lot of money on imports can mean less support for local businesses and industries, which can slow down their own economic growth and development.

To address these challenges, there is a call for regional cooperation among Caribbean nations. By pooling their strengths and resources, these countries can look after their mutual economic interests. Through collaborative efforts, they can design and implement strategies to build self-sufficiency. This involves boosting domestic production, reducing the need for excessive imports, and encouraging regional economic resilience. By collectively investing in sectors such as agriculture, manufacturing and technology, Caribbean nations can decrease their dependency on external resources.

Unemployment and brain drain

Unemployment and brain drain in the Caribbean happens when individuals face challenges in securing meaningful employment, and the region experiences a significant loss of skilled professionals through a phenomenon called brain drain. Brain drain occurs when talented individuals, seeking better opportunities, leave their home countries for employment elsewhere.

This creates a situation where the region loses valuable expertise, particularly among those in productive and reproductive age groups.

To tackle the problem of high unemployment and brain drain, Caribbean countries should join forces to improve the connection between education and job opportunities. They can update school programmes to match the job skills that are in demand, like digital technology, renewable energy and tourism management. Setting up internships and partnerships between schools and businesses can also help. Skills in areas like information technology, sustainable agriculture and hospitality are particularly valuable. By encouraging people to work across different islands and aligning education with these in-demand skills, Caribbean nations can create a vibrant job market that keeps talented workers in the region and strengthens the economy.

National debt and limited private sector growth

The impact of national debt on Caribbean nations is a challenge that significantly influences the growth of the private sector. National debt refers to the amount of money a country owes, and when this debt becomes high, it can have various consequences.

One such consequence is the restriction it places on the growth of the private sector. High national debt often results in increased government spending on interest payments and debt servicing, leaving limited financial resources available for investments and initiatives that support private sector development. This financial strain hampers the ability of businesses to access capital, limiting their expansion and potential contribution to economic growth.

To tackle these challenges, there is a need to prioritise mutual economic interests and collaborative strategies among Caribbean nations. First is the management of national debt. By working together, these countries can find different approaches to reduce debt burdens, such as debt restructuring or negotiation with creditors. This creates an environment where more funds are available for investment in sectors that drive private sector growth.

Encouraging investment is also an important aspect of regional development. Caribbean nations can collaborate to create an attractive investment climate, offering incentives, streamlined regulations and infrastructure support that encourage private sector ventures. This joint effort aims to stimulate economic activities, create jobs and contribute to a more robust and diversified private sector. For example, several Caribbean nations, such as St. Kitts and Nevis, Dominica, Grenada, Antigua and Barbuda and St. Lucia, have implemented Citizenship by Investment (CBI) Programmes. These programmes allow foreign investors to obtain citizenship by making a qualifying investment, often in real estate, businesses, or government funds. This not only brings in much-needed capital but also contributes to economic development.

Crime and social disruption

The issue of crime in the Caribbean has serious implications for development, influencing both investor confidence and social stability. Crime negatively affects investor confidence, making businesses and individuals hesitant to invest in an environment seen as unsafe. This hesitancy to invest limits economic growth and job creation, slowing the overall development of the region.

The social disruption caused by high levels of crime undermines community cohesion and stability. It erodes trust among residents and instils fear, creating a challenging environment for social and economic activities. The consequences include

Figure 14.6 *A property owner takes precautions against crime in Kingston, Jamaica*

movement away from capitals, migration and it stops businesses from establishing or expanding operations in areas of high crime.

To address these challenges, joint strategies for crime prevention and community development are important. Caribbean nations can collaborate on crime prevention measures, including enhanced law enforcement, community policing and social programmes that address the root causes of crime. By building a safer environment, these strategies contribute to increased confidence among investors, encouraging them to participate in the region's economic activities.

At the same time, investing in community development initiatives such as education, healthcare and social services, can address the underlying socioeconomic factors that contribute to crime. This comprehensive approach not only tackles the symptoms but also addresses the root causes of criminal behaviour. Through collaborative efforts in crime prevention and community development, Caribbean nations aim to create a safer, more stable environment that promotes mutual economic interests. This involves not only attracting investments but also ensuring that the benefits of economic development are shared by the entire community, contributing to a more inclusive and sustainable path for the region.

The effects of globalisation, trade liberalisation and trading blocs

The Caribbean finds itself in the midst of globalisation, trade liberalisation, and emerging trading blocs, each influencing its path towards economic progress and wellbeing. To understand its effects, we must look at market expansion, price changes, technology spread and competitive forces.

Here are some of the impacts on the Caribbean region.

- **Brain drain**

    Many talented individuals from the Caribbean are moving to other countries for better job opportunities. This movement is making it tough for local businesses to grow because there are fewer skilled people available to work.

- **Economic vulnerability and economic growth**

    Caribbean countries have made money by selling goods to other places, which has helped their economies. However, because they depend heavily on selling just a few products, a big drop in prices, like with oil, can really hurt their economies. They also face risks from things like bad weather, changes in global prices and economic troubles in countries they trade with.

- **Competition, adjustment and unequal distribution of benefits**

    There is concern that the benefits of globalisation and trade liberalisation have been unevenly distributed across the Caribbean region, with some countries and sectors benefiting more than others. This creates a lot of regional competition. At the individual country level, globalisation and trade liberalisation expose Caribbean industries to increased import competition. This competition can affect domestic sectors, particularly those that need more competitiveness or cannot adapt quickly. Industries like agriculture and manufacturing may face challenges as they compete with cheaper imports from larger economies.

- **Increased market access**

    Trade liberalisation and globalisation have provided Caribbean countries with expanded market opportunities. Caribbean exports can access larger global markets by lowering or removing trade barriers, such as tariffs and quotas, leading to increased trade and potential economic growth.

- **Diversification of exports**

    Globalisation has encouraged Caribbean countries to diversify their exports beyond traditional commodities like sugar and bananas. As trade barriers have been lowered, Caribbean nations have been able to explore new sectors such as tourism, financial services, information technology and creative industries.

- **Development of trading blocs and loss of sovereignty**

    It is argued that participation in regional trading blocs requires Caribbean countries to relinquish some of their **sovereignty**, as they must agree to abide by rules and regulations established by the bloc. Most of these are on an international scale, and not complying can lead to blacklisting and, in extreme cases, embargos. Caribbean countries have formed trading blocs such as the Caribbean Community (CARICOM) and the Caribbean Single Market and Economy (CSME). These regional integration initiatives aim to promote intra-regional trade, economic cooperation and **harmonisation** of policies. Trading blocs can provide a more extensive, unified market for Caribbean producers and enhance their bargaining power in international trade negotiations.

- **Foreign direct investment (FDI)**

    Globalisation has enabled greater inflows of foreign direct investment into the Caribbean region. FDI can bring in capital, technology, managerial expertise and access to international markets, stimulating economic growth and employment opportunities.

Overall, regional integration in the Caribbean helps to protect against the potential adverse effects of globalisation, trade liberalisation and trading blocs by promoting cooperation, increasing regional trade, harmonising policies and strengthening negotiating power. It allows the region to navigate the complexities of the global economy better while safeguarding its unique interests and promoting sustainable development.

The benefits of regional integration in protecting against potential negative impacts

Regional integration in the Caribbean is important for protecting against the potential negative impacts of globalisation, trade liberalisation and trading blocs. Here are a few reasons why regional integration plays a crucial role:

- **Enhancing regional cooperation:** Caribbean countries can unite to address challenges and pursue common goals by fostering regional integration. This cooperation allows them to have a collective voice in global trade negotiations and advocate for their shared interests, including protecting vulnerable sectors and promoting fair trade practices.

- **Increasing regional trade:** Regional integration encourages trade among Caribbean countries, leading to a more diversified and resilient regional economy. By promoting intra-regional trade, Caribbean nations can reduce their dependence on external markets and mitigate some of the risks associated with globalisation. This regional trade can also strengthen industries, create economies of scale and foster innovation and competitiveness.

- **Bigger markets:** Through regional integration initiatives such as the Caribbean Community (CARICOM) and the Caribbean Single Market and Economy (CSME), Caribbean countries can create a larger unified market for their goods, services and investments. This larger market can attract foreign direct investment and increase business opportunities to expand and prosper within the region.

- **Common rules and standards:** Regional integration allows for harmonising policies, regulations and standards among Caribbean countries. This alignment can help the movement of goods, services, and labour across borders, reducing regional trade barriers. It also helps create a more predictable and transparent business environment, attracting investment and fostering economic growth.

- **Strengthening negotiating power:** Globalisation and trade liberalisation expose smaller economies to the influence of larger economies and trading blocs. Caribbean countries can improve their negotiating power in international trade discussions by coming together through regional integration. A unified regional stance can help protect their interests, secure favourable trade agreements and avoid being marginalised in the global economy.

- **Addressing social and environmental concerns:** Regional integration provides a platform for addressing shared social and environmental concerns. Through a united outlook and approach on issues such as climate change, natural resource management and social development, Caribbean countries can leverage their collective resources and expertise to tackle regional challenges more effectively.

Vulnerability to economic shocks, climate change and natural disasters; shared security concerns

Regional integration in the Caribbean is important because countries in our region share the same vulnerabilities to economic shocks, climate change and natural disasters, compounded by mutual security concerns. The region faces economic challenges, and the interconnectedness of economies means that an economic shock in one country can have knock-on effects on others.

For example, the Caribbean region has been significantly impacted by worldwide economic shocks, including the war between Russia and Ukraine, the global COVID-19 pandemic and fluctuations in oil prices. The conflict in Ukraine has had a ripple effect on the global economy, affecting commodity prices and trade relations. The Caribbean is heavily reliant on international trade and vulnerable to external economic influences, and the region has experienced disruptions in export markets and faced challenges in maintaining economic stability.

The COVID-19 pandemic caused widespread disruption to tourism – the backbone of many Caribbean economies – resulting in job losses and economic contractions. The fluctuations in oil prices due to global events have affected oil-dependent economies in the Caribbean, impacting their fiscal health and economic resilience. These demonstrate how interconnected the Caribbean region is with the global economy, emphasising the need for regional cooperation and integration to navigate and mitigate the impact of such widespread economic shocks.

The Caribbean's vulnerability to climate change and natural disasters, such as hurricanes and floods, requires joint efforts in disaster preparedness, response and recovery. Regional integration allows for pooled resources, shared early warning systems and coordinated evacuation plans.

Common security threats, including transnational crime and drug trafficking, call for collaborative security measures. By working together on intelligence sharing, joint law enforcement operations and unified responses to security challenges, Caribbean nations can enhance overall safety and stability.

This sense of shared vulnerability builds mutual assistance and solidarity, leading to more efficient use of resources and a coordinated response during crises. Regional integration helps the Caribbean region to collectively address shared vulnerabilities and promote the wellbeing and development of all member nations.

Case study

GRAND CAYMAN, Cayman Islands (CMC) — The Caribbean Catastrophe Risk Insurance facility (CCRIF) said Wednesday it will pay US$44 million to Grenada as a result of the damage and destruction caused by the passage of Hurricane Beryl last Monday.

It will be the single-largest payout by CCRIF, a segregated portfolio company, owned, operated, and registered in the Caribbean.

The Category 4 storm left a trail of death and damage as it made its way through the Windward Islands on July 1, with the Grenadine islands of Carriacou and Petite Martinique and St Vincent and the Grenadines' Union island severely impacted.

CCRIF said that payout to Grenada will be made this week, adding that Hurricane Beryl totally devastated 90 per cent of all buildings on the islands of Carriacou and Petite Martinique.

It said that there was also significant damage to the agriculture sector as well as the natural environment, including mangrove ecosystems. Electric utilities, mainly the transmission and distribution systems on both islands, also were significantly damaged.

The north of mainland Grenada was also not spared the wrath of Hurricane Beryl, with damage to houses, the agriculture and forestry sectors, and electric utility transmission and distribution, and water distribution systems.

In extending its 'deepest condolences' to the Government and people of Grenada, CCRIF said it is well aware of the impacts on other CCRIF member countries in the region, including St Vincent and the Grenadines and Jamaica.

CCRIF said that its parametric insurance policies make payments based on the intensity of an event and the amount of loss calculated in a pre-agreed model caused by these events.

It said the payout to Grenada on its tropical cyclone policy is the single largest payout by CCRIF. Until now, Haiti had the single largest payout from CCRIF, having received just under US$40 million, following the 2021 earthquake.

"These payouts represent Grenada's first payouts from CCRIF. I commend the Government of Grenada, which has always maintained that despite not receiving a payout, it understood the importance of financially protecting the economy in case a disaster strikes, as it would never want to see a repeat of Hurricane Ivan," said CCRIF Chief Executive Officer Isaac Anthony.

"Countries ought to treat parametric insurance for natural hazards like they treat health insurance. We buy health insurance because it is important to help safeguard our lives. However, we hope we do not need it but when we do, we have the peace of mind that it could help us deal with a more serious illness than a common cold.

"Similarly, we do not want to be negatively impacted by natural hazards and be faced with natural disasters. However, in the case of CCRIF's parametric insurance, the moment we really need it, it is available within 14 days of a triggering event."

Anthony said CCRIF's parametric insurance must be seen as a key component in helping countries to build back better and stronger to withstand future natural hazards, especially within the context of climate change.

CCRIF said that Hurricane Beryl is reminiscent of Hurricane Ivan 20 years ago, which impacted nine Caribbean islands.

Advancements in communication technologies that facilitate the transfer of cultural heritage

Advances in communication technology, particularly the widespread use of social media, helps to promote regional integration in the Caribbean. Social media platforms provide a space for individuals, communities and organisations across the region to connect, share and exchange cultural heritage. The instant and widespread nature of social media fosters a sense of shared identity and promotes a deeper understanding of the diverse cultures within the Caribbean.

Platforms like Facebook, Instagram, and X enable real-time communication, allowing people to share their cultural practices, traditions and artistic expressions. This serves as a powerful tool for breaking down geographical barriers and creating a virtual community that goes beyond national borders.

Educational exchange programmes contribute significantly to regional integration. Collaborative initiatives that encourage the movement of students and teachers between countries encourages teamwork and problem solving, research and new ideas. This strengthens schools and colleges across the Caribbean, connecting them like a bigger team that reaches beyond individual countries. This educational web makes learning better, not just for students, but for the whole Caribbean, making everyone feel more connected and working together.

Social media and student-teacher exchanges are exciting ways to bring Caribbean nations closer. These activities highlight shared heritage and culture, spark joint projects and knit the region into a vibrant Caribbean family.

Tourism and maritime cooperation

Tourism and maritime cooperation are driving regional integration in the Caribbean, with collaborative efforts encouraging a unified approach to harnessing the economic and cultural potential of the region.

Figure 14.7 *A sperm whale swims off the coast of Dominica*

Tourism cooperation

Caribbean Tourism Organisation (CTO): The CTO plays a central role in promoting collaboration among Caribbean nations in the tourism sector. Through the CTO, member countries take part in joint marketing campaigns, presenting the Caribbean as a collective and diverse destination. This cooperative marketing strategy increases the region's global visibility and attracts a broader spectrum of tourists interested in exploring multiple Caribbean destinations.

Caribbean Single Market and Economy (CSME): The CSME encourages tourism cooperation by allowing for the free movement of skilled personnel within the region. This supports the exchange of expertise, creating opportunities for regional tourism initiatives and the sharing of best practices.

Infrastructure development: Collaborative investments in infrastructure, such as regional airports, transportation networks and communication systems, contribute to a seamless and enhanced tourism experience. Shared infrastructure projects make the Caribbean more accessible and attractive to visitors, encouraging exploration beyond individual destinations.

Data and research sharing: The CTO facilitates the exchange of data and research among member countries. This allows nations to make informed decisions about tourism development, respond collectively to changing consumer preferences and adapt to global tourism trends.

Maritime cooperation

Maritime security: Given the geographical proximity of Caribbean nations and the importance of maritime activities, cooperation in maritime security is essential. Joint efforts to combat piracy, illegal fishing and other maritime threats contribute to regional stability and economic sustainability.

Trade and transportation: The Caribbean's reliance on maritime transportation for trade creates opportunities for cooperation in port development and shipping. Shared initiatives can enhance efficiency and reduce costs for participating countries.

Environmental conservation: Maritime cooperation extends to environmental conservation efforts, such as protecting coral reefs and marine ecosystems. Collaborative measures ensure the sustainability of marine resources, in line with the commitment to responsible tourism practices.

The Caribbean Hotel and Tourism Association (CHTA) is an organisation that supports and promotes the tourism and hospitality industry in the Caribbean. It helps members like hotels and tourism businesses work together, improve their skills and advocate for tourism-friendly policies.

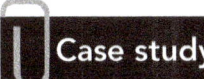

Case study

Dominica Sperm Whale Project

The Dominica Sperm Whale Project focuses on the research and conservation of sperm whales in the waters around Dominica. The project aims to understand the behaviour and social structures of these majestic creatures, promoting their protection and raising awareness about the importance of marine conservation. Through efforts like this, Dominica demonstrates its commitment to preserving marine biodiversity and promoting sustainable tourism practices.

www.thespermwhaleproject.org

Consumer practices in the region

Consumers have rights and responsibilities. They are protected by law when making purchases and should be given ample information about products and services to make informed decisions.

Consumer Protection Interventions such as the CARICOM Competition Commission have been useful in the region to raise awareness and advocate for consumer protection. The Commission, with headquarters in Suriname, seeks to:

- enhance consumer education
- promote fair trading practices among Member States such as discouraging misleading conduct, false and bait advertising
- give details of product safety standards to Member States which would meet the consumer needs
- conduct research to be analysed, keeping the consumer's interest high in the forefront.

There has also been a push towards buying local in the Caribbean among the regional consumers. The obvious advantage here would be the development of local enterprises which would reflect positively on the economy. 'Buy local' campaigns can only work however if the local supply is sufficient, safe and wholesome for public consumption.

Investment promotion has been high on the agenda to promote and safeguard the continuity of local and regional businesses. Organisations such as AMCHAM (The American Chamber of Commerce) serve to promote trade and investments between the US and CARICOM through the CBI (Caribbean Basin Initiative).

Common legal framework

A common legal framework provides a foundation for cooperation and collaboration across member nations. Central to this framework is the Caribbean Court of Justice (CCJ), a regional judicial institution that plays a key role in advancing the principles of legal unity and harmonisation.

The CCJ, established in 2001, is the primary judicial institution for Caribbean Community (CARICOM) member states. It is both an appellate court and an international court which interprets and applies the Revised Treaty of Chaguaramas, which governs the Caribbean Single Market and Economy (CSME).

The CCJ helps to harmonise legal standards across the Caribbean. Its decisions provide interpretations of regional treaties and agreements, ensuring consistency in the application of laws among member states. This harmonisation results in a shared legal understanding and reinforces the commitment to regional integration.

Another common legal framework is the harmonised business regulations, economic and social development.

Efforts to harmonise business regulations, such as standardising company registration processes and business licensing requirements, contribute to a common legal framework. This simplifies the establishment and operation of businesses across the Caribbean, encouraging cross-border investments and economic cooperation.

Agreements within the Caribbean Community (CARICOM) focus on various aspects, including trade, transportation and free movement of skilled persons. The implementation of these agreements creates a legal framework that guides and governs regional cooperation, fostering a shared approach to economic and social development.

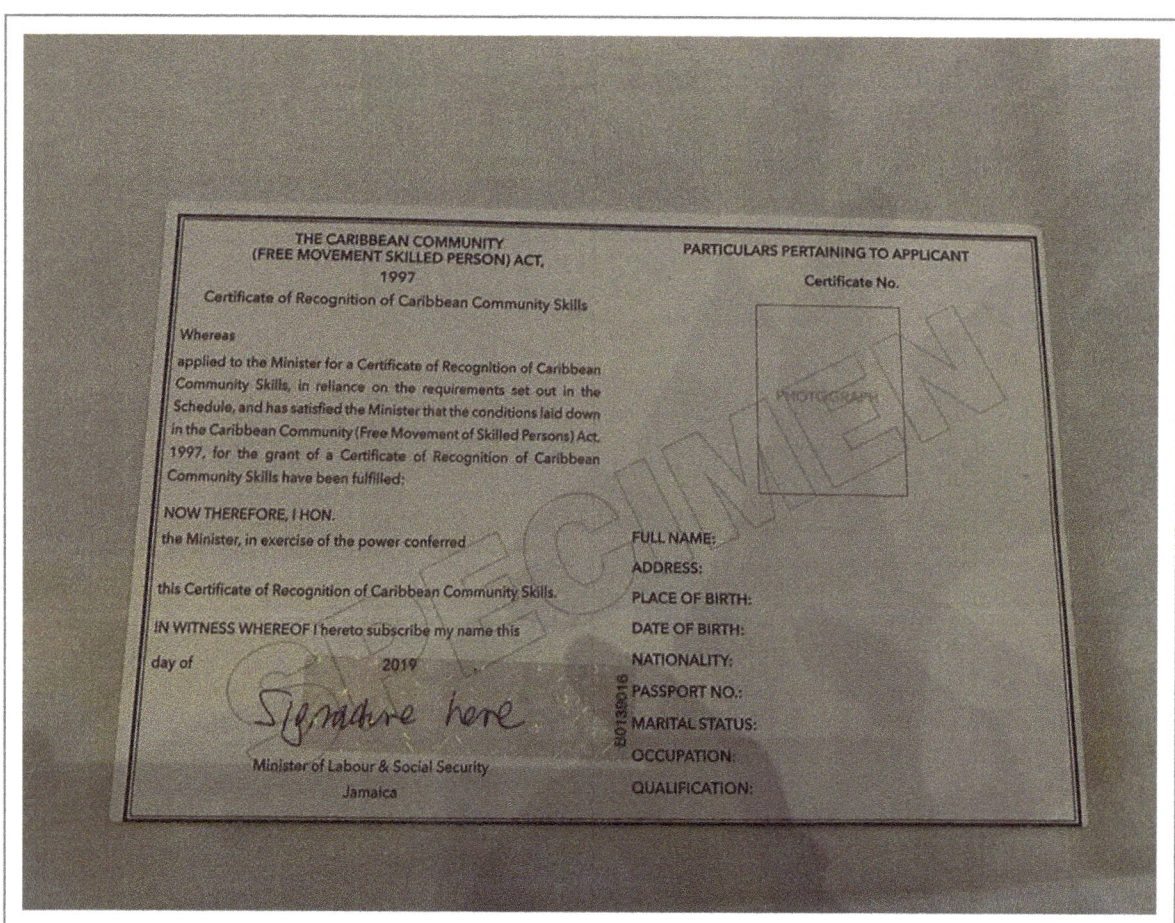

Figure 14.8 *A CSME certificate*

Coordination in immigration procedures contributes to a common legal framework, including the development of standardised visa and work permit regulations. This facilitates the movement of people across borders within the region, supporting initiatives like the CARICOM Single Market and Economy (CSME).

Another important standardisation is that of environmental protocols. Regional environmental agreements and protocols, such as those addressing climate change and conservation efforts, are made possible by a common legal framework. These agreements provide a unified approach to addressing environmental challenges, emphasising shared responsibility and sustainable practices.

Treaties and agreements related to security cooperation, including efforts to combat transnational crime and enhance border security, establish a common legal framework. Collaborative legal measures contribute to the safety and stability of the region, showcasing the commitment to shared security concerns. For example, in 1982 the Regional Security System (RSS) was established. The RSS is a collective security arrangement among several Eastern Caribbean nations.

Youth engagement

Youth engagement fosters a sense of shared identity, collaboration and active participation among the younger generation. The involvement of youth in regional initiatives contributes to the development of a more unified and cohesive Caribbean community. For example, the Caribbean Regional Youth Council (CRYC) was established as a representative body for young people across the region.

Youth engagement provides opportunities for cultural exchange programmes, bringing together young people from different Caribbean nations. These interactions help build cultural understanding, break down stereotypes, and promote a sense of unity and shared heritage among the region's youth.

Additionally, regional educational initiatives and exchange programmes encourage young people to pursue higher education, training and skill development across Caribbean countries. This contributes to the academic and personal growth of individuals and creates networks of young leaders who share a commitment to regional collaboration.

Questions

Multiple choice

1. What is regional integration?

a) The process of combining separate countries into one single entity.

b) The process of different regions within a country coming together for economic purposes.

c) The process of separate countries or territories forming closer political and economic relationships.

d) The process of one country taking over another to form a larger country.

2. Define '**economic interdependence**' in the context of Caribbean nations.

a) The reliance of Caribbean nations on tourism alone for economic stability.

b) The dependence of Caribbean nations on each other for economic stability and growth, involving shared resources and markets.

c) The dependence of Caribbean nations on external financial aid for growth.

d) The reliance of Caribbean nations on agriculture for their economic activities.

3 How does geographical proximity enhance regional integration among Caribbean countries?

  a) By facilitating easier communication and travel between countries, which strengthens economic and cultural ties.

  b) By creating competition among countries for tourist visits.

  c) By isolating the countries from the rest of the world, making them dependent only on each other.

  d) By increasing the likelihood of political conflicts between the nations.

4 How can advances in communication technology promote regional integration in the Caribbean?

  a) By increasing the digital divide between urban and rural areas in the Caribbean.

  b) By sharing cultural heritage and facilitating collaboration across different sectors, fostering a sense of community and shared identity.

  c) By enabling Caribbean countries to rely solely on technology for economic growth.

  d) By reducing the need for physical infrastructure like roads and ports.

Knowledge and comprehension

5 List three key benefits of regional integration for Caribbean countries.

6 Define 'harmonisation' and explain its importance in the context of regional integration in the Caribbean.

7 Match these images with their island of origin and definition

Image	Island	Definition
	Puerto Rico	A symbol of Caribbean music and culture, particularly associated with the vibrant sounds of Calypso.
	Dominica	The national dish of this Caribbean island, made from cornmeal and okra, served with flying fish.
	Jamaica	Spicy, grilled chicken dish. Its unique preparation and flavour makes it a major culinary export of this country.

14 Regional Integration

	Trinidad and Tobago	Percussion instruments made from gourds filled with beads or seeds. They are played by shaking to create a rhythmic sound.
	Barbados	It is a key part of the national dress and worn during cultural celebrations.

Use of knowledge

8 Analyse how the Caribbean Single Market and Economy (CSME) could affect the labour market in the Caribbean.

9 Propose a strategy to enhance maritime security among Caribbean nations to support regional integration efforts.

Major attempts at regional integration

Learning objectives

- Differentiate between bilateral and multilateral agreements and their roles in international relations.
- Outline the evolution and aims of Caribbean integration efforts like the West Indies Federation, CARIFTA and CARICOM.
- Understand the functions of the OECS, ACS and CSME, and their effects on Caribbean economic integration.
- Evaluate the impacts and challenges of these organisations in promoting regional cooperation and trade.

Important definitions

Bilateral agreements – agreements between two nations that can strengthen overall regional integration efforts.

Multilateral agreements – involve multiple nations working together to advance shared interests, essential for regional integration attempts.

Figure 14.14 *Roosevelt Skerrit, Prime Minister of Dominica*

Figure 14.15 *Mia Mottley, Prime Minister of Barbados*

Regional integration has been pursued through various initiatives over the years. From the early attempts of the West Indies Federation to the current CARICOM Single Market and Economy, these initiatives have aimed to foster economic growth, social cohesion and cultural exchange, shaping the Caribbean's evolution into a more interconnected and resilient community.

The Caribbean region shares historical, cultural and economic ties, and regional integration aims to strengthen cooperation, promote economic development and address common challenges collectively. In this section we will look at the various types of agreements and major initiatives that have shaped regional integration in the Caribbean.

Types of agreements between countries and states

- **Bilateral agreements**

    Bilateral agreements involve cooperation between two countries, fostering collaboration on specific issues. For example, a bilateral agreement could be signed between two countries to promote trade in goods or services, or to cooperate on security or environmental issues.

Figure 14.16 *Gaston Alfonso Browne, Prime Minister of Antigua and Barbuda*

- **Multilateral agreements**

    Multilateral agreements extend beyond bilateral interactions, involving multiple countries. These agreements aim to create a framework for regional cooperation, addressing various issues from economic integration to political and social collaboration. In the Caribbean region, multilateral agreements have been used as a means of fostering a unified regional identity. For example, a multilateral agreement could be signed by a group of countries to establish a free trade area or to reduce tariffs on goods and services.

Table 14.1 shows agreements past and present in the Caribbean region.

	Date established	Type of agreement	Goals	Status
West Indies Federation	1958	Bilateral agreement	To create a political union of the British West Indian colonies	Disbanded in 1962
Caribbean Free Trade Association (CARIFTA)	1965	Multilateral agreement	To promote free trade and economic cooperation among Caribbean countries	Replaced by CARICOM in 1973
Caribbean Community (CARICOM)	1973	Multilateral agreement	To promote economic, social and cultural cooperation among Caribbean countries	Still in operation
Organisation of Eastern Caribbean States (OECS)	1981	Multilateral agreement	To promote economic cooperation and integration among the Eastern Caribbean states	Still in operation
Association of Caribbean States (ACS)	1994	Multilateral agreement	To promote sustainable development and cooperation among Caribbean countries	Still in operation
The CARICOM Single Market and Economy (CSME)	2006	Multilateral agreement	To create a single market and economy among CARICOM member states	Still in operation

Table 14.1

Multilateral agreements like CARIFTA, CARICOM and OECS involve multiple independent countries negotiating and cooperating on various issues while maintaining their sovereignty.

In contrast, the West Indies Federation aimed to create a unified political entity under British oversight, making it a unique form of bilateral cooperation between the British government and the collective Federation.

West Indies Federation as a bilateral agreement

The West Indies Federation, established in 1958, is considered a bilateral agreement rather than a multilateral one due to its specific structure and nature of cooperation. While the term 'bilateral' typically refers to agreements between two parties, in this context, it highlights the limited scope of direct cooperation primarily between the British government and the collective entity of the British West Indian colonies.

The West Indies Federation was primarily an initiative by the British government to create a political union among its Caribbean colonies.

The direct interaction was mainly between the British government and the Federation as a single political entity representing the colonies, rather than a multilateral interaction among numerous independent states.

Objectives of the Caribbean regional organisations

Learning objectives

- Understand the objectives of OECS and CARICOM, including their cooperation in education, disaster management and health.
- Describe the creation of a single economy and common foreign policy within OECS and CARICOM.
- Identify the key elements of the CARICOM Single Market and Economy, including free movement of goods, services, capital and skilled labour.
- Explain the role of the Caribbean Court of Justice in resolving disputes among member states.

> **Important definitions**
>
> *Institutional framework* – the organisational structures, like OECS and CARICOM, established to oversee regional integration.

Regional organisations in the Caribbean play a crucial role in fostering collaboration, addressing common challenges, and promoting shared development goals.

OECS and CARICOM

OECS and CARICOM share a common vision of regional integration, with a focus on fostering functional cooperation, creating a single economy and pursuing a common foreign policy.

- **Fostering functional cooperation**

    The primary objective of both the OECS and CARICOM is to foster functional cooperation among member states. This includes collaborative efforts in education, addressing natural disasters, and coordinating health initiatives. By pooling resources and expertise, member states aim to collectively tackle regional challenges.

- **Creation of a single economy**

    An essential goal is the creation of a single economic space within each organisation. This involves harmonising economic policies, facilitating trade and promoting a seamless flow of goods and services. The vision is to enhance economic integration, thereby contributing to the overall prosperity of the region.

Figure 14.17 *The logo of the OECS*

- **Common foreign policy**

  OECS and CARICOM aim to establish a common foreign policy to amplify the collective voice of member states on the international stage. By aligning diplomatic efforts, member states can address global issues more effectively and advocate for shared interests.

Table 14.2 shows the objectives of OECS and CARICOM.

Objectives	OECS	CARICOM
Functional cooperation	Education, natural disaster management and health	Education, agriculture, health, culture, transportation and tourism
Creation of a single economy	Eliminate barriers to trade and investment, harmonise economic policies and establish a common market to facilitate the free movement of goods, services, capital and labour.	Promote economic cooperation and integration among Caribbean countries.
Common foreign policy	Coordinate foreign policy stances to amplify the Caribbean's voice on the international stage and increase its influence in addressing global issues.	Promote a common foreign policy and economic agenda.

Table 14.2

Objectives of the CARICOM Single Market and Economy (CSME)

- **Standardised contingent rights**

  CSME seeks to establish contingent rights, including the free movement of goods and services, the right of establishment and the elimination of trade barriers. This creates an economic environment where businesses can operate seamlessly across member states.

- **Free movement of capital**

  CSME aims to facilitate the free movement of capital, encouraging investment flows across the region. This objective supports economic growth and development by encouraging cross-border investments.

- **Free movement of skilled labour**

  CSME promotes the free movement of skilled labour, allowing professionals to seek employment opportunities within member states. This increases labour mobility, addresses skills gaps and contributes to a more efficient allocation of human resources.

- **CARICOM Development Fund**

  The establishment of the CARICOM Development Fund is a key component of CSME. This fund supports economic development initiatives, particularly in less-developed member states, ensuring a more equal distribution of benefits within the community.

Objectives of the Caribbean Court of Justice (CCJ)

- **Settling disputes among member states**

  The primary objective of the CCJ is to serve as the final court of appeal for member states, settling disputes and ensuring legal consistency across the Caribbean. This promotes the rule of law and contributes to a harmonised legal framework within the region.

- **Harmonisation of policies**

  The regional organisations strive for the harmonisation of various policies to deepen integration. This includes:
  - Immigration policies
  - Fiscal (tax) policies

- Monetary policies
- External trade policies
- Legislation (including customs and companies laws)
- Sectoral policies (for example in agriculture, manufacturing and fisheries).

Evaluating the impacts and challenges of these organisations

These efforts towards regional integration, driven by a shared history and the quest for economic and social development, have culminated in the formation of organisations like CARICOM, OECS, ACS and CSME.

Historical impacts and achievements

CARICOM successfully negotiated favourable trade agreements with international partners, enhancing market access for Caribbean goods. For example, the Economic Partnership Agreement with the European Union boosted Caribbean exports by increasing trade preferences and investment flows.

Figure 14.18 *The logo of the Caribbean Court of Justice*

Table 14.3 shows GDP and export growth percentages for the Caribbean regional organisations.

Organisation	Year	GDP growth (%)	Export growth (%)	Employment rate increase (%)
Caribbean Free Trade Association (CARIFTA)	1965	10	5	8
Caribbean Community (CARICOM)	1973	25	20	18
Organisation of Eastern Caribbean States (OECS)	1981	40	35	28
Association of Caribbean States (ACS)	1994	55	50	38
The CARICOM Single Market and Economy (CSME)	2006	70	65	48
Current	2023	90	85	58

Table 14.3

Challenges and critiques

Political divergence and economic disparities:

Despite the vision of unity, political and economic disparities among member states have posed significant challenges. Differing national interests and varying levels of economic development have prevented some unified policy making and implementation.

Future directions and opportunities

Economic diversification and digital integration:

Future directions could include a greater focus on diversifying economies away from traditional sectors like tourism and agriculture, and leveraging digital technology to create a more interconnected and resilient Caribbean economy.

Questions

Knowledge and comprehension

1. What were the primary goals of the West Indies Federation, and why was it considered a bilateral agreement rather than a multilateral one?

2. Explain how the transition from CARIFTA to CARICOM represents an evolution in Caribbean integration efforts.

3. Discuss the significance of the free movement of goods, services, capital and skilled labour in the objectives of the CSME. How does this facilitate regional integration?

Use of knowledge

4. Assess the role of the Caribbean Court of Justice (CCJ) in advancing regional integration and resolving disputes among member states.

5. Evaluate the challenges faced by Caribbean regional integration efforts, particularly in achieving economic and political cohesion among diverse member states. How have these challenges affected the progress towards integration?

The benefits and successes of regional integration

Learning objectives

- List the benefits of regional integration like better jobs, improved quality of life and stronger international trade.
- Explore how Caribbean countries have successfully worked together in areas like education, finance, health and disaster response.
- Recognise how regional integration helps in sharing culture, sports and education in the Caribbean.
- Know about key Caribbean organisations and their roles in regional cooperation.
- Discuss the good and challenging aspects of regional integration for Caribbean nations.

Important definitions

Inclusive development – promoting equitable distribution of integration benefits, contributing to its success.

The benefits and successes of regional integration

Regional integration strategies in the Caribbean are strategically designed to foster collaboration, economic development and global relevance among member states.

A critical aspect of regional integration lies in its capacity to address labour market challenges. By fostering cross-border employment opportunities, it contributes significantly to the reduction of unemployment and underemployment. This enables a more efficient allocation of human resources, aligning skilled workers with demand across member states.

The successes demonstrate the importance of regional integration in shaping a more prosperous, cooperative and globally influential Caribbean community. By capitalising on shared resources, fostering inclusivity and presenting a unified front, member states continue to navigate complex challenges and advance towards a more interconnected regional future.

Table 14.4 outlines the benefits of regional integration.

Benefit	Description
Reduced unemployment and underemployment	Regional integration can lead to increased economic activity and job creation, reducing unemployment and underemployment rates.
Enhanced response to economic implications of globalisation and trade liberalisation	Regional integration allows countries to collectively address the challenges and opportunities arising from globalisation and trade liberalisation, strengthening their position in the global economy.
Improved quality of life	Regional integration can contribute to higher living standards, improved access to essential services, and enhanced infrastructure, leading to a better quality of life for citizens.
Reduced inequality of wealth distribution	Regional integration initiatives often include measures to address income inequality and promote social equity, contributing to a more just distribution of wealth.
Free movement of goods, labour, and capital	Regional integration facilitates the free movement of goods, labour and capital within the region, boosting economic activity and fostering cross-border cooperation.

Benefit	Description
Increased market size	A larger regional market allows businesses to expand their reach, increase production and achieve economies of scale, leading to lower costs and improved efficiency.
Enhanced international competitiveness	Regional integration strengthens the collective bargaining power and competitiveness of member countries in the international arena, enhancing their ability to attract investment and influence global trade rules.
Expanded trade	Regional integration promotes increased trade flows among member countries, stimulating economic growth and fostering regional economic interdependence.
Increased cooperation among member states	Regional integration encourages collaboration and knowledge sharing among member states, leading to joint solutions to common challenges and shared development goals.
Stronger international presence	A united and cohesive regional bloc gains greater recognition and influence on the international stage, allowing it to effectively advocate for its interests and priorities.

Table 14.4

Case study

Regional integration and the COVID-19 pandemic

Regional integration played a crucial role in the Caribbean response to the COVID-19 pandemic, enabling coordinated action, resource sharing and collective resilience. Here are some specific examples of how regional integration benefited the region's fight against COVID-19.

Coordinated public health measures: Regional organisations like CARICOM and the Organisation of Eastern Caribbean States (OECS) facilitated collaboration among member countries to develop and implement harmonised public health measures, such as travel restrictions, testing protocols and contact tracing strategies. This coordination helped to contain the spread of the virus and protect vulnerable populations.

Resource sharing and procurement: Regional institutions coordinated the procurement and distribution of essential medical equipment, supplies and personal protective equipment (PPE) across member countries. This collective effort ensured that frontline healthcare workers had the necessary resources to effectively manage the pandemic.

Knowledge sharing and exchange of best practices: Regional platforms facilitated the sharing of knowledge, experiences and best practices in managing the pandemic. This exchange of information helped countries learn from each other's successes and adapt their strategies effectively.

Collective advocacy and international representation: Regional organisations advocated for the needs and interests of the Caribbean on the international stage, securing access to vaccines, medical supplies and financial support. This collective voice strengthened the Caribbean's position in global pandemic response efforts.

Overall, regional integration proved to be a valuable asset in the Caribbean's fight against COVID-19. Through coordinated action, resource sharing and knowledge exchange, regional organisations helped to protect public health, mitigate economic hardship, and strengthen the region's resilience in the face of the pandemic.

Regional integration attempts in the Caribbean have produced successes that have positively impacted the lives of Caribbean citizens and strengthened the region's overall development. These successes demonstrate the transformative power of regional integration in the Caribbean, fostering cooperation, enhancing economic opportunities and improving the lives of Caribbean citizens. As the region continues to pursue deeper integration, these achievements serve as a testament to the potential for regional collaboration and the shared aspirations of the Caribbean people.

Here are some more examples of regional integration in action:

Improved access to tertiary education: The establishment of the University of the West Indies (UWI) as a regional institution has significantly expanded access to quality tertiary education for Caribbean students. UWI's presence across the region has provided students with opportunities to pursue higher education closer to home, reducing the financial burden of studying abroad.

Enhanced access to capital: The Caribbean Development Bank (CDB) has played a pivotal role in providing financial assistance and support to Caribbean countries, facilitating infrastructure development, promoting economic growth and fostering resilience in the face of disasters. The CDB's lending and grant programs have contributed significantly to the region's economic development.

Strengthened trading relationships: The CARICOM Single Market and Economy (CSME) has facilitated the free movement of goods, services, capital and labour within the region, expanding market opportunities for businesses and consumers. The CSME has stimulated economic activity, encouraged cross-border investment, and enhanced the competitiveness of Caribbean products and services in the global market.

Improved access to justice and arbitration: The establishment of the Caribbean Court of Justice (CCJ) has provided a regional judicial institution to settle disputes between CARICOM member states, promoting adherence to the rule of law and contributing to regional stability. The CCJ has also offered its services for international commercial arbitration, enhancing the region's reputation as a centre for dispute resolution.

Effective response to health issues: The Caribbean Public Health Agency (CARPHA) has played a crucial role in coordinating regional health initiatives, providing technical assistance and conducting surveillance to address public health challenges. CARPHA's work has significantly contributed to improving the region's health outcomes and preparedness for emerging health threats.

During the COVID-19 pandemic, CARPHA was instrumental in providing timely information, coordinating testing efforts, and supporting the implementation of public health measures across the Caribbean. Their efforts helped to mitigate the impact of the virus and enhance the region's overall response to the pandemic.

Coordinated disaster management: The Caribbean Disaster Emergency Management Agency (CDEMA) has facilitated regional cooperation in disaster preparedness, response and recovery. CDEMA's efforts have helped to strengthen the region's resilience to natural disasters and minimise their impact on communities and economies.

Regional education certification: The Caribbean Examinations Council (CXC®) has established a standardised system of primary, secondary, and post-secondary certification across the Caribbean, facilitating the recognition of qualifications and enabling students to pursue higher education or employment opportunities regionally and internationally.

Cultural exchange and promotion: The Caribbean Festival of Arts (CARIFESTA) has served as a platform for showcasing and celebrating the rich cultural heritage of the Caribbean, fostering cultural exchange and promoting regional unity. CARIFESTA has also contributed to the development of the cultural industries and tourism sector in the region.

Nurturing sporting talent: The CARIFTA Games and the West Indies Cricket Board have played a significant role in identifying, nurturing and showcasing sporting talent in the Caribbean. These organisations have provided opportunities for young athletes to compete at regional and international levels, raising the profile of Caribbean sports and producing world-class athletes.

Promoting regional tourism: The Caribbean Tourism Organisation (CTO) and the Caribbean Hotel Association (CHA) have worked collaboratively to promote the Caribbean as a premier tourist destination, attracting visitors from around the world and contributing to the region's economic growth. Their efforts have helped to enhance the region's tourism infrastructure, improve service standards, and strengthen the Caribbean's global tourism brand.

Factors that hinder the attempts at regional integration

Learning objectives
- Analyse the challenges to regional integration, focusing on geographic, economic and political factors that have contributed to failed integration efforts.
- Evaluate the impact of external influences, such as foreign investment and multinational corporations, on regional integration and resource distribution.

Important definitions

Infrastructure development – creating and improving physical and organisational structures to support economic activities.

Insularity – when persons are only concerned with their own country and are unwilling to consider or accept outside influences or ideas.

Despite the remarkable progress made in regional integration efforts, the Caribbean journey has not been without its challenges. Several factors have got in the way of the full realisation of regional integration goals and slowed the pace of regional cooperation.

Case study

The fall of the West Indies Federation

The West Indies Federation was a short-lived political union of ten British Caribbean colonies that existed from 1958 to 1962. The federation aimed to unify the islands and promote economic and social development. However, it faced several challenges that ultimately led to its dissolution:

- Geographical and cultural barriers
- Economic disparities
- Political fragmentation
- External pressures

In 1961, a referendum was held in Jamaica to decide whether the country should remain part of the Federation. The referendum resulted in a vote to leave the Federation, leading to its collapse in 1962.

The failure of the West Indies Federation serves as a reminder of the challenges and complexities of regional integration. While the federation did not achieve its ultimate goal of a unified Caribbean nation, it provided valuable lessons and experiences that have shaped subsequent regional integration efforts in the Caribbean.

The following factors can hinder the effectiveness of regional integration.

- **Geographical barriers**

    The Caribbean region is spread across a large expanse of the western arm of the Atlantic Ocean, which presents logistical challenges for communication, transportation and coordination. The physical separation between countries can increase the costs of travel, trade and **infrastructure development**, making regional integration a more complex undertaking.

- **Absence of a common development model**

    The Caribbean's diverse economies, with varying levels of development and resources, means forming a unified approach to regional integration can be difficult. The absence of a shared development model can lead to disagreements on economic priorities and stop the implementation of effective regional policies.

    The Caribbean's member states are at different stages of economic development, with some countries more industrialised and others reliant on agriculture or tourism. These differences can lead to competing interests and differing priorities, making it difficult to harmonise economic policies and pursue a common development path.

- **Competition for foreign investment**

    Caribbean countries often compete directly for foreign investment, attracting capital through tax incentives, infrastructure development and favourable investment regulations. This competition can undermine regional solidarity and limit efforts to establish a unified regional investment strategy.

- **Balancing territorial and regional loyalties**

    The strong sense of national identity and territorial loyalty among Caribbean countries can sometimes conflict with the broader goals of regional integration. This tension can manifest in a reluctance to pass authority to regional institutions, slowing down the process of regional decision-making and implementation.

- **Insularities and cultural differences**

    The unique cultural and historical legacies of each Caribbean island can create a sense of **insularity**, making it challenging to establish a cohesive regional identity. These cultural differences can sometimes lead to misunderstandings and hinder effective communication and collaboration.

- **Political will and leadership**

    The success of regional integration relies on the strong political will and leadership of member states. A lack of commitment or political support from national governments can hinder the implementation of regional initiatives and weaken the overall integration process.

- **Interregional transportation challenges**

    The high cost and limited availability of interregional transportation infrastructure can restrict the movement of goods, people and ideas, impeding regional trade, tourism and cultural exchange. Inadequate transportation links can also add to geographical barriers and hinder regional connectivity.

- **Absence of a common currency**

    The lack of a common currency in the Caribbean adds complexity to cross-border transactions and increases the costs of trade and investment. The absence of a common currency can also make it more difficult for countries to coordinate monetary policies and manage exchange rate fluctuations.

Figure 14.19 *Eastern Caribbean dollars*

Table 14.5 shows the different currencies and exchange rates to USD across the Caribbean region.

Country/territory	Currency	Exchange rate to USD
Antigua and Barbuda	Eastern Caribbean dollar (XCD)	2.70 XCD = 1 USD
The Bahamas	Bahamian dollar (BSD)	1.00 BSD = 1 USD
Barbados	Barbadian dollar (BBD)	2.00 BBD = 1 USD
Belize	Belize dollar (BZD)	2.00 BZD = 1 USD
Dominica	Eastern Caribbean dollar (XCD)	2.70 XCD = 1 USD
Grenada	Eastern Caribbean dollar (XCD)	2.70 XCD = 1 USD
Guyana	Guyanese dollar (GYD)	205.85 GYD = 1 USD
Haiti	Haitian gourde (HTG)	111.63 HTG = 1 USD
Jamaica	Jamaican dollar (JMD)	151.66 JMD = 1 USD
Montserrat	Eastern Caribbean dollar (XCD)	2.70 XCD = 1 USD
St. Kitts and Nevis	Eastern Caribbean dollar (XCD)	2.70 XCD = 1 USD
St. Lucia	Eastern Caribbean dollar (XCD)	2.70 XCD = 1 USD
St. Vincent and the Grenadines	Eastern Caribbean dollar (XCD)	2.70 XCD = 1 USD
Suriname	Surinamese dollar (SRD)	14.20 SRD = 1 USD
Trinidad and Tobago	Trinidad and Tobago dollar (TTD)	6.70 TTD = 1 USD

Table 14.5

- **Unequal distribution of resources**

  The uneven distribution of natural resources and economic opportunities across the Caribbean can create disparities in wealth and development levels among member states. These disparities can lead to feelings of resentment and hinder efforts to achieve equitable regional integration.

- **Lack of production diversification**

  The reliance of many Caribbean economies on a limited range of exports, such as agriculture or tourism, makes them vulnerable to external shocks and fluctuations in global markets. This lack of diversification can also limit opportunities for intra-regional trade and economic cooperation.

- **Influence of multinational corporations**

  The presence and influence of multinational corporations in the Caribbean can sometimes overshadow regional priorities and interests. These corporations may prioritise their own profit motives over regional development goals, potentially hindering the implementation of effective integration policies.

Questions

Multiple choice

What was one of the key benefits of regional integration in the Caribbean's response to the COVID-19 pandemic?

a) Decreased tourism

b) Coordinated public health measures

c) Increased regional conflict

d) Reduced cultural exchange

2 The Caribbean Single Market and Economy (CSME) primarily aims to:
   a) Facilitate a single currency for the entire region
   b) Promote free movement of goods, services and labour
   c) Establish a single regional army
   d) Merge all Caribbean countries into a single nation

3 Which of the following is a challenge to regional integration in the Caribbean?
   a) Increased market size
   b) Geographical barriers
   c) Improved access to education
   d) Enhanced international competitiveness

4 How does the Caribbean Development Bank (CDB) contribute to regional integration?
   a) By providing military support to member countries
   b) By facilitating cultural exchanges through CARIFESTA
   c) By offering financial assistance and support for economic development
   d) By organising regional sports events like the CARIFTA Games

5 What was a significant outcome of the dissolution of the West Indian Federation?
   a) It led to the immediate creation of the Caribbean Court of Justice
   b) It highlighted the difficulties of political integration in the Caribbean
   c) It resulted in the unification of all English-speaking Caribbean islands
   d) It prompted the establishment of a common Caribbean currency

Knowledge and comprehension

6 Describe the role of the Caribbean Public Health Agency (CARPHA) during the COVID-19 pandemic. How did CARPHA contribute to regional efforts in combating the virus?

Use of knowledge

7 Considering the benefits of regional integration, explain how the establishment of the University of the West Indies (UWI) has influenced tertiary education accessibility and regional development in the Caribbean.

8 Assess the impact of the Caribbean Disaster Emergency Management Agency (CDEMA) in strengthening disaster preparedness and response in the Caribbean. Discuss specific examples of CDEMA's actions during natural disasters and evaluate their effectiveness.

Integration process in the Caribbean

Learning objectives
- Understand how citizens, businesses, government and media contribute to regional growth.
- Assess the effects of civic participation, business innovation, government policies and media on regional development.

Important definitions

Diaspora engagement – the role of individuals living outside their home countries in supporting integration.

Integration process in the Caribbean

Regional integration in the Caribbean is a dynamic process that involves the active participation of various stakeholders, including individual citizens, business organisations, government entities and the mass media.

- **Role of citizens**
  Individual citizens are vital to the integration process, contributing in various ways. Entrepreneurship, through the establishment of local businesses and initiatives, fosters economic growth and innovation. Supporting regional producers and institutions demonstrates a commitment to the local economy, while showing mutual support towards fellow regional citizens builds a collective consciousness, which is a unifying force. Investing in local and regional businesses enables citizens to actively participate in the economic development of the region. Being informed is equally crucial, as an informed population is better equipped to engage in discussions about integration and make informed decisions.

Role in regional integration	Examples	
Entrepreneurship	Creating innovative businesses and contributing to economic growth	

Section B(ii) Sustainable Development and Use of Resources

Role in regional integration	Examples	
Supporting regional producers and institutions	Purchasing goods and services produced within the region	
Showing solidarity and mutual support	Embracing cultural exchange, celebrating regional achievements and supporting regional initiatives	
Investing in local and regional businesses	Investing financial resources in local and regional enterprises	
Being informed and engaged	Staying informed about integration initiatives and actively engaging in discussions and consultations	

- **Role of business organisations**
  Business organisations play an important role in driving economic integration. Improving competitiveness is crucial, as organisations seek to enhance their ability to thrive in regional markets. This involves increasing the range and quality of goods and services offered, thereby contributing to the overall economic energy of the region. By providing opportunities for investment and employment, business organisations become key contributors to the socioeconomic development of the Caribbean.

- **Role of government**
  Governments play a central role in shaping the integration landscape. Enacting legislation provides the legal framework necessary for the implementation of integration agreements. Harmonising policies across member states ensures consistency and a collaborative environment. Honouring protocols and agreements is crucial for maintaining trust and credibility within the integration

process. Governments also play an educational role by informing citizens about the objectives and benefits of integration, giving them a sense of shared purpose and understanding.

- **Role of mass media**
  Mass media, including broadcast (radio, television, and internet), print and social media, serves as a powerful tool for shaping perceptions and transmitting information. Airing regional programmes promotes a sense of regional identity and highlights the commonalities among member states. Educating citizens about the objectives and benefits of integration is a key function, as informed citizens are more likely to actively engage in the integration process. Mass media platforms also serve as forums for discussion and debate, allowing diverse perspectives to be heard.

The success of regional integration in the Caribbean is linked to the active engagement and collaboration of citizens, business organisations, government entities and the mass media. As these stakeholders play their respective roles, they contribute to the creation of a more interconnected, prosperous and cohesive Caribbean community.

End of chapter questions

1. Define the following terms. (6 marks)
   a) Regional integration
   b) Cultural heritage
2. List THREE heritage links within the Caribbean. (3 marks)
3. What are the main objectives of the Caribbean Court of Justice (CCJ), and how does it contribute to the regional integration process? (6 marks)
4. Identify and explain THREE challenges faced by Caribbean nations in achieving effective regional integration. (6 marks)
5. Explain why regional integration is crucial for Caribbean countries in protecting against the potential negative impacts of globalisation, trade liberalisation and trading blocs. Provide at least two reasons. (6 marks)
6. How does regional integration in the Caribbean enhance regional cooperation? Discuss the benefits of collective voice and advocacy in global trade negotiations. (6 marks)
7. How does regional integration contribute to building a larger market in the Caribbean? Discuss the significance of creating a unified market for goods, services and investments, and its impact on foreign direct investment and business opportunities. (6 marks)
8. Describe the role of harmonising policies and standards in regional integration. Explain how aligning policies, regulations and standards among Caribbean countries facilitates trade and creates a favourable business environment. (6 marks)
9. In what ways do advances in communication technology, such as social media, contribute to the promotion of cultural heritage and regional integration in the Caribbean? (6 marks)
10. Discuss the role of the Organisation of Eastern Caribbean States (OECS) in fostering functional cooperation and how it aligns with the broader objectives of regional integration. (6 marks)
11. Explain the concept of 'trade liberalisation' and discuss its significance in the context of promoting economic cooperation and integration among Caribbean nations. (6 marks)

Summary

Regional integration is a necessary process within the region for a number of reasons. There are many factors that work to deliver services, build relationships and generate levels of development.

We need to recognise our region as unique with its general location and climate vulnerabilities, socio-cultural and economic similarities, trading protocols, global, regional and local networks as well as the opportunities available in the tourism sector and investment.

In order to structure the shared experiences, regional integrative bodies were developed to cater to the region's economic, social and cultural needs. The West Indies Federation was the first attempt at regional integration in 1958 but collapsed due to a number of shortcomings. CARIFTA, then CARICOM followed with the OECS, ACS and the CSME laid the lineup for deep-rooted cooperation.

There are many benefits to be derived from shared experiences which include job opportunities and technical assistance in many facets of life, improvements in the way of life and better, easier trade. However, certain drawbacks take the form of geographic issues, economic and political concerns as well as external influences.

Many other stakeholders such as citizens, businesses, government and the media all have a role in the integrative process and their roles should be identified. Regional integration is ideally a team effort.

Section B: Sustainable Development and Use of Resources
(ii) Regional Development

15 Tourism and Integration

The topics covered in this chapter are:

- the ways in which tourism can be used to promote regional integration
- differentiating between the types of tourism products available in the Caribbean

The ways in which tourism can be used to promote regional integration

Palm trees swaying in the breeze, while the sun lights the crystal-clear waters, creating sparkling jewels. In the background, the rhythms of Caribbean music invite you to dance until dawn. The Caribbean is a paradise that is a dream destination for travellers from across the globe.

In this chapter we will learn how tourism, the lifeblood of the Caribbean, is not just about sun, sand and sea. It's a catalyst for bringing countries together through shared cultures, traditions and economic goals. We will look at the diverse tourism products that define the Caribbean experience.

Important definitions

Regional integration – the collaboration between neighbouring countries to strengthen political, economic and cultural connections, boosting cooperation and mutual benefits.

Tourism products – the diverse offerings and experiences provided by a destination to attract and cater to tourists.

Joint marketing efforts – collaborative promotional strategies used by multiple destinations to enhance the visibility and appeal of a region as a whole.

Cross-border travel – movement of tourists across national boundaries, emphasising the interconnected nature of tourism in the Caribbean.

Aviation hubs – strategic airports designed to facilitate efficient air travel connections, serving as key transit points within the Caribbean.

Economic ties – the interconnected financial relationships and transactions between Caribbean nations, driven by tourism-related activities and economic collaboration.

Communication linkages – the establishment and maintenance of effective channels of communication among Caribbean countries, including information sharing and coordination, which build unity and collaboration.

Tourism development – the systematic planning and implementation of initiatives to enhance the tourism sector, encompassing infrastructure, services and attractions.

Cultural heritage – the collective legacy of a nation's cultural achievements, traditions and artifacts that contribute to its identity and attractiveness as a tourism destination.

Wellness tourism – a segment of tourism focused on promoting health and wellbeing, often incorporating activities such as spa treatments, yoga and holistic experiences.

Event tourism – the travel and engagement associated with special events, festivals and celebrations, contributing to the cultural and economic vibrancy of a destination.

Ecotourism – sustainable and responsible travel to natural areas, emphasising conservation, education and minimised environmental impact.

Caribbean identity – a shared sense of cultural, historical and geographical belonging among the nations of the Caribbean, contributing to the region's unique appeal.

Tourism collaboration – cooperative efforts among Caribbean nations to enhance the overall tourism experience and address common challenges, promoting a sense of unity.

Learning objectives

- Clarify how tourism acts as a driver for regional cooperation and integration in the Caribbean.
- Identify and differentiate between various types of tourism products available in the Caribbean, including their cultural and economic significance.
- Recognise the importance of common economic and marketing policies in promoting a unified approach to Caribbean tourism.
- Evaluate the impact of **communication linkages** in fostering collaboration and information exchange among Caribbean nations.

Types of tourism

Figure 15.1 *An advert for Barbados*

Section B(ii) Sustainable Development and Use of Resources

Table 15.1 shows the types of tourism on offer in the Caribbean.

Type of tourism	Definition	Example
Sun, sand and sea tourism	Focuses on relaxation and leisure activities at beaches and resorts.	All-inclusive resorts in the Bahamas, beaches in Barbados, snorkelling and diving in Antigua and Barbuda
Cultural tourism	Immerses travellers in local customs, traditions and heritage.	Carnival celebrations in Trinidad and Tobago, historical sites in Cuba, Traditional Mas and indigenous communities in Dominica
Adventure tourism	Offers exciting and adrenaline-pumping activities in natural settings.	Hiking and mountain biking in St. Lucia, ziplining and rappelling in Jamaica, kitesurfing and windsurfing in Aruba
Ecotourism	Promotes responsible and sustainable travel that minimises environmental impact.	Wildlife viewing in Belize, rainforest exploration in Grenada, sustainable practices at eco-lodges in the Dominican Republic, the rainforest reserves in Dominica

Type of tourism	Definition	Example
Luxury tourism	Caters to high-end travellers seeking exclusive and personalised experiences.	Private villa rentals in the Turks and Caicos, gourmet dining experiences in Anguilla, luxury spas and resorts in St. Barts
Niche tourism	Targets specific interests and hobbies, such as culinary, wellness, or medical tourism.	Culinary tours in Barbados, yoga retreats in Antigua, medical tourism in Cuba
Cruise tourism	Offers a multi-destination holiday experience at sea.	Cruise ships visiting various Caribbean islands, all-inclusive cruise packages, themed cruises
Sports tourism	Travelling to participate in or watch sports events and activities.	Jamaica attracts sports enthusiasts for events like the annual Reggae Marathon and water sports competitions, other Caribbean islands attract visits to their golf courses and sailing events

Table 15.1

Promoting regional cooperation and integration through tourism

Tourism can encourage regional cooperation and integration through initiatives that enhance economic growth, social progress and environmental preservation. In the Caribbean, where tourism boosts the economy and employs millions, there is substantial scope for improving this sector to deepen regional unity. This could include launching joint tourism marketing initiatives to attract a broader audience, harmonising visa policies to facilitate easier travel around the region, and synchronising emergency response strategies for better disaster preparedness and recovery. These efforts can strengthen the bonds between Caribbean nations, promoting a more integrated and resilient region.

Marketing the Caribbean as a single destination

One of the key strategies for promoting **regional integration** through tourism is marketing the Caribbean as a single, cohesive destination. Instead of competing against each other, Caribbean nations can collaborate to showcase the richness of the entire region. **Joint marketing efforts** can include unified promotional campaigns, highlighting the diverse offerings of each country while emphasising the shared **Caribbean identity**.

Additionally, it is important to navigate political and regulatory differences, tackle environmental challenges, and ensure that the benefits of tourism are distributed equally across all Caribbean nations. These steps are essential for sustaining a regional tourism sector that contributes to the broader goal of integration.

Benefits of marketing the Caribbean as a single destination:

- Increased brand recognition: A unified marketing strategy can improve the Caribbean's brand recognition in the global tourism market. By promoting the region as a whole, Caribbean nations can establish a stronger presence in the minds of potential travellers.
- Enhanced destination appeal: By showcasing the different offerings of each country while emphasising the shared Caribbean identity, the region's unique blend of experiences can be highlighted. This can attract a broader range of tourists seeking a variety of cultural, natural and recreational activities.
- Cost-effective marketing: Collaborative marketing can help reduce individual marketing expenses for each Caribbean nation. By sharing resources and expertise, countries can pool their funds to create more impactful and cost-effective campaigns.
- Improved visitor experience: A single destination approach can offer seamless travel experiences for tourists visiting multiple Caribbean countries. This can include streamlining visa processes, coordinating transportation options and promoting regional tourism packages.
- Strengthened regional cooperation: Marketing the Caribbean as a single destination can enhance cooperation among the nations, encouraging wider regional integration in economic development and environmental sustainability. This unified marketing strategy can help preserve the unique Caribbean identity. It doesn't dilute the distinct nature of each island but rather emphasises the region's collective **cultural heritage**, allowing the individual character of each destination to shine through. This approach not only strengthens the Caribbean's brand but also fosters a sense of unity and shared purpose among its nations.

Recognition of tourism products packaged by each Caribbean country

Each Caribbean country has its own distinct **tourism products**, from eco or nature tourism to health and wellness, sports, cultural heritage and vibrant music festivals. Regional integration can recognise and respect these unique offerings, allowing nations to complement each other rather than compete. Cooperation in advertising these products collectively can create a more exciting and varied appeal for the entire region.

Common economic and marketing policies

Shared economic and marketing policies can streamline **cross-border travel**, investment and marketing strategies. By aligning their efforts, Caribbean nations can create a more attractive and competitive tourism market.

Creating links within the Caribbean – communication

Effective communication is crucial for fostering integration. Establishing strong communication links between Caribbean nations facilitates the exchange of information, ideas and best practices. This interconnectedness contributes to a sense of unity and shared purpose, promoting collaboration in **tourism development** and marketing strategies.

Aviation hubs

Aviation hubs play a vital role in integrating the Caribbean. By strategically developing and promoting aviation hubs within the region, travel between countries becomes more accessible and efficient. This not only boosts tourism but also strengthens **economic ties** by facilitating the movement of people, goods and services.

Tourism products available in the Caribbean and their cultural and economic significance

Tourism in the Caribbean isn't just about beautiful beaches; there are many diverse and vibrant tourism experiences, each with its own unique charm and appeal.

From the exhilarating natural beauty of beachfronts or cascading waterfalls to deep-rooted cultural traditions, Caribbean tourism offers many different experiences for visitors.

Beach tourism

Figure 15.10 *Darkwood Beach, Antigua*

Cultural significance: The pristine beaches offer relaxation and leisure, reflecting the relaxing vacation lifestyle of the Caribbean. These coastal areas often serve as gathering spaces for local communities, hosting cultural events and celebrations.

Economic significance: Beach tourism is a major economic driver, attracting international visitors seeking sun-soaked experiences. Resorts, water sports and beachside businesses contribute significantly to the regional economy.

Nature or ecotourism

Cultural significance: **ecotourism** builds a connection between visitors and the Caribbean's lush landscapes. Indigenous communities often play a role, sharing their knowledge of sustainable practices and traditional ecological wisdom. It gives a glimpse of the natural element of the country.

Economic significance: Preservation of natural resources becomes an economic asset, attracting environmentally conscious tourists. Ecotourism contributes to conservation efforts and provides income for local communities.

Figure 15.11 *Scuba diving in St. Lucia*

Health tourism

Cultural significance: Health tourism often incorporates traditional wellness practices, such as holistic therapies and herbal remedies, rooted in the Caribbean's rich cultural history of natural healing.

Economic Significance: The health tourism sector encompasses spa resorts, wellness retreats and medical facilities, generating revenue and creating employment opportunities in the healthcare and hospitality sectors.

Figure 15.12 *Jungle Bay Resort in Dominica offers wellness treatments*

Sports tourism

Figure 15.13 *Kensington Oval Cricket Ground, Barbados*

Cultural significance: The region is known for its passion for sports, such as cricket tournaments, athletics and sailing regattas, showcasing local talent and traditions.

Economic significance: Sporting events attract participants and spectators, stimulating the local economy through increased tourism-related activities, including accommodation, dining and entertainment.

Cultural or heritage tourism

Figure 15.14 *Carnival in Grenada, known as Spicemas*

Cultural significance: Cultural tourism allows visitors to immerse themselves in the vibrant history, art and traditions of the Caribbean. Historic sites, museums and cultural events showcase the diversity of the region's heritage.

Economic significance: Preservation of cultural sites and the promotion of cultural events contribute to job creation and revenue, fostering a sense of pride and identity within local communities.

Festivals

Cultural significance: Caribbean festivals are more than just parties; they are a celebration of resilience and joy. Despite the challenges they've faced throughout their history, the people of the Caribbean have always found a way to come together and find happiness.

At Caribbean festivals the rhythms of reggae, calypso and soca reveal the soul of the islands. These vibrant events are more than festivities; they're a celebration of the Caribbean's history and culture. Born from a history of African, European and Indigenous influences, these festivals are celebrations of life, showcasing the region's rich heritage and diverse traditions.

Special events, including carnivals and parades, showcase the vibrant colours, costumes and traditions unique to each Caribbean nation, providing a dynamic cultural experience.

Figure 15.15 *Reggae Sumfest is a festival in Jamaica*

Economic significance: These festivals draw international crowds, boosting tourism and local economies through ticket sales, accommodation and associated merchandise. Hosting special events attracts tourists, stimulating economic activity through increased demand for accommodation, local products and entertainment.

Job creation: Festivals generate temporary and permanent jobs across various sectors, including hospitality, food and beverage, transportation, tourism, event management and retail. From vendors selling local crafts to security personnel and entertainers, festivals create a significant employment boost.

Increased spending: Visitors attending festivals spend money on accommodation, food, transportation, souvenirs and other goods and services. This influx of revenue stimulates the local economy, benefiting businesses and entrepreneurs.

Infrastructure development: The need to accommodate large crowds often leads to investment in infrastructure, like improved roads, transportation systems and communication networks. This benefits not only the festival but also the local community in the long term.

Common economic and marketing policies in promoting a unified approach to Caribbean tourism

The Caribbean has the potential to adopt a unified approach to Caribbean tourism. If all the nations adopted common pricing, currency and joint advertising, this could enhance the area's appeal, attract more visitors, and building a resilient, competitive tourism sector. We will now look at the advantages, challenges and strategic moves necessary to transform this vision into reality, ensuring the Caribbean remains a popular destination for generations to come.

Fragmentation and its challenges

Historically, Caribbean nations have taken individual approaches to tourism development, often leading to fragmented marketing strategies and policies. While this independence reflects the diversity and autonomy of each nation, it has given rise to a fragmented landscape in terms of marketing strategies and policies. This fragmentation, although rooted in the desire for individual identity and sovereignty, presents several challenges and implications for the overall success and competitiveness of the Caribbean tourism industry.

Fragmentation can result in inefficient resource allocation, competition rather than collaboration, and missed opportunities to address shared challenges.

Shared vulnerabilities

The Caribbean is susceptible to shared challenges. Among these challenges are the threats of natural disasters, economic fluctuations and global health crises. Geographically situated in the hurricane belt, the Caribbean has a heightened risk of tropical storms and hurricanes, causing widespread destruction to infrastructure and disrupting tourism activities. The region's economic stability is often influenced by external factors, such as fluctuations in global markets and trade conditions. Economic vulnerability is particularly concerning for nations that are heavily dependent on tourism as a primary revenue source.

The Caribbean is not immune to global health crises, as highlighted by events such as the Zika virus outbreak and the COVID-19 pandemic. These shared vulnerabilities emphasise the need for a collaborative and unified approach to address these challenges. By recognising the collective impact of natural disasters, economic uncertainties and health crises, the Caribbean can strengthen its resilience and responsiveness, creating a more robust and sustainable tourism industry for the entire region.

Nations operating independently may struggle to address these challenges effectively, while a unified approach can facilitate coordinated responses and resilience strategies.

Benefits of having common economic policies

Strategic investment and infrastructure

If Caribbean nations join forces to make strategic investment in infrastructure, it can make a big impact on tourism.

- Airports: Smooth, quick check-ins and baggage collection, reducing delays for tourists.
- Roads and transit: Smooth, well-maintained roads and regular, punctual public transport.
- Accommodation and attractions: Luxury resorts and exciting attractions for tourists.
- Employment: More tourists mean more employment opportunities in bars and restaurants, adventure parks and boutique hotels.
- Eco-smart: Sustainable building means looking after our planet, keeping the beaches and waters pristine

Strategic investment and infrastructure in the Caribbean region involves collaborative efforts among nations to enhance tourism infrastructure, including modernising airports, improving transportation networks and expanding hospitality services. These initiatives aim to facilitate easier travel, enrich the visitor experience and improve the region's appeal as a unified tourism destination. Upgraded infrastructure not only supports economic growth and job creation but also encourages sustainable development to preserve the environmental and cultural assets of the Caribbean. By adopting common economic policies and investing in regional transportation, the Caribbean can address fragmented travel systems, strengthening its competitiveness and sustainability as a prime tourist destination.

Caribbean unity on safety and planning

Caribbean unity on safety and planning represents a forward-thinking strategy for the Caribbean to navigate the unpredictable challenges posed by natural disasters and other crises. By pooling resources collectively, Caribbean nations can establish robust financial mechanisms designed to mitigate the economic fallout of unforeseen events. The importance of this approach is underscored by the region's vulnerability to natural disasters, including hurricanes, earthquakes and other climate-related incidents.

In the aftermath of such events, the impact on the tourism industry can be severe. Common economic policies that prioritise risk mitigation and insurance provide a safety net for affected destinations. Pooled resources enable a more rapid response, allowing for the immediate allocation of funds to support recovery efforts. This collaborative approach ensures that the Caribbean can recover from crises quickly, minimising disruptions to the tourism sector and accelerating the restoration of vital infrastructure.

The impact of risk mitigation and insurance extends beyond financial considerations. By sharing the burden of recovery costs, individual nations within the Caribbean can avoid the overwhelming financial strain that may arise from dealing with such crises independently. This collaborative risk management strategy enhances the overall resilience of the region, fostering a sense of unity and shared responsibility.

The establishment of a collective insurance framework creates a sense of confidence among international stakeholders, including tourists and investors. Knowing that the Caribbean has implemented proactive measures to address and recover from crises can enhance the region's reputation as a secure and reliable destination. This, in turn, contributes to the long-term sustainability of the tourism industry, as it reassures both visitors and those considering investments in the region.

Benefits of common marketing policies

Brand unity and positioning

Brand unity and positioning are important to the collective marketing approach for the Caribbean, helping to create a more cohesive and compelling regional identity. The importance of a unified marketing strategy is the ability to craft and communicate a single, powerful brand that demonstrates the different offerings of each individual nation within the Caribbean. Instead of presenting a fragmented image to the global audience, a collective approach can demonstrate the values and aspirations of the entire region.

A cohesive brand identity enhances the global recognition of the Caribbean as a distinctive destination with lots to offer. By aligning messaging, imagery and promotional efforts, the region becomes more than the sum of its parts, creating a holistic and memorable experience for potential tourists. This unified approach allows the Caribbean to compete more effectively in the international tourism market, where consistent and recognisable branding is paramount.

Targeted marketing campaigns

Targeted marketing campaigns can highlight what is special about each Caribbean country. Instead of general advertisements, these campaigns focus on the unique features and attractions of each place. This way, they tell a more interesting story about what visitors can experience in the Caribbean, making it more appealing for tourists.

Collaborative marketing policies should identify and promote the specific attractions, cultural heritage and activities that set each Caribbean nation apart. Rather than presenting a one-size-fits-all approach, targeted campaigns customise messages to advertise characteristics of each destination. This approach resonates more deeply with specific target audiences and ensures that the marketing efforts are relevant and appealing to a wide range of potential tourists.

Figure 15.16 *A Caribbean tourism advert*

Resource efficiency

Resource efficiency means using limited resources for maximum impact ensuring that every dollar invested contributes meaningfully to the promotion of the region as a whole.

Shared marketing strategies allow Caribbean nations to avoid duplication of efforts. For instance, rather than each nation independently targeting the same type of tourist or market, collaboration enables a coordinated effort and reduces the likelihood of competing against one another in the tourism marketplace.

Resource efficiency can also reduce the cost of marketing efforts. By sharing resources, nations can negotiate better rates for advertising space, digital marketing services and other promotional activities. This ensures that each nation benefits from economies of scale, allowing for more extensive campaigns than individual countries could afford.

With a collective approach to marketing, Caribbean nations can pool their resources strategically, targeting emerging markets, adapting to shifting consumer trends and responding promptly to industry changes. This enables the region to stay ahead in the tourism landscape, ensuring that promotional efforts remain relevant and effective.

Challenges and considerations

Figure 15.17 *Visa application*

Despite the potential for tourism integration in the Caribbean, several challenges limit the development of a unified regional tourism strategy. These factors include:

- Lack of harmonised tourism policies and regulations

The lack of harmonised tourism policies and regulations across Caribbean countries creates issues for both tourists and tourism businesses. Varying visa requirements, customs procedures and tourism taxes can put off potential travellers and make it more difficult for tourism operators to expand across the region.

- Inadequate transportation infrastructure and connectivity

Limited transportation infrastructure and lack of connectivity between Caribbean islands pose significant challenges for regional tourism integration. Inefficient and expensive air and sea transportation networks make it difficult for tourists to seamlessly travel between destinations, getting in the way of multi-island itineraries and limiting the scope of regional tourism packages.

- Limited inter-regional collaboration and marketing efforts

Caribbean countries often promote their individual offerings without a coordinated regional strategy. This misses opportunities for joint marketing campaigns, cross-destination promotions and collective branding of the Caribbean as a unified tourism destination.

– Language and cultural barriers

While English is the predominant language in the Caribbean, there are also variations in local dialects and cultural parlance. These differences can sometimes pose communication barriers for tourists and hinder their ability to fully immerse themselves in the region's diverse cultural experiences.

– Economic disparities and development gaps

Economic disparities and development gaps among Caribbean countries can create imbalances in tourism benefits. Some islands may attract a larger share of tourists and generate higher revenue, while others may struggle to develop their infrastructure and attract visitors, leading to uneven distribution of tourism benefits.

– Environmental concerns and sustainability issues

The Caribbean's natural beauty and fragile ecosystems are crucial assets for tourism, but also require careful management to ensure sustainable practices. Over-tourism, environmental degradation and climate change pose significant challenges that demand regional cooperation and action to protect the environment and preserve the region's long-term tourism potential.

– Security and safety concerns

Perceptions of security and safety can influence tourists' decisions, and crime rates can vary across Caribbean islands. While the region has made strides in improving safety, addressing these concerns requires regional cooperation in law enforcement, border security and tourism safety initiatives.

– Limited cross-border investment and collaboration

Encouraging cross-border investment and collaboration in tourism infrastructure, such as transportation hubs, joint marketing campaigns and tourism product development, can strengthen regional tourism integration. However, factors like differing investment regulations and business environments can pose challenges.

Table 15.2 shows the challenges and solutions of harmonisation.

Challenges	Solutions
Lack of harmonised tourism policies and regulations	Establish a regional tourism body to facilitate harmonisation of tourism policies, visa requirements, customs procedures and tourism taxes.
Inadequate transportation infrastructure and connectivity	Invest in regional transportation networks, including upgrading airports, improving seaports and encouraging inter-island ferry services.
Limited inter-regional collaboration and marketing efforts	Develop joint marketing campaigns that promote the Caribbean as a unified tourism destination, highlighting regional themes, diverse cultures and multi-island itineraries.
Language and cultural barriers	Provide cultural sensitivity training for tourism professionals and promote language learning opportunities to enhance communication and understanding with tourists.
Economic disparities and development gaps	Implement regional development programmes that focus on infrastructure development, skills training and tourism promotion in less developed Caribbean countries.
Environmental concerns and sustainability issues	Establish regional environmental standards for tourism development, promoting responsible tourism practices and supporting conservation initiatives.

Challenges	Solutions
Security and safety concerns	Strengthen regional law enforcement cooperation, enhancing border security measures and promoting tourism safety initiatives to address security concerns.
Limited cross-border investment and collaboration	Promote regional investment incentives, harmonising investment regulations and creating opportunities for joint tourism ventures and partnerships.

Table 15.2

Case study

Crafting solutions for Caribbean tourism unity

Scenario:

The Caribbean region wants to transform from single destinations into a unified, world-class travel destination. Despite their individual appeal, the countries struggle with inconsistent policies, disjointed marketing and varying levels of development and infrastructure.

Task:

As a student, you are tasked with developing strategic solutions to foster unity and collaboration among the Caribbean islands, enhancing their collective tourism appeal. Your solutions should address the following challenges:

1. Harmonising tourism policies:
    - Problem: Each country operates under its own set of tourism rules and regulations, causing confusion for travellers.
    - Task: Propose a strategy to harmonise these policies and improve travel across the region.

2. Improving transportation infrastructure:
    - Problem: Inadequate and inefficient transportation options limit inter-island travel.
    - Task: Devise a plan to improve transportation infrastructure and connectivity between the islands.

3. Coordinating marketing efforts:
    - Problem: Limited collaboration on marketing campaigns prevents the region from showcasing its full potential.
    - Task: Create a joint marketing initiative that promotes the Caribbean as a cohesive and diverse destination.

4. Overcoming language and cultural barriers:
    - Problem: Language differences and cultural misunderstandings can detract from the visitor experience.
    - Task: Suggest ways to bridge these gaps, enhancing communication and cultural appreciation among tourists and locals.

5. Balancing economic development:
    - Problem: Economic disparities exist between more and less developed islands, affecting the region's overall growth.
    - Task: Propose a development programme that supports equitable growth across all Caribbean islands.

6. Ensuring environmental sustainability:
   - Problem: The need to balance tourism development with environmental preservation is critical.
   - Task: Outline an approach for sustainable tourism practices that protect the Caribbean's natural resources.

7. Enhancing security and safety:
   - Problem: Varying levels of security and safety across the islands can impact the region's appeal.
   - Task: Recommend measures to strengthen regional security and ensure tourist safety.

8. Facilitating cross-border investment:
   - Problem: Complex regulations and lack of collaboration hinder investment opportunities.
   - Task: Develop a framework to encourage and streamline cross-border investment in the tourism sector.

Assessment criteria:

Your solutions should be innovative, feasible and sustainable, considering the unique characteristics and needs of the Caribbean region. Each proposal should include a clear action plan, potential challenges, and expected outcomes to demonstrate how your strategy will effectively address the identified issues and contribute to the Caribbean's tourism unity and success.

Questions

Multiple choice

1. What is the definition of 'regional integration' in the context of Caribbean tourism?
   a) The process of integrating resort services across the Caribbean.
   b) The collaboration among Caribbean countries to strengthen economic, political and cultural ties.
   c) The development of tourism policies by individual Caribbean nations.
   d) The marketing of Caribbean tourism to international markets only.

2. Which of the following best describes the role of joint marketing efforts in promoting Caribbean regional integration?
   a) Reducing the overall cost of marketing for individual Caribbean countries.
   b) Increasing competition among Caribbean countries.
   c) Highlighting the distinct cultural aspects of each Caribbean nation.
   d) Creating a unified tourism identity to attract a broader audience.

3. In the context of enhancing regional integration, what could be a major impact of establishing common economic policies among Caribbean nations?
   a) Increased regulatory complexities for local businesses.
   b) Harmonised standards and procedures to facilitate easier travel and trade.
   c) Isolation of economically weaker Caribbean nations.
   d) Reduction in tourism due to standardised pricing.

End of chapter questions

1. a) Define 'fragmentation' in the context of Caribbean tourism. (2 marks)
    b) Recall historical reasons for individualistic approaches to tourism development in the Caribbean. (2 marks)
    c) Identify THREE challenges arising from fragmented marketing strategies and policies in the Caribbean. (6 marks)
2. a) Define 'shared vulnerabilities' in the context of Caribbean tourism. (2 marks)
    b) Explain the implications of shared vulnerabilities on the tourism industry in the Caribbean. (4 marks)
3. a) Define the concept of 'strategic investment' in the context of Caribbean tourism. (2 marks)
    b) Identify components of shared infrastructure that can be strategically invested in, such as airports and transportation networks. (4 marks)
    c) Explain how improved infrastructure enhances the visitor experience in the Caribbean. (4 marks)
4. a) Propose solutions to address fragmentation in Caribbean tourism. (4 marks).
    b) Evaluate the benefits of a more integrated and collaborative approach to tourism development. (6 marks)
    c) Formulate TWO strategies for overcoming challenges posed by fragmented marketing in the Caribbean. (4 marks)
5. Propose initiatives for strategic investment in regional transportation, including airlines. (2 marks)
6. Define 'regional integration' in the Caribbean context. (4 marks)
    Explain the concept of regional integration specifically in the context of the Caribbean. Discuss how it relates to the economic, political, and social collaboration among Caribbean nations.
7. Characterise the role of CARICOM in promoting regional integration. (6 marks)
    Describe the role of the Caribbean Community (CARICOM) in advancing regional integration. Highlight its key functions and initiatives that have contributed to the integration process among member states.
8. Evaluate the impact of regional integration on Caribbean tourism. (15 marks)
    Discuss the impact of regional integration on the tourism sector in the Caribbean. Evaluate how policies and collaborative efforts have shaped the tourism landscape, addressing aspects like market access, service standards and regional branding.
9. Explore the significance of common economic policies in the Caribbean. (15 marks)
    Analyse the importance of establishing common economic policies among Caribbean nations. Examine how these policies affect trade, investment and economic growth in the region. Consider both the benefits and challenges associated with such integration efforts.

SBA skills

Title: 'Exploring the link between tourism and regional integration in the Caribbean'

Research question: How does tourism contribute to regional integration among Caribbean countries, and what are the key factors that enhance or impede this process?

Objectives:

To identify the various ways in which tourism acts as a driver for regional cooperation and integration in the Caribbean.

To analyse the role of joint marketing efforts, aviation hubs and economic ties in promoting regional integration through tourism.

To evaluate the impact of communication links and tourism development initiatives on fostering collaboration among Caribbean nations.

To assess the challenges and benefits of marketing the Caribbean as a single destination in terms of regional integration and tourism development.

Methodology:

Conduct a literature review on the role of tourism in Caribbean regional integration, focusing on joint marketing efforts, aviation hubs, economic ties and communication linkages.

Analyse case studies of successful regional integration efforts in the Caribbean tourism sector.

Conduct interviews or surveys with tourism industry stakeholders in various Caribbean countries to gather insights on the effectiveness of current regional integration initiatives.

Evaluate the impact of tourism on regional integration by analysing tourism data, economic reports and policy documents from Caribbean regional organisations like CARICOM and the OECS.

Expected outcomes:

A comprehensive understanding of how tourism acts as a catalyst for regional integration in the Caribbean.

Insights into the effectiveness of current regional integration mechanisms and their impact on the tourism sector.

Identification of the main challenges and opportunities for enhancing regional integration through tourism in the Caribbean.

Summary

Tourism has always played a major role in the region's development. There is a direct relationship between the tourism sector and regional integration as can be seen with the common economic growth policies, the social understanding and the shared environmental awareness.

There are obvious ways to balance regional integration with tourism. Marketing the Caribbean as a single destination helps to maximise collaboration by celebrating the tourism products while at the same time having shared economic and marketing policies.

In the long run, presenting a united front is much better than an individualistic approach as evidenced with fragmentation. Investments and improved infrastructure, together with shared safety protocols and higher levels of sustainability should be more targeted.

Challenges are real situations especially in the Caribbean and take the form of inadequate transportation, limited collaboration and even economic disparities. A conscious effort should be placed to generate awareness, create various programmes and maintain certain standards.

16 The School-Based Assessment

What is the SBA?

The School-Based Assessment (SBA) is an applied teacher-guided/supervised form of non-exam/internal assessment that all CSEC Social Studies students are required to complete. The process is geared towards targeting key areas of deliberate social enquiry, communication of ideas, critical thinking and problem-solving skills among students. The content of the syllabus, paired with the practical nature of the conduct of research, should enhance your performance and assist in your critical skills development.

The SBA is conducted alongside the syllabus coverage to ensure that the syllabus objectives are met and accounts for 20% of a student's final examination mark. This means you can score high marks as the SBA serves as a continuous assessment. The SBA also functions to provide you with various opportunities to demonstrate your proficiency in the subject.

Students are asked to produce an authentic report, individually or in groups, not exceeding 1000 words using the component guidelines given. Group SBAs are also encouraged, where a single SBA is presented by a group of students and the group members are awarded one common mark.

In the CSEC Social Studies SBA you will be unearthing a problem or issue, which can come from any topic of the syllabus.

Managing the project

Planning is key in ensuring that the project is completed within the stipulated time. While it is possible to complete certain sections during normal teaching time, some SBA responsibilities such as data collection, analysis and recommendations will need to be undertaken outside of class time.

Your teacher has an important role to perform in the management of this project. They have to:

- Offer guidance on the range of topics that can be selected and direct you to a researchable issue which may hold personal interest.
- Provide guidance and suitable assistance throughout the SBA experience which is aligned to the specific guidelines and marking scheme outlined in the syllabus.
- Oversee and monitor your progress by explaining the necessary steps to follow together with deadline dates for the completion and review of each task.
- Provide timely and constructive feedback to you at every stage of your work to ensure improvements can be made. This will ensure that the final SBA product is your best work.
- Ensure that the project is your own work and does not contain any instances of plagiarism (work copied from somebody else).
- Assess the project/report based on the CXC Social Studies mark scheme and submit your mark to CXC, together with your project, if requested.

Choosing a topic

Selecting an issue or problem to research is one of the most important tasks as it provides the basis for the entire project report. The topic can be based on social and economic processes, situations or problems in the school or immediate community, all of which are covered throughout the syllabus.

In choosing a topic you should consider:

- The relevance of the CSEC Social Studies syllabus so that you can apply the content and problem-solving skills to studying the issue and its socio-economic impacts on your school or community.
- The value that the outcome of the research would have on your community, family, school or even the wider society.

- The practicality of the research. Do I have enough time to conduct the research? Do I need additional resources to conduct the research? Do I have access to the resources I may need throughout the process?

In order to focus on a given idea for a project, you could reflect on the following questions:

1. Can I apply the subject knowledge gained from Social Studies to investigate the problem or issue?
2. Will I learn something that could have a meaningful impact on myself, my school or my community?
3. Will it be possible for me to collect the data I need?

Here are some examples of topics with notes on whether they meet the guidelines for the Social Studies SBA.

EXAMPLE 1

What effects does unemployment have on familial relationships in the Pomegranate community?

1. Can I use the knowledge content from Social Studies to investigate this?
   Yes: I can apply the knowledge on the concept of unemployment among the labour force in relation to the provision of family needs.
2. Will I learn something from this SBA that I can use to improve how I act or direct the action of others?
   Yes: I will be able to observe any relationship between unemployed people and familial issues to possibly raise awareness/reduce such occurrence in the community.
3. Will it be possible for me to get the data I need for this?
   Yes: I will be able to gather data from households in the community to look for any relationship between the two variables.

Generally, this topic will be classified as a good topic for the SBA project as it meets the outlined guidelines.

EXAMPLE 2

What impact does flooding have on the social and emotional wellbeing of Peppertop villagers?

1. Can I use the knowledge content from Social Studies to investigate this?
   Yes: I can apply the knowledge from natural resources to make links about the effects of flooding on the human resource.
2. Will I learn something that could have a meaningful impact on myself, my school or my community?
   Yes: Flooding is a national, regional and international issue that affects all, not only those living in flood prone areas.
3. Will it be possible for me to collect the data I need?
   Yes: I am able to target/source individuals from Peppertop who have been significantly and continuously affected by this social issue.

Generally, this topic will be classified as a good topic for the SBA project as it meets the outlined guidelines.

EXAMPLE 3

To investigate the purchase of sugary foods among the student population at RiverRoad Academy.

1. Can I use the knowledge content from Social Studies to investigate this?
   Yes: I can apply the knowledge about health and education in the human resource component of the syllabus.

2. Will I learn something that could have a meaningful impact on myself, my school or my community?
   No: I will only collect data on the type of sugary foods bought by students. The cafeteria staff would be guided by the data collected for repurchase purposes but the school community generally will not benefit.

3. Will it be possible for me to collect the data I need?
   Yes: I will be able to collect the data from the participating students.

This topic will be viewed as limited as it lacks depth concerning the effects of the sugary foods on students' concentration levels at school. The topic will also not direct the school to possible solutions.

EXAMPLE 4

What impact did the portrayal of 'Barbie' in the 2023 movie have on gender roles among the female population at Richworth High School?

1. Can I use the knowledge content from Social Studies to investigate this?
   Yes: I can apply the knowledge about family and the changing roles of members in the household.

2. Will I learn something that could have a meaningful impact on myself, my school or my community?
   Yes: In society, there is a tendency to view women as the weaker sex and this movie raised important questions about women's role in the home and in the wider society.

3. Will it be possible for me to collect the data I need?
   Yes: I will be able to collect the data from the participating students.

This will be viewed as a good topic as all the guidelines were met.

Planning and executing your SBA

After selecting the problem or issue which will serve as your research project, you will need to plan your route through the fixed tasks. Your teacher should be made aware of each step in your planning stage so that achievable deadlines can be set. The steps below should help you in the execution of your report.

Write out your statement of problem and reason for selecting the area of research

You must write a statement of problem which can use a statement or question format. It should include no more than two variables which identify the issue or problem selected. You are also asked to specify the target population.

Once your statement of problem is confirmed by your teacher, you can shape your reason for undertaking this study. This section can include definition of key terms, recent and relevant statistics as well as the core justification for the topic at hand. You are encouraged to express yourself in third person and avoid using 'I' and 'my' when justifying the topic selected.

Identify your methodology and sample selection

You are required to explain how the data would be collected and the particular research tool which is appropriate for use in the study of the topic. You are able to select from a number of research tools such as questionnaires, interviews, observation checklists or even documentary searches. These should be carefully identified and described.

The sample should then be chosen, which consists of the individuals who will be participating in your study/investigation. A brief description of the sampling method should be included together with the sample size. The participants can originate from the school or the residential community, depending on the statement of problem.

Present your data collection instrument with informed consent

This task covers the actual data collection tool that you will be using to gather the data from the sample. If you have opted to use a questionnaire or interview schedule, you need to ensure the items (questions) are well sequenced, clear and relevant to your variables in the statement of problem.

Questionnaires can include an assortment of questions such as close-ended, open-ended and with the use of a Likert scale. The table below gives some useful ideas.

Table 1 gives an overview of the variations in questions.

Close-ended questions	Open-ended questions	Likert scale questions					
		Statements	Strongly disagree	Disagree	Neutral	Agree	Strongly agree
1. What is your age? O 14–15 O 16–17 O 18–19	1. What were some of the problems encountered during online/ remote teaching during 2020? _____ _____ _____ _____	I feel like I belong to the school community					
		I like the school community					
2. What is your highest level of education? O Primary O Secondary O Bachelor degree O Postgraduate O PhD	2. What did the government do after the last flood in your area? _____ _____ _____ _____						

When administering a questionnaire or conducting an interview, it is best practice to obtain consent from the participant/respondent. This can be done via a cover letter where the participant should be made aware of:

- the name of the researcher and the organisation they represent or are attached to
- the intention of the research
- what the results will be used for
- the preservation of personal data such as name, age, date of birth, etc. through anonymity and confidentiality clauses
- the instructions on answering the questionnaire.

Other data collection methods

If your study lends itself to an observation technique, you can employ a checklist format in the form of a table to gather your data. Your predetermined areas would be located in the left column of the table while the right columns would contain the options for checking. You can also include a column for additional comments.

Collect your data

Once you have completed the previous sections and secured permission from your teacher, you can then proceed to administer your questionnaire/interview. This can be conducted either face to face or via an online method. Email addresses from the respondents would need to be requested if using an online method. There should be a confirmed deadline date for participants to submit completed questionnaires. Any other data collection methods such as observations would be conducted and results recorded.

Present your data

At the end of the data gathering period, you must collect the completed forms from your sample. If you used observation checklists, you would now have to sort through all the data. This process culminates in the construction of THREE different and appropriate ways of presenting the data. The selected diagrams should be labelled correctly, given suitable titles and presented accurately. You are able to use software to assist you with the diagrams which can take the form of bar charts, pie charts, tables and histograms.

Writing your project report

At this point you would have covered the practical components of the investigation. The next step is to work on the general layout of the report and ensure that all tasks are included in formal sections such as a cover page, a table of contents, a bibliography and appendices. All pages should be numbered which should correspond to the table of contents.

Marks are awarded for both writing skills (4 marks) and overall presentation (4 marks). It is important that you maintain a word count of 1000 words, excluding charts, graphs, tables, pictures, the bibliography and appendices, as exceeding this by 150 words can lead to a penalty of a 10% deduction from your final score. Further guidance about the word count is given below.

This section addresses each task and should guide your report. You should adopt these major formatting elements throughout the body of the report.

- Times New Roman using 12-point font
- Double space line spacing
- Uniform one-inch margin

Cover page

This page can be personalised to include an appropriate picture of the topic under study as well as a page border. You must include:

- Name of candidate
- Candidate number
- Name of school
- Centre number
- Name of teacher
- Title/topic of study
- Subject
- Territory
- Date/year of submission

Table of contents

The table of contents should be correctly formatted with the headings and the corresponding page number. A table can be used with appropriate formatting.

Acknowledgements (not compulsory)

This section conveys gratitude to the persons who were instrumental in the completion of the project report.

Statement of problem (2 marks)

This is the issue or problem which you selected to investigate written in the form of a question or statement. This question or statement should include the specific target population being used.

Reason for selecting the area of research (2 marks)

You are asked to reflect on the issue or problem to account for its selection. You can give a reasonable justification which can be based on personal preference or a social concern. You can include key terms as well as relevant, reliable and recent statistics about the social phenomenon. Secondary sources can be used for emphasis which will be a useful reflection in the analysis stage. You are encouraged to write in the past tense.

Method of investigation (4 marks)

This gives an overview of how you plan to conduct the study, including the procedures and the appropriate data collection instrument. Please ensure that you identify and describe the data collection instrument giving a reason for its use. You also need to identify and describe the sample selected giving adequate details about the sample size.

Data collection instrument (4 marks)

You are to place a copy of your data collection instrument together with a cover letter which indicates the respondents' consent. The data collection instrument should comprise of a series of items addressing the variables you are studying. The items should be clear, progressively organised and constructed with the intended variables in mind.

Presentation of data (6 marks)

This section requires that you present your captured data using appropriate and clear illustrations, tables and charts. The data must be accurately represented in THREE different ways, such as tables, bar graphs, histograms and pie charts. Three of the same diagrams are not permitted. All illustrations should have an appropriate title, a neat border around the diagram and a brief description under the diagram.

Tables

Tables should be clear, highlighting the variables under investigation. Data should be represented in percentages. Colour can be used for emphasis.

Pie charts

A range of colours can be used to display the different segments for visibility purposes. Avoid using varying shades of one colour as it might be difficult to observe the differences. The accompanying percentages should be included in each segment and a key should be present.

Bar graphs

Ensure that both axes are labelled correctly and where appropriate, a scale is given. Use of colour is highly recommended with accompanying percentages.

Analysis and interpretation of data (8 marks)

You must give an overview of the data collected with the use of percentages through calculations and statistics. You should explain what the data means in a comprehensive manner while addressing the statement of problem. You can also identify trends and refer to the presentation of data and the secondary sources for added emphasis. Some suggestions for starter sentences include:

- It was determined that ...
- Figure 2 illustrated ...
- 20% indicated that ...
- Table 1 showcased ...

Statement of findings (3 marks)

You must make THREE definitive statements about your discovery from the investigation of the problem. You can include percentages here. You should use the statement of problem as a guide, together with the presentation of data.

Recommendations and implementation strategy (3 marks)

You are to make TWO recommendations based on your findings which can serve as plausible solutions. These realistic proposals should match your research. You should also outline how any ONE recommendation could be applied/implemented within the confines of the selected community.

Bibliography

This section contains a list of all the sources of information that you referred to when conducting the research. You should keep track of all the sources that you used throughout the research period to include at the end when you are writing up the report. The list should be in alphabetical order following the American Psychological Association (7th edition) format.

– **Citing a book**

Author's last name, initial(s). (Publication date). *Title of source*. Publisher.

– **Citing a website**

Author's last name, initial(s). (Year and month published). *Title of web page*. Name of website. URL

Appendices

Your appendices should be used to include any items related to your research that are too big to be placed in the report itself. Items which could aid in the understanding of the issue or problem such as images and journal entries could also be included here.

SBA mark scheme

The following table summarises the mark scheme that your teacher will use to mark your SBA report. The total number of marks for each of the criteria is given in brackets, with the accompanying breakdown. A suggested word count is also given.

Specific guidelines

Tasks/sections/SBA component	Breakdown description	Marks	Proposed word count
1. Statement of problem (2 marks)	– Problem expressed clearly in the form of a question or statement with the issue and target population clearly specified	2	25
	– Problem statement unclear (issue or target population not specified)	1	
2. Reason for selecting the area of research (2 marks)	– Reason clearly stated, is appropriate and relevant	2	50–75
	– Reason unclear or not very relevant	1	
3. Method of investigation (4 marks)	– Method identified and justified, sampling procedures identified and described; award marks as follows:	(4)	75–100
	– Method identified	1	
	– Method justified	1	
	– Sampling procedures identified	1	
	– Sampling procedures described	1	

Tasks/sections/SBA component	Breakdown description	Marks	Proposed word count
4. Data collection instrument (4 marks)	– Data collection instrument consists of clearly stated, well sequenced items which address all relevant variables	4	150
	– Data collection instrument consists of clearly stated, well sequenced items but does not address all relevant variables	3	
	– Data collection instrument satisfactorily constructed and sequenced	2	
	– Data collection instrument poorly constructed	1	
5. Presentation of data (6 marks)	– Data presented in three different ways which are appropriate	2	
	– Data presented in two ways which are appropriate	1	
	– Three charts/graphs/tables that are appropriately labelled and titled	2	
	– Two charts/graphs/tables that are appropriately labelled and titled	1	
	– Three charts/graphs/tables that are accurately presented	2	
	– Two charts/graphs/tables that are accurately presented	1	
6. Analysis and interpretation of data (8 marks)	– Analysis and interpretation relevant and well developed	7–8	400
	– Analysis and interpretation relevant and adequately developed	5–6	
	– Analysis and interpretation moderately relevant and moderately developed	3–4	
	– Analysis and interpretation show limited relevance and development	1–2	
7. Statement of findings (3 marks)	– Three statements of findings based on data presented	3	100
	– Two statements of findings based on data presented	2	
	– One statement of findings based on data presented	1	
8. Recommendations and implementation strategy (3 marks)	– Two recommendations and one associated implementation strategy	3	150
	– Two recommendations and no implementation strategy	2	
	– One recommendation and one implementation strategy	2	
	– One recommendation only OR one implementation strategy	1	

Tasks/sections/SBA component	Breakdown description	Marks	Proposed word count
Writing skills (4 marks)	– Excellent organisation (paragraphing), use of language, spelling and grammar	4	
	– Good organisation, use of language, spelling and grammar	3	
	– Satisfactory use of language and grammar and several spelling errors	2	
	– Poor use of language, poor grammar and many spelling errors	1	
Overall presentation (4 marks)	– Appropriate layout with four elements such as acknowledgements, table of contents, bibliography, cover page, appendices	4	
	– Appropriate layout for the most part with three of the elements	3	
	– A moderate presentation with only two of the elements	2	
	– An unsatisfactory presentation with only one of the elements	1	
TOTAL		40	

Examples of possible SBA topics

The following are some examples of the statement of problem that you could use or modify for your SBA research project.

- To what extent has remote teaching been supported by parents in the Village community?
- What are the effects of sleep deprivation on the emotional wellbeing of Form Four students at Summertime High School?
- What is the impact of the use of social media on communication habits among Grade Seven students at Orangeville Academy?
- What impact does the use of social media have on beauty standards among Form Five students at Hatfelt Convent?
- What are the factors influencing the level of religiosity among the Springtime youth community?
- What are the emotional/financial effects of criminal activity on Popeye Hill residents?
- To what extent does the use of social media influence cyberbullying among the students of Flower Academy?
- What impact do different family forms have on the academic performance of Mangrove High School students?
- What impact did the pandemic have on the members of the Eagle Warriors Football club?
- What role do peer dynamics among the Grade Eight year group at Academy High have on their sense of self?

Sample Social Studies SBA

Name of candidate: Clarissa Bhayers

Candidate number: 1212121212

School: Station Academy, Port Fernando

School code: 121212

Territory: Sapphire

Topic: The Use of Social Media and its Effects on Face-to-Face Communication

Subject: Social Studies

Subject teacher: Mrs Smith

Year of the exam: 2025

Date of submission: 12th April, 2025

Table of Contents

Title	Page
Acknowledgements	1
Statement of Problem	2
Reason for Selecting Area of Research	3
Method of Investigation	4
Data Collection Instrument	5
Presentation of Data	10
Analysis and Interpretation of Data	14
Recommendations and Implementation Strategy	15
Bibliography	16
Appendices	17

Acknowledgements

I would like to thank the Fifth form students of Summertime High School for their generous support and time spent responding to the questionnaires. I also want to thank God and members of my family who have been my constant source of motivation. I extend a special thanks to my teacher for her time, patience and guidance during the entire experience. The completion of this report would not have been possible without your kind assistance and cooperation.

Statement of Problem

What impact does the use of social media have on the face-to-face communication among the Fifth form female students at Summertime High School?

Reason for Selecting the Area of Research

The topic was chosen because of a special interest in the growing number of online platforms worldwide. Due to the proliferation of these platforms, online communication among social groups has become easier. This form of connection may be dangerous and unsuitable for some but acceptable and helpful to the social development of others. Therefore, the desire to investigate these highly networked social groups among the student population was of great interest.

Method of Investigation

Quantitative research was desired as numerical data can be collected and analysed easily. It can be used to find patterns, averages and produce suitable representations. A questionnaire, which is a pre-set list of questions, was designed by the researcher for the purpose of data collection. It proved to be efficient in capturing and analysing the data. Form Five students were selected using a systematic random sampling method where every 5th student from each class was chosen. As such, the sample comprised of 20 respondents. The questionnaires were distributed on Monday 10th December and students were requested to return them by Friday 14th December.

Cover Letter

Social Studies Research SBA Questionnaire on

'What impact does the use of social media have on the face-to-face communication among the Fifth form female students at Summertime High School?'

#15 Café Pinto,

Picachun

Dear Participant,

     This survey is being carried out among the fifth form students of Summertime High School to determine the impact of the use of social media on face-to-face communication. This study is being conducted for my Social Studies SBA which is currently ongoing. The questionnaire consists of a total of 11 questions. You are required to answer by checking a box, selecting an option based on level of agreement and answering in your own words.

     This is for research purposes only and results will be used to inform school officials. There are no wrong or right answers and you are kindly asked to complete the questionnaire truthfully. A reminder that your name is not required during this time therefore your response will be completely anonymous and responses will be kept confidential. Thank you very much for your cooperation and participation.

Yours Respectfully,

_____

Clarissa Bhayers

Data Collection Instrument

1. Do you use any social media platforms?
   - ☐ Yes
   - ☐ No

2. How many hours do you spend on social media daily?
   - [ ] 1–4
   - [ ] 4–8
   - [ ] 8–12

   Other: _____

3. Do you use social media to communicate with friends and/or family?
   - [ ] Yes
   - [ ] No

4. Do you prefer to use social media to communicate with friends and/or family?
   - [ ] Yes
   - [ ] No

5. Is it easier for you to communicate a message via social media or face-to-face communication?
   - [ ] Social media
   - [ ] Face-to-face

6. a) Does the use of social media to communicate affect the receipt of your messages?
   - [ ] Yes
   - [ ] No

   b) Please state the reason for your answer in part 6. a) above.

   _____
   _____

Please answer questions 7 and 8 by ticking your appropriate response in the table below

7. Do you agree that social media increases social interaction more than face-to-face communication?

8. Do you agree that online communication is responsible for lack of face-to-face communication?

Question	Strongly Agree	Agree	Neutral	Disagree	Strongly Disagree
7	☐	☐	☐	☐	☐
8	☐	☐	☐	☐	☐

9. a) Do you think students are becoming introverts due to the use of online communication instead of face-to-face communication?
   - [ ] Yes
   - [ ] No

   b) Please state the reason for your answer in 9. a) above.

   _____
   _____

10. a) Do you think face-to-face communication is vital for the development of your personal social skills?

   ☐ Yes

   ☐ No

   b) Please state the reason for your answer in 10. a) above.

11. Suggest one strategy you would employ to reduce the negative effects of the use of these social media platforms on communication.

   _____

   _____

Presentation of Data

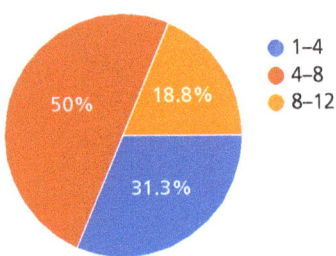

Figure 1

Figure 1 above indicates the length of time spent on social media daily. Fifty percent (50%) of the sample used social media for an average of 4–8 hours, 31.3% used social media for 8–12 hours and 18.8% used social media for 1–4 hours.

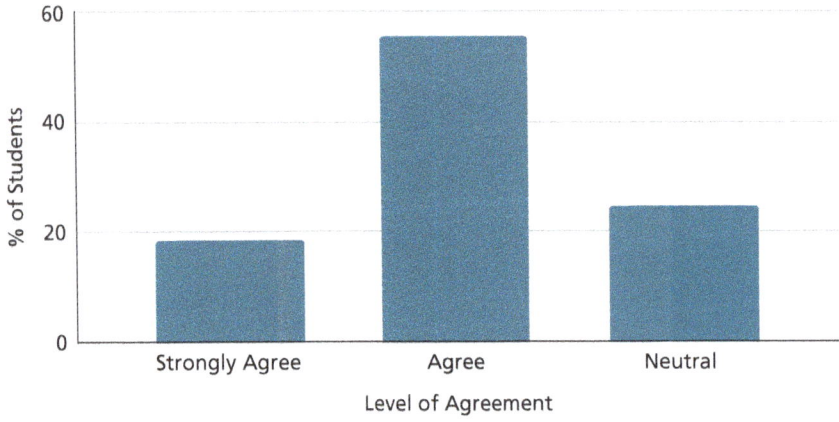

Figure 2

Figure 2 illustrates students' agreement that social media increases social interaction more than face-to-face communication. Twenty-five percent (25%) of girls felt neutral, they neither agree or disagree with the statement, whereas 18.75% strongly agreed and 56.25% agreed with the statement.

Table 1: *Do you think students are becoming introverts due to the use of online communication instead of face-to-face communication?*

Responses	Tally	Total %
Yes	||||| ||||| |||	81.3
No	|||	18.8

Table 1 above shows that the sample perceive that students are becoming introverts due to the use of online communication instead of face-to-face communication. The majority, 81.3%, said yes and 18.8% said no.

Analysis and Interpretation of Data

The data collected showed that 100% of the fifth form students use a social media platform. When asked if they used social media to communicate with friends and family, 100% said yes, but 37.5% preferred to use social media to communicate whereas 62.5% did not. Among the students, 56.3% thought it was easier to communicate via social media while 43.8% believed it was easier to communicate via face-to-face interaction.

Students were asked if the use of social media to communicate affected the receipt of their messages and 81.3% said yes, with the average reason being how the sender intended the message may be different from how the receiver interpreted it. This left 18.8% who responded in the negative. When asked if they agreed that social media increases social interaction more than face-to-face communication, 18.75% strongly agreed, 56.25% agreed and 25% were neutral. Students were asked if they agreed that online communication is responsible for lack of face-to-face communication, 62.5% strongly agreed, 18.75% agreed and 18.75% were neutral.

The sample was asked if they thought the use of social media to communicate causes students to become introverts and 81.3% said yes and 18.8% said no. The prevalent reason for the response of yes was that students spent more time away from real people and face-to-face conversations, therefore they were more comfortable in communicating online. Finally, students were posed with the question of whether face-to-face communication is vital for the development of personal social skills and 100% indicated positively. The general reason being that without face-to-face communication they would not be able to adapt to the various characteristics and/or personalities displayed by people.

Statement of Findings

This survey has revealed deficiencies with respect to the impact the use of social media has on the face-to-face communication among the fifth form female students at Summertime High School. These are as follows:

1. One of the main disadvantages of students using social media to communicate instead of face-to-face communication is that students are becoming introverted.

2. The convenient access to online communication is responsible for lack of face-to-face communication.
3. The use of social media to communicate affects the receipt of messages whereas face-to-face communication ensures a clearer reception and interpretation.

Recommendations and Implementation Strategy

Using social media to communicate more than face to face can cause students to suffer from a lack of communication skills and have difficulties in adapting to the various characteristics and/or personalities displayed by people. When persons are incapable of meeting in a real-life forum, it is recommended that students use interactive platforms for instance Zoom or Google Meet. There will still be face-to-face communication and persons can express their ideas thoroughly.

Secondly, since there is easy access to social media platforms, students would find comfort in online communication and would eventually shy away from face-to-face communication. To combat this problem, it is recommended to use timers or shut down sequences for social media apps in order to force people to revert to interacting face to face.

One way to implement the second strategy is by informing the students and their parents of the effects of the prolonged use of social media on face-to-face communication. They can then be made aware of the timers or shut down sequences for social media apps. With this applied behaviour, parents can hold their children accountable and manage the amount of time they spend on social media.

Bibliography

Gayah M., Hyacinth, M. (2024) *CSEC Social Studies* HarperCollins Publishers, 978-0-00-866705-4.

Gestier, E (2010). Social Media impact on existing social relationships. Retrieved from https://www.slideshare.net/EGestier/social-media-impact-on-existing-social-relationships on January 12th, 2025.

Hanke, S (2018). How Social Media Affects our ability to communicate. Retrieved from www.thriveglobal.com on January 13th, 2025.

Appendix

Students should include their questionnaire data in their appendix.

Index

Figures and tables are indicated by an f and t following the page number.

A

accessibility, ICT, 297
active listening, 5
adults
    as nurturers, 21
    as providers, 20
adventure tourism, 358
African enslavement in Caribbean, 68–74
    language evolution, 69–70
    linguistic legacy, 68–69
    musical expressions, 71–73
    religious syncretism, 70–71
after-school programmes, 46
agents of transmission, 80–81
age-sex pyramid/age structure, 178–179
agricultural development, 289–290
agricultural land, natural resources, 249–250, 254
agriculture industry, 238–239, 240t
Antigua and Barbuda Electoral Commission (ABEC), 146
Arcaico, 60
assimilation, 74
asylee, 208–209
asylum, migration and, 213–214
asylum seekers, 211
authority, family, 8
authority, social group, 102
aviation hubs, 360–361

B

banking industry, 242
Barbadian education, 49
Barbados Secondary Schools Entrance Examination (BSSEE), 49
basic education, human resources development, 227
bauxite, 253
beach tourism, 361
bicameral legislature, 126–127
bigotry, 209
bilateral agreements, 338
biochar, 266, 269
biodiversity, 261
birth and death rates, 177, 197
birth rates, 197
bleaching, 268
blended families, 12–13
Bouyon music, 73
brain drain, 209, 210, 302, 326–328
budget management, governments, 133
business cost, ICT, 297

C

Cadence music, 73
campaign advertising, elections, 162–163
campaign strategy, elections, 165
capital availability, employment, 234
carbon footprint, 269
carbon neutral, 270
Caribbean Community (CARICOM), 90, 333–334
    impacts and challenges, 342–343
    vision of regional integration, 340–341
Caribbean Conservation Association (CCA), 263
Caribbean Court of Justice (CCJ), 341–343, 346
caribbean culture, migration and, 214
Caribbean Development Bank (CDB), 346
Caribbean Disaster Emergency Management Agency (CDEMA), 346
Caribbean Examinations Council (CXC®), 346
Caribbean family
    adult roles and responsibilities, 20–21
    African enslavement in, 68–74
        language evolution, 69–70
        linguistic legacy, 68–69
        musical expressions, 71–73
        religious syncretism, 70–71
    blended families, 12–13
    case study, 21–25, 24f
        social issues, 38–43
    changes in roles and responsibilities, 26–30
        causes of, 27–29
    child abuse, 21
    children's roles and responsibilities in, 23–25, 24f
    Christianity to, 63–64
    culinary practices, 76
    cultural diversity of, 58–78
        European colonisation, 61–68
        indigenous peoples, 59–61
    cultural identity, 77
    cultural imperialism, 80
    cultural practices and customs, 73–74
    extended family, 9–10, 12, 20
    globalisation, 8, 27, 39, 41, 79–84, 82
        cuisine, 83–84
        dance, 83
        fashion, 83
        literature, 83

music, 82–83
   sport, 84
indentureship, 75
legal roles and responsibilities, 21
linguistic diversity, 75
migration, 77–78
musical enrichment, 76–77
nuclear family, 12
parenting within, 31–33
reorganised families, 13
resistance and cultural retention, 74
social issues in, 38–43
   solutions to, 49–52
tourism, 80
understanding family dynamics, 20–21
Caribbean Festival of Arts (CARIFESTA), 346
Caribbean integration, 302
Caribbean Public Health Agency (CARPHA), 346
Caribbean Regional Youth Council (CRYC), 335
Caribbean Single Market and Economy (CSME), 50
Caribbean Tourism Organisation (CTO), 332, 346–347
CARICOM (Caribbean Community), 280
CARICOM Single Market and Economy (CSME), 236, 334
   impacts and challenges, 342–343
   objectives of, 341
cartographers (mapmakers), 195
case study
   Caribbean family, 21–25, 24f
   COVID-19 pandemic, 345
   developmental challenges, Caribbean, 307–311
   development, Caribbean, 274–275
   electoral processes, 146
   fall of the West Indies Federation, 347
   governments, structure of, 130–132
   industry development and economic contributions, 290–292
   justification of strategies, 314
   migration, 208
   The Programme of Advancement Through Health and Education (PATH), 45–46
   social issues, 38–43
   tourism, 370–371
Casimoroids, 60
Catholicism, 63
CCCCC (Caribbean Community Climate Change Centre), 271
child abandonment, 37
child abuse, 21
child development, 43
child labour, 25
child protection, 22, 52
choropleth map, 194

Christianity, 63
Ciboney, 59–60
citizens/citizenship, 137–138
   characteristics of, 140
civil/public service, 129
civil registrations, 185
Climate Action Network (CAN), 269
climate change, 265. *See also* global warming
   causes of, 267
   consequences of, 267–268
   coral reefs, destruction of, 268
   extreme weather, 267
   health related concerns, 268
   impact of
      agriculture, fishing and forestry, 268
      tourism, 268
      water supply, 269
   responses to
      agricultural communities, 269
      government, 270
      individuals, 269
      organisations, 269–270
      regional and international bodies, 270–271
   rising sea levels, 267
coalition, 151
cohabiting couples, 10
commercialisation, 80
commitment, social group, 102
commodification, 80
common-law unions, 13
common legal framework, 333–335
Commonwealth Caribbean countries, 127–128
Commonwealth of Dominica, 130
communication links, tourism, 360
community-based support systems, 46
competition, social group, 106
compromise, social group, 107
Conditional Cash Transfer (CCT) programmes, 50
conflict resolution, 5
conflict, social group, 106–107
conservation, 257
constitutional monarchy government, 124
construction industry, 240–241
contour ploughing, 258
contract workers, 238
controlled logging, 258
cooperation and collaboration, social group, 107
cooperation, social groups, 93
cost of living index, 285
counselling and therapy services, 46
creativity and problem solving, social group, 107
creolisation, 58, 62–63

crime
    and social disruption, 327–328
    and violence, 37
criminality and violence, 305
crop rotation, 258
crown colony government, 124
cruise tourism, 359
cuisine, 83–84
culinary practices, 76
cultural adaptation, 30
cultural and creative industries, 292–293
cultural diversity, 58
    European colonisation, 61–68
        economic impacts, 67–68
        linguistic transformations, 62–63
        religious influences, 63–65
        traditions and cultural practices, 65–67
    reasons for, 59
cultural heritage, 360
    regional integration, 322–324
    tourism, 363–364
cultural identity, 43, 64, 77
cultural imperialism, 80
cultural influence, migration and, 215
cultural practices and customs, 73–74
cultural preservation, 63
cultural resilience, 74
cultural tourism, 358
culture, human resources development, 231
customs and immigration records, 185–186
cyclical unemployment, 236

D

dance, 83
data analysis, election processes, 167
    conclusive statements, 169–172
    managing data, 167–169
death rate, 177, 198
debt burden, 312, 314
decision-making process, 160–165
deforestation, 266–267
delayed parenthood, 29
democracy, 122–123. *See also* government
demography, 176
dependency ratio, 179
depopulation, 209
desalination, 250
development, Caribbean, 274
    case study, 274–275
    challenges to, 302–303
        case study, 307–311
        disaster preparedness and management, 307
        economic, 304
        investing in research and technology, 307
        physical, 303–304
        political, 305
        promoting environmental sustainability, 307
        social, 305
    Eastern Caribbean, 279
    economic integration, groupings by, 280
    Greater and Lesser Antilles, 275, 278
    Guyana, Suriname and Belize, 279
    historical creation, 277
    indicators
        global partnerships, 289
        international comparisons, 287
        policy planning, 286–287
        resource allocation, 287–289
    industry development and economic contributions
        agriculture, 289–290
        case study, 290–292
        cultural and creative industries, 292–293
        manufacturing and mining, 291
        tourism, 290
    Information and Communication Technology (ICT), 296–298
    justification of strategies, 312–317
    language, groupings by, 279–280
    Leeward and Windward Islands, 278–279
    measuring, 281
        economic measures, 282–285
        Human Development Index (HDI), 285–286
        social measures, 285
    migration policies, 313
    targeted strategies, 314–316
    territorial dynamics in, 276–277
diamonds, non-renewable resource, 253
direct democracy, 122
direct taxation, 133
disaster preparedness and management, 307
discrimination and social injustice, 37
disrupted family dynamics, 42
diverse family types, 13
divorce, 37
divorce rates, 29
domestic violence, 51–52
Dominican education, 49
dot map, 194
dual-income households, 29
Dutch-speaking Caribbean (Suriname), 280

E

Eastern Caribbean Currency Union (ECCU), 280
ecological systems, 262
e-commerce, 297
economic challenges, 28
economic developmental challenges, 303
economic institutions, 117–118

economic integration, 280
economic measuring, Caribbean development, 282–285
economic provisioning, 4
economic status, electors, 165
economic vulnerability and economic growth, 328
economy, migration and, 214
ecotourism, 356, 358, 361–362
education, 22, 27
    elections, 164
    and government, 133
    human resources development, 227
    migration and, 213, 215
    parenting techniques, 31
    social issues, 37, 49
educational initiatives, 47
educational institutions, 114, 114t–115t
    financial resources and scholarships, 230
    functions of, 116
    pre-primary, 228
    primary, 228
    secondary, 228–229
    tertiary, 229–230
    types of, 227
effective parenting, 32–33
Election Day, 149–150
election observation, 148
elections. *See also* electoral processes
    decision-making process, 160–165
    electoral processes, monitoring of, 157
    outcomes of, 161
        age, 164
        campaign advertising, 162–163
        campaign strategy, 165
        COVID-19 pandemic, 164
        economic status, electors, 165
        education, 164
        media coverage, 162
        national issues, 165
        party loyalty, 164
        public opinion polls, 163
    preparation for
        campaign activities, 156–157
        campaign finance, 156
        candidates selection, 155–156
        commissioning opinion polls, 157
        facts, opinions and propaganda, 158
        manifesto, 157
        party structure, 155
Elections Commission/Electoral Office, 146–147
electoral processes. *See also* data analysis, election processes/results
    case study, 146

    dissolution/prorogation of parliament, 145–146
    Election Day, 149–150
    Elections Commission/Electoral Office, 146–147
    free and fair elections, 147
    independent observer mission, 148
    political parties, 148
    polling station, 149f
    Prime Minister/President, selection of, 150
    quantitative and qualitative data, 148
    swearing in ceremony, 150
    voters, 148–149
    winning party, 150
electoral systems, 150
    first-past-the-post system, 150–151
    Proportional Representation system, 151
emergency assistance programmes, 46
emigration, 210
emotional readiness, parenthood, 31
empathy, 5, 32
employment, 234. *See also* unemployment
    capital availability and use, 234
    entrepreneurial opportunities, 237
    gender and, 237
    industries
        primary, 238–240
    skills demanded *vs.* available skills, 235
    trained human resource, 235
    women's rights, 237
    WOW (world of work) ready, 237–238
employment, migration and, 212
employment opportunities, 50, 132
empowerment, 5
energy forms, natural resources, 252
English-speaking Caribbean, 279–280
enslavement, 9
entrepreneurial opportunities, employment and, 237
entrepreneurship, ICT, 298
environment and population practices
    ecological systems, 262
    forest reserves, 260
    zoning, 259
environment and population practices, sustainable development
    contour ploughing, 258
    controlled logging, 258
    crop rotation, 258
    reforestation, 258
    terracing, 258
equity, 33
European colonisation, 61–68
    economic impacts, 67–68
    linguistic transformations, 62–63

religious influences, 63–65
traditions and cultural practices, 65–67
executive, separation of powers, 128–129
extended family, 9
    Caribbean, 12, 20
    family trees, 13, 14f

F

facts, electoral processes, 158
family, 2. *See also* Caribbean family
    aspects of, 7–8
    community-based support systems, 46
    cooperation and interaction, 47–48
    cultural perspectives, 9–10
    definitions, 2, 8–10
        sources for, 8–9
    diverse family types, 13
    functions of, 2
        emotional and psychological support, 4–5
        procreation, 3
        socialisation and nurturing, 3–4
    globalisation, 8
    legal perspectives, 10
    policy advocacy, 47
    as social group, 8–9
family bonds, 9–10
family diversity, 8
family resource centres, 47
family rights, 52
family trees, 13–15, 14f
fashion, 83
fertility rate, 197
festivals, 364
financial planning/support, 22, 32, 49–50
financial resources and educational scholarships, 230
financial support, 49–50
first-past-the-post system, 150–151
fishing industry, 239, 240t
folkways, 103
food security, 224
forced/involuntary migration, 199
foreign direct investment (FDI), 329
forest reserves, 260
forests, natural resources, 250–251, 255
formal education, 114
formal social group, 90, 93t
fossil fuels, 265
free and fair elections, 147
freedoms, 137
frictional unemployment, 236
full-time workers, 238
fundamental human rights, 137

G

gender equality, 27
gender roles, 43
general election, 145
generational wealth, 4
generation gap, 37
geographical location, regional integration, 321–322
geothermal energy, 252
globalisation, 8, 27, 39, 41, 328–330
    Caribbean cultural forms on, 82
        cuisine, 83–84
        dance, 83
        fashion, 83
        literature, 83
        music, 82–83
        sport, 84
    and cultural imperialism, 79–84
        agents of transmission, 80–81
        media, 80
        tourism, 80
        transformation, 81–82
global musical landscape, 82–83
global partnerships, development indicators, 289
global warming, 266–267
goals, social groups, 93
gold, 253
good governance, 127
    characteristics of, 138–139
governments, 122
    forms of, 122–123
    functions of, 132–134
    responsibilities of, 137
    separation of powers, 126–132
        bicameral legislature, 126–127
        civil/public service, 129
        executive, 128–129
        head of state, role of, 127–128
        judiciary, 129
        legislature, 126
        making laws, 126–127
        office of the president, 128
        opposing groups, 127
        unilateral legislature, 126
    structure of, 125
        case study, 130–132
greenhouse effect, 266–267
greening, 140
Gross Domestic Product (GDP), 282–284
Gross National Product (GNP), 282–284
group cohesion, 100
    authority, 102
    commitment, 102
    control of, 101

cooperation, 102
folkways, 103
laws, 103
leadership, 100–101
loyalty, 102
mores, 104
norms, 103–104
requirements for, 100–102
rules, 103
social control, 102
group dynamics, 112
Guanahatabey, 60
guardianship, 23

H

habitats, 247, 251
healthcare decisions, 22, 28, 43, 132
health emergencies, 305
health, human resource development, 225
health status and education, 183
health tourism, 362
hidden curriculum, 116
hierarchical structure, institutions, 119
housing development, 261
Human Development Index (HDI), 285–286
human dignity, 137
human resources, 222
    development of, 222
        culture, 231
        education, 227
        educational institutions, 227–230
        health, 225
        nutrition, 223–225
        primary/preventive healthcare, 225–226
        secondary/curative healthcare, 226
        sports, 230–231
human rights, 137
human trafficking, 41
hung parliament, 151
hydroelectric power, 252
hydropower, 257

I

identifiers, social groups, 94
ideological approach, family, 8
Igneri, 60
immigrants, 209
inadequate food systems, 224
inclusive education, 227
income inequality, 224
income level and employment status, 183
indentureship, 75
Indian culinary traditions, 76
Indian musical traditions, 76–77
indigenous peoples, 59
    with Maroon communities, 60–61, 74
indirect democracy, 123
indirect taxation, 133
individual migrant, 209
industries
    agriculture, 238–239, 240t
    banking, 242
    construction, 240–241
    fishing, 239, 240t
    information technology, 242
    manufacturing, 240
    mining, 239–240, 240t
    primary, 238–240
    quaternary, 242
    research and development, 242
    secondary sector, 240–241
    tertiary, 241–242
    tourism, 241–242
infant mortality rate, 198
informal social group, 90–91, 93t
Information and Communication Technology (ICT), 296
    impact of, 296f
        accessibility, 297
        business cost, 297
        e-commerce, 297
        entrepreneurship, 298
        greater efficiency, 297
        research and development, 297
information technology, 242
institutions, 114
    characteristics of, 119–120
    economic, 117–118
    educational, 114, 114t–115t, 116
    political, 119
    recreational, 118
    religious, 116
    social, 114
integration process, 351–353
interest social group, 92
internal migration, 198–199
international comparisons, development indicators, 287
international migration, 199
interns, employment, 238
interpersonal relationships, 42
intragroup/intergroup relations, 106
intraregional migration, 199
involuntary social group, 91
Iron Band music, 73

J

Jamaican education, 49
Jamaica Promotions Corporation (JAMPRO), 291–292

joint marketing efforts, 359–360
justification of strategies, 312
    case study, 314
    debt burden, 312, 314
    migration policies, 313
    research activity, 313
    underemployment, 312
juvenile delinquency, 38

K
Kalinago, 59–60
Kizomba music, 73

L
labour market statistics, 39–41
land and marine life, natural resources, 251–252, 255
language evolution, 69–70
language groupings, 279–280
law enforcement practices, 50–51
leadership, 100–101
legal aid and advocacy services, 47
legislation/legal consent:, 22–23, 28, 103
lifelong learning, 227
limited private sector, 327
linguistic diversity, 75
linguistic legacy, 68–69
literature, 83
longevity, institutions, 119
Lower House (House of Representatives/House of Assembly), 126–127
loyalty, social group, 102
luxury tourism, 359

M
malnutrition, 224–225
manufacturing industry, 240
maritime cooperation, 332–333
Maroon communities, 60–61, 74
media coverage, elections, 162
membership, social groups, 93–94
Members of Parliament, 126–127
mental health, 37
mentoring programmes, 46
microfinance programs, 50
migrants, 206, 208–209
migration, 28, 77–78, 198–199
    Caribbean culture, spread of, 214
    case study, 208
    causes of, 206–208
    consequences of, 208–211
    country of origin, 210
    cultural influence, 215
    economy, 214
    educational influence, 215
    global impact of, 214–215
    host country, 211
    individual, 209
    political influence, 214–215
    push and pull factors, 207–208
    reasons for
        asylum, 213–214
        education, 213
        employment, 212
        natural disaster, 213
    social services, 213, 215
    sociocultural, economic and environmental effects of, 211
migration influx, 305
migration policies, 313
mining, 239–240, 240t
modernisation, 39, 41
monocropping, land resources, 260
moral and ethical guidance, 23
moral education, human resources development, 227
multilateral agreements, 338–339
music, 82–83
musical expressions, 71–73

N
national census, population statistics, 184
national debt, 309, 312–314, 327
national issues, elections, 165
national security, 133
National Trusts, 263
national unity government, 151
natural disaster, migration and, 213
natural hazards, 303
natural resources
    alternative energy, 256–257
    environment and population practices
        contour ploughing, 258
        controlled logging, 258
        crop rotation, 258
        ecological systems, 262
        forest reserves, 260
        improper practices on, 260–262
        reforestation, 258
        terracing, 258
        zoning, 259
    location of the Caribbean, 247–248
    mineral resources, 255–256
    non-renewable resource, 249
        bauxite, 253
        diamonds and other minerals, 253
        gold, 253
        petroleum, 253
    renewable resource, 248–249

agricultural land, 249–250, 254
forests, 250–251, 255
forms of energy, 252
land and marine life, 251–252, 255
water, 250
and sustainable development, 257
tourism products, 256
uses of, 254–257
nature/ecotourism, 361–362
new family bonds, 9–10
Niche Tourism, 359
non-renewable resource, 249
bauxite, 253
diamonds and other minerals, 253
gold, 253
petroleum, 253
norms, community cohesion., 103–104
nuclear family
Caribbean, 12, 21
family trees, 13, 14f
legal definition, 10
Western perspective, 9
nurturing, 3
nutrition, human resource development, 223–225

O

open communication, 4
opinions, electoral processes, 158
opposing groups, government, 127
Organisation of Eastern Caribbean States (OECS), 340–341
Otoroids, 60
overcropping, land resources, 260
overnutrition, 224
overpopulation, 177
oxygen cycle, 266–267

P

parenthood, 31–33
parenting education programmes, 46
part-time workers, 237–238
party loyalty, election campaign, 164
patience, 32
peer social group, 91
per capita income, 284–285
percussion instruments, musical expressions, 71
petroleum, 253
physical developmental challenges, 303–304
policy advocacy, 47
policy planning, 286–287
political developmental challenges, 305
political influence, migration and, 214–215
political institutions, 119
political parties, electoral processes, 148

polyrhythms, musical expressions, 71
population, 176
age, 176–177
defining, 176
ethnicity, 182
gender distribution, 177
health status and education, 183
income level and employment status, 183
occupation, 178–179
pyramids, 178–179
religion, 182
population change, 196
birth rates, 197
deaths, 198
factors influencing, 197
fertility rate, 197
forced/involuntary migration, 199
infant mortality rate, 198
internal migration, 198–199
international migration, 199
intraregional migration, 199
migration, 198
seasonal migration, 199
statistical diagrams, 201–202
population density/population distribution, 182–183
population distribution and density, 191
factors influencing, 191–194
country's development, 192
human factors, 192
physical factors, 192
interpreting maps, 194
Jamaica's population distribution, 194f, 195f
map reading skills, 195
population statistics
civil registrations, 185
customs and immigration records, 185–186
development planning using, 188
national census, 184
religious institutions, 185
uses of, 186–187
positive reinforcement, 5
poverty, 224
poverty and economic inequality, 37
pre-indigenous peoples, 59
pre-primary educational institutions, 228
primary educational institutions, 228
Primary Exit Profile (PEP) exam, 49
primary industry, 238–240
primary/preventive healthcare, 225–226
primary social group, 90
procreation function, family, 3
economic provisioning, 4
emotional and psychological support, 4–5
socialisation and nurturing, 3–4

professional training, 227
The Programme of Advancement Through Health and Education (PATH), 45–46
promoting environmental sustainability, 307
propaganda, electoral processes, 158
Proportional Representation system, 151
protections, 137
Protestantism, 63
providers, 20
psychological readiness, parenthood, 31
public opinion polls, 163
pure democracy, 122

Q

quality education, 36, 42, 227
quantitative and qualitative data, electoral processes, 148
quaternary industry, 242

R

recreational institutions, 118
referendum, 122–123
reforestation, 258
refugee, 208–209
regional integration, 320
   advancements in communication technologies, 331–332
   benefits and successes of, 344–347
   bilateral agreements, 338
   Caribbean Community (CARICOM) and, 340–343
   CARICOM Single Market and Economy (CSME) and, 342–343
   common legal framework, 333–335
   consumer practices in, 333
   and COVID-19 pandemic, 345
   crime and social disruption, 327–328
   cultural heritage, 322–324
   economic development and import dependency, 326
   economic vulnerability and economic growth, 328
   fall of the West Indies Federation, 347
   geographical location, 321–322
   globalisation, trade liberalisation and trading blocs, 328–330
   hinder effectiveness of, 347–349
   increased market access, 328
   maritime cooperation, 332–333
   multilateral agreements, 338–339
   national debt and limited private sector, 327
   Organisation of Eastern Caribbean States (OECS) and, 340–341
   socio-economic challenges, 325
   tourism and (*See* tourism and integration)
   tourism cooperation, 332
   unemployment and brain drain, 326–327
   youth engagement, 335
rehabilitation, 227
religious influences
   spread of christianity, 63
   syncretism, 63–64
religious institutions, 47, 116, 185
religious practices, 29
religious syncretism, 63, 70–71
renewable resource, 248–249
   agricultural land, 249–250
   forests, 250–251
   land and marine life, 251–252
   water, 250
reorganised families, 13
representative democracy, 123
Republic government, 124
research and development
   ICT, 297
   industry, 242
resistance and cultural retention, 74
resort development, 261–262
resource allocation, development indicators, 287–289
resource efficiency, 367
retraining, 227
revenue generation, 133
rituals, institutions, 120
rule of law, 140

S

Saladoids, 60
same-sex marriage, 10
SBA. *See* School-Based Assessment (SBA)
scamming, 41
School-Based Assessment (SBA), 375
   examples of topics, 384
   mark scheme, 382–384
   planning and executing, 377–382
   project planning, 375
   sample Social Studies, 385–390
   topic selection, 375–377
seasonal migration, 199
seasonal unemployment, 235
secondary/curative healthcare, 226
secondary educational institutions, 228–229
secondary sector, 240–241
secondary social group, 90
secondary socialisation, 140
secularisation, 116
Senators, 126–127
separation of powers, 126
   bicameral legislature, 126–127
   civil/public service, 129

executive, 128–129
head of state, role of, 127–128
judiciary, 129
legislature, 126
making laws, 126–127
office of the president, 128
opposing groups, 127
unilateral legislature, 126
single-parent dynamics, 20
Soca music, 72, 73
social aggregate, 92
social control, 102, 112
institutions, 119
social developmental challenges, 305
social groups. *See also* group cohesion
aggregates and categories, 92
behaviour, patterns of, 95
characteristics of, 92–96
common goals, 93
cooperation, 93
diversity and inclusion, 95–96
identifiers, 94
interaction in and between, 106–107
membership, 93–94
needs, interests and values, 94
rules and regulations, 94–95
sanctions, 95
structure, 93
technological impact, 96
types of, 89–90
formal group, 90, 93t
informal group, 90–91, 93t
interest group, 92
involuntary group, 91
peer group, 91
primary group, 90
secondary group, 90
voluntary group, 91
social institutions, 114
social interaction, 106–107
socialisation, 3, 101
social issues, 36
on Caribbean family life, 41–43
case study, 38–43
child development, 43
cultural identity, 43
economic disparities and poverty, 38
emerging social issues, 41
gender roles, 43
globalisation and modernisation, 39
historical and cultural influences, 39
labour market statistics, 39–41
policy and advocacy, 43
sociopolitical factors, 39
solutions to
community-based support systems, 46–47

cooperation and interaction, 47–48
educational initiatives, 47
education and training, 49
employment opportunities, 50
financial support, 49–50
law enforcement practices, 50–51
legal system, 51–52
policy advocacy, 47
religion, 47
social services and institutions, 51
types of, 37–38
social measures, Caribbean development, 285
social movements, 28
social safety nets, 50
social services
institutions and, 51
migration and, 213, 215
social solidarity, 116
social welfare, 132
socio-economic challenges, regional integration, 325
sociological approach, family, 8
soil erosion, land resources, 260
solar energy, 252
Spanish-speaking Caribbean (Greater Antilles), 279
sports, 84
human resources development, 230–231
tourism, 359, 363
Steel Band/Steel Pan music, 73
stress management, 5
structural unemployment, 236
substance abuse, 37, 46
Sub-Taíno, 60
summer camps, 46
sun, sand and sea tourism, 358
supervisory and regulatory functions, governments, 134
sustainable development, 320
symbols/emblems/logos, institutions, 119
syncopation, musical expressions, 71
syncretic religious practices, 63, 70–71

T

Taíno, 60
targeted marketing campaigns, 366
taxation, 133
technical and vocational education and training (TVET), 227
Technical and Vocational Education and Training (TVET) programmes, 49
technological/technical unemployment, 236
technology, social groups, 96

teenage pregnancy, 37
temporary workers, 238
terracing, 258
tertiary educational institutions, 229–230
tertiary industry, 241–242
therapy services, 46
tillage/ploughing, land resources, 260
tourism, 80, 241–242, 256, 262, 268, 283, 290
    aviation hubs, 360–361
    brand unity and positioning, 366
    case study, 370–371
    challenges and considerations, 368–370
    communication links, 360
    economic and marketing
        policies in, 360, 364–367
    investment and infrastructure, 365
    products, 360
        beach tourism, 361
        cultural/heritage tourism, 363–364
        festivals, 364
        health tourism, 362
        nature/ecotourism, 361–362
        sports tourism, 363
    promoting regional cooperation and
        integration, 359–361
    resource efficiency, 367
    targeted marketing campaigns, 366
    types of, 357–359
    unity on safety and planning, 366
tourism cooperation, 332
trade barriers, 302
trade liberalisation, 328–330
trading blocs, 328–330
traditional caribbean genres, 71–72
trained human resource, 235
transnational families, 30
Trinidadian education, 49

U
unconditional love, families, 5
underemployment, 312
unemployment, 234–237, 326–327
UNICEF (the United Nations International Children's Emergency Fund), 24
unilateral legislature, 126
United Nations Framework Convention on Climate Change (UNFCCC), 270
Universal Secondary Education Programme (USEP), 49
University of the West Indies (UWI), 346
Upper House (Senate), 126–127
urbanisation, 27

V
value system, institutions, 119
visiting unions, 13
voluntary social group, 91
volunteers, employment, 238
voter apathy, 164
voters, 148–149
    electoral decisions, 163
    turnout/participation, 163–134

W
water, 250
wind energy, 252
women's rights, employment and, 237
WOW (world of work) ready, 237–238

X
xenophobia, 206, 209

Z
zoning, 259
Zouk music, 72

Acknowledgements

We are grateful to the following for permission to reproduce copyright material:

Extract from "Breakdown of social norms" *Guyana Chronicle*, 08/07/2011, guyanachronicle.com/2011/07/08/breakdown-of-social-norms/. Reproduced with permission; Extract from "Barbados becomes a republic" by David Torrance, UK Parliament, House of Commons Library, 29/11/2021, copyright © House of Commons 2024; Figure 8.5 'Number of marriages by region, Guyana 2015-2022', Bureau of Statistics, Government of Guyana, statisticsguyana.gov.gy. Reproduced with permission; Figure 8.6 "Source countries of immigrant stock in Trinidad & Tobago" from *Migration in Trinidad and Tobago: current Trends and Policies*, UNDP LAC PDS No.37, undp.org/latin-america/publications/migration-trinidad-and-tobago-current-trends-and-policies, fig 8, p.15. Source UN DESA Population Division - International Migrant Stock 2020; Extract from "Country analysis. Trinidad and Tobago", ACAPS, acaps.org/en/countries/trinidad-and-tobago. Reproduced with permission; Figure 8.8 "Suriname: Population Distribution and Density map of Suriname at District level (22 Jun 2021)" MapAction, mapaction.org/. Reproduced with permission; Figure 8.9 "2011 Jamaica population dot distribution" and Figure 8.10 "2011 Jamaica population density" from *2011 Population and Housing Census, Statistical Institute of Jamaica*, statinja.gov.jm. Statistical Institute of Jamaica; Figure 8.12 "Numbers and share of immigrants and emigrants in Caribbean countries" and Figure 9.3 "Trends in total numbers of emigrants and immigrants in the Caribbean region, 1990–2020, a. Total numbers of emigrants, Caribbean region" from *International Migration in the Caribbean. Background paper for the World Development Report 2023: Migrants, Refugees, and Societies, April 2023* by Pascal Jaupart, Table 1, Figure 2. Sources: UN DESA 2020; World Bank, World Development Indicators 2022. Reproduced with permission; Figure 8.14 "People of Trinidad and Tobago, age breakdown 2022", by Arthur Napoleon, Raymond Robinson, David Watts and Bridget M. Brereton, updated 10/07/24; and Figure 8.15 "Grenada. of ethnic composition 2011" by Eric V. B. Britter, Encyclopædia Britannica Inc., britannica.com/. Reproduced with permission; Figure 9.2 "Refugees, IDPs, migrants… what's the difference?" Concern Worldwide, concern.net/news/refugee-idp-migrant-difference, 22/04/2022. Reproduced with permission; Figure 9.10 "History of Migration in Jamaica" from *Migration in the Caribbean: contributions, good practices and challenges Jamaica* presentation (Santiago, Chile, ECLAC Regional Seminar, June 14 & 15, 2023), slide 3. Planning Institute of Jamaica. Reproduced with permission; Figure 10.3 "Infant and child nutrition stats Jamaica" from 'Burden of malnutrition', *Country Nutrition Profiles: Jamaica*, Global Nutrition Report, globalnutritionreport.org/resources/nutrition-profiles/latin-america-and-caribbean/caribbean/jamaica/. Data source: Unicef/WHO/World Bank, May 2022, Accessed November 2022; Extract from "$1B To Address Learning Loss" by Chanel Spence, 18/03/2022, The Jamaica Information Service (JIS) jis.gov.jm/1b-to-address-learning-loss/. Reproduced by permission of Jamaica Information Service; Figure 11.14 "Map of bauxite mining in Jamaica" The Jamaican Caves Organisation, jamaicancaves.org/bauxite-mining.jpg. Reproduced with permission; Figure 11.15 "Modern simplified geologic map of the Guiana Shield" from *A Look at Diamonds and Diamond Mining in Guyana*, Figure 3, https://www.gia.edu/gems-gemology/summer-2022-diamonds-from-guyana, first published in *Gems & Gemology*. Reproduced with permission from the Gemological Institute of America (GIA); Figure 11.19 "Energy Generation by Source 2015" beltraide.bz/uploads/6/4/9/6/64967361/chart.png?373, Ministry of Energy, 2015. Reproduced by permission of Ministry of Public Utilities, Energy, Logistics & E-Governance; and Figure 11.28 'Climate change graphic' US Environmental Protection Agency, copyright © 2017.

In some instances we have been unable to trace the owners of copyright material, and we would appreciate any information that would enable us to do so.

Images

We are grateful for the following for permission to reproduce their images:

p.29 Art Directors & TRIP / Alamy Stock Photo, p.35 Danita Delimont / Alamy Stock Photo, p.38 Tryphosa Ho / Alamy Stock Photo, p.59 World History Archive / Alamy Stock Photo, p.60 Image provided by the author, all rights reserved, p.71 Paul Thompson Images / Alamy Stock Photo, p.71 Pictorial Press Ltd / Alamy Stock Photo, p.72 Abaca Press / Alamy Stock Photo, p.74 SEAN DRAKES / Alamy Stock Photo, p.74 Author's own image, p.76 SEAN DRAKES / Alamy Stock Photo, p.80 Pictorial Press Ltd / Alamy Stock Photo, p.81 Karol Kozlowski Premium RM Collection / Alamy Stock Photo, p.82 Associated Press / Alamy Stock Photo, p.83 Album / Alamy Stock Photo, p.84 Associated Press / Alamy Stock Photo, p.91 Associated Press / Alamy Stock Photo, p.93 Nandani Bridglal / Alamy Stock Photo, p.95 Independent Photo Agency / Alamy Stock Photo, p.103 Mikko Palonkorpi / Alamy Stock Photo, p.115 © Bill Bachmann / Alamy Stock Photo, p.115 Robert Landau / Alamy Stock Photo, p.116 Sean Sprague / Alamy Stock Photo, p.117 Arterra Picture Library / Alamy Stock Photo, p.117 Art Directors & TRIP / Alamy Stock Photo, p.118 Findlay / Alamy Stock Photo, p.118 robertharding / Alamy Stock Photo, p.119 SEAN DRAKES / Alamy

Stock Photo, p.122 SEAN DRAKES / Alamy Stock Photo, p.132 The Canadian Press / Alamy Stock Photo, p.133 AB Forces News Collection / Alamy Stock Photo, p.134 PA Images / Alamy Stock Photo, p.144 Mark Summerfield / Alamy Stock Photo, p.146 tina norris / Alamy Stock Photo, p.147 Imago / Alamy Stock Photo, p.148 Image from CARICOM Election Observation Mission's preliminary statement to the General Elections of the Commonwealth of Dominica (6 December 2022). Permission granted by CARICOM, p.150 Art Directors & TRIP / Alamy Stock Photo, p.150 Imago / Alamy Stock Photo, p.151 Image courtesy of Jamaica Observer from the article Watch Carnival Atmosphere: Manchester Central Nomination Day. Used with permission., p.156 Associated Press / Alamy Stock Photo, p.157 Art Directors & TRIP / Alamy Stock Photo, p.157 Roi Brooks / Alamy Stock Photo, p.163 Image from the official JLP Jamaica webpage. Used with permission from JLP Jamaica., p.175 megapress images / Alamy Stock Photo, p.176 Image reproduced with permission from UNFPA's Dominica National Report 2020 , p.179 Map of Suriname population distribution and density (22 Jun 2021), reproduced with permission from ReliefWeb, p.180 Image courtesy of the Statistical Institute of Jamaica (STATIN). 2011 Jamaica Population Dot Distribution Map., p.181 Image courtesy of the Statistical Institute of Jamaica (STATIN). 2011 Population Density Map., p.214 US Coast Guard Photo / Alamy Stock Photo, p.226 Art Directors & TRIP / Alamy Stock Photo, p.228 SEAN DRAKES / Alamy Stock Photo, p.239 Universal Images Group North America LLC / DeAgostini / Alamy Stock Photo, Figure 10.7 Primary school technology lesson in St Lucia. Reproduced with kind permission from Mrs. Fontenelle, Principal, Belle Vue Combined School, Figure 10.9 Woodworking from "TVET helping to curb school drop-out" Guyana Chronicle, 24/09/2016, Figure 10.10 from "Badminton's future" Barbados Today, 28/08/2019 https://barbadostoday.bb/2019/08/28/badmintons-future/ p.239 Arterra Picture Library / Alamy Stock Photo, p.241 Ingolf Pompe 10 / Alamy Stock Photo, p.246 , p.251 imageBROKER.com GmbH & Co. KG / Alamy Stock Photo, p.252 Arterra Picture Library / Alamy Stock Photo, Figure 11.11, The Wigton wind farm at Rose Hill, Manchester, from "Wigton in talks to replace Phase One turbines" The Gleaner, 07/11/2021, https://jamaica-gleaner.com/article/business/20211107/wigton-talks-replace-phase-one-turbines#slideshow-1, p.291 Jon Arnold Images Ltd / Alamy Stock Photo, p.301 Associated Press / Alamy Stock Photo, p.303 Associated Press / Alamy Stock Photo, p.315 Rodney Legall / Alamy Stock Photo, p.319 Associated Press / Alamy Stock Photo, p.323 blickwinkel / Alamy Stock Photo, p.324 ZUMA Press, Inc. / Alamy Stock Photo, p.324 CHRIS ARJOON / Alamy Stock Photo, p.327 Image provided by author, p.336 Gibson Blanc / Alamy Stock Photo, p.337 imageBROKER.com GmbH & Co. KG / Alamy Stock Photo, p.338 Imago / Alamy Stock Photo, p.338 UPI / Alamy Stock Photo, p.340 fabrizio annovi / Alamy Stock Photo, p.342 Jon Arnold Images Ltd / Alamy Stock Photo, p.352 Arterra Picture Library / Alamy Stock Photo, p.357 Retro AdArchives / Alamy Stock Photo, p.358 Mark Graf / Alamy Stock Photo, p.358 Kate Hockenhull / Alamy Stock Photo, p.358 Sabena Jane Blackbird / Alamy Stock Photo, p.359 Colin Anthony Photography / Alamy Stock Photo, p.359 Planetpix / Alamy Stock Photo, p.363 Roger Lee / Alamy Stock Photo, p.364 UPI / Alamy Stock Photo, p.367 Patti McConville / Alamy Stock Photo.

All other photos © Shutterstock.com.

The publishers have made every effort to trace and acknowledge all copyright holders of the images used in this textbook. However, in some cases, it was not possible to trace the source. If any copyright holders have not been properly credited, the publishers would be grateful if they would contact us, so we can make the necessary corrections in any future editions of the book.